Reconstructing Biology

Reconstructing Biology

Genetics and Ecology in the New World Order

JOHN VANDERMEER

Department of Biology
University of Michigan

John Wiley & Sons, Inc.

New York • Chichester • Brisbane • Toronto • Singapore

Library of Congress Cataloging-in-Publication Data:
Vandermeer, John H.
     Reconstructing biology : genetics and ecology in the new world
     order / by John Vandermeer.
          p.   cm.
     ISBN 0-471-10917-7
     1. Biology—Social aspects.   2. Human ecology.   3. Genetics—
     Social aspects.   4. Evolution (Biology)—Social aspects.
     I. Title.
     QH333.V36   1996
     304.2—dc20   95-12076

For Ivette, Jason, Jaime,
Elsie, Harry, Erin, Cass, and Tina,
with some of whom I share genes,
with all of whom I construct my world.

Contents

Preface

I was born just before the last "new world order." Many of my formative years were spent under its aegis. When George Bush announced we were entering a new new world order, I took note, not just as a loyal subject, but also as a practitioner in one of the institutions that are widely believed to form a foundation for all sorts of world orders. As a university professor of biology, I had seen my discipline called on to solve real problems as well as provide an ideological bulwark for all sorts of nefarious projects of a new world order type. Would this new new world order try once again to draft us? Just in case it would, I decided to write this book.

In a sense, I am a converted foot soldier in this ideological war. While most conversions may be sudden and spiritual, mine was rather a gradual and intellectual one. And there is something quite special about the converted, isn't there? As an ex-smoker, for example, I have been quite annoying to my many friends who still enjoy that most dangerous of all drugs. When I first adopted atheism, I could hardly contain my enthusiasm for bashing organized religion. It's as if the experience of having been wrong provides insight into how to make right. Perhaps this is the secret of success of many organizations of exes—ex-cons help other ex-cons go straight, ex-alcoholics, ex-spouses, and so on. Perhaps this helped me write this book.

My historical trajectory began as a young boy fascinated with animals. But my first significant academic transformation occurred as I confronted the evidence for evolution, as a beginning university student. My religious upbringing bounced between Lutheran and Charismatic Christian, and I brought to my first zoology class the background of a born-again Christian who believed the current manifestation of Satan was international

Communism. Evidence from the fossil record and comparative anatomy, and especially the logic of natural selection based on Mendelian genetics, were simply too much cognitive dissonance. My fundamentalism was defeated, although it would be several years before my religious atheism managed to finally win over my spiritual belief system.

As I matured as a biologist, I rapidly came to adopt certain religious and habitual aspects of the discipline: not the published results of critical experiments, but rather the unwritten set of traditions that those who fulfilled all the requirements of becoming members of the fraternity seemed to share. At some deep, almost psychological, level, those traditions reflect certain assumptions that emerge from the culture in which the science is embedded—in this case, the culture of modern western civilization. It seems that we biologists begin adult life with the same set of assumptions as everyone else about how biology relates to society. As we study and become professionals, we accumulate detailed knowledge of the critical experiments and important theories that make up the science of biology. But our assumptions need not change, and on some counts they certainly do not. Yet, because we are professionals, the society around us sees these assumptions as informed knowledge.

In the best of all worlds, as one matures in an academic discipline, the lay assumptions that relate that discipline to the everyday world are challenged, and one's careful academic work serves to modify those lay assumptions. It may be obvious to all observers that the sun goes around a flat earth, yet careful study long ago dispelled such misconceptions from our popular culture. But careful academic work is not necessarily aimed directly at the underlying assumptions of a discipline, nor should it be. Consequently, academic professionals gain public credibility but not necessarily any special understanding. Their proclamations thus may have no more truth value than those of the lay public, but the perception is that they do.

As I accumulated the tools of the world of the professional biologist over four years of undergraduate training and my first few years of graduate school, I saw ever more clearly the relationship between my academic discipline and my social and cultural background. Like all academics, I wanted my professional life to have meaning and significance, so I naturally began applying biology to everyday life. And it was remarkably successful. The theory of evolution through natural selection, perhaps the most powerful idea since Newton's laws, could explain everything. What a device for cocktail parties! Everyone was interested in hearing a young professional biologist tell tales about how evolution had molded everything about life, including all of those mysteries of the personality that make supermarket tabloids and soap operas the major icons of the modern world. Aggression? Our most aggressive ancestors left more offspring. Family? We share more genes with family members, and thus have a stake in having them be more successful. Sex roles? Females and males contribute in different ways to the reproductive process and evolution has favored the specialized roles that tend to promote more offspring. I could explain everything!

But my passion was not really in evolutionary biology, but rather in ecology. And here I would countenance no opposition. I had grown up believing in the "balance of nature," and my new understanding of evolution simply reinforced that notion—ecosystem components had also evolved, or rather coevolved, with one another. One thus had to expect an optimum relationship among those components. My lay idea of the balance of nature was strongly reinforced by my new-found inspiration—evolutionary biology. I had worshiped the natural world ever since my youth, and it was certainly an inspiration to find scientific rigor in my prejudices.

And, finally, my youthful concern for fighting Communism gave way to my biologist's concern for the obvious environmental destruction going on around me. And the most obvious cause of this destruction was the only thing that was "unnatural," the only thing that disturbed the wonder of the coevolved balance of nature—*Homo sapiens*. Because we, as a species, had gone beyond our evolutionary endowments and developed modern society, our effects on the natural world were out of the ordinary and certainly not in line with the coevolved nature of the rest of the natural world. Thus, the sheer presence of a population of humans was enough to threaten the natural world. If that population got very large, those effects could only become worse. I had already read an important pamphlet by Henry Fairfield Osborn before Ehrlich's *Population Bomb* appeared, and I devoured the latter with the enthusiasm of a groupie.

These three issues became something of a new religion for me: the natural world created through evolution to be a perfectly balanced entity, threatened by large numbers of *Homo sapiens,* whose activities were also dictated by the laws of evolution. The solution to the world's problems seemed to be first, an acceptance of the evolutionary heritage and adjustment of ethical, moral, and legal systems to its reality; second, a curbing of the rampant population growth of this one deviant species, *Homo sapiens;* and third, a return to the deep appreciation of nature that was most surely also a natural heritage of our evolutionary past—genetic determinism, neo-Malthusianism, and nature worship.

My first break with this trinity was, perhaps surprisingly, not at the hands of careful scientific thought, but rather by some rather simple commentary from my first wife, a high-school speech teacher. We had just returned home from a party in which I had held forth on the nature of the human psyche, explaining with evolutionary reasoning everything from homosexuality to female submission. My arguments were super-logical and held the persuasive power of the authority of a biologist talking about psychology and sociology—i.e., a "real" scientist talking about the "soft" sciences. Upon returning to our apartment and unwinding from the heated discussions, my wife suggested that my method of argumentation could not fail to explain whatever conceivable observation one might make. She then noted that a method that explains all conceivable things really explains nothing—sort of like religion, she said. Her words ring true to the present, although I reacted with scorn at the time.

Regardless of my scorn, my wife's observations represented the first major insight for me into the subtle problems associated with what I believed to be the major theoretical connection between the science of biology and the common opinions of the lay public. As it turns out, this theoretical connection has its modern roots in the latter half of the nineteenth century, and has changed little since then. Unfortunately it is only marginally related to modern biology, even though the latter is held up as its justification. On the other hand, it remains part and parcel of the public's vision of what biology has to say about human society. That the modern science of biology is actually either contradictory to these ideas or has nothing to say at all, is not well understood in popular culture.

This defines one of my aims in writing this book. The trinity of genetic determinism, neo-Malthusianism, and nature worship has been socially constructed, first, by popular culture and second, by biologists themselves (independently of what the science of biology actually says). Given that this position has been socially constructed, it is clear that it can be deconstructed also. That is the first purpose of this book.

But deconstruction should not leave a void. If it is true that biological determinism cannot tell us much about race and racism, then what can? If it is true that neo-Malthusianism has nothing to do with environmental destruction, then what does? If a return to nature (or "family values" or "that old-time religion" or whatever the new euphemism might be) is not the solution to contemporary problems, then what is, and what, if anything, does modern biology have to say about it? This collection of questions forms the second purpose of this book.

Even a single-authored text is really a social phenomenon. I cannot really lay claim personally to the ideas in this one—they are the result of the myriad social connections that form my life. The list of actual contributors to the ideas herein might thus be the size of a small book, if I could remember all of them. Of particular importance have been conversations with Ivette Perfecto, Peter Rosset, Kristen Nelson, Richard Levins, Richard Lewontin, Joe Scanio, Troy Keller, Brian Hazlett, Margaret Reeves, Douglas Boucher, Kathrine Yih, David Andow, Alison Power, Robert Rice, Alan Wald, Brian Schultz, Jim Beaver, Jerry Urquhart, Hugh McGuiness, Nancy Scheferly, Skip Rappaport, Paul Richards, Bill Friedland, Larry Bush, Baldemar Velasquez, Fred Buttle, Iñigo Granzo de la Cerda, Jorge Siman, Cass VanDerMeer, Miguel Altierri, Kay Dewey, Dan Janzen, and several others I really ought to cite, but my memory wanes. Furthermore, while I follow current academic tradition in accepting responsibility for all errors, I cannot help but thinking that, since all intellectual endeavor is ultimately social, some errors really ought to be shared with others.

ONE

Introduction

A NEW WORLD ORDER OR A CURIOUS STENCH?

The Stalinist systems of eastern Europe collapsed, the Soviet Union self-destructed, the largest army in the Third World was soundly defeated in Kuwait, Panama was placed under massive military attack to arrest a non-cooperative dictator, and Croatians fought Serbs, who "ethnically cleansed" Muslims. Yes, the Cold War ended in 1989. Yet, six years after the real and metaphorical victory parades, the winners of the Cold War cannot help but note some obvious problems. Paraphrasing Kurt Vonnegut, it's as though we're at a cocktail party and everyone is engaged in polite conversation, but a curious stench seems to be emanating from somewhere, and no one wants to be the first to point it out.

And despite the expectations (positive or negative) provoked by either Bill Clinton's victory in 1992 or the Republican victory in 1994, 1995 has done nothing to quench that stench. Spontaneous uprisings in places like Venezuela and Mexico, thought to be perfectly secure especially now that the "Commie" menace is gone, as much as ethnic conflict in much of eastern Europe and bloodbaths in Bosnia-Herzegovina and Rwanda, suggest that, worldwide, the stench is getting increasingly difficult to ignore. The 1992 uprising in Los Angeles following the Rodney King incident was quelled, but only after 30,000 arrests, more than 50 deaths, and military mobilization. The most powerful country in the world is now the largest debtor country in the world, with a crisis in the banking industry so large that a solution has not even been theoretically proposed. The billions of dollars necessary to resolve just the savings-and-loan scandal will be a drop in the bucket compared to the multi-billions necessary to clean up the thousands of toxic waste dumps in the United States, which themselves are paralleled only by their cousins in the states formerly known as the Soviet Union. Simultaneously, changes on a global scale, such as continually increasing carbon dioxide emissions and destruction of the ozone layer, threaten not only us but future generations, and the loss of biodiversity worldwide narrows the future options for our grandchildren, as noted in the 1992 Global Summit in Rio. Yet, George Bush, president of the most powerful country on earth, apparently felt that his system of government could not survive if it was restrained from destroying the planet, and he became, in Ibsen's famous words, the man who stood most alone.

The 1992 U.S. political campaigns perhaps signaled something new on the horizon. Bill Clinton emerged as the victor for the political insiders, but only after Jerry Brown denounced the political system from the left, Pat Buchanan denounced the political system from the right, and Ross Perot claimed more than a third of the electorate in early polls, based on denouncing the political system from somewhere that no one quite understood. The political mainstream seems to have been forced to take notice of the stench.

As many authors have noted, the West has been in an ideological confusion since the collapse of Stalinism. The last half century has been defined by the Cold War, with all real problems being cast, frequently falsely, as a mortal struggle between two ideologies. Most palpably, this distortion has been felt in the Third World, which was unfortunate enough to find itself in an era of national liberation that happened to fall into the time frame of the great ideological struggle between two countries that had nuclear weapons pointed at each other. Thus Cuba, Vietnam, Nicaragua, and many others, while engaging in the same behavior the United States had engaged in a couple of centuries earlier, were cast in the framework of the defining struggle of the times—the Cold War. Similarly, movements to redefine racial relations and gender relations, and to clean up the environment, were frequently cast in the same framework. Anyone, from Martin Luther King Jr., to Ralph Nader, to Gloria Steinem, were sometimes cast as either Communists or Communist dupes.

Many have written on this issue in the past few years. Perhaps the main glue that held the society of the West together was the mortal struggle against the great Satan—Communism. In some ways, history suggests that societies are frequently held together by Satans (interestingly, probably more than by gods), be it the infidels the Muslims chased out of Jerusalem or the infidels the Crusades sought to chase out of Jerusalem again, or the infidels recently chased out of Jerusalem, or the infidels who may get chased out of Jerusalem in the future. The pattern exists throughout the world and throughout history—the Chinese confronting the Mongols, the Masai confronting the Kikuyu, the Spanish clergy confronting the Moors, the American revolutionaries confronting the British crown, the Bolsheviks confronting the Czar, the Serbs confronting the Croats—the list could go on for a very long time. What is apparent in the United States and Britain today (and to a lesser extent, but nevertheless evident, in France, Germany, and other western European nations), is that a certain social and political emptiness is forcing us to recognize problems that in the past were easily shrugged off as a necessary consequence of the fight against the great Satan, Communism.

A NEW GLUE?

There is slowly emerging, in the midst of the metaphorical stench, a new defining character for the world—a new "new world order," so to speak, based not on empty rhetoric, but on the acknowledgment of shared world problems whose solutions ought to determine how we organize ourselves and where we focus our energies. First are the massive, and sometimes baffling, ethnic conflicts occurring in eastern Europe and central Asia, which have their counterparts in the West in the persistent and worsening racism in the United States and other developed countries, to say nothing of parallel problems in Third World countries such as Guatemala, Bolivia, Malaysia, Kenya, Rwanda, and others. Second are the conflicts associated with the environment, broadly defined. Global warming, destruction of the ozone layer, deforestation, biodiversity loss, toxic waste production, solid waste disposal, and a variety of other problems threaten to severely restrict the options for future generations and greatly alter the way of life of the youth of the present generation. Third is a collection of problems whose existence has been acknowledged mainly in the developed world of the West: the oppression of women, the social disease called homophobia, the denial of society's rewards to differently abled people, and a variety of related issues. Fourth is the classic problem of equality of opportunity. It has always been the case that a person born in the streets of Calcutta or the inner city of Washington, D.C., could not aspire to the same life goals as a person born in the mansions of an oil-rich Texas billionaire or to the family of the Prince of Wales. But the uniqueness of the new world order is that such divisions in the world seem to be getting worse, not better, perhaps for the first time since the Industrial Revolution.

This four-part classification of world problems may soon congeal into the defining nature of the post–Cold War. All four problems have important, if not generally acknowledged, connections with the science of biology—the subtle biological differences that are sometimes assumed to exist when racial and ethnic tensions flare, the ecological "balance" that has become so distorted by human activities, the biological essence presumed to underlie gender differences, and questions of individual human inequality still tied, in some parts of the world, to assumed biological differences among people. In this sense, the new world order certainly connects with the science of biology.

Yet, to a biologist, much of what is explicitly stated, and even more of what seems to be implicitly assumed, seems oddly reminiscent of that stench that Vonnegut noted. In so many ways, biology is being either misused or ignored—listen to what the German Nazi skinheads say about the Romanian Gypsies, or what George Bush said about biodiversity, or an unfortunately uncountable number of other examples that could be cited. In many ways, biology is being either misappropriated or ignored. As an antidote, the following chapters are offered. Together, they are intended to deconstruct the pseudo-biology that has been socially constructed and inform the biological ignorance that remains rampant.

RACISM AND ITS RELATIVES

The most dramatic evidence of biological essentialism reverberates in images such as swastikas painted on synagogues, burning crosses, and German skinheads. Such hate-mongering, while certainly born of ignorance, either explicitly or implicitly relies on biological ideas. While most rational humans reject such "extremes," it is most surprising to find pieces of the same feelings deep within ourselves, even the most unprejudiced of us. Uncontrovertable facts are that African Americans really do score (on average) lower on standard IQ tests, Puerto Ricans really do have greater difficulty holding onto jobs in New York, women really are more emotional, Native Americans really are more stoic, and Europeans really do tend to dominate others more. What does biology have to do with this? The answer, ultimately, is probably nothing at all. But the important point is that most people assume, even if they won't say it out loud, that just a little bit of biology is probably (or possibly) involved in one or a few of these assumptions.

Such ideas cut across all political spectra. Former U.S. Vice President Dan Quayle seems to have felt that women are biologically destined for specified roles within his peculiar notions of family values, yet some feminists argue that female humans have biologically determined superior talents in what are probably the most important human skills. While right-wing white racists (the subtle kind) have become so common in universities one hardly takes notice when they speak, a whole new generation of scholarship, dominated by left-wing African American scholars, is promoting biological explanations for the peculiar habits of Europeans (either the European, American, Australian, or Canadian forms). Biology thus cuts both ways politically. Both ways are incorrect.

In all of this there is a profound misunderstanding of a particular field of biology, genetics. And here much can be gained from historical reflection. When many of these ideas, or their immediate predecessors, were developed, the science of genetics was young and underdeveloped. Because of the dramatic advances in this discipline over the past 25 years, the bogus assertions of nineteenth-century biologists can be easily put to rest, but not, of course, without some minimal background. That background is provided in chapters 3, 4, 5, and 6.

ENVIRONMENTAL DEGRADATION

Environmental problems are of increasing concern in popular culture, from municipal solid waste management to the destruction of tropical rain forests. Unfortunately, what is emerging with this new-found concern is a rather naive view of what the science of ecology actually is. This naive view can lead to overly pessimistic attitudes about environmental destruction or overly optimistic visions about what we might be able to do about environmental problems. So, for example, a popular response to the destruction of tropical rain forests is to plant trees—restore the forest by replanting it. This response stems from a naive interpretation of how ecology works. At the opposite extreme, in 1968 a U.S. Marine Corps general told me that the rain forests of Vietnam would recuperate rapidly after the U.S. Air Force sprayed them with herbicides, because tropical vegetation had an immense capacity for growth—again, a response generated from a misunderstanding of how ecology works. Both positions were incorrect.

The science of ecology is more misunderstood than similar sciences, partly because its youth generates principles and laws that are less than scientifically accurate, prompting skepticism among colleagues in other sciences and self-doubt among ecologists themselves. Perhaps when ecology has had a history as long as physics, its principles will be just as useful (although there are substantial reasons to expect that the level of precision achieved by physicists will never be within the reach of ecologists—their subject matter is considerably less well-behaved). Nevertheless, there is a distinct body of published work that defines the science of ecology, and part of the purpose of this book is to describe exactly what some of that work says. This description is presented in chapters 8, 9, 11, and 12.

THE HISTORICAL CONTEXT

There is, of course, a history to all of this—or rather, several histories. First is a scientific history, involving some critical experiments, some critical insights, several important debates, and the usual fare of patient plodding mixed with blinding insight. Much of this unfolds as the text is developed, especially in the more technical information.

Second, there are chains of events, historical narratives, that lay bare how current conditions came to be the way they are. Three particularly important historical narratives are included in this text—Chapter 4 on the evolution of *H. sapiens,* Chapter 10 on the evolution of the hydrocarbon society, and Chapter 13 on the development of agriculture. In all three cases, it is good to bear in mind that these narratives are told from a specific point of view (as are all historical narratives), and that a different observer might choose to tell a different narrative, albeit about the same subject.

Third, and finally, there is the general development of European thought concerning nature and *H. sapiens* subsequent to Darwin. This development has been channeled into two distinct traditions. The first tradition holds that human beings are embedded in natural structures that provide the primary limiting factors for progress, that our evolutionary heritage and ecological connections with nature provide certain limits that we would be fools to try to transcend. It is a kind of biological essentialism. The second tradition holds that human beings socially create structures, that these human-created structures impose whatever limits appear to exist, and they can thus be transcended with sufficient effort. These traditions are clearly recognizable in much of the environmental movement, with an understandable emphasis on one or the other, depending on one's conditions in life. This is the introductory topic (chapter 2) of this text, and represents a theme that resurfaces throughout.

A NOTE ON EPISTEMOLOGY

According to Gail,

> Walking down a darkly lit street, a large form hunkers in the shadow ahead of me. No one is around. A single street light illuminates ever so faintly. The form moves as I approach. I make a move to cross the street, the form rises from the shadow and appears to begin crossing the street, but becomes hidden among some parked cars. It is so dark. I continue walking. A sudden movement in the bushes next to me, something grabs my arm, I scream. It is only a branch touching my arm and the large form is an old man who I now see walking some distance ahead of me. Yet my adrenalin, like so many nights before, is at a high level.

Gail understands the feeling of walking alone on a dark street in the social climate of the times. It would be difficult for a male to understand that feeling in the same way that Gail does.

Beth testifies that "If you sum up the squares of two sides of a right triangle you get the square of the hypotenuse of that same triangle."

Beth understands the Pythagorean theorem.

Edward tells that

> Every Sunday we went to church. I don't go to church much anymore, but I remember Momma and Daddy taking all of us kids to church, and the pastor making me feel so good and so wanting to do good. And then I remember the singing and the indescribably ecstatic feeling I got when the pastor yelled "Praise the Lord!" after the choir finished, and I would sometimes yell "Amen," and "Tell it," and things like that. I may not go to church much anymore, but I still feel it and it feels good. It's what I call my religious tradition or religious upbringing and it helps me understand and cope with what's going on in the world.

Edward understands a part of the world that someone raised an atheist or Catholic or Muslim probably would find a bit foreign.

Marvin says, "I never would have thought that I could become so totally immersed in anything at all, but having my son Robert has changed my outlook on everything. I see what is meant by the joys of parenting and I also see that there was no possible way for me to see that before. I would do anything for Robert; indeed, I'm not sure I had much of a life before he was born."

Marvin understands fatherhood like no childless male possibly could.

Betty reports that "Enzyme activity was severely reduced in the high pH treatment."

Betty understands the effect of acidity on a particular enzyme.

Radnish tells me, "If you put a statue of Ganesh on your window sill and burn incense in front of it every day, you will have good luck. I know, because I have been doing it all my life."

Radnish understands the power of the god Ganesh like no one raised outside of the Hindu tradition possibly could.

All of the above vignettes are examples of knowing. There should be no question that all are legitimate. It used to be that philosophers would separate the Pythagorean theorem and enzyme activity examples and call those material knowledge, while all the other examples would be known more as spiritual or experiential knowledge. Thus is the standard classification of dualism: a dual system of knowledge, one scientific and mathematic, the other experiential and spiritual.

Since the advent of systematic thought (whenever that was), the human animal seems to have had an unswerving desire to fit all forms of knowledge under one umbrella, to reject the dualist philosophy. This has become an especially intense desire since the advent of modern science as a coevolutionary product of the Industrial Revolution, and in some ways culminated in the German monist movement (see chapter 2).

It is my position that the tendency toward monism is futile at best, and is probably pernicious. Indeed, a new philosophical tendency can be seen in many parts of the world, aligned with the basic tenets of philosophical dualism but more encompassing than previous forms. That tendency goes by the name of cultural diversity, cultural democracy, multiculturalism, and several others. It acknowledges that Gail's life experiences suit her to a particular kind of understanding of what it feels like for a woman to walk alone at night. Her knowledge is legitimate—like that of Edward, Marvin, and Radnish.

Epistemology is like a blind mountain climber. There is an ineluctable tendency to move upward, despite the fact that the top of the mountain is largely invisible. All new information, of whatever form, is incorporated into the information already constructed in one's memory, mainly information that comes from experience, but also much that has been abstractly constructed in the absence of experience (part and parcel of being *Homo sapiens*). Thus all new information is inevitably filtered through a set of preconceived notions, yet simultaneously contributes to changes in that set of notions. Faced with the obvious similarity between the skeletons of *Australopithecus* and *Homo sapiens,* a deeply religious Baptist steeped in the tradition of creationism sees those similarities quite differently from someone raised in an atheist tradition. The bones are clearly the same, but they have a different impact on the two people because of their background information.

It is unfortunate that many people, mainly those associated with the natural and physical sciences, tend to devalue knowledge that is not strictly material (although it could ultimately be argued that experiential knowledge is quite material anyway). Since such "non-material" knowledge accounts for more human behavior than the more clearly material knowledge, such an attitude simply creates narrow-mindedness. To be sure, the classic scientific method, of which natural and physical scientists are so proud, is exceedingly powerful when applicable. The problem is that it is not always applicable.

The scientific method is, in a sense, the great democratizer of knowledge. It is a recipe for knowledge. Given a problem, the scientific method gives a set of rules for solving it, and a very clear set of criteria for deciding when, in fact, the problem is solved. In a sense, it makes the creation of knowledge accessible to anyone. Just follow these rules, and you will get your answer. Science, from this point of view, is a way of knowing for those who are not very smart. It is so powerful that you don't have to think too much about what you're doing to get the right answer. But, indeed, it is a powerful method.

Unfortunately, the scientific method simply does not work for most types of knowledge that are important. This is why today's epistemology must be dual, or, better said, eclectic. It is also why I offer no apologies for the methodological and philosophical eclecticisms so evident in this text.

While different ways of knowing are certainly legitimate, it is nevertheless an error to assume that knowledge is all relative. All knowledge, including scientific knowledge, should be subject to question, challenge, and modification. An innocent child, brought up in a family that happens to believe that the earth is flat, will be disoriented when confronted with a society that generally believes the earth is round. The child's knowledge, based on family tradition, is legitimate but certainly not "correct" in any interesting sense of the word correct. The child will undoubtedly be challenged in the contemporary world, and more than likely will change his or her knowledge about the shape of the earth. So it is not the case that knowledge is completely relative, and it is most definitely the case that some things are wrong and others right.

A NOTE ON METHODOLOGY

This text ranges from some relatively technical expositions in chapters 3, 6, 8, 11, and 12, to the inclusion of *H. sapiens,* which changes not only what we understand but how we go about understanding it, in chapters 4, 5, 7, 9, 10, 13, 14, and 15. Here we begin to see a fundamental methodological problem that must be dealt with. Part of biology is clearly associated with topics that use standard scientific methods in the tradition that grew from the Industrial Revolution and, perhaps, even earlier. Although photosynthesis may seem like chemistry and orographic lifting like physics, when *Homo sapiens* comes onto the scene, special conditions arise, both for the environment itself and for the way we pursue an understanding of it. Unfortunately, beginning with the methodology of the natural sciences, it is easy to simply lapse into a use of the same methodology when dealing with human systems. This tendency is known as "positivism" and was largely discredited a hundred or so years ago, so we certainly do not want to repeat that error. What methodology, then, is to be used when studying biology, when that biology includes human beings?

Although we can easily dismiss positivism as inappropriate, it is not so easy to describe what methodology should, in fact, be used. It is tempting, especially for a biologist, to descend into another form of essentialism, interpreting human structures in terms of genetics and evolution, which are ultimately just as deceptive as positivism and just as seductive, if not more so. Since the transition from prehuman to human was so clearly a consequence of natural selection, it seems quite natural that the social world of that species should also be amenable to interpretation through natural selection. This line of reasoning is as old as the theory of natural selection itself, and has been discredited in much the same way as positivism—in fact, human beings create social structures that supersede their genetic structures so completely that new rules must be sought for understanding this unique species. As discussed in chapters 4 and 6, the tendency toward positivism generally and essentialism of the natural-selection sort should be rejected.

All of this still leaves us with the problem of what methodology really ought to be used in the study of *Homo sapiens*. My tendency, made clear as it develops (especially in chapters 4 and 9), is to emphasize the way in which human social structures dictate how humans transform material things, effectively, what Marvin Harris calls "cultural materialism." Yet I am aware of the limitations of this viewpoint.

Once *Homo sapiens* evolved language, various institutions arose from the social interactions of the members of the species (institutions that I later incorporate in the more general category of discourses). Whether such institutions in a primitive form actually existed in the times of *H. erectus* is completely unknown, but they certainly must have had their beginnings there if language itself had its beginnings there. Once human institutions become established, they seem to take on a life of their own. In dealing with this topic, there seem to be two rather extreme positions.

On the one hand is cultural materialism—the position that human institutions have some material justification at their foundation. For example, the phenomenon of India's sacred cows, when examined carefully, reveals all sorts of material reasons that cows should be preserved—they provide milk on a regular basis, they provide meat on an occasional basis (to be sold to Muslims), they are walking garbage disposals, and they provide dung that fuels thousands, if not millions, of small cooking fires each day. Could it be that all human customs, traditions, rules of conduct, world views, have similar simple functional rationales in real resources? This is the materialist extreme of the argument.

On the other hand is the position that human institutions take on an importance in and of themselves. Institutions think for themselves, as Mary Douglas titled her excellent book. I was told once in India that if I lit incense beneath a small statue of the god Ganesh, I would have good luck. As to why the god Ganesh cares about my incense, or whether he has the ability to affect my fortune, we would be hard pressed to imagine a material basis for such a belief. We might be able to imagine how some sort of material concern gave rise to the belief in Ganesh in the first place, but those who believe in the divine truth of this deity will undoubtedly have some behavior patterns that result from the reality of this institution, independent of its potential material origins.

There is a third position, I think; it is a somewhat more intermediate position. In the spirit of what some of the less relativistic postmodern thinkers have been writing, it is possible to understand human institutions as both material and non-material, if we examine the interrelations between the two. Thus, even in the case of the obviously material sacred cow of India, at least part of the farmer's willingness to abstain from the slaughter, even in the face of clearly visible Muslim customers, is more usefully viewed as a non-material-based behavior. Its material consequence is that the cow becomes an emergency resource (i.e., in an economic emergency, the cow can be slaughtered and sold to the Muslim). So we could imagine a sequence in which cows are said to be holy, but everyone knows that the reason is to stop people from slaughtering them, so there will be milk. The tradition is thus established of not slaughtering cows. As the tradition becomes older, the material reason may become submerged, and farmers will refrain from slaughtering cows because they are sacred, not because they give milk. But now, because of the custom, the cow actually becomes a different material thing, a hedge against economic emergency.

I take the position that while many human institutions have clear contemporary material foundations, many others have lost whatever material foundation they may have had in the past, and some may have never had such a foundation in the first place. What seems clear is that in many ways humans behave in accordance with tradition, custom, or habit, without the slightest notion of what might be the underlying or original material basis for the behavior.

Humans construct amazing institutions at an amazing rate, in diverse situations, and come up with a bewildering array of different forms, each of which is only partially understandable. Indeed, social scientists have long marveled at this diversity, and regularly lament their inability to devise a general approach that would make all that diversity make sense. Yet there is a particular form of human institution that seems to transcend all cultures, and would appear to be very old, perhaps as old as language itself. As humans go through life engaging in inevitable social interactions with one another, they develop some sort of world view, a way of understanding their surroundings without specifically thinking about them. This notion takes on different nomenclature in different disciplines—the world view, the conventional wisdom, the received wisdom, the paradigm, the conceptual scheme—but the general idea is quite similar in all. The idea can be traced to earlier thinkers. For example, Douglas notes,

> According to Durkheim, . . . individuals come to think alike by internalizing their idea of the social order and sacralizing it. . . . the shared symbolic universe and the classifications of nature embody the principles of authority and coordination. In such a system problems of legitimacy are solved because individuals carry the social order around inside their heads and project it out onto nature.[1]

Douglas also quotes the philosopher Fleck,

> The individual within the collective is never, or hardly ever, conscious of the prevailing thought style which almost always exerts an absolutely compulsive force upon his thinking, and with which it is not possible to be at variance.[2]

While other authors could be cited in diverse fields, perhaps the most challenging and important interpretation of this old idea is the recent voluminous work of Michel Foucault. Citing Foucault is likely to be controversial, for he, more than any other, has come to symbolize the recent trends in postmodern relativism. Nevertheless I choose to jump into this controversial morass, just for a moment, since I feel that Foucault has provided the most penetrating insights, at least recently, into this very difficult terrain.

Foucault identifies the phenomenon of concern as the discourse.

> . . . discourse is constituted by the difference between what one *could* say correctly at one period . . . and what is actually said.[3] [Emphasis added.]

In addition to recognizing the phenomenon and casting it in its broadest framework, Foucault has illustrated in several key cases how the discourse is altered and, in some cases, dramatically changed ("ruptured"). Chapter 4 speculates on the evolutionary origins of discourse formation (and, consequently, the formation of institutions, conventional wisdoms, and the like), likely a far more important human characteristic than bipedalism or primitive tool use.

Thus, from the natural selectionist to the cultural selectionist, and later from the materialist to the institutionalist, and even from the contemporary economistic to the historical developmentalist, the general methodology used in this book can only be described as eclectic. To adopt an eclectic strategy implies studying subjects that have been relegated by the academy to different "disciplines."

Thus, we are immediately faced with what has become a classic problem—how to speak interdisciplinarily when disciplinary languages are so specialized. The standard solution to this problem is to define every project as one of separate subprojects, each subproject associated with a recognized discipline. So, for example, a so-called interdisciplinary development project in Africa will have an agronomist, a sociologist, an entomologist, an economist, and probably some other ists, each well versed in his or her field, and each bent on doing his or her project independently of the others. My experience with such projects is that the various specialists not only do not talk to each other, but also really do not take the other specialists very seriously in the first place—the entomologists think that the sociologists just talk a lot of bull and the sociologists think the agronomists are incapable of thinking beyond their statistical designs. While I can think of exceptions to this rule, it seems that most attempts at incorporating separate disciplines into a project by tapping individual experts have been comical failures.

Yet we are faced with the clear quandary that many problems we wish to solve are poorly understood, and those knowledge gaps cry out for information and analysis that typically resides in several different disciplines. Some sort of interdisciplinary focus is clearly required, yet its exact form is elusive. Anthropologist Alan Wolf (1989) has written brilliantly on this topic regarding the human sciences, and I can only urge compliance with his point of view, when he laments,

> If there are connections everywhere, why do we persist in turning dynamic, interconnected phenomena into static, disconnected things.

Since my purpose is to understand the relationship between the species *Homo sapiens* and its environment, both ecological and social, those connections that exist everywhere must be the focus of the study. Some subjects will appear to be economic, others sociological, others historical, and so on. Yet it is the connection among them that forms the basis of a true understanding of humans and their environment, and it is that sort of interdisciplinary focus that I seek. Thus, the usual compliance with and respect for disciplinary boundaries will not be a goal of this text. Indeed, I struggle to break these boundaries down.

One final methodological note is worthy of mention here. The traditional notion of the scientific method, in its simplest form, includes three stages: (1) observation ("Good grief, look at that. Why does it do that?"), (2) hypothesis formation ("It does that because the third gizmo on the left has not been oiled"), and (3) hypothesis testing ("That makes sense, but I just oiled the gizmo and it still does that. I reject your hypothesis."). In the real world, the scientific method is a lot more complicated than this schoolroom version, but supposedly operates on these three basic principles: First, make an observation about nature; second, tell a story about why the observation is the way it is; and third, gather evidence to support the veracity of your story. All too frequently, in the sciences related to humans, the third part of the scientific method is given short shrift. When reading a text (any text, including this one), the wise reader will always repeat to himself or herself, "What is the evidence for that?" All too frequently, the answer will be "none," or effectively none (watch for euphemisms like "the evidence is weak, but . . . ," "scholars are in disagreement but . . . ," "the small amount of evidence that we have been able to obtain indicates that . . ."). Much that we would like to be able to submit to real scientific scrutiny is not possible when studying humans, and we resort to a great deal of speculation to fill in obvious gaps in knowledge.

Respecting at all times the well-founded criticisms of positivism and the rampant fear that positivism will creep into the human sciences any time a natural scientist puts his or her foot in, reliance on evidence is a piece of the traditional scientific method that ought to be adopted. Indeed, some would argue that the most important contribution made by the Western scientific tradition is not a reliance on testing of predictions generated by theories, but rather a change from relying on authority to relying on evidence. A natural scientist never (or should never) asks, "Who's your authority on that?" but rather asks, "What is your evidence for that?"

This proposition is the piece of the Western scientific tradition that is most important in approaching subjects involving the species *Homo sapiens*. One should be relatively free to speculate about function and origin, but the constraints of available evidence ought always be part of the methodology. We do not use evidence from DNA with respect to the common ancestor of *Homo habilis* and *Homo erectus* simply because that evidence is unobtainable, and, thus, all of us who are interested in that question realize that one of our constraints is that a whole class of evidence we may wish to consider is simply not at our disposal. The rest of the evidence—stone tools, campfire remains, and skeletons, for example—are at best imperfect classes of evidence, but they are all that is available.

Thus, the general methodology employed in this text can be summarized as: (1) human affairs are structured in great part by the way in which humans have come to transform material resources (cultural materialism); (2) the subject matter is too complex to remain within traditional boundaries (multidisciplinary); and (3) we shall try to rely on evidence, rather than authority, in trying to understand this most complicated of all animals.

Any attempt at understanding *Homo sapiens* faces an additional epistemological problem, especially when we arrive at an interpretation of contemporary structures. One is tempted to use a weak metaphor of the Heisenberg uncertainty principle (you cannot simultaneously know the position and velocity of a subatomic particle) by noting that it is difficult to maintain one's social and cultural being while trying to understand that being. You cannot be a person and understand that person at the same time. Such a constraint is to be attacked, it seems to me, but frequently the attack hits too close to home. If it is true that much of what we regard as the essence of our own humanness begins to appear more myth than reality, myth created by someone or some group that wishes to maintain power over us, or advantage over us, we are challenged to change, or should be. And while humans frequently seem to resist change, we know that they in fact do so, sometimes radically.

TWO

Biological Essentialism Versus Social Construction: The Legacy of the Nineteenth Century

History is a great teacher, partly because it repeats itself, but mainly because it provides a context for the present. Just as the archaeologist is unable to find meaning in an ancient sculpture if it is not found in the context of other artifacts, analysts of current events must be able to contextualize if those events are to have meaning. If ignorance of history is lack of context, then those ignorant of history will never find meaning.

This book is about the present. It is partly about biology, and partly about how biology affects and is affected by society. As an ancient sculpture in the hands of an archaeologist, without context there can be no meaning.

The context for biology as a science involves not only the historical sequence of *Homo sapiens,* but also all of life's history, spanning a period of more than three billion years. But the intellectual discipline called biology is really a product of the modern era. Certainly Greek philosophers were biologists in their own right (indeed, much of today's natural history was first done by Aristotle), Egyptian mummifiers were in some sense anatomists, and groups in prehistory undoubtedly had medical procedures that were, in a vague way, based on biological principles. But the science of biology would not be fully constructed until Western science itself was constructed, and this certainly did not happen in any significant way before the modern period.

While medicine and nature study flourished in China and Europe before and during the early years of the modern period, the watershed event for biology was the publication of Darwin's *On the Origin of Species* in 1859, marking the beginning of modern biology. We thus look to the latter half of the nineteenth century to understand the origin of modern biology, and to appreciate how some subtle and not-so-subtle ideas about biology came to be—how biology became involved in contemporary human affairs.

Pondering the human condition in the nineteenth century must have been quite disturbing for anyone with even slightly humanistic tendencies. European industrial capitalism had, in a sense, matured, and the conditions of the working class were nothing short of scandalous.[1] Worse, if one took a serious look at the colonies and the quality of life there, a humanist could get downright depressed. The world had become one, but the various fiefdoms of financial power remained as much at odds with one another as they had been when they were concerned with castles and kings. The changes induced between 1450 and 1550 had come home to roost, and the ugly underbelly of the modern period became exposed.[2]

Within this social and political cauldron, great intellectual changes were stirring, changes that remain part and parcel of fundamental contemporary debates. Two main intellectual themes emerged in their modern form during this time. They reflected, in part, much older themes, but they took on a new, more "scientific" character. They were based, to a large extent, on distinct views of how the Darwinian revolution should influence our interpretation of human society. One theme was something of a literal translation of Darwinian principles to human social operations, in which the human condition was seen as a simple outgrowth of natural selection, no different from the history of any other species. The remarkable intellectual success of Darwin's theory in a sense gave license to relegate all human existence to an essential biological nature. This was not the first time that the human condition had been thought of as composed of "essential" elements (that which God put on earth with Adam and Eve, for example). But such essentialism gained new respectability. A new school thus emerged that a cynic might say simply reiterated much of the prejudices of the clerics, but with a veneer of scientific authority. This school of thought I call the "natural structures" school, to distinguish it from earlier forms of biological essentialism.

Another theme was something of a metaphorical application of Darwin's ideas to human social structures, in which purely social formations, such as social classes, could be seen vying for the right to survive and reproduce in a manner reminiscent of individual lions vying for the tenderest piece of zebra meat or zebras competing for the crucial corner of lion-free space. This school of thought I call the "human structures" school. It did not regard the human condition as emanating from anything essential, either biological or religious, but rather saw the bulk of human affairs resulting from the way people interact with one another. It was concerned with things like the social transformation of resources, general social construction, and the formation of discourses.[3]

THE NATURAL STRUCTURES SCHOOL OF THOUGHT

As a scientific theory, the theory of natural selection was not particularly controversial, as Darwin had taken great pains to accumulate mounds of evidence before publication (indeed, the simultaneous formulation of the theory of natural selection by Alfred Russel Wallace finally pushed Darwin to finish his opus).[4] It was its particular application to human society, a topic that Darwin had not really dealt with, that was most controversial.

The natural structures school, developed originally in England and Germany, was the outgrowth of the thoughts of many people. But two figures stand out as especially important: Herbert Spencer in England and Ernst Haeckel in Germany. Of their many writings, and of those of their followers, it is possible to identify three interrelated tendencies: (1) genetic determinism, (2) Malthusianism, and (3) nature worship.[5]

Genetic Determinism

Haeckel was perhaps the most influential biologist in nineteenth-century Germany, and was a prolific writer, not only of scientific papers but, most importantly, of many popular books. His most influential work was *The Riddle of the Universe,* in which he laid out his overall theory of the natural unity of everything, what he called "monism" (as contrasted to dualism, in which part of the world was interpreted as material and part as spiritual), and which became something of a bible for the influential organization called the Monist League.[6]

The monists saw everything as decipherable through physical and biological laws, something that does not surprise anyone today, but that was antithetical to nineteenth-century Judeo-Christian thought. However, it is not this central point of the monists that distinguishes them from the "human structures" school of thought, but rather their particular adoption of Darwinism in a direct, non-metaphorical, manner. Human beings were just like other animals, they argued, our level of consciousness and social organization being only quantitatively different from what exists in other mammals. According to Haeckel,

> The higher vertebrates . . . have just as good a title to "reason" as man himself, and within the limits of the animal world there is the same long chain of the gradual development of reason as in the case of humanity.[7]

Hitler's *Mein Kampf* was strongly influenced by the German Monist League, at times sounding even logical from a biological point of view. Hitler noted, for example, that the normal course of events in animal populations is for subpopulations to form, usually through some form of physical isolation. The animals in those subpopulations then slowly diverge in appearance from one another, eventually forming physically distinguishable races. When (or if) the physical barrier is later removed, the races come in contact and either (1) the better-adapted race eliminates the inferior race through competition, or (2) the intermingling of the two races forms a new race that is intermediate between the two, better adapted than the lower race, but more poorly adapted than the higher race. While such thinking may appear quaint to a modern evolutionary biologist, it is not really that far off the mark. While we rarely talk of "races" any longer, we certainly do recognize genetically distinct subpopulations having arisen through various mechanisms, including natural selection, and we certainly recognize that when two subpopulations overlap in their ranges they typically form intergrades that are generally intermediate between the two physical types. In short, Hitler was close to, if not right on the money with regard to possible scenarios in the evolution of subpopulations of nonhuman animals, something most likely gleaned from the German Monist League.[8]

It was when he extended his analysis to the level of *Homo sapiens* that he erred. He reasoned that human subpopulations must have formed in the past, similarly to other animals, but unlike other animals, humans, with their gift of language and culture, engaged in productive activities that required socially organized labor. When one race encountered the members of another race, rather than killing them (either directly or indirectly) as other animals would do, the superior race enslaved or otherwise captured the labor power of the inferior race.[9] In so doing, the races were forced to physically intermingle, which inevitably resulted in inter-breeding and the eventual "mongrelization" of the race. One event that occurs regularly, as a normal course of nature, is the elimination of one race by a better-adapted one, just as within populations better-adapted individuals gradually eliminate less-adapted ones by leaving more off-spring. Because of human culture, and especially because of the Christian religion, according to Haeckel, *Homo sapiens* averts this eventuality, thus short-circuiting its own improvement.

> The artificial selection practised in our civilized states sufficiently explains the sad fact that, in reality, weakness of the body and character are on the perpetual increase among civilized nations, and that, together with strong, healthy bodies, free and independent spirits are becoming more and more scarce.[10]

According to Haeckel, the superior (better adapted) races have something of a biological or moral responsibility to eliminate the inferior (more poorly adapted) races, just as happens in other species.

It would not be difficult to guess which race was the "better adapted" according to Haeckel:

> The difference between the reason of a Goethe, a Kant, a Lamarck, or a Darwin, and that of the lowest savage, . . . is much greater than the gradua-ted difference between the reason of the latter and that of the most "ratio-nal" mammals, the anthropoid apes, or even the papiomorpha [baboons], the dog, or the elephant.[11]

What this means, in practice, is,

> . . . [since the] lower races are psychologically nearer to the mammals than to civilized Europeans, we must, therefore, assign a totally different value to their lives.[12]

And what race sat atop the hill? Based partly on the idea of a common stem in the evolutionary tree of languages, the original stem of human racial groups was thought to represent the original European race, the people who invented "civilization and dignity," European style. That stem was called Aryan. All other "races" (Slavs, French, Mediterraneans, Jews, and so on) were deviations from this stem, and had been protected from what would have been their natural fate, extermination by the superior Aryans, because of the very civilization those Aryans had created. A "realistic" look at inevitable natural processes would reveal that the same civilizing influence of the superior Aryan race was a stumbling block to further advanced civilization. As part of the baggage of the high civilization of the Aryans, they had evolved a moralistic and humanistic attitude toward other races, and this was their ruin. A realistic program would mold politics on the hard facts of science, one of which was that the Aryan race was superior to all other races and had the right, even the obligation, to suppress their advancement.

Identical arguments were posed for "inferior" individuals in the population of the Aryans themselves, most dramatically illustrated by Haeckel's lauding certain Spartan customs:

> the most "remarkable" aspect of Spartan history, Haeckel wrote, was their "obedience to a special law" whereby "all newly-born children were subject to careful examination or selection." Then, those children who were "weak, sickly, or affected with any bodily infirmity were killed." It was only the "perfectly healthy and strong children [who] were allowed to live, and they alone afterwards propagated the race." In this way the Spartans were "not only continually in excellent strength and vigor," but they also perfected their bodies and increased their strength with every generation. Haeckel concluded, therefore, that the "destruction of abnormal new-born infants" could not be "rationally" classified as "murder" as is "done in modern legal works." One should regard it rather, he wrote, as a "practice of advantage both to the infants destroyed and to the community." Haeckel, therefore, advised the Germans to emulate the example of the ancient Spartans. Was it not, he argued, only a "traditional dogma" that life had to be sustained under all circumstances.[13]

Such ideas certainly seem harsh by today's standards, but they are based on biological ideas that still enjoy wide acceptance among the public, if only subconsciously. Much like Malthusianism and nature worship, as described below, biological determinism is alive and well in much of the contemporary world, having adapted itself to new political conditions, and performing the same pernicious function it did in Germany. First, in the developed world, the generally lower social class position of people defined as belonging to "other" races (and the definition itself is, of course, arbitrary and without biological merit)[14] is thought to be "at least partly" determined by their less well-endowed genetic makeup. Subtle assumptions about African Americans in the United States, or Pakistanis in England, or Chinese in Japan, retain the same racist flavor so characteristic of the German monists, and scientists in all of those countries are busily elaborating theories that serve to justify those subtle assumptions. For the most part, such scientists are in the minority today, receiving little encouragement from the scientific community in general, but nevertheless sometimes capturing the lion's share of public attention.[15]

Second, between the developed and Third World countries, racist assumptions, again usually subtle, underlay imperialism in the same way they did in Germany. It is assumed, with very little questioning, that the United States has the right to dictate what political structures are allowable in the countries of Latin America. Why? The popular debate is structured along the lines of how the United States should go about its objectives of dictating to the Latins, soft-hearted liberals suggesting that we accomplish it through diplomacy and economic pressures, and hard-line realists demanding a certain degree of saber rattling and gunboat realism, but no one in the mainstream questioning the ultimate right of the United States to dictate the limits of political philosophy to Latin Americans.[16]

Third, and frequently least recognized and appreciated, but perhaps strongest in practice, within the Third World itself racist assumptions are rampant, not only in places like Guatemala and Bolivia, where large populations of indigenous people remain, but also in completely Westernized countries, such as El Salvador. A Nicaraguan once told me, for example, that most of his country's problems were due to its "*indi*osyncracies," and, most disturbingly, even Latin American peasants themselves frequently identify much of their social position with the fact that they are cursed with their Indian heritage.

Fourth, while in the eighteenth century it hardly needed to be articulated that biology was destiny for the female of the species, such ideas are rampant today as well. Women are thought to be "by nature" more intuitive, more caring, less "linear," and the like. Or, if your politics are different, women are less capable, more dependent, and sillier than men—by their "nature," of course. Carol Tavris dissects these ideas in great detail.[17]

Malthusianism

The Reverend Thomas Malthus laid the groundwork for notions of how the size and/or rate of growth of the human population would determine the human condition. At a simple mathematical level, Malthusian ideas are obviously correct and hardly earth-shattering as intellectual currency—the world is finite, a growing population will eventually become crowded. It was the political implications of the ideas that became part and parcel of the natural structures school of thought. To this day they retain their sinister potential.

Malthus took a phenomenon of social relations and biologized it. The trading of goods and services, the basis of what the science of economics is all about, is a profoundly social activity. Economists before and since have sought to understand how this remarkably complicated social activity actually functions. Malthus was the first to interject an important nonsocial component into the equation. He noted two very simple facts: one, food is necessary for survival, and the production of food is ultimately limited; and two, the "passion between the sexes" leads inevitably to the growth of the population. Thus, two profoundly biological forces, agricultural production and human population growth, were brought into the equation. Human population growth would inevitably exceed the capacity to produce food and, thus, produce human misery. Biology was introduced into the social equation as an underlying, or essential, force.[18]

This biological essentialism directly determined, according to Malthus, what certain aspects of public policy should be. For example,

> . . . whatever steps may be taken [to relieve the suffering of the poor] . . . it is necessary to be fully aware of the natural tendency of the labouring classes of society to increase beyond the demand for their labour or the means of their adequate support, and the effect of this tenedency to throw the greatest difficulties in the way of permanently improving their condition.[19]

The inhuman conditions in which the laboring masses lived could thus be written off as a consequence of the operation of natural biological laws, something that social policy could do little about; indeed, something that ill-considered social policy might actually exacerbate.

Malthus and his followers thus effectively created a convenient scapegoat for many social problems.[20] They took a simple biological/mathematical truism and extended it to account for the growing social problems of the day—as biological organisms, the "passion between the sexes" would always cause population growth, yet the capacity to produce food and other necessities was ultimately limited. The condition of society's underpriviliged derived from the fact that they had so many babies, not from any possible structural defect in the system.

These ideas have been largely rejected, at least in their crudest form, by modern analysts.[21] *Homo sapiens* is a complicated species that engages in resource use patterns unlike any other, and it is simply not possible to simplify what it does in order to analyze it as if it were a population of fruit flies. But in the nineteenth century, such arguments seemed compelling to many. Indeed, they were a central building block of Herbert Spencer's application of Darwinian principles, applying the ideas in a practical form to England, but theoretically proposing them as universal laws of human society.

Spencer focused on the Malthusian character of Darwin's theory, but combined it with strong biological determinism. Having promoted Malthusian ideas before Darwin's ideas were made public, he found in the principle of natural selection a powerful *raison d'être* for political power differentials in modern societies. Overpopulation, according to Spencer, was an inevitable consequence of the human tendency to reproduce, leading to the inevitable consequence that some members of the society would survive, while others would perish. Who would survive? Obviously the fittest, leading to the ever-popular phrase "survival of the fittest," which was coined by Spencer, not Darwin. The biological determinist tone of Spencer's Malthusianism cannot be overestimated, as, for example, when he states,

> The poverty of the incapable, the distresses that come upon the imprudent, the starvation of the idle . . . are the decrees of a large, far seeing benevolence, [which also] brings to early graves the children of diseased parents, and singles out the low-spirited, the intemperate and the debilitated as the victims of an epidemic.[22]

Spencer's form of Malthusianism and genetic determinism caught on like wildfire in the United States, where the unbridled greed of robber barons clashed with underlying principles of egalitarianism on which the U.S. Constitution was based. Foremost amongst its proponents was the distinguished Yale professor William Graham Sumner, who, perhaps more than Spencer himself, united the two principles of Malthusianism and genetic determinism. According to Shipman,

Sumner . . . sprinkled the fertilizer of the Protestant work ethic onto the soil of Malthusian economics in which Darwinian evolution was rooted. . . . It was readily apparent to him that people were biologically and, more important, morally unequal. Natural selection must be left to take its course, he maintained, and he felt a deep animosity for the social meddlers who were always trying to help the unfit. Poverty was simply the natural result of innate inferiority and a lack of thrift, industry, honesty, and sobriety. To alleviate it was to encourage bad behavior, to foster the spread of undesirable traits in the population, and to burden unfairly those who had succeeded through hard work.[23]

The connection between genetic determinism and Malthusianism continued through the earlier parts of the present century. For example, Fredrick Osborn, cofounder of the Pioneer Fund in 1937,[24] combined eugenics and population as part and parcel of the same determinism. In his influential 1958 essay, for example, he wrote,

. . . excessive fertility by families with meager resources must be recognized as one of the potent forces in the perpetuation of slums, ill health, inadequate education, and even delinquency. . . . The characteristics of each new generation . . . include hereditary factors that are often transmitted with remarkable constancy through innumerable generations.[25]

As with Spencer, American Malthusianists' vision corresponded well with the vision of laissez-faire economics so prominent among the rising entrepreuneral class of the youthful United States. Many rich industrialists could be cited, but probably the most famous is John D. Rockefeller:

The growth of a large business is merely the survival of the fittest. The American Beauty rose can be produced in the splendor and fragrance which bring cheer to the beholder only by sacrificing the early buds which grow up round it. This is not an evil tendency in business. It is merely the working out of a law of Nature and a law of God.[26]

I am not really sure how God gets thrown in, but the sense of Mr. Rockefeller's quote is clear. Just as biology justified the expansion of Nazi Germany throughout Europe, it also apparently justified the growth and expansion of U.S. corporations.

One would think that ideas that appear so ludicrous today would be detectable only on the lunatic fringe, but this is not so. The philosophy expressed by Garrett Hardin, a respected ecologist from California, repeats the arguments of *Lebensraum* almost word for word,[27] using the crude example of a lifeboat (we, in the developed countries, are in a lifeboat with large numbers of people drowning in the ocean around us. If we let them in the lifeboat, our lifeboat will become overcrowded, sink, and we all will perish. Thus, we are compelled to protect our lifeboat from those who would seek to overpopulate it). According to Hardin:

> ... the allocation of rights based on territory must be defended if a ruinous breeding race is to be avoided. It is unlikely that civilization and dignity can survive everywhere; but better in a few places than in none. Fortunate minorities must act as the trustees of a civilization that is threatened by uninformed good intentions.[28]

And such ideas remain popular among many professional biologists (but not the majority, by any means).

Nature Worship

German neo-romanticism grew out of a sense of frustration with the social problems arising from industrial capitalism—the problems of urbanization, pollution, poverty, and the like. One could hardly avoid despair when viewing such problems, and such despair permeated the intellectual thought of the time. A feeling that somehow things would get better, or looked at in another way actually were better than they seemed, or could be made better if we only understood how, was perhaps a necessary antidote to the readily observable problems of the day. When clouds were so dark, could not a silver lining be found?

For some, the silver lining was in the ultimate and inevitable overthrow of the capitalist system, followed by the construction of a society in which social classes no longer existed and ever-increasing material wealth paired with human equality to form a socialist utopia. For others, like Haeckel and the monists, the evils of industrial capitalism were contrasted to the beauty of the natural world. Nature, unspoiled by *Homo sapiens,* was a picture of harmony and perfection. Rabidly anti-religious, the monists identified their new religion openly and vigorously as "science" and nature. In a chapter in Haeckel's *The Riddle of the Universe* entitled "Our Monistic Religion," he explains,

> ... it is of the first importance that modern science not only shatter the false structures of superstition [i.e., of religion] and sweep their ruins from the path, but that it also erect a new abode for human emotion ... the Trinity of "the true, the good, and the beautiful."[29]

Admitedly, it is difficult to criticize someone who seeks to base a philosophy on that which is true, good, and beautiful. I should only point out that such wording is a clear reflection of the neo-romanticism alluded to earlier. And what is truth? According to Haeckel,

> . . . truth unadulterated is only to be found in the temple of the study of nature . . . The paths which lead to the noble divinity of truth and knowledge are the loving study of nature and its laws.[30]

With regard to what is good, the monists differed little from the Christians, but with regard to beauty,

> [t]he diametrical opposite of this dominant Christian art is the new artistic tendency which has been developed during the present century in connection with science. The remarkable expansion of our knowledge of nature, and the discovery of countless beautiful forms of life, which it includes, have awakened quite a new aesthetic sense in our generation, and thus given a new tone to painting and sculpture. Numerous scientific voyages and expeditions for the exploration of unknown lands and seas, partly in earlier centuries, but more especially in the nineteenth, have brought to light an undreamed abundance of new organic forms. The number of new species of animals and plants soon became enormous, and among them . . . there were thousands of forms of great beauty and interest, affording an entirely new inspiration for painting, sculpture, architecture, and technical art.[31]

And he goes on,

> All these sources of the keenest enjoyment of nature have only recently been revealed to us in all their splendor, and the remarkable progress we have made in facility and rapidity of conveyance has given even the less wealthy an opportunity of approaching them. All this progress in the aesthetic enjoyment of nature—and, proportionately, in the scientific understanding of nature—implies an equal advance in higher mental development and, consequently, in the direction of our monistic religion.[32]

The monists, probably through a combination of the neo-romanticism growing in Germany at the time and the biological prejudices of Haeckel, developed a sense of the natural world that was self-consciously religious. Nature, untouched by the unnatural hand of *Homo sapiens,* was the essence of truth, good, and beauty, and became the new religion of the rabidly anti-Christian monists.

It merits considerable reflection that this extreme nature worship was part and parcel of the monists' world view (along with Malthusianism and biological determinism), and that it has become so popular in the developed world today. First, we should reflect on its practical utility as a philosophy. Some of us find nature beautiful indeed. But there is certainly no basis in science for suggesting that nature is more beautiful than a Frank Lloyd Wright building, or the pirouette of a ballerina, or the solution of a complex equation, or even the beat of a heavy-metal rock band. While human activity creates certain things that almost everyone agrees are ugly (I have yet to hear anyone suggest that the *Valdez* oil spill was pretty, or that the Chernobyl explosion was aesthetically pleasing), there is, according to most people, great beauty in things that humans do. Indeed, the very notion of beauty could not exist at all without human consciousness.[33]

But, second, we should reflect on a frequently unstated assumption of nature worship that probably originated with the monists, that the love of nature must imply something of a hatred of humanity, something that some of the contemporary popular ecology movement seems to viscerally adopt, and something that is neither necessary, nor, in my opinion, desirable.

HITLER, EUGENICS, AND NATURAL STRUCTURES

It is, I think, always a useful exercise to imagine what future historians will say. As the noblemen led the crusades in the Middle Ages, I have no doubt they saw future historians lauding their bravery as they saved the Christian world. Few of them imagined that their escapades might be seen in the future as pointless expenditures of human lives, and certainly none of them could have predicted that the thieves and terrorists of Sherwood Forest would fire the imagination of adventurous young people more than the legend of King Arthur. Similar scenarios could be constructed around Caligula, or Hatshepsut, or, for that matter, probably Moses, Jesus, or Mohammed.

As we come to the end of the modern era, we might reflect on how we will be treated 2,000 years hence. Certainly ours will be a highly analyzed half-millennium, and our wars and technical advances will almost certainly be major foci. But stepping back and honestly reflecting on our modern era, three astonishing subjects have always struck me. The Europeans, founders of the modern civilization of which we are so proud, murdered millions of the natives of America, they enslaved millions of Africans, and they annihilated six million Jews. The modernism we all take for granted would certainly not have developed the way it did if the first two of these events had not been permitted to happen, and the Holocaust must be seen as an outcome of modernism itself. While the genocide of the people of the American continents and the enslavment of the people of the African continent are events that deserve a great deal of personal reflection on the part of all Europeans and their descendants, the Holocaust is on another level entirely. While the former two phenomena were precursors to, and probably prerequisites to, the development of modernism, the Holocaust was an outcome, a result of something operative within the system we call modern.

In fact, the Holocaust was the final stage of a journey that began a half-century earlier, in some ways the direct descendant of the monists and their philosophy, yet gaining its original justification from earlier trends that took hold in England.[34] Darwin's cousin, Francis Galton, used his considerable wealth to promote an idea that seemed so obvious as to need little scientific justification. The idea was twofold: first, that human characteristics such as intelligence, thrift, aggression, and the like, were subject to the same laws of natural selection as characteristics such as coat color, tail length, or body size in other animals; second, it should be possible, perhaps imperative, to direct the course of natural selection of these characteristics, which is to say, convert the natural selection of these characteristics to an artificial form, by choosing which individual people should be allowed to breed. Thus was born the field of eugenics.

Galton, whose brilliance is certainly more debatable than his wealth, was soon joined by the clearly brilliant Karl Pearson, a renowned statistician. Pearson entered the fray and, in the course of trying to promote eugenics as a respectable science, developed several statistical techniques that remain in use even today. Together, Galton and Pearson developed most of the ideas that became the bulwark of eugenics. It is worth noting that much of this scientific (or pseudo-scientific) framework was established well before the rediscovery of Mendel's work, and thus had to develop without a firm foundation in genetics. This was not seen as a problem, and the ideas of eugenics developed rapidly under the creative leadership of Galton and Pearson. Two currents developed simultaneously. First was the idea that a great many human characteristics were assumed to have a genetic basis. Large databases were accumulated on the distribution of these characteristics in human populations. Second, and far more pernicious, was the idea that we could, and perhaps should, intervene in the process of human reproduction, for the genetic health of the population.

From the second of these currents arose two methodological points of view, positive eugenics and negative eugenics. Positive eugenics was simply the encouragement of "good" gene stock to breed more frequently, while negative eugenics was the encouragement of "poor" gene stock to breed less frequently or not at all. The extremes of negative eugenics would be experienced a short half-century later in Nazi Germany.

While eugenics originated in England, its most enthusiastic development, prior to the Nazis, was in the United States. If in England there had been major concerns about the great conflicts that were growing between the working and bourgeois classes, in the United States such concerns were focused quite differently. At the turn of the century, the United States experienced waves of immigrants. The knowledge that the rapid industrial growth of the country required such an immigration to fill the rapidly expanding job base did not curtail the popular feeling that there was a general problem brewing as a consequence of allowing foreign workers into the country. Would this be the feared "mongrelizing" factor that would dilute the fine genetic stock of "real Americans"? Would the famous melting pot turn out to be a cauldron of genetic deterioration? As a sign of the times, consider the thoughts of Madison Grant, author of *The Passing of the Great Race,* an immensely popular book, reprinted at least seven times. Grant writes,

> What the Melting Pot actually does in practice can be seen in Mexico, where the absorption of the blood of the original Spanish conquerors by the native Indian population has produced the racial mixture which we call Mexican and which is now engaged in demonstrating its incapacity for self-government.[35]

And about the newly arriving immigrants in the United States he writes,

> These new immigrants were no longer exclusively members of the Nordic race as were the earlier ones . . . The transportation lines advertised America as a land flowing with milk and honey and the European governments took the opportunity to unload upon careless, wealthy and hospitable America the sweepings of their jails and asylums . . . Our jails, insane asylums and

almshouses are filled with this human flotsam and the whole tone of American life, social, moral and political has been lowered and vulgarized by them.[36]

Grant finally concludes,

We Americans must realize that the altruistic ideals which have controlled our social development during the past century and the maudlin sentimentalism that has made America "an asylum for the oppressed," are sweeping the nation toward a racial abyss. If the Melting Pot is allowed to boil without control and we continue to follow our national motto and deliberately blind ourselves to all "distinctions of race, creed or color," the type of native American [he is not talking of American Indians] of Colonial descent will become as extinct as the Athenian of the Age of Pericles, and the Viking of the days of Rollo.[37]

It was into this atmosphere that the biologist Charles Davenport stepped. Davenport convinced the Carnegie Institute to fund a center for the study of human heredity. He was granted rather lavish funding and became the director of the new laboratory at Cold Spring Harbor in New York. Davenport's institute was responsible for the original idea of a national immigration policy based on genetics, although his genetics, by modern standards, was a bit crude. For example, he felt that Italians were prone to "crimes of personal violence," while Poles were "independent and self-reliant though clannish." Greeks and Serbs were "slovenly"; Swedes, Germans, and Bohemians were "tidy," but occasionally given to "thieving." Hebrews were "intermediate" between the Greeks and Germans.[38] Davenport was an advocate of both positive and negative eugenics, and his influence was to have two practical consequences in the United States, sterilization laws and immigration restriction. Sterilization laws were eventually enacted in 22 states and produced some of the worst, and to this day relatively unknown, violations of human rights within the country. The culmination was probably the Supreme Court's upholding of the Virginia sterilization law in the celebrated case of Carrie Buck.[39] Both Carrie Buck and her mother were judged as feebleminded, and the court-ordered sterilization of Carrie was upheld by the Supreme Court. A key piece of evidence was Carrie's daughter, who was also judged to be feebleminded—she was examined when she was seven months old. Justice Oliver Wendell Holmes presided over the case. For good measure, Carrie's sister Doris was also forceably sterilized after doctors told her she was going to have an appendectomy. Doris only learned what had been done to her some 50 years later. Her response was, "I broke down and cried. My husband and me wanted children desperate—we were crazy about them. I never new what they'd done to me."[40]

As cruel and inhuman as the eugenics movement in the United States may seem to us today, its real importance lies in the effect it had elsewhere, in Germany. While the biological background for Nazism had been laid down by Haeckel and his monists, the practical aspects of the Nazis' sterilization program was strongly influenced by the sterilization laws and eugenics movement in the United States.[41] The evolving German racial policies were lauded by leading U.S. eugenicists, and no wonder, as they were initially patterned after similar laws in the *U.S. Eugenic News,* of which Davenport was one of the editors. The *Eugenic News* reported, in 1934,

> One may condemn the Nazi policy generally, but specifically it remained for Germany in 1933 to lead the great nations of the world in the recognition of the biological foundations for national character. It is probable that the sterilization statues of the several American states and the national sterilization statute of Germany will in legal history, constitute a milestone which marks the control by the most advanced nations of the world of a major aspect of controlling human reproduction, comparable in importance only with the state's legal control of marriage.[42]

While most U.S. eugenicists eventually broke with, and even condemned, Nazi policies, their initial enthusiasm was hardly a secret.

But Nazi policies were not driven by genetic determinism alone. A derivative of Malthusianism, *Lebensraum,* was one of the ties that bound the German people under Hitler. As Hitler wrote in *Mein Kampf,*

> [We have] an annual increase in population of nearly nine hundred thousand souls. The difficulty of feeding this army of new citizens must grow greater from year to year and ultimately end in catastrophe, unless ways and means are found to forestall the danger of starvation and misery in time. . . . The productivity of the soil can only be increased within defined limits and up to a certain point. . . . It is therefore illusory to hope that an increase in production can provide the basis for an increase in population.[43]

And, tying his Malthusian position with his well-known racism, he notes,

> Instead of expanding geographically, instead of exporting men, the white race has exported goods and so has built up a world economic system, the

characteristic of which is that in Europe, and lately also in America, is to be found a gigantic world scale level of manufacture while the rest of the world provides vast markets and sources of raw materials. The white race can . . . only maintain its position so long as differences in the standard of living persist in various parts of the world. Depending on their innate capabilities the various nations have taken differing steps to safeguard this predominant position.[44]

While the events leading up to World War II and the Holocaust were complex and even today are not fully understood, few doubt that certain components of underlying German ideology promoted the war and permited the Holocaust. Among those components must be included the very biological determinism discussed in this chapter. The biological ideology spawned in the nineteenth century easily oozed its way into the twentieth, and the world witnessed the horrendous consequences. That is why some of us are concerned today.

THE HUMAN STRUCTURES SCHOOL OF THOUGHT

Social Darwinists, characterized by Herbert Spencer and his followers, were distinct from the German monists on one critical point. Monists decried the excesses of industrial capitalism and sought to analyze and change the system for the better,[45] while the followers of Spencer felt that the natural laws exposed by Malthus and Darwin (they apparently had little to say about the beauty of nature) justified an unbridled capitalist exploitation of everyone and everything.

An alternative point of view, the human structures school of thought, emerged parallel with the German monists, and drew its main strength from a similar vision of industrial capitalism. However, this school began the analysis with a fundamentally different point of view concerning the nature of *Homo sapiens:* The human species differed from all other animals in that it had language and culture, and participated in the directed modification of the natural world. Directed modification meant that, while many, if not most, animals and plants modify the environment in which they live, humans are unique in that they construct an abstraction before they act. The human, before acting, constructs a mental image of the act, conducting a mental experiment before taking action.

In addition to the construction of an abstraction before action, humans are fundamentally social, but, unlike other social animals, are also social about their abstractions. Thus, one person may construct in his or her imagination a cocktail party or vacation trip, and then talk with a companion about the plans. The party or trip is not only constructed abstractly before it is actually done, it is constructed both socially and abstractly. This trick, that only the species *Homo sapiens* happened to evolve, makes the process whereby resources are obtained and used qualitatively different from the way other organisms do it.[46]

Beginning, thus, from biological assumptions critically different from the natural structures school, the human structures school builds up a totally different interpretation of the way humans and the environment interact, an interpretation that makes it difficult to apply the normal rules of biology to the activities of humans. For example, the Malthusians treat humans as though they utilize resources just like any other animals, whereas the more complicated view sees humans as organizing socially, modifying resources into products, using those products as new resources, organizing socially again, modifying those new resources into products, and so on. The monists saw nature as the ultimate expression of beauty; the human structures school sees the environment as a social construct of human abstract thought.[47]

The human structures school ultimately arrives at a necessarily more progressive political philosophy than does the natural structures school, almost by definition. The natural structures school sees what exists as natural, perhaps with recent undesirable innovations that must be squelched in order to return to the perfect natural state, whereas the human structures school sees what exists as a product of human social activity, and thus perfectly changeable if the will exists to make changes. Because of this fundamental difference in programmatic consequences, it is not in the least surprising to find that those receiving the bulk of the "goodies" produced in society should be tempted to adopt the natural structures point of view, while those not so well-rewarded should tend toward the human structures school. Black female activists in urban ghettos usually talk about changing structures. White male corporate executives usually talk about the inevitability of the human condition. The debate is alive and well.

NATURAL STRUCTURES IN CONTEMPORARY DISCOURSE

In many ways the natural structures school—Malthusianism, genetic determinism, and nature worship—defines biology's role in human affairs. Malthusianism arises—sometimes openly, sometimes subtly—as we try to grapple with the immense environmental and social problems facing us today. Rather than deal with the complex and perplexing human social relations that create pesticide poisonings, hazardous waste, urban riots, and Third World revolutions, it is tempting to suggest that those poisoned by pesticides, or contracting cancer from PCBs, or living in the street because their home was recently trashed in urban revolt, are themselves responsible for their fate, or at least their parents are. There are simply too many people demanding food, energy, and space. Agriculture thus must expand to accommodate so many people, fossil fuels must be burned to supply so many people with energy, and they all need space, which is why they crowd into places like south-central Los Angeles. The explanation is obvious, straightforward, and seductive in its simplicity. It is also wrong.[48]

Similarly, genetic determinism is brought to bear on parallel problems. The underclass in urban America is mainly African American and Latino. Could it be that there is something "deep" that is causing their condition? Compare them with the Koreans, also generally poor people, who have managed to make a go of it in opportunity-rich America. Could the African and Native American heritage of blacks and Hispanics actually have something, if ever so subtle, to do with their predicament? The Southerner's lament that their Negroes are just too lazy to be given much self-responsibility has its modern and respectable counterparts in those who seek to explain African Americans' predicament by something in their genes that predisposes them to living in tenements, or that Latinas are somehow hotheaded and emotional by temperament (the Puerto Rican spitfire, the hot-blooded Latin lover), or women belong in the home and not in executive suites.

I do not speak here of the notorious hate groups, whose recent growth worldwide is especially scary, but rather of the subtle forms of the same ideas that affect all of us daily, and also ultimately give aid and comfort to their more extreme counterparts—the black executive who believes deep down that his Jewish banker's refusal of a loan is because Jews are inherently avaricious, the white liberal intellectual (this is a real example) who learned to expect less of his adopted African children because the black race (whatever that is) has been endowed with lower intelligence, the father who encourages his son to play baseball and his daughter to help Mommy cook because "it's natural that way." These are assumptions that pervade daily life in the late twentieth century. They occasionally become exaggerated in hate groups like the Klu Klux Klan or the American Nazi Party or their equivalents in Europe, but, perhaps more importantly, they have a driving effect on daily life, affecting what we do and how we act with one another in subtle and usually subconscious ways. These ideas seem obvious, straightforward, and seductive in their simplicity. They are also wrong.

As something of an antidote to the persistent problems of the human condition, a feeling of returning to nature, an unfettered nature where human beings have not mucked things up so much, is a very popular current in the late twentieth century. In so many ways it hardly differs from the romanticism of the nineteenth century, and sees much beauty in nature and frequently in "traditional" values. Depending strongly on one's political persuasions and/or cultural heritage, the utopian solution to the world's problems may seem like a return to the natural world, or traditional values, however defined by one's politics and culture. It is a soothing notion that there is some safe haven, even if we cannot get there, where the world's problems cannot reveal themselves to us, where we can sit back and relax and just be happy and content. For some, that vision is an outback wilderness, for others a scene from a romantic landscape painting, for others traditional family values. It is an escape that seems obvious, straightforward, and seductive in its simplicity. It is also wrong.

The alternative analysis is far more complex and difficult to understand, which is one of the things that makes the essentialist position (i.e., the natural structures school) so attractive. Consider, for example, the spectacular events in Los Angeles in 1992 in response to the Rodney King verdict. That Koreans owned the shops that were burnt out by African Americans and Latinos is very easy to understand if you believe that blacks and Hispanics are genetically dumb and predisposed to live in poverty and become violent, while Koreans have that Asian genetic structure that makes them industrious. But if you have to grapple with the fact that slavery, the production system brought here by the Europeans, was what caused millions of Africans to be enslaved, thus breaking up culture, family, and tradition; that sugar and cotton production could never have provided the backbone of European expansion into the Americas without slavery; that the sharecropping following abolition was a racist system that evolved from slavery; that the northward migration of African Americans was conditioned by the needs of burgeoning industry in the wake of the total destruction of Germany and Japan; that institutions were subsequently established to maintain people of African ancestry in an outcast position; that Chicanos were originally deprived of their land by military subterfuge; that Aztlán remains a dream of many Chicanos; that contradictory politics sometimes characterizes the relationship between Chicanos and Mexicans living in Los Angeles; that Salvadorans regard themselves as a distinct culture within Los Angeles; that Korean immigrants to California originate from generally entrepreneurial family histories in Korea; that Korean American family structure evolved partially from Korean traditions; and so on, it is not an easy and pat picture. But if you want to understand the response to the Rodney King verdict, these are the complexities you must understand. The situations of African Americans, Korean Americans, and Latinos living in Los Angeles are complex consequences of human social and political structures that defy easy characterization, and require a great deal of effort to even begin to understand. It is easier to think that blacks have a lazy gene, Hispanics a hot-tempered gene, and Koreans an "I'm going to open a corner grocery story" gene; that there are too many people in Los Angeles and/or Korea and/or Mexico and/or El Salvador, and anyway a refuge exists at a backyard barbecue in the suburban bliss that God intended for us and ours.

Thus, we remain in the throes of resolution of these two intellectual traditions. While Hitler's deviation of the "natural structures" lineage was resoundingly defeated in the 1940s, and Stalin's deviation of the "human structures" lineage was likewise defeated when the Soviet Union fell a half-century later, the two general intellectual traditions are nonetheless discernable in a variety of forums. At times their apparition is blatant and obvious, as in recent arguments about lifeboat ethics versus calls for structural reform in Third World lending.[49] At other times, they manifest themselves in very subtle form, with corporate executives justifying lower pay scales in Third World countries based on the "natives'" acceptance of routine and monotonous work.

In its crudest, yet most pragmatic, state, this dual tradition is the underlying basis for economic policies, both within regions and between regions. While the details of any given situation are always complex, rendering each economic problem enigmatic, the underlying tension between these two world views is inevitably one of the forces driving much of the hidden agendas of the game's players. For essentialists, the extant structure of political power, economic advantage, personal influence, and the like, is taken as a given scenario within which planning must be confined. This tradition holds (if ever so quietly) that such extant structures are (at least partly) determined by unalterable biological forces, and are thus quite resistant to change. To be realistic, it is argued, one must promote economic policies that recognize the naturalness of this order. Thus, for example, the notion that it is proper for the United States to dictate what forms of government are acceptable for the nations of Latin America is rooted in a past that we now recognize as racist, and fully established in a present that we must admit retains some of the essential features of that racism.

On the other hand, these same structures of political power, economic advantage, and so forth, are viewed quite differently by those more influenced by the human structures tradition. Structures of inequality are viewed as arising from past decisions about how humans organize their productive activities, and plans for the future must include changes in the way these activities are organized. Thus, the backdrop automatically accepted by the natural structures school is the very focus of change for the human structures school.

Many of today's most critically important issues, and especially many of the apparent paradoxes that emerge, are a consequence of the current tension between these two schools of thought.

ARGUING THE EXTREMES

There is always some danger in casting such a problem as one of extremes. More often than not, the driving forces in human relations are far too complex to be captured as simply one or the other end of a continuum, and a more nuanced analysis comes closer to a representation of the truth. With the subject matter treated here, however, it would appear that in both its historical and contemporary contexts, the extremes act as attractive poles. While any particular person undoubtedly harbors a complex set of ideas regarding the topics, it seems that those ideas are, in a sense, pulled in opposite directions. Thus, the rush to find a biological basis for homosexuality, for example, is usually tempered with a disclaimer, acknowledging that "environment plays a role, too."[50] Similarly, few neo-Malthusians now argue that the size of the human population can be thought of as the single determining factor of environmental degradation, but they also acknowledge the role of social relations.[51]

Thus, the debate about essentialism versus social construction, in either its historical or its contemporary form, is not ultimately a debate about which extreme is correct, but rather a metaphorical contest in which both extremes provide poles of attraction. Individual analyses wind up influenced to some degree by both extremes, but are ultimately some complex combination of the two. Recognizing this dynamic, it is worthwhile to characterize and analyze these extremes, not as the positions actually taken, but as influential attractive poles in the debate.

THREE

Natural Aristocracies: Genetics and Evolution

The great American revolutionary, Thomas Jefferson, advocated rule by a "natural aristocracy" so that the dangers of "slaves, paupers and destitute laborers" attempting to control their own lives could be properly administered.[1] He was also a principal architect of U.S.-style democracy, which normally is not thought of as admitting anything like a natural aristocracy. Such fundamental contradictions are characteristic of almost every society that persisted more than a few decades—Stalin eliminated the small family farms since he was leader of the vanguard party, which naturally knew better than the ignorant masses; feudal lords had a natural right and responsibility to "care" for their subjects. The masses are always there, with seemingly natural rights to strive for goals such as self-determination and the pursuit of happiness. Yet there also is always some "natural aristocracy" that lays claim to know best how to accomplish those goals, even if it means suppressing those very masses.

Rarely is this contradiction faced forthrightly, but when it is, one can almost always detect an underlying assumption about biology, a usually tacit assumption that the "natural" in natural aristocracy comes from a source that cannot be denied or controlled. Before Darwin, the authority usually was some sort of divine decree or god. In the contemporary world, the authority seems to come, ultimately, from modern biology. It is a subtle effect, we seem to think, but in the end, not all people are created equal or born with the same capabilities, and within these differences there is a "natural hierarchy." Given such natural diversity, as we go about the business of deciding how we should organize our society, we obviously want to be sure that the "men of best quality" rule.[2] Otherwise, we would face disaster. Today few would assert that a god determines who is born as a "man of quality," but the basic ideology has not really changed. If, formerly, it was thought that the good lord blessed certain folks with the wisdom and decency to rise above the fray and become leaders, today it is believed that the genetic heritage of some people predisposes them to be such leaders. Such ideology is deep, and I am constantly amazed at the number of seemingly well-educated people that, although they are embarrassed to say it publicly, believe in their hearts that such genetic differences really exist and account for some—perhaps only a small amount, but nevertheless some—of the differences we see in the capabilities of different people.

Frequently similar attitudes emerge regarding different groups of people—Jews versus Arabs, African Americans versus European Americans, Bosnian Serbs versus Bosnian Muslims, men versus women, gays versus straights; the list goes on. As with men of quality, in the contemporary world it is rarely articulated openly, but is frequently deeply felt, that the differences between such groups is, at least partly, based on biology. That feeling is both right and wrong, right about many features that don't matter much, wrong about almost all characteristics that matter. Modern biology has been able to say quite a lot about this issue, but the popular media and general attitudes have changed little, and the echoes of the nineteenth century are, unfortunately, still loud.

At the other end of the spectrum is an attitude that is even more difficult to deconstruct, an attitude not about the differences between individuals or groups, but rather about the sameness of everyone—the nature of human nature.[3] Humans are aggressive or non-aggressive, avaricious or sharing, warlike or peaceful, xenophobic or gregarious, competitive or cooperative; the list goes on. It seems that almost every trait ever recognized as part of the human condition has, at some point, been claimed as part of our natural biological heritage. Consequently, many human conditions are thought of as somehow inevitable because they stem from the basic nature of *Homo sapiens*. If we are by nature competitive, selfish, and avaricious, why try to fight our natural tendencies? Alternatively, if we are cooperative and sharing by nature, let us try to recapture that essence of humanness. It turns out that the distinction between a competitive, avaricious society and a cooperative, sharing one is not something about which biology has anything to say. As far as we can tell, for the traits that we are interested in, biology offers virtually nothing with which to inform us, except to the extent that we can now say with relative confidence that biology is probably all but irrelevant.[4]

Thus, we see three levels of thinking about biological determinism: first, that some individual people are biologically destined to be of higher quality than others; second, that a group is biologically destined to be of higher quality than another group; and, third, that all individuals of *Homo sapiens* have particular qualities that are fixed biologically. As we shall see in later chapters, for all practical purposes, these attitudes are wrong. They have a long history, have been repeated in world literature and popular science, and, until recently, have been widely believed. Given what we know about genetics today, most of these attitudes can be dismissed as either wrong or unknowable. To see how this is so, a short (more or less) detour into some technical aspects of genetics is unavoidable. The rest of this chapter is that detour, and should be understood as preparatory to the material presented in subsequent chapters. Remember, as you wade through what perhaps may seem a bit arcane, it all comes together in the two chapters that follow. But for now we shall concentrate on three of the most essential components of modern biology: (1) the notion of particulate inheritance (Mendelian genetics), (2) the role of deoxyribonucleic acid (DNA) in inheritance and protein formation, and (3) the nature of organic evolution. Those readers already familiar with Mendelian genetics, protein synthesis, and evolutionary theory can easily skip this chapter.

THE GENE—AN ABSTRACT CONCEPT

Most readers will have had an introduction to genetics, if not in high school biology, then on the evening news. What with DNA fingerprinting and biotechnology, not to mention *Jurassic Park,* the modern world has been bathed in information about genetics for the past 20 years. It bears considerable reflection that this entire field began with what must have seemed, at the time, a rather unlikely speculation. In the next few paragraphs, we trace the general form of the observations and speculations that eventually led to the development of modern genetics. To make the story interesting, I shall assume that biological understanding is more or less at the level of the early nineteenth century, such that all we have to go on are the trivial and obvious observations one can make about the surrounding world.

Children resemble their parents. Furthermore, a child frequently looks very much like a cross between its mother and father. It would seem most obvious to suggest that something from the father is blended with something from the mother to produce the child. Indeed, this was the common view during the nineteenth century. It was known as *blending inheritance* and was thought to be so obvious that one would have been labeled a bit loony had one suggested it was not true.

To see how, in fact, it is wrong requires what may be the greatest single insight in history of biology, if not in all of science. It was an insight gained by an Augustinian monk, Gregor Mendel, working in a monastery garden.[5] Living in a world that believed almost instinctively in blending inheritance, he had naturally made all of the normal observations one would make of parent-offspring relationships. He was also a gardener, and many of his observations were made on plants. If one collects seeds from a tall plant and sows them, one usually gets tall plants from those seeds. If the flowers of a plant are white, the seeds sown from that plant generally produce plants with white flowers. Mendel had developed the same bag of tricks that any gardener would have developed at the time, a general sense of what aspects of particular pea varieties one could expect to be reproduced in the offspring of that variety—more or less. It was this "more or less" that fascinated Mendel, and he sought to discover how one might be able to predict not only that the offspring of a white-flowered plant produced mainly white flowers, but exactly what fraction of the offspring would have white flowers (he had already observed that there were sometimes a significant number of purple flowers among the majority of white-flowered offspring produced when two plants with white flowers were crossed).

Mendel developed an abstraction, a key step in the evolution of any scientific theory.[6] The reasoning was as follows: We already know that hereditary information is received from both father and mother; let us suppose that the information is passed on to the offspring as small packets of information, a packet from the father in the pollen or sperm, and a packet from the mother in the ovule or egg. What might be the nature of this packet? A white-flowered male passes on information that says "make white flowers" and the white-flowered female does the same, thus forcing us to conclude that the offspring should always make white flowers. But Mendel already knew that sometimes a white-flowered male, when crossed with a white-flowered female, produced a significant number of offspring with purple flowers. Therefore, the packets of information must say something like "make white flowers, except sometimes make purple ones."

The next part of the abstraction is obvious. The parent sometimes passes the white-flower information and sometimes the purple-flower information. The only question remaining is, what causes it to pass one or the other signal? Mendel took a guess—suppose that each parent has an equal number of each of these alternative signals, "packets of information," so to speak, and suppose that these packets are passed on to the offspring at random.[7]

Mendel invented some names for his observations and abstractions. The packets are known as genes, each of which has a couple of alternative states, known as alleles (e.g., the "flower color" gene has two alleles, the white allele and the purple allele). The genetic message (the alleles received from each of the two parents) is called the *genotype* and the physical representation of the genotype is the *phenotype*. The distinction between genotype and phenotype is quite important, and will be discussed in more detail in a later chapter. If both parents give the offspring the allele for white flower, the offspring contains the genetic message white-white (or ww for short) while it contains purple-purple (pp) if both parents give it the allele for purple flower. The genotype may be ww and the phenotype white flower, or the genotype may be pp and the phenotype purple flower. The distinction between genotype and phenotype becomes critical when the father gives a white allele and the mother gives a purple one, making an offspring with a wp (white-purple) genotype. What will be the phenotype, which is to say what will be the actual physical color of the flowers of this offspring? White? Purple? Intermediate?

While this question is somewhat more complicated than indicated here, one of the alleles frequently dominates the other, so that an individual with a wp genotype will produce purple flowers. The purple allele is "dominant" over the white allele. Today we understand a great deal about how such dominance comes about, some of which is presented below, but in Mendel's time, he could only speculate that sometimes one allele dominated the other.

This, then, is an outline of the foundations of genetics, normally referred to as Mendelian genetics. There are three possible genotypes associated with flower color (or many other characteristics)—ww, pp, and wp. But there are only two phenotypes, white flower or purple flower. The ww genotype causes a white phenotype, while the pp and wp genotypes cause a purple phenotype because purple (p) is dominant.

It is worth a moment of historical reflection to contemplate the revo-

a. Blending inheritance model.

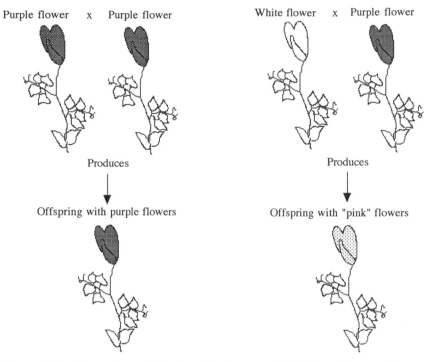

Purple flower   x   Purple flower

White flower   x   Purple flower

Produces

Produces

Offspring with purple flowers

Offspring with "pink" flowers

Figure 3.1. Comparison of blending inheritance with the Mendelian model. (a) The expectation from two different crosses under the assumption of blending inheritance. (b) The expectation of a particular cross under the assumption of the Mendelian model.

lutionary nature of this theory. If two white-flowered individuals are crossed, they produce white-flowered offspring, just as anyone would expect. If two purple-flowered individuals of the pp genotype are crossed they produce purple-flowered offspring, just as anyone would expect. But what happens if two purple-flowered individuals of the wp genotype are crossed? Since both parents have purple flowers, the old ideas of blending inheritance suggest that all offspring should have purple flowers.[8] But it doesn't happen that way. The father contributes either a w or p allele to

b. Mendelian inheritance model.

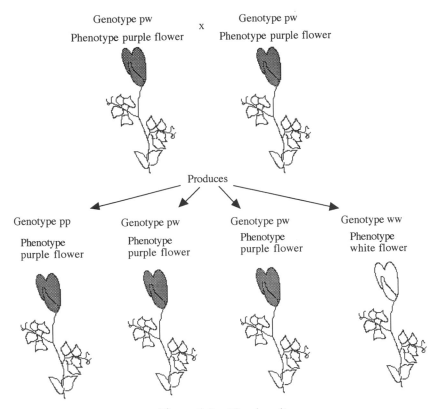

Figure 3.1. (*Continued*)

each offspring and the mother does the same. Thus, offspring may be pp, or wp, or ww, which means that the offspring can have either purple or white flowers. This is a dramatic result in a world that believed to the core that inheritance was through the blending of characteristics of mother and father. Here was a theory that destroyed what appeared to be common sense.[9] Two parents could produce offspring that were totally different in appearance from either of them (see Figure 3.1). And Mendel carried out extensive experiments that left little doubt that his view was correct and that the then-prevalent view of blending inheritance was wrong.[10]

Deoxyribonucleic Acid—The Material Basis of the Abstraction

By the end of the nineteenth century, Mendelian genetics was accepted throughout the world as the fundamental principle of inheritance, and has been the basis for the science of genetics ever since. But by this time the gene itself was still something of an abstraction, little more than Mendel's original "little packets of information." Discovering what constituted the physical makeup of the gene became an obsession of biologists.

What clues were available to the geneticists of the early twentieth century in their quest for the physical nature of the gene? Some initial observations were quite obvious. The genotype contained two messages, two alleles (for each characteristic), one from the father and one from the mother. Where could those messages be? To come from the father the message had to be contained in the sperm or pollen. Both sperm and pollen contain virtually nothing except the nucleus of the cell. Thus, the message must be located in the nucleus, reasoned the early geneticists, quite correctly. What, then, was in the nucleus? Not much was known about the chemicals in the nucleus, other than that they were organic acids and very simple molecules. Their very simplicity suggested that they were not likely candidates for the genetic material, since the genetic material contained so very much information. Not much else was known about them, other than that they were simple acids and they were located in the nucleus—thus, they were called nucleic acids.

As biochemists made further advances in characterizing the nucleic acids, they discovered that there were two major types. One occurred only in the cell nucleus, while the other type was found both in the nucleus and in other structures in the cell. Both types contain sugar. In one case, the sugar is ribose, thus giving rise to the term ribonucleic acid (i.e., the nucleic acid that contains ribose). The other form, the one that occurred only in the nucleus, is just like the other, except its sugar lacks an oxygen and is thus called deoxyribose (ribose without an oxygen). The nucleic acid restricted to the nucleus was thus called deoxyribonucleic acid. Deoxyribonucleic acid became known as DNA—maybe you've heard of it.

Then, in 1954, two young biologists, Francis Crick and James Watson, discovered the chemical structure for DNA, which not only led to an understanding of how DNA is reproduced, but also enabled us to understand exactly how the genotype determines the phenotype.[11] This amazing discovery changed biology, if not the world, in ways that we are still trying to understand. The knowledge it provided permitted us to think of new technologies that previously never would have entered our minds, and led to a technological revolution that we are currently only beginning to experience.

FROM MENDEL TO WATSON AND CRICK—THE CENTRAL DOGMA EMERGES

The combination of Mendel's brilliant abstractions and Watson and Crick's remarkable detective work has led to a fundamental picture of how biological reproduction occurs and provides us with the centerpiece of modern biology, what is referred to as the central dogma. In its most simplified form it almost seems trivial—parents pass on information to their offspring through genes, the genes are composed of DNA, the DNA causes the formation of specific chemicals, and the specific chemicals cause the offspring to develop in certain ways. Taking the above example of the white and purple flowers, (1) the parent gives the offspring its DNA, (2) particular parts of the DNA differ depending on whether the "signal" they give is "purple flower" or "white flower," (3) in the offspring's body, the DNA directs the formation of specific chemicals that go into the flower, and (4) the chemicals "paint" the flower either purple or white.

The details of this pattern are fascinating,[12] although to grasp in principle the significance of the central dogma, one must simply understand that Mendel's genes are actually composed of DNA structured the way Watson and Crick suggested and that the DNA in an organism's body directs the formation of all the chemicals in that body, which in turn determine everything about the body. This general picture is correct as far as it goes, and is intellectually accessible with little knowledge of anything technical. However, some details of the process are quite important to an understanding of how all this relates to human affairs, such as, for example, the determination of "men of best quality." To see such details, we must introduce two pieces of technical information: (1) the structure and reproduction of DNA, and (2) the structure and production of proteins. The following section is a bit technical, but in the end is quite simple. It will help if you read it twice, once rather quickly to get the general idea, and once more, with feeling, so to speak. The key points to remember are (1) *DNA,* which is composed of a *sugar backbone* (a deoxyribose sugar) plus a series of *bases* (adenine, thymine, cytosine, and guanine); (2) *RNA,* which also is composed of a *sugar backbone* (a ribose sugar) plus a series of *bases* (adenine, guanine, cytosine, and uracil); (3) RNA comes in various forms, two of which are important to the present discussion—*transfer RNA* (tRNA) and *messenger RNA* (mRNA); and (4) *proteins,* the major chemicals of life's processes, which are composed of long strings of *amino acids* (the particular sequence of amino acids ultimately determines the function of the particular protein).

THE CENTRAL DOGMA IN OUTLINE

Watson and Crick suggested that DNA is composed of two backbones and a series of connectors, much like a railroad track with its ties (but in this case, the railroad track is twisted so that it appears like a helix, which is what gave rise to the name the "double helix"). The chemical composition of the individual parallel tracks is unimportant for our purposes, but the ties connecting the tracks are critical. The ties are composed of "bases" (the technical chemical term), and there are four of them—adenine, guanine, cytosine, and thymine.[13]

When a cell divides to produce two cells, what does the DNA do? Since everything about the cell is reproduced, the DNA itself must be reproduced. How does the DNA reproduce itself at the time of cell division?

Because of their chemical structure, the bases (the ties in the track) are able to pair with one another in a restricted fashion. Adenine is able to pair with thymine and cytosine with guanine, but never the reverse (i.e., you cannot get adenine to pair with cytosine nor guanine with thymine). As you cross the "tracks" of the DNA molecule, you encounter the backbone followed by a base followed by another base followed by the backbone again (see Figure 3.2a), and the two bases may be AT (i.e. adenine attached to thymine) or TA or CG or GC (never AC, TG, AG, GA, GT, CA, TC, or CT). As the cell begins to divide, the two tracks separate, each taking with it a single member of the base pair, as illustrated in Figure

---

Figure 3.2. Diagrammatic illustration of DNA replication. (a) Diagram of complete molecule, the double helix form (at bottom) straightened out and magnified to see the base pairing rules. (b) The two strands begin to separate. (c) The two strands are completely separated. (d) Two identical completed molecules.

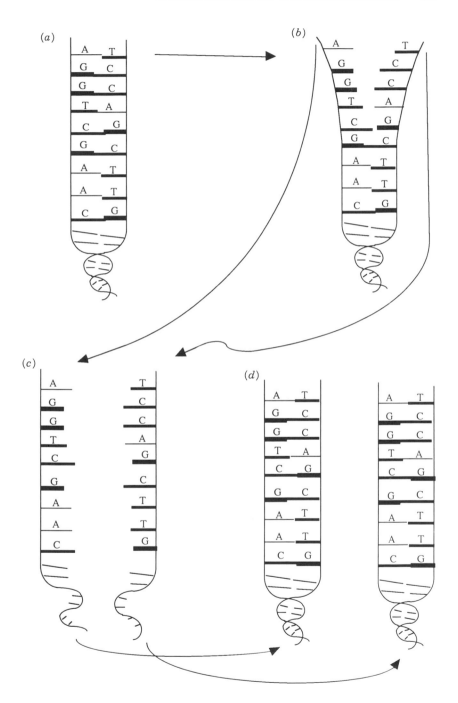

3.2*b*. Thus, we are eventually left with two strands of half-DNA. These two strands of half-DNA act as templates and attract new bases, which are freely floating in the nucleus. The new bases line up at the points where the base pairs originally split (see Figure 3.2*c*), form a new backbone, and thus are produced two exact duplicates of the original DNA (Figure 3.2*d*). Naturally, as the cell divides, one copy goes to one cell and the other copy goes to the second cell, and both cells thus receive exactly the same genetic information.

The next issue is how the genetic material is translated into the phenotype—how the particular strand of DNA that says "make a white flower" actually gets translated into the visible white flower. At this point the other nucleic acid comes into play—ribonucleic acid, or RNA. RNA is structurally similar to DNA, with an important exception: It usually occurs as a single strand (a train track with only one rail).

Contained in the cytoplasm (i.e., the part outside the nucleus) of the cell is a particular form of RNA known as transfer RNA (or simply tRNA for short). The tRNA is composed of a backbone, similar to one of the tracks of the DNA, but much shorter,[14] and containing an unusual structural feature that "exposes" exactly three bases on the "wrong side" of its sugar backbone, as illustrated in Figure 3.3. That is, at one point on the molecule of tRNA, a triplet of bases is chemically active, ready to combine with a triplet of bases elsewhere, following the basic recipe that adenine combines with thymine and cytosine with guanine.[15]

There is another important component of the tRNA molecule, at the

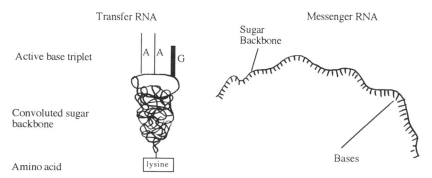

Figure 3.3. Diagrammatic representation of the two main types of RNA molecule.

opposite end of the molecule from where the three active bases are located. At that end, the tRNA molecule is attached to an amino acid, which is particularly associated with the three bases on its other end (see Figure 3.3). Thus, for a specific triplet of bases (say cytosine, adenine, guanine) a specific amino acid (in this, case glycine) is attached to the tRNA. So the combination "base triplet-RNA-amino acid" forms a sort of natural unit that floats around in the cytoplasm (not in the nucleus). And remember, a specific sequence of three bases always codes for a specific amino acid. That is, for a given threesome at one end of the tRNA molecule, a given amino acid is always found at the other end of that molecule.

Yet another form of RNA, a much larger form than tRNA, is known as messenger RNA or, simply, mRNA. The messenger RNA brings the information from the DNA in the nucleus to the cytoplasm, where the protein eventually is assembled. The protein is assembled in the cytoplasm simply by lining up the appropriate tRNA molecules along the mRNA molecule, and combining the amino acids that are thus lined up, as shown in Figure 3.4. The connected string of amino acids is a protein. Note how the exact sequence of amino acids in this protein was ultimately specified by the sequence of bases on the mRNA molecule.

But exactly where did the mRNA get the information, which is to say, how did the bases come to line up on the mRNA molecule in some specific way? Recall that during the normal cell replication sequence the

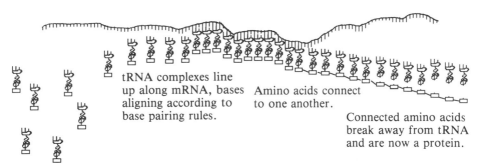

tRNA complexes line up along mRNA, bases aligning according to base pairing rules.

Amino acids connect to one another.

Connected amino acids break away from tRNA and are now a protein.

Base triplet/tRNA/amino acid complexes are attracted to the mRNA molecule.

Figure 3.4. Schematic of the process of protein synthesis.

DNA molecule splits into its two component strands (the two tracks come apart), and bases are positioned along each of the separated tracks to make two replicate copies of the original DNA molecule (refer back to Figure 3.2). In a very similar fashion, when it is time to make a protein, the DNA molecule in the nucleus begins unzipping its two strands, but rather than making two new molecules of DNA as pictured in Figure 3.2, a strand of RNA is produced, simply by lining up the bases according to the normal base-pairing rules on one of the unzipped strands, and connecting them with ribose (rather than deoxyribose) sugars. Thus, we have a strand of RNA whose base sequence is the exact complement of the original strand of DNA (i.e., it has an adenine where there used to be thymine and vice versa, and a cytosine where there used to be guanine).

Now all the pieces of the central dogma are in place, if in a very simplified fashion.[16] First, we have the creation of the genotype, the genetic definition of the individual (or of some characteristic of the individual). The DNA in a cell's nucleus normally replicates itself by unzipping its two strands, attracting complementary bases to the bases on each of the strands and thus making two identical molecules, one of which goes to each of the cells resulting from cell division. That is how the genetic information is transferred to all the cells in the body from the initial fertilized egg. Second, we have the translation of the genotype into the phenotype, the physical appearance of the individual (or of some characteristic of the individual). The DNA in the cell's nucleus unzips just like it does when replicating, but this time, in attracting complementary bases to its own bases, the complementary bases are linked together with a ribose sugar, and we have a strand of RNA. This strand takes the genetic message out of the nucleus, and thus is called messenger RNA. Once in the cytoplasm, the mRNA attracts the much smaller tRNA complexes such that particular base triplets on the tRNA line up with complementary base triplets on the mRNA, bringing their associated amino acids in contact with one another. The amino acids, thus lined up according to the information contained on the mRNA (which was dictated by the information on the DNA in the nucleus), are connected together forming a specific protein (remember, it is the specific sequence of amino acids that determines what kind of protein it is). The procedure of protein formation is illustrated in Figure 3.5.

At this point it probably makes sense to reread this section, if this was your first time through.

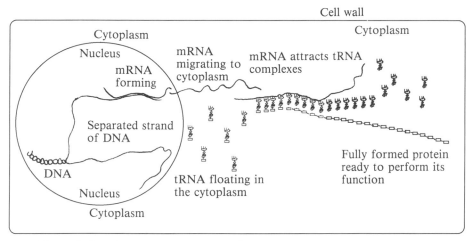

Figure 3.5. Diagrammatic summary of the central dogma of modern biology.

MORE ABOUT PROTEINS

Proteins are a class of chemicals that are involved in life's processes in several crucial ways. They are structural, contributing to the structural integrity of everything from your muscles to the minute scales on a butterfly's wing. Proteins as structural components frequently dictate something much more visible than the somewhat abstract "sequence of amino acids." For example, the particular wavelength of light that reflects from the scale on the butterfly's wing (i.e., its color) may be determined by the exact kind of protein that goes into making the scale itself. Thus is the butterfly's color genetically determined.[17] One very important class of proteins contains "enzymes," which are chemical catalysts. Just as our commonsense notion of a catalyst is something that causes something else to happen, a chemical catalyst causes a chemical reaction to proceed at a much faster rate than it would without the catalyst (the catalyst itself is not changed in the course of the action, but simply acts to accelerate the chemical process). Chemical processes that may take days or weeks to complete in the absence of enzymes may happen in seconds or minutes when the proper enzyme is present. For all practical purposes we could simply think of these processes as not happening at all if the proper enzyme is absent.

Particular enzymes may have slightly different arrangements of amino acids, yet perform the same general function. But the exact nature of that function may vary depending on the amino acid sequence. In Figure 3.6, for example, we illustrate the activity rate of an enzyme that is involved in the promotion of cell division (for simplicity here called the cell division enzyme—not its real name). Note that the rate of activity depends on the environment in which the enzyme is found (in this case, the environment is the acidity of the medium), and on the phenotype, that is, on its exact arrangement of amino acids. Form A has a slightly different sequence of amino acids from form B, although both forms perform the same function in promoting cell division. But form A performs better (has greater activity) at slightly lower acidity levels than does form B. This phenomenon, to which we will return in later chapters, is a critical component of our understanding of modern genetics. The environment (in this case, acidity) interacts with the genotype (form A or form B), to make the phenotype (in this case, the enzyme activity). The graph shown in Figure 3.6 is frequently referred to as a norm of reaction, and is useful to emphasize that

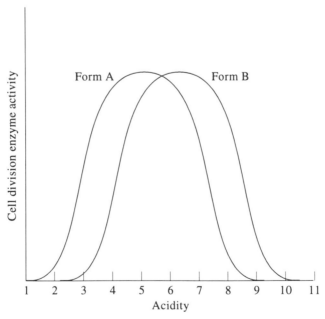

Figure 3.6. Activity rates of two forms of an enzyme involved in the promotion of cell division.

the phenotype is realized as a combination of a genotype operating in a particular environment.[18]

For evolutionary biologists, proteins take on another significance. Since we now know that proteins are explicitly synthesized from instructions in the DNA, and the DNA contains the genes, we can get very close to studying the genes directly by studying the proteins—only one step removed, so to speak. Indeed, the understanding of protein synthesis at this level has enabled biologists to hone the very definition of what a gene is in the first place, and when most modern biologists speak of genes, they are no longer talking about those abstract entities that Mendel invented, but rather about a length of DNA that codes for a single protein. The protein becomes the phenotype and the particular strand of DNA that stipulated its exact amino acid sequence is the genotype.

Finally, there is something about proteins that becomes crucially important for studying genetic topics in the natural world. As discussed above, proteins can occur with different structures, yet do exactly the same thing. This is not to say that any protein will perform any enzymatic activity; that is most definitely not true. Indeed, specific chemical reactions require enzymes with particular structures. But within each enzyme there is usually only one or a few sections of the molecule that are especially active and give the protein its particular function. A useful analogy is a tangled clothesline. Since a protein is a long chain of amino acids, it can be thought of as a clothesline all tangled up.[19] Suppose that, amidst the big tangle of the clothesline, there is a loop that sticks out of the tangled mess (see Figure 3.7). We can use this loop to hang up the tangled mess on a barn rafter, and let us suppose that the entire function of the clothesline is to hang up on a barn rafter. What would happen if we changed the details of the tangle, perhaps loosening it a little, perhaps distorting it somewhat, but all the time retaining the integrity of that loop on the top that we use to hang it from the barn rafter? In so doing, we could change the formal structure of the tangle, but retain its function (to hang from the rafter).

This little analogy is useful to understand one of the most important tools biologists use in studying the genetics of animals and plants in the natural world. Indeed, it is true that the "tangles" of proteins come in all sorts of shapes and sizes, even though the "loop" remains constant. That is, there are frequently several different forms of the protein (different

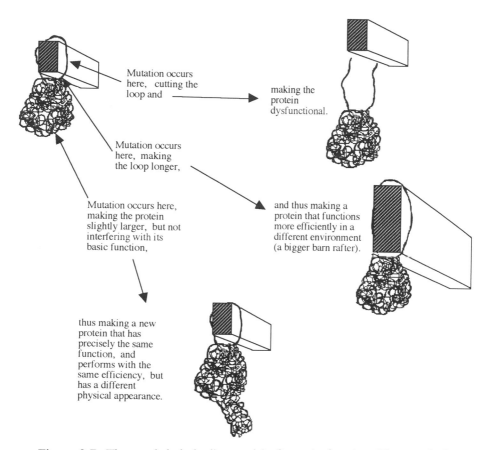

Mutation occurs here, cutting the loop and

making the protein dysfunctional.

Mutation occurs here, making the loop longer,

Mutation occurs here, making the protein slightly larger, but not interfering with its basic function,

and thus making a protein that functions more efficiently in a different environment (a bigger barn rafter).

thus making a new protein that has precisely the same function, and performs with the same efficiency, but has a different physical appearance.

Figure 3.7. The tangled clothesline model of protein function. The protein is conceived as a tangled mass of clothesline with a large loop that allows the tangle to be hung on a barn rafter. The "function" of the protein is to hang on the barn rafter. The various consequences of mutations at different points in the protein are illustrated.

configurations of the tangle) that make no difference to the protein's function (do not change the nature of the loop). These different forms exist in the natural world and can tell us a great deal about the genetics of animal and plant populations. The study of these protein polymorphisms[20] will be critical, for example, when we look at the genetics of human races.

It is not really difficult to see how protein polymorphisms arise. Mutations, or changes in the structure of DNA, are continually happening, albeit at a very low rate. For example, if you examine a particular protein in a population of 100 million fruit flies, you might find that a different form spontaneously appears in a single individual every other generation. In other words, mutations occur all the time over the long run, but only rarely over the short run. A mutation is most frequently a change in a single base on the DNA molecule. Since the code that translates base triplets into amino acids is redundant (several different codes normally code for a single amino acid), many mutations really do absolutely nothing as far as the protein is concerned. For example, the base triplet adenine-adenine-adenine codes for the amino acid called lysine. If the third base is changed so that the triplet is adenine-adenine-guanine, the associated amino acid is still lysine. But if the change is such that we get adenine-adenine-cytosine, the associated amino acid is aspartic acid. So some mutations actually do not change the protein at all, while others cause a particular amino acid to be replaced by another amino acid in the amino acid chain that is the protein.

Considering only those mutations that cause a change in the amino acid, sometimes the change occurs within the active site of the enzyme (i.e., sometimes there is a "cut" in the loop of the tangled clothesline), naturally resulting in a loss of function of the enzyme. If such a mutation occurs, and if that point on the DNA (that gene) is the only one that makes that protein, and that protein is essential for life, that mutation will result in the death of the individual that contains it—it is called a lethal mutation. But if the change in amino acid is in the tangle and causes only a reorientation of the tangle itself, leaving the loop intact, the mutation is neutral as far as function is concerned, and what we have is an alternative protein (almost identical to the original one) that performs the same function, yet has a different form or morphology. These concepts are summarized in Figure 3.7.

THE GENES THAT GET TO THE NEXT GENERATION—DEDUCING DARWINISM

The Darwinian Revolution has become almost folk knowledge. Accounts of this event abound, not only in biology texts, but in texts of many other fields, and innumerable popular accounts feature the same actors and the same chronology. What was the evidence Darwin used? What was the role of the geological record, the finches on the Galapagos, or the unique contributions of Susannah Wedgwood? Indeed, it is a fascinating historical narrative.

There is an alternative pedagogy. Modern biology has made tremendous progress in the past 100 years. Our knowledge of genetics is to Darwin's knowledge as nuclear physics would be to Newton. We are now at a point of understanding in which it is quite possible, indeed simple, to deduce the basic elements of evolution from first principles. That is, it is no longer necessary to ask questions about the fossil record or animal and plant breeding as Darwin had to do. We can simply take what we know for certain about genetics and demonstrate quite clearly that Darwin's principal notion, that of evolutionary change through natural selection, is a necessary consequence of what we know to be true. That is the approach we shall take here.

The genetic material is continually undergoing mutation, the substitution of one base for another on the DNA molecule. Most of the mutations occur in such a way that either the amino acids in the inactive part of the protein are the ones that are changed, or the base substitution does not change the amino acid, and, thus, not much of anything happens. These are called neutral mutations. Occasionally, a mutation causes the active site of a protein to change such that it can no longer function properly. If that is the only piece of DNA that codes for that protein, and that protein is required for life's processes to work, the mutation is lethal. But what about those inevitable (although rare) mutations that change the active part of the protein, but only slightly, such that the protein still functions, but slightly differently than before—the tangled clothesline with a bigger loop, as pictured in Figure 3.7. What will happen to such a mutation?

If the protein functions differently, that implies that it is either a little more efficient or a little less efficient than it was before the mutation changed it. It is still the same protein in that it performs the same biochemical function, but the change in an amino acid has changed its performance ever so slightly so that its efficiency of action is slightly altered, much as was the case with the cell division enzyme of Figure 3.6.

The next step in the logic is to relate the enzyme efficiency to the life of the animal or plant in which the enzyme is acting. Consider, for example, a colony of bacteria living in a medium with an acidity of 5. Suppose all the bacterial cells have the cell division enzyme Form A (Figure 3.6), but that a recent mutation has resulted in a small fraction, say 1 percent, of the cells having form B. Suppose that a sample of this population is now put into a petri dish with a medium at acidity 7. A glance at Figure 3.6 suggests what might happen. The cell division enzyme activity of the few cells that contain form B will be much more active than the enzyme of the other cells (since they have the A form of the enzyme, which has its peak activity in a different environment—one of acidity 5). If the cell division enzyme form B acts about twice as fast as form A in this new environment, the next generation of cells will have about 2 percent of the cells with form B. In subsequent generations we expect about 4 percent, 8 percent, 16 percent, and so on. In just seven or eight generations, the bacterial culture will have changed the fraction of form B from just 1 percent of the cells to 100 percent. The population has changed—evolved—to a different genetic makeup than it had, as illustrated in Figure 3.8.

This very simple example illustrates the basic idea of organic evolution. A genotype confers a reproductive advantage over alternative genotypes (i.e., one genotype tends to leave more offspring per generation than its alternatives), and thus increases its frequency in the population. In this case, we had two forms of a cell division enzyme that conferred different rates of cell division depending on the acidity of the environment. We also see from this example how a knowledge of modern biology inexorably leads us to the conclusion that evolution is inevitable. If it is true that proteins dictate life processes (which they do), and it is true that DNA dictates the structure of proteins (which it does), and it is true that mutations in the DNA occasionally alter the proteins (which they do), it is inevitable that the genetic structure of populations must change over time, if ever so slowly. This change in the genetic structure of populations is evolution.

Such is the crux of the theory of evolution through natural selection, a theory that was controversial in its day only because the field of biology had not yet come to understand the science of genetics. With a knowledge of modern genetics, Darwin's scheme of evolution through natural selection is a necessary consequence of well-known facts and has ceased to be controversial, at least in academic circles.

It may seem unusual at first, but understanding the basic idea of the evolution of a population of bacterial cells provides one with an understanding of the evolution of all life forms, although it gets quite complicated and sometimes even enigmatic with more advanced organisms. As mammals evolved from their tiny, insectivorous state through the primates

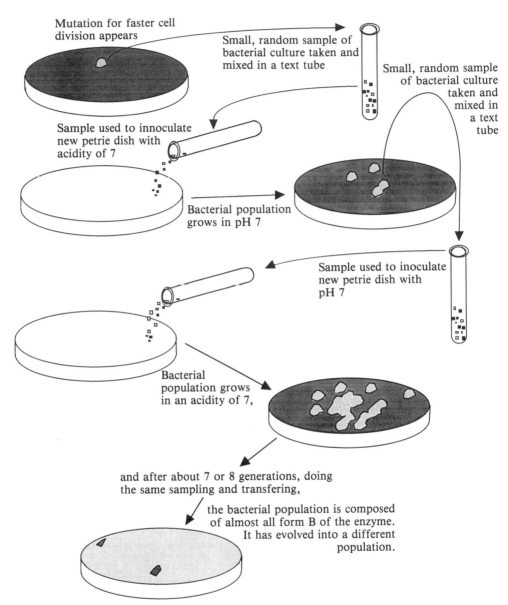

Figure 3.8. Evolutionary change in a bacterial culture. Beginning with a culture that has been kept at pH 5, a mutation arises in a cell division enzyme so that one cell has a different form (form B of figure 3.6). When a new culture is initiated in an environment of pH 7, the cells with the new enzyme form multiply more rapidly than the other cells and, after several cultures are initiated, the bacterial population becomes dominated by this new form of enzyme. The bacterial population has changed its biological character; it has evolved.

to the great apes and to *Homo sapiens,* the same fundamental process was presumably involved: Mutations in the DNA created alternative forms of proteins that did things a little differently, giving a selective advantage to those harboring such proteins. Simply multiply that process millions of times and you have the evolution of limbs from fins, of feathers from scales, of bones from cartilage; in short, of all the biological diversity in the world today.

THE EVOLUTION OF BIODIVERSITY

The biological world has fired our imaginations for at least as long as recorded history. Much of that imagination is fear, as certainly it must have been as we evolved from our Australopithecine ancestors. And, sometimes, that fear is indeed justified. The menacing crocodile in Figure 3.9a is not just the mythology of Crocodile Dundee. In Figure 3.9b, the stomach contents of a single Nile crocodile are displayed, and unless a single, hapless individual was weighted down with 20 or so necklaces, this crocodile had consumed a good number of specimens. Perhaps the most romantic symbol of all is the African lion (Figure 3.9c), which may not be the king of the beasts, but is certainly a danger, and has been since Eve wandered around the Rift Valley. It is said that some 60 or 70 Englishmen were killed by lions during the construction of the railroad from Mombasa to Nairobi (of course, the number of black Africans killed was not recorded).

Usually the danger posed by the natural world is more myth and romance than fact. For example, the little peanut bug (Figure 3.9d) of Costa Rica has some remarkable folk knowledge associated with it. According to tradition, if you are bitten by a peanut bug, you must have sex before nightfall or you will die. I can imagine all sorts of possible social consequences of this particular myth—"Excuse me, you don't know me, but I wonder if you could help me. I've just been bitten by a peanut bug and . . ." Actually, in this case, modern science cannot claim that the myth is false, since in fact peanut bugs do not bite.

The danger, romance, mythology, and aesthetics of nature are certainly part of the modern world, as partially suggested in the previous chapter. But it is well to recall that most of the earth's life has already passed on. Somewhere on the order of 99.9 percent of all species that have ever existed have already become extinct. A true appreciation of the

Figure 3.9. Some views of nature. (a) Salt water crocodile. (b) Stomach contents of a single Nile crocodile (display at India National Museum, Calcutta). (c) The "lion king" on the Serengeti of Kenya. (d) A peanut bug from Costa Rica (photo by Jerry Urquart).

(c)

(d)

world's biodiversity thus cannot really be gained by looking only at today's very tiny sample of biodiversity, but must be appreciated in its historical context, as popular culture has recently reminded us in the popular film *Jurassic Park*. The biodiversity produced by the evolutionary process is remarkable indeed.

At a micro level, it is really quite easy to understand the principles of organic evolution through natural selection, as indicated in the previous section. But when we arrive at macro levels, when we wish to understand how the evolutionary process created all of the diversity of life we see in the world today, we face a daunting task. When the genotypes in question stipulated two forms of enzymes, one of which caused more rapid cell division than the other, deducing the evolutionary pattern was really quite obvious. But when we extend this basic idea to more complicated patterns, the causes of these patterns are not nearly as easy to see, and we are forced to make rather weak claims of generalization.

Even though the causes are less than fully understood, the patterns of evolution are themselves quite well known. Because we have such a long history of the study of fossils, and because modern methods of dating ancient materials are remarkably sophisticated, we now have a relatively complete and accurate picture of evolutionary history. Those who have had the privilege to travel through western North America have, whether they know it or not, seen much evidence of that pattern. The multicolored rocks that attract thousands of visitors each year to the Grand Canyon of Arizona contain abundant clues to the evolutionary history of life on earth (Figure 3.10). At the base of the canyon, the Colorado River cuts through rocks that were formed prior to the existence of the world's plants and animals, and the various layers of different colored rocks above it were deposited at later times. Thus, as your eye moves from the river basin upward, you are moving from past to present.

If you examine the dark grey rocks on the river's edge (see Figure 3.10), you find remnants of tiny, single-celled organisms. Bacteria first evolved billions of years ago (earliest fossils are about 3.5 billion years old). They are thus the most successful form of life on earth, if we judge success in terms of how long something survives. All the world's bacteria, including all species that have become extinct, are grouped in one large category, the kingdom Monera. The Monera have a simple structure: each individual is a single cell, which lacks many of the structural details of more recently evolved life forms. Most importantly, these cells lack a nu-

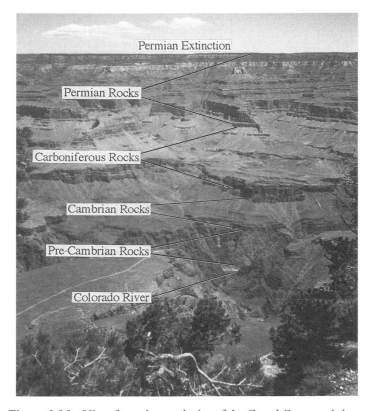

Figure 3.10. View from the south rim of the Grand Canyon, Arizona.

cleus. Indeed, modern biologists divide life into two major groups, the prokaryotes (meaning "without a nucleus" and including all the bacteria) and the eukaryotes (with a nucleus, and including all other life forms).

While the first great revolution in life was clearly the origin of life itself, the second was undoubtedly the evolution of the eukaryotic cell. Most biologists are now in agreement that this origin was actually the result of a parasitism or mutualism of one prokaryote by another. That is, the eukaryotic cell can be thought of as one organism, the cell, being parasitized by another organism, the nucleus; since, in this case, the "parasite" is actually beneficial to the host, and the host beneficial to the parasite, we refer to the relationship as a mutualism.[21] All other eurkaryotic life forms apparently arose from this evolutionary invention that occurred about 2.5 billion years ago. This eukaryotic revolution produced two major forms of life, those that are capable of photosynthesis (the algae) and those that are not (the single-celled animals), grouped together in the kingdom Protista.

Thus, by the time the red rocks were formed on top of the black rocks on the banks of the Colorado River, at least two of the five great kingdoms of life had already been formed, the Monera (bacteria) and the Protista (algae and single-celled animals). As your eye moves from the shores of the Colorado River up to the first reddish layer of rocks above, you have gone from the phase of life dominated by small, one-celled animals to an assemblage of animals that includes all the fundamental forms we know today. This is what is known as the Cambrian explosion (called Cambrian because the first well-known group of fossils from this period was discovered in Cambria, England). All the animals living today—the insects and their relatives, the clams and snails and their relatives, the earthworms and their relatives, the corals and jellyfish and their relatives, the mammals and their relatives—had their origins at this point in time. At their point of origin, they were all very small and they all lived in the ocean, but all the basic body plans that we see in all the animals in the world today were established at that time. And it was a true revolution: It occurred in a geological instant, perhaps only a few million years.

Actually, the Grand Canyon is not really a good place to look for Cambrian fossils. A variety of other sites that contain fossils from this period have been discovered all over the world, and, despite its great age (it began some 600 million years ago), the kinds of animals that lived then are quite well known. Drawings of some of those animals are shown in Figure 3.11, and a recreation of what a Cambrian sea may have looked like is presented in Figure 3.12. Note that we can identify several of these

---

Figure 3.11. Drawings of some of the animals of the Cambrian. (a) *Pikaia*, the form that was on the same lineage as modern chordates, which, of course, includes us. This, then, was one of our earliest ancestors. (b) *Amiskwia*. (c) *Nectocaris*. (d) *Hallucigenia*. (e) *Wiwaxia*, perhaps an early form on the same lineage that led to modern mollusks. (f) *Yohoia*. (g) *Marrella*. (h) *Opabinia*. (i) *Lenargyrion*. (j) *Odontogriphus*. (k) *Dinomischus*. (l) *Anomalocaris*. (m) *Sanctacaris*, an early member of the lineage that gave rise to some of the modern arthropods. All drawings from Gould, *Wonderful Life: The Burgess Shale and the Nature of History*, Copyright 1989 by Stephen Jay Gould, with the permission of W. W. Norton & Co., Inc. Illustrations by Marianne Collins.

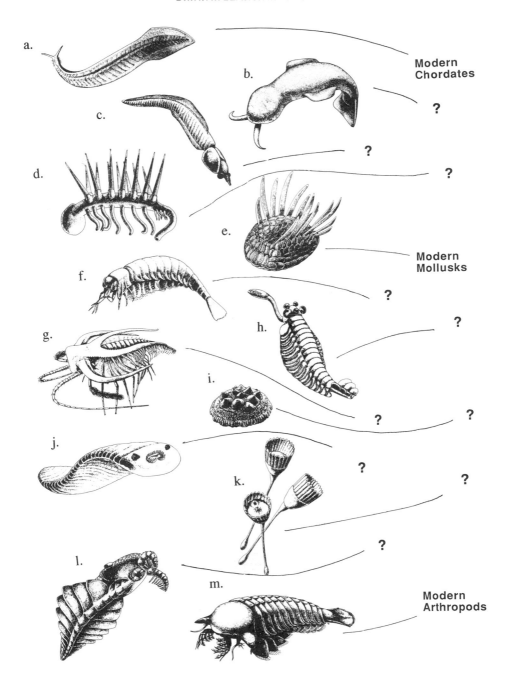

a.

b.

c.

d.

e.

f.

g.

h.

i.

j.

k.

l.

m.

Modern
Chordates

?

?

?

Modern
Mollusks

?

?

?

?

?

?

?

Modern
Arthropods

Figure 3.12. Diorama of the Cambrian sea (*Courtesy of the Exhibit Museum of Natural History*, University of Michigan, Ann Arbor). Note the school of *Marrella* (see Figure 3.11g) in the lower part of the photograph.

creatures as similar to ones we are familiar with today. Indeed, when you stop to think about it, of the common animals that exist today we only really have eight major types.[22] The eight major groups are (1) the corals and their relatives, immensely important as the major land-mass builders in the world; (2) the roundworms and (3) the flatworms, many of which are important human parasites; (4) the starfish and their relatives, recognizable mainly because of their radial symmetry; (5) the vertebrates and their relatives, interesting principally because they include us; (6) the clams and snails and their relatives; (7) insects, spiders, crabs and their relatives, the most diverse animal group, by far, in the world; and (8) worms, such as those that come out on sidewalks after a spring rain.[23] The amazing thing about the organisms that lived in the Cambrian is that these eight basic body plans were already present 600 million years ago, but that simultaneously there were many other body plans coexisting with these eight (see Figure 3.11). All but these eight have disappeared, while no new body plans have come into being again. Granted, there has been a great amount of diversification—for example, an organism similar to one identified as *Piakia* in the Cambrian probably gave rise not only to fish, but to dinosaurs, birds, and humans as well, while something similar to *Sanctacaris* probably gave rise to all the world's species of spiders, mites, scorpions, and the like. So the diversification of life has proceded during the past 600 million years, but all of the basic body plans had already evolved at the Cambrian explosion—the "big bang" of zoology.

Starting with the Cambrian period, which you can see in the Grand Canyon as the first layer of reddish rocks directly above the blackish rocks on the banks of the Colorado River (see Figure 3.10), the record of fossils in the various strata of rocks is really quite good, and it is possible to discern a great deal of pattern in the history of life. One of the patterns that has been known for quite some time are cycles of "radiation" and extinction. About every 100 million years, a major extinction event occurs—a large number of species disappear, followed by rapid evolution of different forms of life from the ones that remain. While no subsequent radiation has been quite as spectacular as the Cambrian explosion, each of the major extinction events has been followed by some major radiation, the evolution of new species of life.

The Cambrian Period began with the famous Cambrian explosion and ended a short 100 million years later with a massive extinction. Following this extinction, a new radiation occurred, the most obvious characteristics of which were the appearance and diversification of fish, the first land animals and plants, and the first appearance of insects. This time frame includes what geologists have named the Ordovician, Silurian, and Devonian Periods, and is marked by a mass extinction at the end of its 100-million-year period.

The radiation that follows the Devonian Period is especially important for *Homo sapiens* today. This 110-million-year time frame includes the geological periods known as the Carboniferous and the Permian, and is characterized by forests occupying all of the world's terrestrial habitats. Especially important were extensive swamp forests. These were the habitats in which complete biological decomposition did not always occur,[24] and, thus, organic material became fossilized in a partially decomposed state, eventually becoming the world's coal supplies. Furthermore, during this period, all of today's continents had come together into one very large continent, known as Pangaea. The extinction that marks the end of the Permian was the greatest extinction in all history, in which over 90 percent

Figure 3.13. Dinosaur footprints from the Navajo reservation in Northern Arizona.

of all animal species disappeared, as well as a large fraction of the plant species that made up the great coal-forming Carboniferous forests. And at this point we have come to the top of the rim of the Grand Canyon.

So, from the banks of the Colorado River, where the rocks were all older than the Cambrian time (generally referred to as pre-Cambrian), through the radiation of the fishes (in the Ordovician, Silurian, and Devonian periods), through the formation of coal from extensive swamp forests (the Carboniferous and Permian), to the final Permian extinction at the top of the canyon, we can see the remains of the geological era generally known as the Paleozoic (old animals) Era, encompassing the above five geologic periods. As we arrive at the end of the "old animals" era, we also arrive at the top of the Grand Canyon. Since later strata are always above earlier strata, we must travel elsewhere to see the later strata. Traveling east, we arrive at the Navajo reservation, and sandstone deposits that date from the end of the Permian to about 66 million years ago. In that sandstone, we can find telltale fossil footprints that look very much like the footprints a giant turkey would make (see Figure 3.13). Finally, if we wish to travel yet further toward today, we travel further east until we come to the famous Badlands of South Dakota, and fossil bones that look very much like our own. All of this is summarized in Figure 3.14.

The radiation that occurred at the end of the Permian, that of the animals that caused the giant turkey footprints (Figure 3.13), is the one that fires the imagination of school children the world over. This was the radiation of the dinosaurs. During the almost 200-million-year-old time frame of the Mesozoic Era (composed of the Triassic, Jurassic, and Creta-

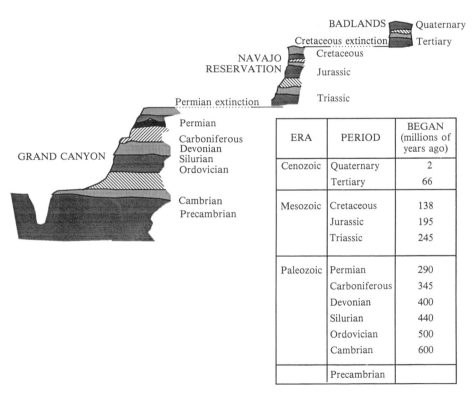

Figure 3.14. Schematic representation of the rock formations in the western United States, with the appropriate geological eras and periods.

ceous Periods), dinosaurs were the most conspicuous land animals in the world. This is also the period in which the continents were moving apart. And then, at the end of the period, we have the famous Cretaceous extinction, in which the dinosaurs became extinct, and for which we now have a great deal of evidence as to its cause. Apparently, a spot on the earth now covered by the Yucatan peninsula of Mexico was the site of impact of a massive meteorite that hit the earth, 66 million years ago. The explosion that resulted was far greater than anything we could imagine, even in an all-out nuclear war, and caused a dark haze to cover the earth. The climatic changes caused by this haze is thought to have caused the massive Cretaceous extinction, thus giving rise to the evolutionary radiation that effectively gave us the forms of life we see around us today.

The radiation that has been going on since the Cretaceous extinction encompases the past 66 million years, is still going on, and is known as the Cenozoic era. Its first geological period, the Tertiary, saw the continents drawing near to their current positions, and the dominant forms of terrestrial life, plants, and their pollinating insects, radiate to approximately their current form. Its second geological period, the Quaternary, began only 2 million years ago and is characterized by the advance and retreat of massive glaciers (the ice ages), and, at its end, the evolution of *Homo sapiens,* the subject of the next chapter.

FOUR

Human Origins

Considering the entire history of life on earth, the human species is hardly worth the trouble; it originated a geological microsecond ago, and will soon become extinct anyway. But here we are, near the turn of the century, and those of you reading this are all members of that species, and as insignificant as we are in terms of the evolution and history of life in general, we certainly are dominating things now. It seems somehow important, therefore, to take a close look at some of our special properties and offer some speculations on where they may have come from.

Any group of three or more people gathered together to answer the question, "What is a human being?" would likely begin in harmony (a special species of primate), but end in disagreement (the essence of humanness is love—no, it is understanding and compassion—no, it is warfare, and so on). That unique collection of things that makes us human is a subject that has caused considerable debate, as much among the world's greatest philosophers as among undergraduate students in college dorms. And what a fascinating debate it is!

To understand the relationship between *Homo sapiens* and the environment in which it lives, certain things about which we debate are critical, others less so. In this chapter we examine the origin of humanness within the context of its articulation with the natural world. I am in broad agreement with the position of the anthropologist Marvin Harris that the best way to understand *H. sapiens* is through an understanding of its interaction with material resources, an approach he labels "cultural materialism." [1] While I may have some differences associated with which particular research strategies are allowable, it seems true to me that one critical component must somehow be interaction with material resources. At least it presents us with one avenue of understanding, admittedly only one in a potpourri of other possibilities. As will become evident in this chapter, with the evolution of language and culture, it becomes ever more difficult to relate the salient features of this species directly to material resources. The very nature of human social organization is dictated, in great part, by the way we talk to one another, the way we construct social realities, such that much of what we regard as essential to our being may have lost all recognizable connection to any material resources. So, a central feature of the following overview of human origins will emphasize the utilization of resources, but clearly will have to include other elements that go into the grab-bag of things normally thought to characterize the human species. Chapter 9 will be devoted entirely to the question of the material transformation of resources.

With respect to origin and evolution of the human condition, we can identify six key elements that define humanness: (1) bipedalism, (2) tool manufacture, (3) concentrated energy use, (4) social resource transformation, (5) language and abstract thought, and (6) discourse and social construction. One might argue that elements 1 and 2 are simply precursors to what makes us human, while 3, and especially 4, are the essence of the cultural materialist approach, leaving 5 and 6 in the epistemological arena of deciding whether or not 4 is the best approach for studying humans. Regardless, for purposes of this chapter I include all six as being the essence of humanness, and seek to present as coherent a view as possible of the origin of each.

BIPEDALISM AND TOOL MANUFACTURE

About 12 million years ago, the African continent had an accident: It collided with Europe. That collision resulted in the uplifting of virtually all of the eastern quarter of the continent. The western edge of this great convulsion is marked by the famous Rift Valley, itself bordered on the west by mountains and on the east by the East African highlands.

This most dramatic geological event had important climatological consequences. The mountain chain bordering the western edge of the Rift Valley acted as a barrier to the waterladen air making its way up the Congo basin, such that by the time an air mass reached the Rift Valley, most of its water had been removed. Thus, all of eastern Africa within the latitudinal limits of the tropics falls within a massive rain shadow, making it far drier than would be normally expected for a land mass within the tropical belt.[2]

This dry region set the stage for the development of a unique habitat, caused by a combination of large grazing herbivores and naturally-oc-curring fire. The herbivores (e.g., rhinoceros, gazelles, and zebras) contin-ually cropped the vegetation, thus preventing the formation of a canopy of trees. Without a canopy, the remaining vegetation lost its moisture dur-ing the dry season. This dry vegetation burned easily. Burning promoted grass growth, since the underground stems of the grasses survived the burning and new shoots easily emerged after the fires. Thus were formed the large expanses of African grasslands.

Some 10 million years earlier, a special type of monkey evolved. The details of its structures, the details that make it different from monkeys per se, are not important. What makes it important for us is that it gave rise eventually to the four species of great apes—the gorilla, the chimp, the orangutan, and the human.[3] For the next 10 million years a great deal of evolution occurred, resulting in a significant diversity of these creatures, most of which became extinct. But two major lineages remained, one of which presumably remained a forest animal and eventually gave rise to present-day orangutans and gorillas, while the other moved into the newly created grasslands of East Africa and gave rise to present-day chimpanzees and humans.

Then, about 4 million years ago (as far as we know), a particular ape appeared that did something that no ape had ever done before—it "stood up." It is not that a particularly intelligent individual suddenly decided to stand up, but, rather, over many generations, the habit of upright ambula-tion slowly evolved, eventually resulting in a species that was completely bipedal. For the first time in the history of mammals, a species did almost all of its walking on its hind legs. This great ape never did have a common name, so we are forced to refer to it by its generic scientific name, *Australo-pithecus.*

We know little of any of the species of *Australopithecus.* That they walked upright is noncontroversial, not only from their skeletal configu-ration but also from the remarkable excavations of Mary Leakey, which uncovered the fossilized imprint of footprints of an adult and juvenile, tramping through the mud some 3.5 million years ago, leaving not even a hint of the use of forelimbs in locomotion.[4]

There has been a great deal of speculation and debate about the advantages that may have accrued to *Australopithecus* from its bipedal habit. The most obvious is to to be able to see over the grass. Many other animals of the African grasslands—such as baboons, mongoose, and vervet monkeys—stand up to do this, and one certainly cannot forget Gary Larson's classic cartoon of the giraffe standing on a chair looking for lions. Being able to see better has its advantages (Figure 4.1), but it must be admitted that such cannot represent an obvious advantage for walking upright all the time, rather than occasionally standing up to look around. What seems a more important advantage to bipedalism is freeing of the hands for other than locomotor activities. If one normally walks on the hind legs, the forelimbs are available for carting bits of meat that were scavenged, using sticks to probe termite nests, transporting fruits and nuts gathered on the ground—in short, for carrying things.

The original *Australopithecus* was called *Australopithecus afarensis,* and appears in the fossil record about 4 million years ago. The fossil record is always a fickle scribe, and we thus have no idea of when the Australopithecines began diverging. Nevertheless, it is clear that by about 3 million years ago we can recognize two distinct species of *Australopithecus,* one called *A. robustus,* the other called *A. africanus.* The *robustus* line had large molars and facial musculature, perhaps associated with utilization of coarse plant material for food, while the *africanus* line had dental and facial muscle structures more in keeping with the use of meat. One hypothesis suggests that this latter form was a scavenger in the grassland, competing with hyenas for the scraps of zebra and gazelle left by lions and cheetahs.[5]

By 2.5 million years ago, a second robust species had appeared in the fossil record, *A. boisei,* perhaps similar to *robustus* in its eating habits. Thus, by 2.5 million years ago, the African grasslands were inhabited by at least three distinct species of *Australopithecus (robustus, boisei,* and *africanus),* each of which likely viewed the others as distinct organisms, much like we view chimpanzees, despite the fact that they lived in the same habitat and walked upright, and to our eye appear quite similar to one another.

It was actually quite recently that the first (we presume it was the first) species of our own genus was discovered, first a skull fragment about 1.7 million years old found by Louis Leakey in Tanzania, and, later, an almost complete skull by his son Richard in Kenya, both in the middle of the Rift Valley. This new species was characterized by a very large cranial capacity, almost the same proportion to body weight as our own, and was thus clearly distinguishable from all species of *Australopithecus.* It was cata-

Figure 4.1. The African savannah as viewed from a crouching position (top photo), and from a standing position, illustrating the potential benefit of a small creature's being able to see beyond the tall grass.

logued as being in a different genus, *Homo,* and was named *Homo habilis* ("practical man"). This marks the first appearance of our genus in the world, some 2 million years ago, possibly derived from *A. africanus.*

But the really interesting thing about *Homo habilis* is not the collection of bones unearthed over the past 25 years in East Africa, but, rather, the things that were found with those bones, stone tools. This is the first case we have of a major manufacturing process where resources were dramatically altered to produce commodities that were usable for the transformation of other resources—the first machines, so to speak. Conceptually, it represents the first time that a machine, in any significant sense, actually took the place of human labor, a factor to which we return later for considerable detailed analysis.[6]

It is worth noting that many other animals use tools. Captive bluebirds have been seen using pieces of newspaper to get at food that is out of their reach. Sea otters regularly use stones to break the shells of the mollusks they eat. Almost all primates use tools of one sort or another, and chimpanzees even manufacture tools as they strip the bark from small twigs to make probes for capturing termites. But when we begin talking of the stone tools of *Homo habilis,* the scale of tool manufacture is spectacularly different from the sort of tool use and/or manufacture of other animals. It is true that a chimpanzee can catch as many termites in an hour with a twig probe as it might take 5 hours to do without that tool (thus substituting a machine for labor), but consider the time it would take to skin a buffalo and cut its meat into the pieces necessary to hand out to the extended family without the stone knives that were used for that purpose, or the time it would take to stalk a wildebeest and kill it by stoning (if that were even possible), compared to killing it with a spear fixed with a stone spearhead. The manufacture and use of stone tools by *Homo habilis* is, indeed, qualitatively distinct from the simple modification of a twig by chimpanzees.

Mary Leakey argues that it is quite important to distinguish between simple modification of resources and purposeful manufacture. Chimpanzees do "manufacture" a termite probe, but it is with a simple modification of a twig they invariably find nearby. *H. habilis* brought special rocks, sometimes from large distances, and modified them according to a prescribed plan. Even the earliest, most primitive, stone tools of *H. habilis* seem to have been produced in this manner—purposeful manufacture, rather than simple modification.[7]

Furthermore, with *H. habilis,* we find the first time that an animal used a tool to make another tool. Could the bluebird use the paper to drag a stick into its cage in order to use the stick to get at the food? Could the sea otter use the stone to break the mollusk shell in a specific form in order to use it to scoop out the mussels it captures? This notion has been cited as possibly indicating the first precursor to language facility, in that a tool is "seen" as embedded in another structure.[8] Perhaps more indicative of primitive language abilities, or at least their precursors, is an interesting collection of stones arranged in a circle from a *H. habilis* site, apparently arranged to stabilize some sort of shelter. If this is really what these stones represent, I find it much easier to imagine them being constructed if some sort of language were available to the construction crew. It need not have been a spoken language, but could have been some form of relatively complicated communication (more than "Look out, snake,") perhaps with hand signals, but enabling the practitioners to say things to one another, such as, "Let's put the rocks in a circle," "But why should we do that?" "Let's make our house for the night," and so on.

CONCENTRATED ENERGY USE AND SOCIAL RESOURCE TRANSFORMATION

The ability to rapidly release stored energy from biological material outside of the body was a human development that was unparalleled in any other species.[9] The ability to control and use fire represents just such an invention. A tree that may have required 30 years to accumulate all the energy contained in its trunk could now be used as an energy source, releasing 30 years' worth of stored energy in a few minutes—i.e., it could be burned for the creation of heat. In a sense, the control of fire made *Homo* a superior herbivore. Beetles may bore into a tree's trunk, termites may slowly eat it from within, grasshoppers eat leaves, and many moth larvae grow inside seeds. But with the ability of *Homo* to control fire, for the first time there was an "herbivore" that could chop a tree down and burn it, releasing decades of the tree's energy storage for immediate use.

The evidence for use of fire comes from archaeological sites associated with yet a new species of *Homo, H. erectus.* Ancient campfires are clearly associated with this species, and there is little controversy over the fact that it used fire, at least in the later stages of its existence.

At least some of the reasons for using fire can be reasonably guessed: warmth as the species spread northward, cooking meat, keeping predators away from the campsite at night, and so forth. But the real importance of using fire is that it set the stage for the development of energy-intensive societies. From the burning of firewood, to the manufacture of charcoal, to the use of fossil fuels, the harnessing of biologically stored energy out-side of the body represented a discovery that had a tremendous influence on future development, whatever its influence on *H. erectus* itself may have been.

H. erectus may have evolved from *H. habilis* or may have evolved from some yet-undiscovered line of *Homo*. The only evidence one way or an-other is that *H. erectus* appeared at approximately the same time as *H. habilis* disappeared. *H. erectus* is physically very similar to us. Besides using fire, it was characterized by the development of stone tools that were much more sophisticated than those of *H. habilis*. On the all-important question of the development of language, we have no evidence. One can speculate that during its exceptionally long history (about 1.5 million years), the process of language evolution was continuously unfolding, or one could speculate that *H. erectus* remained with a primitive language system until modern language emerged quite suddenly, marking the end of *H. erectus* as a species. Bickerton argues that the use of fire implies some sort of "representational system," since it is difficult to imagine gaining control over something that all other animals fear without some form of commu-nication, representing to others in the group what it might look like to have a campfire, for example.[10] This will be discussed further in the next section.

What we know for sure that characterized *H. erectus* was its spread out of Africa. First appearing in the fossil record about 1.6 million years ago, the species apparently remained in the African grasslands for more than half a million years, but then began a massive migration northward. Specimens have been found in Europe and Asia as far as Peking and Java, the first time that a human-like organism spread significantly on the globe.

At some point in its evolutionary history, *Homo* began a process of socially transforming resources. Since *H. erectus* developed the ability to control fire, certainly developed the ability to spread northward, probably lived in social groups, and hunted socially, one is tempted to speculate that it was about at the time of *H. erectus* that a new form of resource transformation began to take shape. If it is true that language began evolving at this time, this is all the more reason to suspect such a change.

When ecologists think of resource transformation they usually think of three factors: the resource itself, its transformed state, and the supply of energy that goes into making the transformation. This way of thinking dominates, whether talking about lions and zebras or photosynthesis—energy is applied to a resource to create a product. The lion supplies the energy to transform the resource "zebra" into the product "zebra meat," and the sun provides the energy to transform carbon dioxide to energy-rich compounds (see Figure 4.2*a*). When thinking of *Homo sapiens,* and perhaps even when thinking of *H. erectus,* such a basic plan is no longer useful. The facts of humanness (language, abstract thought, consciousness, social construction, discourse) are so overwhelmingly determinate that trying to apply the resource–energy–product formula is like trying to understand not only the football game, but also the school spirit, tailgate parties, and drunken aftermaths of a college football game from a detailed analysis of the physics of the ball–throw–recieve sequence. Clearly, a different model, a different *minimal* model, is required for understanding resource transformation under the special case of *H. sapiens,* perhaps originally developing with *H. erectus.*[11]

It is useful to begin with the basic ecological transformation "resource–applied energy–product," albeit for purposes of modifying it to fit into what *Homo* does. In the human case, the applied energy is purposeful and social. Individual humans "see" the product before it is produced. They then organize themselves to apply energy to resources in order to get the material product. Thus, the product begins, even before it is produced, to affect the social organization that creates the applied energy. That socially organized energy then is applied and the product emerges, presumably resembling that which had been envisioned before the process began.

The product is then "consumed," in a very general sense of the word. A stone tool is consumed as it is used, acorn bread is consumed as it is eaten, the consumption of roasted meat is initiated even before the meat itself is roasted. In this variety of pathways, the notion of consumption affects the way the socially organized energy is actually organized. So, we best conceptualize the whole process as (1) a product that results from the application of (2) socially organized energy applied to (3) a resource. The product is subjected to (4) consumption, which in turn affects the nature

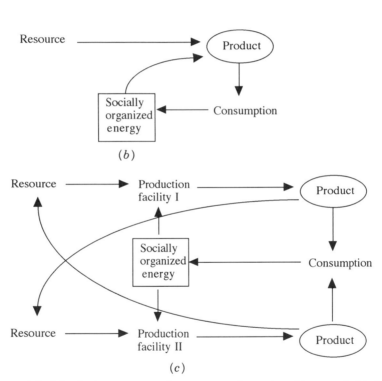

Figure 4.2. The basic processes of energy transformation. Top graph (a) illustrates the process as a general ecological rule. Middle graph (b) illustrates the addition of sociality. Bottom graph (c) is the "minimal" model for the process in *Homo sapiens*.

of the social organization. This basic configuration is illustrated in Figure 4.2*b,* as distinguished from its non-human counterpart in Figure 4.2*a.*

But the special situation of *Homo* does not end here. In all cases we know of (and here, we really have no idea regarding *H. erectus*—it's all speculation), products are produced both for direct consumption of those engaged in the act of applying socially organized energy, and for use as resources in other resource transformation processes. Furthermore, resources are usually brought together in some sort of central location, a "production facility," whose exact nature depends on the resource transformation process involved. We could imagine a hunting group of *H. erectus* bringing a recently killed antelope to the campfire for roasting, in which case the campfire would be the production facility. In modern societies, the factory or farm or office might be the production facility, depending on which resources and products were under consideration. At any rate, the socially organized energy is brought to bear on the resource in the production facility, from which results a product that is used as a resource in another transformation process. The basic structure is illustrated in Figure 4.2*c.*

This, then, is the minimal model for primitive resource transformation, probably as practiced by *H. erectus,* certainly as practiced by the later species *H. sapiens.* It is explored in more detail in chapter 9.

LANGUAGE STRUCTURE AND ABSTRACT THOUGHT

It is ironic that in the era for which the fossil evidence is best, the last half-million years, the actual sequence of events is most controversial. As described above, about a million years ago, *H. erectus* dispersed throughout the Old World, having well-established populations in Europe, Africa, and Asia. They never were abundant by current standards, and certainly did not have a very large impact on the global ecosystem.[12]

Until a few years ago, it had been assumed that this highly-dispersed population somehow evolved all in the same direction to become the same species, *H. sapiens.* Thus the general population that inhabited eastern Asia became a "Mongoloid" version of modern *H. sapiens,* those that inhabited Africa became a "Negroid" version, and those that inhabited Europe became a "Caucasoid" version. But an alternative view, not really new but recently bolstered by some controversial data from molecular biology, was that the initial dispersion of *H. erectus* was ultimately a failure. According to this view, those 40,000 or so bands of *H. erectus* all became extinct, and the spread of *H. sapiens* throughout the old world was far more recent, perhaps as recent as 200,000 years ago, originating from a population located in the grasslands of eastern Africa. The data from molecular biology concern the configuration of DNA in samples of people whose origins are from around the globe. In a watershed paper published in 1987, Rebecca Cann, Mark Stoneking, and Allan Wilson calculated that all contemporary humans derive from a single population located in Africa some 200,000 years ago. At the time of this writing, the "timing" debate has not yet been convincingly resolved.[13]

What is it that characterizes *H. sapiens* and makes it so distinct from the previous *Homos,* or, for that matter, from *Australopithecus?* We are now on much better grounds than before because we are talking about a species that still exists and, more importantly, one that we can talk to. And that is just the point. *H. sapiens* is characterized by language, which means socially constructed abstract thought, which leads ultimately to the formation of discourses (as discussed in the next section). It is difficult to emphasize too strongly the importance of this collection of traits. If individuals of early *H. sapiens* (or even *H. erectus,* if it were possible) could ask each other questions, how long could it have been before one of them asked, "Why does the sun come up each day?" or, "What causes lightning?" or, "Why did the flood kill my infant?" To a mind like that of early *H. sapiens,* likely as sophisticated in a physiological or neurological sense as our own, but certainly without the tens or hundreds of thousands of years of storytelling about the sun and lightning and the causes of floods, what kinds of answers were available? Obviously, there could not have been any but very simple answers. Yet even the simplest of answers would have begun an important human process. Why does the sun rise every day? Because some force we cannot see causes it to do so. Once we postulate a force we cannot see, we have begun the development of a parallel world— a spiritual world, so to speak—the world that provides a mirror to define our own consciousness. Once we answered, "A force we cannot see causes floods," we set up a framework in which the essence of us became that which was responsive to another, unseen but powerful, force.

That both a spirit world and consciousness itself may have arisen at this time is perhaps less important than the very likely prospect that social construction and discourse may have their origins here. The question-and-answer pair that produced "God makes the sun rise," might very well have been the first of our social constructions (albeit somewhat more modest constructions, such as "If we put the stones in a circle they'll form a stronger base," may have been more likely). At any rate it is clear that abstract thought, language, social construction, and discourse form a sort of continuum that, in a sense, defines the very essence of the species *Homo sapiens*. How might they have come about?

First, consider language.[14] *Homo sapiens* stands alone as having fully developed language. Other animals have vocalizations, some seemingly can form abstractions in their minds, and others can put abstract symbols together in meaningful strings. Perhaps the most famous animal example is the vervet monkey, in which at least three different vocalizations mean three different things. One sound apparently means "python," and causes all the animals in the troop to look downward as they climb higher up into the trees. A second sound means "hawk," and causes the troop members to look upward and move down in the tree. A third sound means "leopard," and causes an anxious looking around, neither up nor down necessarily. But no vervet monkey can ever put those vocalizations together to mean, for example, "the python ate the hawk."

On the other hand, several celebrated examples of chimpanzees have suggested that chimpanzees have capacities similar to ours for language. The problem, it is argued, is that chimps cannot vocalize, so that in order to teach them language up to their capacity, one must provide them with some way of signing. This has been done with computer symbols, with little plastic tokens that represent different words, and with hand signals. The result is that chimps have a remarkable capacity not only for abstractly representing images in their mind, but also for stringing words together seemingly to form sentences, and even using what appears to be language to engage in such human activities as lying.

Despite all the impressive talents displayed by the various chimpanzees in the various labs around the world, the final word seems to be that their language capabilities are a far cry from those of *Homo sapiens*. A couple of simple examples will suffice to demonstrate the difference. A chimp can be taught the subject-object distinction through the simple device of word order. "The python ate the hawk" will be correctly interpreted by the chimp that has been taught subject is always before object (as will the simple string "python eat hawk"). But that same chimp will either be confused or get it backward when faced with "The hawk was eaten by the python." Even worse, could anyone imagine a vervet monkey distinguishing between "The leopard that saw the python ate the hawk" and "The leopard saw the python that ate the hawk"? The words of the two sentences are identical, the order is nearly identical (only one word has had its position changed), but the meaning is totally different. Yet even the most uneducated person, save those with specific language disabilities, will not fail to easily and automatically sense the difference in the meaning of those two sentences. Of all animals that ever lived, only *H. sapiens* (and perhaps *H. erectus*) could do that.[15]

Language clearly requires abstract representation, but the reverse is not true. Substantial evidence exists that a variety of animals—from pigeons to dolphins to primates—are capable of representing images in their minds. Representation of abstract images is an important prerequisite to language, but it must also be noted that language permits far more complicated abstractions than would be otherwise possible. For example, no one has any problem constructing a mental image when we say "the golden mountain," or "the unicorn in the garden," or the "auditorium filled with naked people," despite the fact that no one has ever seen one. To my knowledge there is no evidence even suggesting that other animals are able to engage in abstract representation of this sort of complexity.

Such complex representation suggests the possibility that the primary function of language may not simply be communication (although that is clearly one of its functions), but rather a system of representation. If I can say "a golden mountain," even if I do not say it to anyone else, I can envision such a thing even though I have never seen it. Such capacity allows for the mental construction of things never seen before, but possibly achievable. Did that band of *H. erectus* have an individual who first saw "a circle of rocks" in her head before she placed them in a circle? Of course, it is conceivable to imagine the construction of relatively simple abstractions like circles of rocks without the symbolic representation of the things that go into the phrase that describes them with language. But what about "children laughing because of the funny clown suit I am going to wear" or "a computer program that I will write that will enable me to predict the future behavior of the stock market"? Clearly, a prerequisite for language requires the capability of abstract representation to start with, but its existence makes that abstract representation infinitely richer, encompassing actions, things, and states of being that never existed before, including many that cannot exist in material fact.

To see where this system may have come from, we must describe in outline form what language structure is about, beginning with a distinction between different basic forms of a representational system. A useful analogy is an atlas versus a list of itineraries. The atlas provides maps of geographical areas, whereas the list of itineraries provides the possible routes that might be taken around the geographical area. We can locate Cairo and Casablanca on a map of the world, but to travel from one to the other we need to have instructions as to which roads to take, which bridges to cross, which boats to take, and so on. It would not do to simply draw a line from Cairo to Casablanca, take a compass reading, and start walking. Rather, we would consult a book of itineraries indicating a system of roadways that take us along the southern shores of the Mediterranean, or flight schedules that fly us directly (quite similar to a compass reading, but it is necessary to check the flight schedules), or we could take a boat to Athens, drive a car to Madrid, hitch a ride to Gibraltar, and take a short boat ride to Casablanca.

The analogy to language is that the atlas is the representational system in static form, formally referred to as the lexicon—the phonemes, which are limited to just a few, the words the phonemes are allowed to create, the concepts the words indicate. This atlas has certain restrictions. For example, words generally fit into hierarchies ("all things" is broken down into the "concrete and the abstract." "Concrete" is broken down into "animate and inanimate." "Animate" is broken down into "invertebrate and vertebrate." "Vertebrates" into "mammals and others." "Mammals" into "cats, dogs, horses, etc." "Cats" into "lions, leopards, etc."). While it is doubtful that vervet monkeys have such a lexical atlas, substantial evidence exists that chimpanzees do, to some extent.

The other aspect of language, the itineraries, is strictly limited to humans. It is what allows us to create virtually an infinite variety of sentences from our lexicon, what permits us to say things like, "Absence makes the heart grow fonder," and tells us not to say, "Persistence makes the lungs turn sad." It is what makes us, almost automatically, see the difference between "With the knife brought for the steak, Jane was cut by the man," and "With the knife brought by the man, Jane cut the steak." Without thinking twice, we immediately distinguish the knife that was brought by the man from that which she brought, "cut" the steak rather than "cut by" the man, the activity being aimed at Jane rather than at the steak, and the man's action bringing the knife or cutting Jane. How do we automatically see such differences when we form sentences?

There are three sorts of structural consistencies involved in sentence formation: predicability (not predictability), grammaticization, and syntax. The first of these is somewhat flexible in use, but the other two are seemingly fixed and unalterable, perhaps representing something that might be called underlying structure.

With regard to predicability, we can say "the story is fascinating" or "the story is true," but we cannot say the "the story is tall" or "the story is sorry." We can say "Jane is tall," "Jane is fascinating," or "Jane is sorry," but we cannot say "Jane is true." We have two entities and four qualities. The relationship between an entity and a quality is predication. As can be seen from these examples, all qualities cannot be predicated by all entities. Indeed, there appear to be fairly strict rules about what can be predicated from what. Yet this is the one aspect of the language itinerary over which we do have some flexibility. Most people would reject, for example, that a tree could be hungry, but foresters concerned with a tree's nutrition might very well come to speak normally of trees being hungry. A calculator cannot be asleep, but portable computers (like the one I am writing on now) are fitted with a feature that automatically puts the computer to "sleep" when it is not used for a while. Indeed, predication can evolve with use. According to some linguists, predication is defined by use in the first place, and while we currently see strict limits, those limits are arbitrarily defined.

A far more complicated aspect of the itinerary is grammar. Virtually any sentence you might think of is composed mainly of elements that are not demonstrable. Take that last sentence, for example. The words sentence, composed, elements, and demonstrable are at least referentiable— that is, you could point to one of them or demonstrate them. But the other 12 words are only indicators of the sentence structure itself, and are referred to as grammatical items. In most languages, more than half the words are such grammatical items—when we speak, then, more than half the time is spent structuring the language rather than referring to persons, places, things, concepts, or actions. Sometimes grammatical items can be omitted, sometimes they will be assumed if omitted, but for the most part, the omission of a grammatical item from a sentence makes the sentence meaningless, incorrect, or both, or may change its meaning entirely (as with the leopard that either ate the hawk or saw the python eat the hawk, or Jane's unfortunate incident with the knife).

Grammatical items vary from language to language. In some languages, it is possible to express things that are inexpressible with other languages. For example, in several languages, verbal inflections exist that specify whether information has been personally obtained or gathered secondhand, something we cannot do in English. Yet it is even more interesting to speculate on why all human languages grammatize so few of the potentially grammaticizable items. All languages deal with one versus many or present versus past versus future, but none deal with, for example, whether a thing is edible or not, or whether it is hostile or not. Why can we distinguish grammatically between "I go to the store" and "I went to the store," but not between "Here comes an animal I can eat" and "Here comes an animal I cannot eat"? We could imagine, for example, "Here comes an animaled" versus "Here comes an animalin," where -ed refers to edible and -in refers to inedible. Why are we spared the need to say, "I go to the store in the present" and "I go to the store in the past?"

Such questions are fascinating and, to my thinking, totally baffling. But the critical point about grammatical items is their importance within all languages. We use them all the time without even thinking about them, and language as we know it would not be possible without them.

The third structural consistency existing in all language is syntax. Consider that sentence. It has ten words, and, therefore, there are exactly 3,628,800 ways you could rearrange it. Very few of those ways, however, give a sensible sentence, which means that about 3,600,000 are wrong. We automatically know which of that more than three and a half million possibilities are the correct ones—no one has to teach us how to recognize them. Indeed, we appear to have a recipe for structuring sentences, a recipe so rich and efficient that it automatically rules out the more than 3,600,000 wrong combinations and effortlessly recognizes the right ones. What is more amazing is that we apparently develop that recipe without the slightest active effort, as part of the normal development sequence. As much as we crawl and then walk, we babble and then talk. By the time we talk, we seem to have developed the complicated formula that allows us to recognize correct structure. What does that formula look like?

A great deal of effort has gone into this question in the last 20 years. It is not appropriate to summarize that research here, but it is worthwhile to introduce two of the salient features to give the reader a feel for the complexity of the subject. First, there is a particular way in which phrases are structured that appears to be common to all languages. Noun phrases and verb phrases are not strung together as we tend to think of chimpanzee language; they are, rather, inserted into one another much like the famous Chinese boxes. So, for example, "The vervet monkey that saw the python that ate the large hawk was frightened by the leopard" is not just a string of words, but, rather, phrases within phrases within phrases. At the highest level we have a noun phrase (The vervet monkey that saw the python eat the large hawk) followed by a verb phrase (was frightened by) followed by a noun phrase (the leopard). The first noun phrase is composed of a noun phrase (the vervet monkey) followed by a verb phrase (that saw) followed by a noun phrase (the python that ate the large hawk). The latter noun phrase is composed of a noun phrase (the python), a verb phrase (that ate), and a noun phrase (the large hawk). Phrase structure in all languages has this hierarchical structure.

Second, argument structure is consistent from language to language. Arguments depend on verbs, and each verb categorizes for a fixed number of arguments (usually). For example, leave, arrive, sleep, awaken, and many others take a single argument (I leave, he arrives, Jill sleeps), while others take two arguments (he dropped the cup, she sings the song, Joe beats his dog, etc.), while yet others take three (I gave him his due, she brought me flowers, etc.). The remarkable fact about arguments is that they appear to be universal. Thus, for example, any non-English language that has a word that means arrive, will allow one argument for that word, while any non-English word that means brought will take three. This is a remarkable consistency.

Fully-developed human language can thus be thought of as composed of a lexicon and a set of itineraries, the latter of which are composed of predications, grammar, and syntax. While other animals have primitive lexicons, only *H. sapiens* (and, to some unknown degree, possibly *H. erectus*) contains the itineraries. This species produced Shakespearian sonnets, *The Autobiography of Malcom X,* the speeches of Albizu Campos, the poetry of Emily Dickinson, the writings of Rigoberta Menchú. The longest utterance on record from a chimp was "give orange me give eat orange me eat orange give me eat orange give me you," which leaves little doubt about what he wants, but is a far cry from the beauty, erudition, or elegance of any of the above authors.

THE EVOLUTION OF LANGUAGE AND ABSTRACT THOUGHT

To approach the question of how language may have evolved, it is useful to first distinguish between protolanguage and language. By the age of two, most children speak a sort of language, but it is a language with little grammatical or syntactic structure. Shortly after that, language rapidly flowers into its complete adult structure. What might happen if the two-year-old remained at that level? A partial answer is provided by the case of Genie, now quite famous among linguists. Genie was found, at the age of 13, wandering with her mother, having been isolated from the age of 20 months by a tyrannical father who kept her locked up and isolated from human contact all her life. He literally treated her as an animal, apparently barking at her like a dog. Her language skills were nil when she came to the attention of linguists. Despite a great deal of subsequent tutoring, Genie was never able to develop language skills beyond the capabilities of a typical two-year-old.

A further piece of information is supplied by so-called pidgin languages. Due to the conditions of European colonialism, several places in the world were forcibly stocked with unwilling conscripts to the slavery or semi-slavery system. Places like Haiti, Jamaica, Belize, Hawaii, and others were sites to which slaves or itinerant workers were brought from several different places. Even in a place like Jamaica, where all slaves were from West Africa, they were drawn from a variety of cultures with a variety of languages. The only language that seemed to be common to all of them was the language of the master—English, for example, in the case of Jamaica. But because the slaves or itinerant workers typically outnumbered the masters, even though they spoke their native tongue fluently, the brand of colonial language they developed was significantly lacking in complex grammar and syntax. It was a kind of language known as pidgin and commonly developed in the colonies of the French, English, Spanish, and Portuguese, although the phenomenon is known from substantially earlier times. The children of pidgin speakers developed a new language, based on the pidgin of their parents, but with all the grammatical and syntactic structure of normal human language, and they did it automatically, without special tutoring. This language—which spontaneously develops among the children of pidgin speakers—is known as Creole and can be heard yet today in places like Haiti (French Creole), Jamaica, and much of the West Indies (English Creole). The remarkable fact is that with no special tutoring, within one generation, a complex grammar and syntax were added to what is not exactly a language, pidgin, to make all the structural attributes of human language.

The type of language spoken by typical two-year-olds, the language eventually learned by Genie, and the pidgins developed by many adult people forced to cope in an environment in which their own language is not understood, all provide something of an insight into what Derek Bickerton calls "protolanguage." It is a language that may be very rich in lexicon, but poor in or void of grammar or syntax—it has a large atlas, but no particular itineraries. One might speculate that protolanguage developed as a precursor to real language, again, perhaps with *H. erectus*.

The fully complex itineraries of human language then somehow evolved from this protolanguage. Exactly how that may have happened remains a mystery, but certain clues from normal language development suggest a possible pattern. After a relatively long period of protolanguage development, the normal developing child acquires the full itinerary of language (predicability, grammaticization, and syntax) with blinding speed. It is frequently the case that biologists use the developmental sequence of an organism as a clue to its evolutionary history. If we follow this tradition here we might conclude, as did Bickerton, that the itineraries evolved very rapidly once protolanguage had fully evolved. Of course it would be difficult to imagine, from one generation to the next, the sudden appearance of full language in one or two generations, just as a child does not develop its final grammar-rich adult language pattern from one day to the next. However, just as the rapidity of the development of language itineraries has enthralled psycholinguists for ages, the evolution of this advanced language capicity may have been very rapid, as argued by Bickerton. Bickerton's argument has been questioned by some and even ridiculed by others,[16] but to a biologist who recalls the power of ontogeny recapitulating phylogeny from embryology courses years ago, a soft version of Bickerton's rapid evolution of language's itineraries does not seem so far-fetched.

DISCOURSE AND SOCIAL CONSTRUCTION

If protolanguage preceded language, we then ask what might be the relationship of protolanguage to abstract representation, social construction, and discourse. At the most elementary level, these three elements are so obviously part of the human condition that it almost seems trivial to point them out. In the fog of my pre-coffee morning hours I begin planning what I will do during the day—an abstract construction. I speak with my partner about her plans, and based on that dialogue I may modify my plans—a primitive social construction. I hear of my son's planned day, which may cause me to modify my plans further. Eventually I have a picture of what my day will look like, based on (1) my ability to construct the day in my head, abstractly, and (2) my dialogue with others about their own abstract constructions. I have engaged in dialogue that has led to a social construction. The carpenter constructs beam fits and saw angles in his or her head before fitting and sawing, and may ask for input from a coworker about the abstract plans. An architect conceives of a floor plan, and changes it after talking with the customer; a house painter conjures a picture of the painted house before ever opening a can of paint and communicates this image to the homeowner; a cook invents a new recipe by imagining how a particular dish would taste with twice as much garlic, and confers with a friend on the virtues of more garlic taste in this particular dish—and millions of other examples. At this most simple level, social construction is an obvious and clearly ubiquitous human characteristic, made possible by abstract thought and language.

But social constructions do not exist in a vacuum. Context is always important, and that context determines not only what is transmitted in a dialogue, but also what is received. This context is sometimes referred to as the "discourse," and is a somewhat slippery concept.

One of the more interesting and universal, yet poorly understood, features of modern *Homo sapiens* is the general formation of "discourse," not in the sense of a simple interchange or conversation, but rather in the sense used by post-modern thinkers such as Foucault.[17] The discourse is the collection of assumptions, metaphors, topics, rules of interchange, and other characteristics, that form the way we think about things without questioning. Similar concepts are well known to most of us. For example, some years ago, Galbraith introduced the notion of "conventional wisdom," to account for the set of unquestioned assumptions we have about politics and the economy.[18] Kuhn popularized the word "paradigm" to indicate the set of assumptions, problems, acceptable modes of analysis, and agreed-upon sets of questions that one was allowed to ask within the sciences.[19] Kuhn's ideas have become somewhat generalized, and one typically hears talk of the "current paradigm" in many fields other than the natural and physical sciences. Sometimes it is common to speak of the "received wisdom," which simply means the accepted version of the way things work. Chomsky frequently talks about the "limits of the debate," noting how in political debate there are those things that are "acceptable" to debate, and those things that are beyond the agreed-upon limit.[20] One can, for example, debate whether or not the United States could have won the war in Vietnam, but one may not debate the ultimate goal of the United States (i.e., it is an agreed assumption that the United States' goals in Vietnam were noble, but that we made a lot of mistakes—you can talk about the mistakes all you wish, but those who begin questioning the goals themselves rapidly encounter social and political isolation in respectable circles, outside the limits of the debate).

Foucault's notion of the discourse is somewhat more overarching than any of these other formulations, although they are all quite similar. The discourse is the collection of things we don't question, and in many ways represents the things that run most of our lives. Most of what we do each day, what we think about, what we desire, the form of interactions we have with others, are all determined to some extent by the discourse. Furthermore, while the discourse gives ultimate form to our lives, it also occasionally changes quite dramatically—ruptures, so to speak. It is this rupture in discourse that provides much of the fodder for grand historical changes, both in the lives of individuals and in the society at large.

At the personal level, we can all feel this notion (the personal discourse). The rules of engagement with our friends, enemies, and strangers are set by our former experiences and training. The way we see the world is conditioned by our assumptions about it, with one person seeing the work of God in nature's beauty, another the results of Darwinian natural selection, another the untamed wilderness, red in tooth and claw. In many ways, the phenomenon of personal growth is tied to this personal discourse. For example, many of us raised in the 1950s were personally filled with the discourse of anti-Communism, to the point that we saw almost everything that was evil as associated with the bogeyman of Communism. But for most of us, this discourse was dramatically ruptured either by the vicious activities of the McCarthy hearings or the political discussions surrounding the Vietnam war, so common on campuses in the 1960s. Many of us experienced a major rupture in our personal discourse during this time. The process of changing religion (or giving up religion altogether) is frequently a momentous occasion in one's personal life. Going from loving a spouse or companion to hating him or her is frequently accompanied by dramatic and sometimes violent changes in points of view. All of these examples are included in the notion of the rupture of the discourse at a personal level.

A parallel process occurs at a social level. The discourse of a society changes through time, always evolving slowly, but occasionally undergoing dramatic shifts. This has always happened, it happens before our eyes in other societies, but it is almost always assumed not to be possible from within a particular social discourse. For example, we all recently saw a major rupture of the discourse of Communism in the Soviet Union. Undoubtedly, until the day before the collapse of the society, there were individuals in the Soviet Union who were assuming that "while we certainly have problems in our country, our basic structure is sound and the underlying principles of our political, social, and economic system will always remain the same." So strong is the discourse that individuals living under it sometimes refuse to recognize its rupture even when it is collapsing all around them, and most frequently the signs of rupture are evident only to those living outside it.

Much remains to be done before we completely understand this most complex of all characteristics of *Homo sapiens*. While we can see quite clearly that the concept is key to forming the way we "make our way in the world today," and that frequently sudden and dramatic shifts have occurred in the past, exactly how the discourse is formed, how it maintains such a strong hold over our lives, and how it eventually ruptures are all points that are under debate and analysis at the current time. For our purposes in this chapter, we only wish to acknowledge the existence of the social discourse, for the purpose of speculating on its possible origins within the context of the evolution of *H. sapiens*. It is to that speculation that we now turn.

While abstract representation was likely a precursor to language, its relationship to protolanguage is simply a matter of speculation. Chimps are capable of language that is close to protolanguage, but there is no evidence that they naturally engage in this. Could a protolanguage have led to social construction and discourse formation in anything resembling the modern sense of those concepts? Evidence is totally lacking, but speculation is always fun. About all we can expect from *H. erectus* endowed with protolanguage might be a sequence something like "Stones, circle make,"

"Circle hard, line easy," "House, circle strong." Did a social construction result from that dialogue? Perhaps a primitive one. Did it lead to a discourse? Did the two or three individuals engaging in it eventually come upon a mental image, more or less consistent among them, of what their night's shelter would look like? Did they approach the next night's shelter differently, with a new background, a "protodiscourse"? I leave it to the reader to ponder these questions.

Whatever its origin, discourse and social construction are clearly part and parcel of contemporary *Homo sapiens,* even though coming to grips with exactly how they work has been less than successful thus far.

One of Foucault's major contributions (in my opinion) is the identification of power with discourse.[21] For him, there can be no discourse without the development of power relations (by power, we mean one person's or one group's ability to restrain the action of another individual or other group, without resort to violence, yet clearly against the will of the latter). The husband, with no threat of violence whatsoever, compels his wife's acquiescence by force of the history of their interaction plus society's underlying assumptions about spousal roles—the prevailing discourse. A subgroup, clearly allied with management, may exert concessions in bargaining from another subgroup in a union mass meeting, by virtue of its perceived potential to "deliver" for the union. The capitalist class, through philanthropic activities, receives support from other classes because of its perceived ability to marshal resources for the "general good." High officials of the Communist party are repeatedly elected to office based on a general fear that uninformed younger members would cause undesirable deviations in party ideology. All of these represent power relations that emanate from human discourse. Foucault argues that it is not possible to have human discourse without the generation of power relations, and this implies that all of our social constructions are products, at least in part, of unequal (perhaps undeserved?) power relations among individuals and could very well take on very different forms if the power relations were reversed or constituted differently.

A corollary to the "power is automatically involved in human discourse" theme is that rebellion is also automatically involved. Whenever unequal power is involved in human social structure, if history is to be believed, rebellion against that power seems to be frequently just under the surface. This is a point worthy of a great deal of reflection.

However little we understand about discourse and social construction (and I argue that we are just beginning the journey), two things are abundantly clear—first, social constructions are vivid and appear somehow beyond their reality (i.e., they may appear to be natural structures or God-given properties, etc.),[22] and, second, they are frequently altered, sometimes very dramatically.

A NOTE ON METHODOLOGY

In the above description of human origins I have explicitly used two dramatically different methods of analysis. From the diversification of the apes to somewhere along the *Homo* line leading to *sapiens,* I have presented developments as though they obeyed Darwinian laws of evolution. I believe this is noncontroversial. But at the point we begin talking about social transformation of resources, language, abstraction, social construction, and discourse, a reliance on Darwinian interpretations begins to be submerged. And there is a concrete reason for this.

Characteristics of *Australopithecus* changed over long periods of time mainly because individuals of the species who contained particular forms of the characteristic produced more surviving offspring than individuals who did not contain those particular forms. As long as those characteristics were specified by genes, all the rules of Darwinian evolution are perfectly applicable. Indeed, one evolutionary biologist, Richard Dawkins, has suggested that a useful way of understanding Darwinian evolution is to think of the genes themselves as trying very hard to reproduce themselves—metaphorically of course.[23] Each gene (which translates into a phenotype like hair color or eye color, or perhaps enhanced musculature of the left biceps) selfishly attempts to outproduce its competitors. Because the genes must be contained in individuals, it is the ones that are contained in those individuals that leave more offspring that, in fact, are most successful. But it is a useful metaphor to think of the gene as "trying" to outcompete its competitor genes, even if the only way it can do so is by being contained in an individual that leaves more successful offspring than the individuals containing the competitor gene. It is a useful metaphor, if not pushed too far (some argue that Professor Dawkins indeed did push it too far).

By the time we reach *H. sapiens,* the rules have changed dramatically. I have tried, in the above discussion, to indicate how these changes may have come about. As tentative as the points of origin of human characteristics must be because of the weak database, it is clear that by the time we reach modern *H. sapiens,* all of those characteristics are there. Human society had the rules of evolution changed on it because it became structured by socially organized resource transformation, abstract thought, language, social construction, and discourse. Could one seriously say that the expansion of Islam occurred because Islamic people left more offspring? Or that Christians succeeded because they left more offspring than believers in other religions? Or that spear throwing became common because spearthrowers left more offspring than non-spearthrowers? Such statements would be preposterous. Once human culture evolved, as it certainly had by the time *H. sapiens* emerged (perhaps even earlier), Darwinian evolutionary reasoning no longer is useful for explaining human evolution. The rules are simply different.

Some anthropologists, thinking of a loose metaphorical relationship between characteristics under genetic control versus those under cultural control, have coined the term "meme" as a sort of cultural gene. It is perhaps a useful metaphor, especially if one adopts Dawkin's metaphor on top of it. We can think (very loosely, I might add) of "selfish memes." That is, we have cultural characteristics that "try" to outcompete other cultural characteristics. But unlike genes, the cultural characteristics are not contained in the bodies of individuals, but rather lie somehow among the individuals in the population. Thus they can reproduce, mutate, and migrate immensely more rapidly than can genes. A mutated meme can permeate the population in a matter of minutes or days, whereas a mutated gene will take generations to achieve the same ubiquitousness. Furthermore the notion of fundamental change—mutation—clearly happens millions of times faster among memes than among genes. All in all, if one thinks of Darwinian evolution as competition among selfish genes and cultural evolution as competition among selfish memes, it is quite clear that any characteristic that could be controlled either by genes or memes is likely to come under the control of the latter. A gene that dictates holding the arm up high with a rock in the hand, dropping the arm rapidly, propelling the rock forward (such a gene never could exist in the first place, but ponder it anyway—use your ability to abstractly represent something that is clearly impossible), may spontaneously arise in the population every tenth generation. If it conferred an advantage (as it probably would) to individuals possessing it, it would spread through the population rapidly, with only 10 or 20 generations required for the spread. Later, another mutation might occur that would cause the snapping of the wrist as the arm was being lowered, thus propelling the rock forward much faster. Again such a mutation might arise every tenth generation, and, presuming it conferred an advantage, might spread rapidly, in only 10 or 20 generations. Now imagine a dialogue "Hey, if I put my arm up in the air with a rock in my hand and bring it down rapidly, releasing the rock, look what happens!", "Wow, that's cool but I wonder what would happen if you snapped your wrist at the same time?" The equivalent mutations of the memes happened in less than a minute (rather than in about 20 generations), and we can presume that the new characteristic would spread through the population in a matter of months rather than in 10 to 20 generations. For this reason, the evolution of memes will most likely take over whatever can be taken over, as long as there really are memes. And here is the catch. Humans are the only animals that have memes. That is why they are the only animals whose most important features are simply not understandable through the vehicle of Darwinian evolution. Thus, while the above discussion began with a standard Darwinian explanation of changes in *Australopithecus,* gradual changes in the fundamental nature of the species, initially through Darwinian evolution, ultimately render that same Darwinian interpretation with little merit for the species *H. sapiens.*[24]

The Origin of Human Races and Racism

Abraham Lincoln stated publicly, "There is a physical difference between the white and black races which I believe will forever forbid the two races living together on terms of social and political equality. And inasmuch as they cannot so live, while they do remain together there must be the position of superior and inferior, and I as much as any other man am in favor of having the superior position assigned to the white race."[1] Of course, such ideas are not restricted to the past, nor are they the exclusive domain of the white race. François Karera, a senior politician with the former Rwandan government, stated recently that, "The Tutsi are *originally* bad. They are murderers. . . . Physically they are weak—look at their arms and their legs. No Tutsi can build; they are too weak, [therefore] they just command. The others work."[2] [Emphasis added.]

While few would doubt that race plays a dominant role in contemporary culture, the concept itself is rather slippery. On the most trivial level, race is a categorization, a pigeonhole in which to put someone. The pigeonholes are frequently based on characteristics that are clearly genetic, and therefore it seems obvious that racial categories are biologically meaningful. But there is an implication of race that is far more profound than a simple categorization of physical types. We categorize people according to many physical features such as hair color, eye color, portliness, and the like. But when we categorize racially, we feel our categorization goes somehow further—redheads and short people are categories that do not connote the same meaning as black people and white people. Members of the same race, whatever it is, share a great deal with one another, and differ significantly from those who are not members of the race—or at least that is what seems to be understood. Race is, in this sense, akin to family. African Americans, it is thought, are more like other African Americans than they are like European Americans. We can thus identify two levels of understanding of race here, at least as it relates to biological factors. On the one hand, race is a category, while on the other hand, race membership says something deep and abiding about one's self and about how one differs from outsiders.

In this chapter I will first talk about the problems with making racial classifications, and follow with a discussion of the origins of major patterns of human physical variation. These patterns of variation are what make it so difficult to make racial classifications meaningful. But constructing the classification based on physical features is only the first step. Understanding what people think those categorizations mean is the next, and more important, step. How you determine that a person is in a particular race is usually straightforward. What you conclude about the person because of that race membership is something altogether different. It is frequently assumed that racial categorizations reflect ancestral similarities and, thus, that different races are characterized by deep differences. If the categorization itself is genetic, so the argument goes, then there are likely to be deeper abiding differences among the races.

After dealing with the problems of categorization and the presumed meaning of deep racial differences, I will proceed to a discussion of some background material that is necessary to evaluate the assumptions of deep racial differences with the tools of modern biology. This includes a rather detailed study of the concepts of species, subspecies, and geneologies, as well as the statistical subject of within- versus between-group comparisons.

With this basic background I will continue with the question, "Are human races true subspecies that represent deep differences?" As will be clear, data from molecular biology find little evidence for assumptions of deep differences among races.

RACE AS A BIOLOGICAL CATEGORY

The idea of race is fraught with conceptual difficulties—the concept itself is formulated in a nonscientific manner, varies from place to place, and is different in the minds of different people.[3] Thus, when a plant breeder speaks of a race of corn, he or she is referring to a genetically distinct is not obvious when a group of genetically distinct plants ought to be called a race.[4] Most Americans would find it unusual to speak of Jewish or Gypsy people as belonging to a distinct race, yet Nazi skinheads focus much of their racial hatred on these people. And Mr. Karera's characterization of Tutsis suggests a belief in biological differences between Hutu and Tutsi that puts tribal identity in the same ballpark as race.

In the United States, there is a great deal of confusion about what race means in the first place. Many government forms explicitly state that "Hispanics" may be of "any race," while many Texans are clear about the "Miskins" in their state being racially distinct,[5] and many people from Latin America, especially Mexico, actively promote the notion of "la raza" (the race) to indicate that they are a distinct race, born of a mixture of other "races," but, nevertheless, today a distinct, and indeed proud, race. The past five hundred years have produced a remarkable mixing of people from all over the planet, and present races, no matter how defined, are frequently amalgams of something that existed before (although, as discussed below, this is nothing qualitatively new in the history of our species).

But this should not confuse us. From a biological perspective there are no meaningful races in the first place, and what we today recognize as races are entirely social constructs. Indeed, there is nothing wrong with speaking of the Latino race or the black race. Latinos are various combinations of European, African, and Native American people, but form a cultural entity that only rarely is difficult to identify. Latinos have sets of customs and values that are plainly recognizable to anyone within their group, and by all we understand of racial formation, there is nothing incorrect about regarding them as a race, U.S. government forms notwithstanding. The same could be said of the black race, although here there is arguably less basis for making a racial classification, since African blacks share little culturally with American blacks. Of course, a similar mixing of people has occurred within African American people as among Latinos, and very few African Americans can boast of pure African heritage. Nevertheless, we seem to have little trouble identifying and accepting that anyone with even a small amount of genetic heritage from Africa belongs to the black race.

Indeed, the issue becomes confusing when we try to base a racial classification on some sort of simple biological rationality. The categories that humans normally identify as racial simply cannot be identified with strictly biological categories. The list of entities that are considered to be races, at least by some people in some places, is enormous (Black, Latino, Chinese, Oriental, Asian-Indian, Pakistani, Jew, Roma, Slav, Slovak, Bohemian, Azerbaijani, Hmong, Filipino, Tasaday, Tutsi, the list goes on). Given such a diversity of viewpoints, we might expect that races, as we actually define them today, really ought to have little to do with biology. As far as we can tell, from currently available hard scientific evidence, that is quite true. It is also not very surprising if we simply acknowledge that race is a socially constructed category in the first place.[6]

THE ORIGIN OF HUMAN DIVERSITY

The history of *Homo sapiens* has been one of migration and mixing ever since we left Africa some 200,000 years ago.[7] Later, Arab trading routes in the Indian Ocean and Mediterranean, as well as the overland routes through the Sahara and through Central Asia, caused further admixtures. Indeed, the only relatively complete isolations resulted from the New Guinean/Australian migration about 30,000 years ago and the American migration, about 12,000 years ago. So the only potentially "pure" biological races that are even theoretically possible are Native American, Native Australian/New Guinean, and European/African/Asian.

Nevertheless, there are obvious subgroups of the above three, and these subgroups clearly have some biological differences from one another. Subsaharan Africans all have much darker skin than Europeans; east Asians have a fold on their eyelids that south Asians lack; southern Europeans tend to have black hair, in contrast to the lighter hair of northern Europeans.

This human diversity is a consequence of migrations. While humans have been migrating throughout their history, the global distribution of this species is mainly the result of three major migratory events, the exact timing of which is under debate, and the exclusiveness of which is quite unknown. The first major migration occurred either a million years ago or 200,000 years ago (all such dates are very approximate, at any rate) and involved a migration out of eastern Africa into western and southern Africa, Europe, and Asia. We do not know how long it took, nor how many "waves" of migrants it involved, nor if the actual behavior was really migratory rather than diffusive, but it is fairly clear that what was a relatively isolated population in eastern Africa eventually moved out to colonize much of Europe, Africa, and Asia. Undoubtedly, many migratory events followed, migrating to different places within Asia, Europe, and Africa, and likely migrating among these three places quite frequently. Yet enough isolation was preserved so that certain characteristics, most probably those under genetic control, came to dominate certain areas. For example, southern Asians evolved dark skin (they probably had lighter skin before they migrated southward), and a high percentage of sickle cell genes evolved in many African populations. Thus, many biological characteristics evolved during this period of 200,000 (or a million) years, at least some of which are closely correlated with racial classifications. Undoubtedly, we would expect a great deal of biological diversity to be associated with this first major migration, since it occurred, comparatively, so long ago.

The second and third migrations occurred much later, and both arose from eastern Asia. About 30,000 years ago, much of what we now consider the East Indies were connected by a land bridge (the sea being much lower then, due to the expansion of the ice sheets). Along this land bridge, a series of migrations from China and other parts of eastern Asia populated New Guinea, Australia, and many of the Pacific islands. Finally, about 12,000 years ago, with the seas again lowered, a land bridge formed between eastern Asia and North America, and people from northeastern Asia migrated to the Americas.[8]

With this now well-known history of human migrations, it is relatively clear what to expect biologically, at a very general level. The migrations that occurred very long ago (200,000 or a million years ago) could have produced three general categories: European, African, and Asian. The second set of migrations, to Australia and America, could have produced three different categories, European/African/Asian, Australian/New Guinean, and Native American. But if we begin fine-tuning these gross divisions, it is not all that obvious what we should expect biologically. Migrations apparently occurred quite frequently and over long distances. For example, some of the migrations to Australia occurred from northern China, through Taiwan, and down through the Philippines, while others occurred from southeast Asia, through Borneo. Archaeological evidence indicates trade between West Africa and the Middle East at least 30,000 years ago. For example, extensive excavations in the Hotu cave, located on the banks of the Caspian Sea, record extensive human activity and likely migrations to and from Asia beginning more than 10,000 years ago, with continuous evidence of migration until the present day. Most recently, genetic evidence has suggested that a major migration occurred from the Middle East to Europe, associated with the spread of early agriculture about 10,000 years ago.[9] The picture that emerges is, thus, one of biological changes, to be sure. But with so much admixture, even before the expansion of Europe 500 years ago, it would not be at all surprising to find that the biological differences among races are largely insignificant. The only racial groups that have been relatively isolated are the Australian and American groups, and both are probably results of multiple migrations anyway. If we expect major racial differences at all, the most likely place to look for them would probably be in small indigenous populations that have been isolated for long periods of time.[10]

Knowing what we now know about migratory patterns, it would be rather surprising if we were to find large biological differences among the various races. In fact, the hard evidence from genetics indicates that there is no general biological difference among the races, despite the fact that certain cues we use to classify them (e.g., skin color) have a biological basis themselves. Today, it is possible to make such a strong statement precisely because we understand so much more about the fundamentals of biology[11] than we did back in the late 1800s, when many of our contemporary intellectual traditions had their beginnings.[12]

Nevertheless, in a sense it is self-evident that the differences among certain races are biologically based, in that the cues we use to distinguish races are themselves sometimes biological in origin. There are difficulties here in that many individuals who clearly belong to one or another race do not have the proper characteristics for that race, yet they obviously belong to it. The main distinguishing feature for the black race, for instance, is skin color, yet we all can cite examples of African Americans with lighter skin than some of our Italian American or Pakistani American friends. Nevertheless, it is generally true that biological differences must exist to the extent that the characteristics we use to classify races are themselves biological. But please note the arbitrariness here. We could, if we wished, define a racial category based on eye color. The blue-eyed race versus the brown-eyed race, or the tall race versus the short race, or, for that matter, the male race versus the female race, would be just as "biologically based" as the black race versus the white race. In this sense, the notion that racial categories are biological may be true formally, but it is a rather trivial truism. It becomes important only in that it sometimes implies something rather more profound, the ideology of "deep difference."

DEEP DIFFERENCES

A persistent idea that manifests itself in all sorts of subtle and non-subtle forms is that there are some biological essences that "show through," that can be detected in the character of the African American or the Korean American, that date back to the genetic instructions passed on by the great-great-grandfather. Surely the current stock of Chinese Americans is an admixture of people originally from China with those originally from Europe, but the industriousness of Chinese Americans must have something to do with that part of their genetic heritage that comes from China, so the story goes. African Americans may contain significant numbers of European genes, yet our culture tends to associate Africa with the problems it attributes to this race. The lower scores of African Americans on IQ tests, for example, is never attributed to their European ancestry, nor to the possible effects of mixing European with African, but rather to some imagined shadowy genetic contribution from the African side.

In this sense, racial categories are thought of as biological in a somewhat deeper form than simply the fact that the physical characteristics used to classify them are biological. It is assumed that the classifying characteristics are merely indications of yet other, deeper, differences, which are also biological. The indicators that we use to categorize the races are reckoned to be the tip of the iceberg of biologically-based racial differences, such that deep down, the biological heritage permeates a great deal of the differences among races. This is the ideology of deep difference.

For example, it is true that African Americans score lower on IQ tests, on average, than European Americans. Since blacks and whites have different ancestries, presumably accounting for various biological differences such as skin color, it might seem to be a reasonable assumption that other differences between these two races also have biological bases. Therefore, both the differences in IQ scores and the difference in skin color might simply be reflections of a more general biological difference between blacks and whites.[13] If this is true, other characteristics, such as criminality, industriousness, sexuality, and many other characteristics thought to differ between the black and white races could also be part of this general biological difference. Indeed, there is a school of thought growing within the African American community that basically accepts this ideology of deep difference, but focuses on the positive aspects of the black race and their putative biological basis—for example, whites have a tendency to conquer other people and rob S&L's, while blacks are cooperative by nature and build sustainable, healthy communities.[14]

It is worth some reflection as to how ethical and moral considerations might be affected if it were discovered that racial differences really were deep and biological. In fact a variety of human conditions —Tay-Sachs disease, diabetes, and many others—are known to be caused by genetic factors. Having identified the disease, the reasonable medical researcher seeks to learn what it is about the phenotype that causes the disease, so the disease can be cured. Knowing that it is genetic helps mainly in family counseling, but little, if at all, in treatment. And here it is remarkable how much politics can obscure one's logic. For example, the psychologist Arthur Jensen implied, that, since IQ was largely inherited (it probably isn't, but that is what he said), we should simply expect less of African Americans and stop spending money on special programs for them.[15] Such a conclusion is exactly the opposite of what a responsible medical researcher would suggest (imagine, having discovered that diabetes is genetic, suggesting that diabetics should no longer be given insulin!).[16]

So if, in the future, someone should discover that all we have come to understand about the biology of races is false, and that there really are deep biological differences among the races,[17] the conclusion still should not be that current policies about race are correct. Quite the opposite: If Europeans are really less industrious than Asians because of some gene, we should seek ways of intervening in the environment to correct that deficiency. If African Americans really cannot learn calculus as quickly as European Americans because of a gene, our philosophy of providing all with equal opportunity should require us to give African Americans special attention when teaching calculus.

While it is true that "naturalness," or the assumption that racial characteristics have a biological basis, frequently is nothing more than an attempt to bolster and obscure what are effectively political arguments, and that whether or not a characteristic is genetically determined has little to do with how that characteristic should be dealt with in a medical, sociological, or humanistic sense, it is nevertheless interesting simply as an academic exercise to examine the credibility of the assumption that there is something biological about presumed deep racial differences. Here we can enlist some of the results of modern biology to rigorously investigate the assumption of a biological basis. To do so, we must understand two sets of concepts: (1) the interrelated biological concepts of species, subspecies, and geneology and (2) the statistical concept of intra- versus inter-group diversity.

SPECIES, SUBSPECIES, GENEOLOGY

The concept of species seems commonsense. A lion is a lion, clearly different from a leopard, and few have trouble distinguishing a gorilla from a chimpanzee. But what about a Great Dane and a Mexican Chihuahua? They certainly look more different from one another than a gorilla and chimpanzee, but they are members of the same "biological species," whereas chimpanzees and gorillas are not. At times it is really quite difficult to determine whether a particular population of animals and plants represents a distinct species from some other population. Nevertheless, the underlying biological reasoning that theoretically separates them is unambiguous. If two individuals can pass genes to one another under normal circumstances, they are members of the same species, while if they normally cannot, they are regarded as members of different species. We sometimes simply refer in a sort of shorthand way to the principle of reproductive isolation—if two individuals are not capable of interbreeding, they are members of separate species.[18]

With this definition, one might naturally wonder about the example of the Great Dane and Chihuahua, since I doubt there is a case of any two members of these two races directly interbreeding. While it is difficult to imagine such a small dog interbreeding with such a large one, it is easy to imagine a chihuahua breeding with a dachshund, the latter with a toy collie, the latter with a German shepherd, the latter with a Doberman, and the Doberman with a Great Dane. By successive breeding with slightly larger breeds, a gene originally located in the Chihuahua can be easily transferred to a Great Dane, although it might require a number of generations. So, in recognition of the ready possibility of transferring genes in a population (even if it might have to be done through various individuals over various generations) the species *Canis familiaris,* the domestic dog, is a biological species. Both Great Dane and Chihuahua are members of this noble species.

Yet, simply because all individuals in a given population are of the same species, we cannot conclude they are biologically equivalent, as the example of Chihuahua and Great Dane suggests. Indeed, there is great genetic variation among individuals in a normal animal or plant population. While almost any pattern of variation is possible, considering the enormous number of living organisms in the world, most variation in populations of animals and plants has a geographic basis to it, and, consequently, biologists have recognized and studied that variation. In the 1940s and 1950s the study of "subspecies," subpopulations of species that share certain characteristics not shared by other subpopulations of that species, was very popular. Even though one rarely hears a professional biologist speaking of subspecies any longer, it is worthwhile reviewing some of the scientific debates that raged in the 1950s and early 1960s over the concept of subspecies.[19]

The importance of geographic variation is its consistency. If an animal population is larger in the north than in the south, we might be tempted to suggest that there is a northern subspecies or race and a southern subspecies or race. But if that same species is darker in coloration in the east than in the west, should we base a subspecies division on the east-to-west variation or the north-to-south variation? And, if you suggest that we make up four subspecies (the northwest one, the northeast one, and so on), what happens if we find another characteristic that varies from the center of the range outward? Evidently, in order to make a biologically interesting classification of subspecies, we require that various characters vary "concordantly." Northern and southern subspecies thus imply, say, that northern ones are bigger, huskier, and browner than southern ones, and that few other characteristics show variation in other directions. In Figure 5.1 are examples of two populations of imaginary animals, illustrating geographic variation in three different characteristics—body color, snout length, and tail length. On the left-hand map all three characters vary concordantly, which means that we could define northern and southern subspecies. The northern subspecies is lighter in color, and has a larger snout and a shorter tail than its southern cousin. But now, consider the case of the map on the right. If we choose color as a characteristic we can, as before, define a northern and southern subspecies. But if we choose tail length as a characteristic, we wind up with an eastern and western subspecies. And snout length varies all over the place, making a short-nosed subspecies have no geographic location at all. In this situation (which is by no means unusual in animal and plant populations), it simply makes no biological sense at all to define subspecies.

A note of caution is in order here. In all of the above examples, we are making the assumption that the characteristics under study are controlled genetically in the first place. If, in fact, the characters are simply reflecting plasticity to environmental differences, the question of whether or not there are meaningful subspecies should never arise in the first place.

One way of understanding the importance of character concordance is by asking the question, "How predictable will a subspecies categorization be?" Suppose I hold two individuals behind my back and give you some genetic information about them—they both have short tails and long noses, for example. Now, I ask you, do they come from the same subspecies or not? Clearly, if the two individuals are from the first example in Figure 5.1, you can answer immediately that both are from the same subspecies, while no matter what might have been the definition of subspecies in the second example, you would have no idea whether they came from the same or different subspecies, even though all their given characteristics were the same.

The job of putting people into racial categories and then trying to figure out how those racial categories are related to one another is effectively a problem of subspecies classification. One might argue that finding the correct subspecies for the various extant human populations would enable us to understand questions of deep difference better. Indeed, what is done in popular culture is an informal taxonomic analysis of human populations, identifying the "black" subspecies, the "white" subspecies, and so on. The idea is not necessarily all that bad in principle, although ancestry is always a fickle indicator—sometimes it provides clues as to deep differences other times it is irrelevant. It all depends on how much evolu-

---

Figure 5.1. Theoretical example of geographic variation in an imaginary rat. Example on the left shows the three pertinent characters (color, snout length, tail length) varying concordantly, thus making the classification into a northern and southern species possible. Example on the right shows the same three characters varying in a discordant manner, thus making classification into two subspecies impossible in principle.

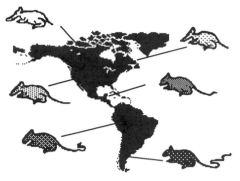

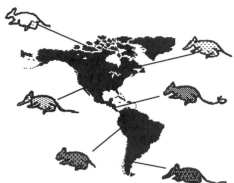

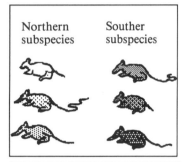

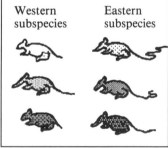

Northern subspecies   Southern subspecies

Northern subspecies   Souther subspecies

Western subspecies   Eastern subspecies

Short-nosed subspecies   Long-nosed subspecies

tionary change occurred since the split in the lines of evolution leading to the subspecies.

What, precisely, is intended when we invent particular racial categories? Naturally, we hope that the racial classification "makes sense." But in what way should it make sense? Consider four people: Misha, Rose, Jennifer, and Jodi. Let us suppose that we wish to establish a racial system in which two individuals are in each of two races. Suppose Rose and Misha have darker skin, while Jennifer and Jodi have lighter skin, so we initially decide that we will have a dark-skinned race and a light-skinned race. To what extent does this classification make sense?

At one level it makes quite a lot of sense. Since we have chosen the characteristic—skin color— that is readily observable, we therefore should encounter no difficulty in establishing a person's race simply by visual examination. Naturally, we also could have used hair color, or eye color, or a variety of other physical features, and at this level of judgment the resultant categories would make just as much sense.

But there is a different connotation in which we may ask the question, "To what extent does this classification make sense?" Having categorized Misha and Rose into the same race, can we now say something else about them? Will there be other features that we might expect Misha and Rose to share simply because they belong to the same race? Can we predict anything about these people simply because they have been put in a similar racial category?

There are two ways in which this question might be answered. First, having grown up in a society that recognizes these racial categories, Misha might be expected to share some behavioral characteristics with Rose, while Jennifer will likewise share them with Jodi, simply because of their upbringing as members of a recognized race. If society expects, for example, that dark-skinned people will score lower on IQ tests than lighter-skinned people, that very expectation may cause the former to be treated differently from the latter and, thus, the expectation acts as a self-fulfilling prophecy. Simply because of society's expectations, it may turn out that both Misha and Rose score lower than Jennifer and Jodi, and clearly it is because of their racial membership that they do so. So the answer is, "Yes, there are a certain number of things we can predict about these people based on their racial category."

Yet, there is a second sense in which the key question is frequently asked. If Misha and Rose are related to one another by virtue of ancestry—

that is, they share an ancestor in common sometime in the past (a grand-parent, a great-grandparent, or even further back)—and Jennifer and Jodi are related to one another by virtue of a different ancestry, then it may be possible to say that there is some predictability based on biology. Misha and Rose may share certain traits because of their biological ancestry, and Jennifer and Jodi may likewise share traits because of their biological an-cestry. It may, in effect, suggest that there are deep similarities that each pair shares, and deep differences associated with a comparison between the two groups (of course, it need not mean that such deep differences exist, but certainly the relationship by ancestry must be there before we can ask whether those ancestral differences imply the long-sought deep differences).

Thus we can imagine (at least) three ways to answer the question, "To what extent does our racial classification make sense?": (1) simply to distinguish people from one another, (2) to be able to predict certain com-mon patterns, either physical, psychological, or social, that may have arisen from the fact of the classification itself, or (3) to be able to predict certain patterns that are the result of ancestral biological similarities among individuals within a racial category. The first level is perhaps the easiest to satisfy, although certainly the most trivial. The "black" race and the "white" race, defined principally based on skin color, provide for a relatively easy identification of people belonging to one or the other. In the United States, for example, one can predict with substantial accuracy whether an individual is black or white simply by looking at him or her (probably in 80 to 90 percent of cases). On the other hand, if we define Hispanic as a race, our ability to place a person in the proper racial cate-gory simply by looking at him or her is probably no better than 5 or 10 percent.

The second level is also equally easy to satisfy. A person raised in the cultural traditions of the black race in contemporary U.S. culture fre-quently has physical, psychological, and social features that are quite char-acteristic. These are the features that modern society usually calls "eth-nicity" or "cultural characteristics." Similarly, Hispanic people are sometimes recognizable for their taste in music, language, dress, and the like.

But both of these levels, while certainly legitimate, are not particularly controversial. The one that causes all the controversy, and the one most frequently misunderstood, is the ancenstral level. Based on the racial classification, can one make any predictions about a person because the racial categories represent something about the person's ancestry?

To answer this question, we must establish relationships for the question to make sense in the first place. To ask whether or not we can predict anything from ancestry presumes we know the ancestry. If Jennifer and Jodi are sisters, for example, we know that they share ancestry and we can go on to ask whether their similar appearance or behavior is or is not a consequence of their biological ancestry. But first, we must know that they are sisters. In the context of race, the equivalent prerequisite is, first we must know if they share biological ancestry. That is, do the racial categorizations that we have made have any basis in true biological ancestry?

Going back to the racial categories that place Misha and Rose in the dark-skinned category and Jodi and Jennifer in the light-skinned category, let us suppose that the true ancestry of these four individuals is as in Figure 5.2. This arrangement would mean that the biology was consistent with the racial classification, and suggests that perhaps (certainly not necessarily) there would be a certain predictability, based on biological ancestry, associated with the racial classification.

But the arrangement of Figure 5.2 is not the only possibility; there are two others. All three possibilities are illustrated in Figure 5.3. In the absence of any information about the true ancestry of these four individuals, we are really at quite a loss to determine which of these three genealogies would be correct. Naturally if the last one were correct (the one originally shown in Figure 5.2), we would say that our racial classification made sense biologically. If one of the other two were correct, we would

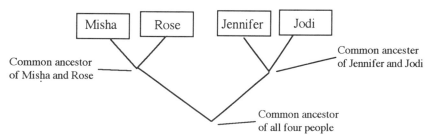

Figure 5.2. Hypothesized ancestral relationship between the four individuals in the example.

be forced to conclude that our racial classification had no basis in biological ancestry.

If, in fact, we knew nothing whatsoever about these four individuals other than the darker skin of Misha and Rose and the lighter skin of Jennifer and Jodi, how would we determine which of these geneologies is correct? In other words, how would we figure out if our racial categorization were anything more than skin deep? Today, because of many advances in biology, we do have the tools to asess which of these geneologies is correct. We can examine the genes of the individuals (or the closest things to the genes, the proteins that are dictated by the genes). Let us imagine a particular scenario with regard to the genetic constituency of these four individuals. Suppose we sample a strand of DNA from each, and obtain the following:

Misha   AAA TTC CGG GGA TGC CCG TTT AAG GGC TGC TTG CTA

Jennifer   AAA TTC CGG GGA TGC CCG TTT AAG GGC TGC TTG CTA

Rose   TAA ATC CGC CGT AGG GGC AAA TAC CGC AGG AAC GAA

Jodi   TAA ATC CGC CGT AGG GGC AAA TAC CGC AGG AAC GAA

In 100 percent of the cases, the bases of Misha and of Jennifer are perfectly concordant, as are those of Rose and Jodi. But comparing Misha with Rose or Jodi, or Jennifer with Rose or Jodi, we see large differences. If our racial categories had been Misha and Jennifer in one race and Rose and Jodi in the other (the first geneology in Figure 5.3), the genetic diversity within a race would be very small (it would be zero, in fact, since

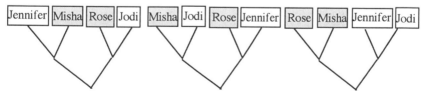

Figure 5.3. The three possible ways of defining two races with two people in each one.

Misha and Jennifer are exactly the same) and all the diversity would be between races. We would thus judge that this racial categorization is good, from the point of view of biological ancestry. That is, there might very well be deep differences between the races. However, the classification that we actually made (Misha and Rose in one race and Jennifer and Jodi in the other) indicates that the genetic diversity within race is large (i.e., there are big differences between Misha and Rose, as well as between Jennifer and Jodi), and between races small (in the particular example, it is zero). We are forced to conclude that this racial classification has no significant basis in biological ancestry.

This, in essence, is the geneological problem. When we define categories, do they really represent significant biological categories? We can actually answer that question if we can compare the genetic similarity of people within the categories to the genetic similarity among the categories themselves. This is the technique of comparing "within" versus "between" variation, and has, in fact, been done for the major racial groupings in today's world.

WITHIN- AND BETWEEN-GROUP DIVERSITY

This, then, brings us to one final background point, one that is not really biological, but, rather, statistical. When speaking of the imaginary animals above, we asked the simple question, "given a set of quantitative measurements about two individuals, is it possible to say whether the two individuals belong to the same group (subspecies) or to different groups?" Recall that in the second example in Figure 5.1 it was not possible to tell, while in the first example it was. The procedure that we used to decide whether it was possible or not to tell involved a comparison of the diversity of characteristics within groups related to the diversity between groups, the groups in this case being the defined subspecies.[20] Precisely the same comparison was made when trying to decide whether our racial categories of Misha, Rose, Jennifer, and Jodi were correct.

Under a variety of circumstances, we are faced with the task of deciding whether observable differences between two groups are real or simply due to chance. For instance, consider a human population that has a higher cancer rate when located near a toxic waste dump than when located near a golf course, a group of rats that was subjected to a particular pharmaceutical versus a control group that wasn't, or a group of students that studied for an exam versus another group that didn't. In such cases, the response of the groups may be a result of the factor of interest, or it may not. Suppose, for example, that the group of students that studied received 80, 79, 78, 77, and 76 as scores on the exam, while those who did not study received 72, 71, 70, 69, and 68 (as shown graphically as example I in Figure 5.4). It is fairly clear that studying made a difference. But if both the group that studied and the group that did not study got 90, 80, 70, 60, and 50, it would be clear that studying did not make a difference. But a more likely result would be something a bit less obvious—perhaps the group that studied got 98, 88, 78, 68, and 58, while the group that did not study got 90, 80, 70, 60, 50 (as shown in example II of Figure 5.4). Did studying make a difference?

The normal way of treating such a problem is to examine the diversity of the scores from two points of view—within a population and between populations. The studious students in the second example got exam scores that ranged from 58 to 98 (a 40-point range), while those who did not study obtained scores ranging from 50 to 90 (also a 40-point range). The average score for the first group was 70 and for the second group 78, an 8-point range between the group averages. We would likely conclude that studying didn't make much difference, since the range of values within populations was 40 and that between populations only 8. You could say that the total diversity of scores was $40 + 8 = 48$, and the proportion of that diversity that occurred within the population was $40/48 = .83$. Thus, 83 percent of the total diversity of the scores occurred within the population and 17 percent between populations.

Now, consider the first example, in which the group that studied scored 80, 79, 78, 77, and 76 and the group that did not study scored 72, 71, 70, 69, 68. Again, there is an 8-point difference between populations, but this time, the average difference within each group is 4. So the overall diversity in scores is $8 + 4 = 12$, which means that the proportion of that diversity that occurs within the population is $4/12 = .33$. Thus, 33 percent of the total diversity was within the population and 67 percent between populations.

These two examples are intended to provide a feeling for the importance of between-group and within-group comparisons. The formal statistical techniques for dealing with such comparisons are beyond the intentions of this book,[21] but with these simple examples one can, hopefully, gain an intuitive grasp of the idea. Focus on the proportion of diversity

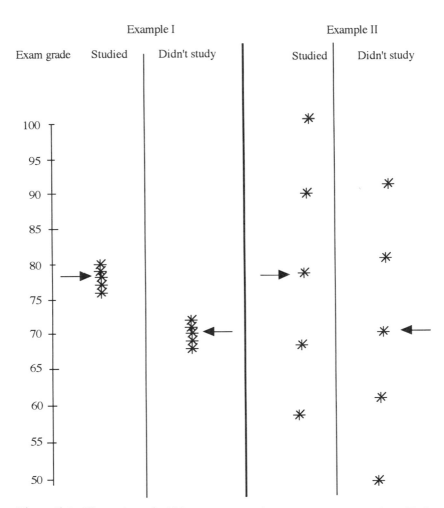

Figure 5.4. Illustration of within-group versus between-group comparison. Each asterisk represents an exam score and the arrows indicate the averages of each of the groups. In Example I the within-group variability is small compared to the between-group variability. In Example II the within-group variability is large compared to the between-group variability.

that is accounted for within populations and compare it to the proportion accounted for between populations. As a very rough rule of thumb, when the proportion of diversity between groups begins approaching 40 or 50 percent, we begin thinking that the between-group differences may be important.[22]

With that background information, recall the above query about deciding whether two individuals come from the same group or not. Let us say that I have two students in my office, and the difference in their scores on that test is 8. From that information, are you able to tell me whether these two students belong to the same group (either studiers or non-studiers)? Of course, the answer depends on the within-group diversity of scores. If the proportion of within-group diversity is large (say 83 percent, as in the example), both students could have come from either the same or different groups—it is not possible to say because of the high within-group diversity. But if the average within-group diversity is small (say 2 percent, as in the above example), it would seem most likely that the students were, in fact, from different groups. And that is the fundamental question that is answered by comparing within- and between-group diversity—if I have two individuals and I give you their scores, can you tell me whether they are in the same or different groups?

ARE HUMAN RACES TRUE SUBSPECIES THAT REPRESENT DEEP DIFFERENCES?

We now proceed to apply the above ideas to the question of human races. The fundamental question is, "If I have two individuals and I tell you all about their genetics, can you tell me whether they belong to the same or to different races?" We thus use the basic concept of within- and between-group comparison to investigate the question, "Do human races correspond to sensible subspecies that have diverged significantly from one another?" which is simply a modern way of formulating the nineteenth-century question of deep difference.

As noted in detail earlier, some human races are defined by particular features that themselves are known to have genetic bases, and if this is all one means when one claims the races are biologically different, there is nothing really to study. It is the same as saying that all blue-eyed people are genetically different from all brown-eyed people—a truism, but hardly interesting. What we are concerned with is the notion of the deep difference. To get at the question of deep difference, the presumed factors that we cannot see but nevertheless are basic to the race and genetically determined, we must somehow get away from simple phenotypes such as manner, intelligence, aggressiveness, and the like, and get closer to measuring the genetic material itself. Recall that modern biology tells us that the underlying function of each gene is to produce a protein, and that sometimes the protein can have a different form (different "morphology"), yet perform the same function. That the same functional protein can have a variety of different morphs is known as protein polymorphism (poly = many; morph = forms).[23] We can thus ask the question, "Does protein polymorphism vary more within racial categories or between racial categories (much like the exam scores above were compared between and within study categories)?" Harvard geneticist Richard Lewontin did just such a study, and his results are summarized here.[24]

In order to do the study, it was first necessary to define which races were to be studied, a daunting task, as suggested above. First, it was assumed, without much fanfare, that the new racial classification hardly merited study in the first place (the Latino race is so obviously not a biological category that its inclusion in the study was never contemplated). But even assuming the old classification, it was not always clear which race was which. For example, Turks, Hungarians, and Finns all appear to be Caucasoid, yet their language affiliates them with the Mongoloid tribes of Central Asia. The people of India who speak Hindi and Urdu are historically derived from south Asian aborigines, Persians, and central Asian Aryans (who are related to Caucasians). Are they Europeans because Hindi and Urdu are close to European languages, or south Asians because of their dark skin? Such problems make a serious study of human races very difficult (mainly because the human races don't make any biological sense to start with), and the study had to begin by making some rather arbitrary assumptions (for example, Turks were treated as Mongoloids, but Hungarians and Finns as Caucasoid). After making a number of these arbitrary assumptions (it turns out that the results are the same if you reverse those assumptions), seven major human races were recognized: Black Africans, Amerinds, Australian Aborigines, Caucasians, Mongoloids, South Asians, and Oceanians.[25]

In addition to these seven races, several subpopulations—nations or tribes—were distinguished within each of them. For example, the Finns and the Hungarians were included as separate subpopulations within the

Caucasians. This subdivision permitted the estimation not only of variability within and between major races, but also within and between subgroups of the major races.

In comparing the races or subpopulations within the races, we must first decide on which genes to base the comparison. For about 75 percent of all human genes, there is no variation at all. Naturally, we could learn nothing of racial differences by looking at such genes. We need to restrict the study to only those genes that show some variability—that is, those genes that occur as alternative forms in different people, such that some people have one form of the resultant protein, while other people have an alternative form. We then seek to learn whether the alternative forms occur in a "sensible" pattern, given our racial classification. If we have a biologically meaningful racial classification, as explained above, we would expect that most of the variation would be between races—that is, one morph of the protein would be mainly found in one race, while the other morph would be found mainly in another race (recall the example of Jodi, Jennifer, Rose, and Misha from the above discussion).

At the time of Lewontin's classic study, 17 polymorphic genes had been studied sufficiently intensively to provide data on all eight races. The results of the study on these 17 genes are presented in Table 5.1.

It is clear from Table 5.1 that the vast majority of the genetic diversity is within populations—differences from person to person—regardless of their race, nation, or tribe. On average, 85 percent of the diversity is to be found on a person-to-person basis, and only 6 percent on a race-to-race basis. The difference between populations within races is approximately the same as the difference among races (8 percent and 6 percent), suggesting that it makes about as much genetic sense to classify Hungarians and Finns in different races as it does blacks and whites.

These data tell us, in no uncertain terms, that in examining the underlying genetics of human beings through protein polymorphisms, we fail to detect evidence for a potential "deep difference" associated with racial differences.

Of course, it could always be argued that these particular genes are unusual, and that if another study is done, the results could be different. That is possible. But there is no reason to suspect that these genes were in any respect special, and every reason to assume they, in fact, are a relatively random sample of the general genome of *Homo sapiens*. Others may argue that the deep difference is associated with some specific gene or group of

Table 5.1. **Percentage of genetic diversity between and within human groups, for 17 genes.**

Gene	Within Populations	Within Races between Populations	Between Races
1	89	5	6
2	83		
3	94		
4	100		
5	93	6	1
6	88	6	7
7	94	3	2
8	85	2	13
9	74	2	5
10	64	10	26
11	97	3	0
12	90	7	3
13	69	21	9
14	95	3	2
15	91	4	5
16	67	7	25
17	91	6	3
Average	85	8	6

genes that have not yet been sampled. This is also possible. But suggesting there is a gene or small group of genes that are responsible for deep racial differences actually negates the entire philosophy of "deep difference." The deep difference is supposed to be a generalized genetic tendency. We already know that there are some genes that are specific for particular racial groups (sickle cell, for example), but outside of the particular function of those genes, there is nothing about genetics to suggest that other, more general, functions will be dictated by them. Available evidence suggests just the opposite. Indeed, modern biology seems to have the answer fairly well established. There is no gene (or small groups of genes) for racial quality, nor is there a general genetic tendency that suggests some sort of deep difference.

In the end, after a great deal of serious study with regard to the notion of deep difference among the races, our conclusion has to be that such differences simply have no biological basis whatsoever. We always have to admit that some future studies may find this "holy grail," but as of now, the evidence is quite strong and incontrovertible. The races of *Homo sapiens,* do not represent differentiated subspecies. Race, as used in the case of *Homo sapiens,* is not a biological issue. We are drawn inexorably to the conclusion that race is socially constructed.

On the other hand, an interesting question arises from this fact. Granted that current racial classifications make no biological sense, might it be possible to create ones that do make sense? The answer is yes, but the particular classification is not likely to please anyone searching for a biological justification for current political arrangements. While the bulk of humanity has been intermingling for perhaps hundreds of thousands of years, a large number of very small inbred groups exist all over the world. Partly because of their size and partly because of their isolation, these groups are frequently characterized by unusual gene frequencies. For this reason, one could define races as follows: Race number 1 would include 99.99 percent of all humans on earth, race number 2 might be a single population of 400 or 500 people isolated on a South Pacific island, race number 3 might be a single population of 400 or 500 people isolated in the Amazon rain forest, and so on. We might eventually have a few hundred distinct races, but 99.99 percent of all people would be in one of them, and tiny fractions of percents in each of the others. These racial classifications would not really be very good (i.e., the within-race variability would still be relatively high), but it would be, biologically, a much better approximation to a true ancestry-based classification than the one we currently use.

Fanciful new constructions of race aside, modern biology leaves little doubt that our classification of races is not biological at all. Blacks having dark-skin is of as much interest as blue-eyed people having blue eyes. The immense political and emotional baggage we carry with the concept of human race, despite what might seem intuitively obvious to some people, is, in fact, a consequence of our own social relations, and is simply not a biological topic.

The Elusive Transformation: Genes Dictating Development in an Environment

MODERN BIOLOGY AND MODERN GENETIC DETERMINISM—QUESTIONS THAT OUGHT NOT BE ASKED IN THE FIRST PLACE

L et us attempt an historical thought experiment. Imagine the world before Hitler, and an international discourse that, however subtly and unspoken, included strong anti-Semitic currents. In that world of the 1920s and 1930s, most Jews lived in less than desirable circumstances, many were involved in banking and commerce, and almost all lived in a diaspora. From the perspective of most of the world's gentiles, Jews had certain behavior patterns that were different from those of gentiles. Jewish families tended to be, on average, very close, emphasizing personal achievement, scholarly study, and extended family solidarity. Jews were very clever in business, tended to be in the financial sectors of national economies, and tended to form cartels with other Jews in many business deals. Of course, even further anti-Semitic currents were quite popular (Jews cheat, steal, can't be trusted, and so on), but I wish to be concerned with the softer side of the anti-Semitic argument, a side that characterized many Europeans, even those who regarded themselves as not anti-Semitic.

Given such a background, it is not difficult to imagine how certain questions might sound quite reasonable, especially if posed by respectable scientists. For example, imagine, "I'm not saying there is anything at all genetic about Jewish behavior; indeed, I don't think there is. But it is a valid scientific question to ask whether there is a genetic basis, however slight, to the behaviors we have come to understand as typically Jewish." Who could be against such a reasonable statement, especially from someone who himself does not personally feel there is any sort of genetic basis? However, it is a series of small steps from "if there is a genetic basis, certainly it is a small one," to "we know that genes are not the only factors," to "the underlying genetic factor can be overwhelmed by environmental variables," to "clearly, there will be occasions in which the environmental variables are not the real driving force," to "it is those typical behaviors that are controlled mainly by genetic forces that we wish to study," to "it is well known that there are various behaviors that are profoundly influenced by genetic factors," to "if the genetically controlled behaviors are in the genes, continued procreation will continue those behaviors in the population," to "we must be concerned if our national policy actually encourages behaviors that the majority of our population is against," to "controlling reproduction is the only way we can avoid the progressive genetic deterioration of the human population," to "under some circumstances genetically defective people ought to be encouraged or, if necessary, forced to undergo sterilization operations," to "unable to control births, we may eventually be forced to a more aggressive means of genetic hygiene."

If the above scenario sounds outlandish, listen to a few quotes from respected U.S. scientists of the time (all taken from the important work of Stefan Kühl[1]):

> Racial hygiene in Germany remained until 1926 a purely academic and scientific movement. It was the Americans who . . . proved (with impeccable precision) Galton's thesis that qualities of the mind are as heritable as qualities of the body; they also showed that these mental qualities are inherited according to the very same laws as those of the body. (p. 20)
>
> *   *   *
>
> The racial hygienist as a biologist regards the development of eugenic sterilization as the effort of the state "organism" to get rid of the burden of its degenerate members. (p. 25)
>
> *   *   *
>
> . . . the national sterilization statute of Germany will . . . constitute a milestone which marks the control by the most advanced nations of the world of a major aspect of controlling human reproduction, comparable in importance only with the state's legal control of marriage. (p. 46)
>
> *   *   *

The new law [the Nazi sterilization law] is clean-cut, direct and a "model." (p. 49)

*   *   *

That nation [Germany] in this particular field of applied negative eugenics has evidently made substantial progress in its intention to act fundamentally, on a logterm plan for the prevention, so far as possible, of hereditary degeneracy. (p. 49)

*   *   *

It is from the synthesis of the work [of many eugenicists] that the leader of the German nation, Adolf Hitler, ably supported by the Minister of Interior, Dr. Frick, and guided by the nation's anthropologists, its eugenicists, and its social philosophers, has been able to construct a comprehensive race policy of population development and improvement that promises to be epochal in racial history. It sets the pattern which other nations and other racial groups must follow, if they do not wish to fall behind in their racial quality, in their racial accomplishment, and in their prospect of survival. (p. 34)

But now, we must step back from this historical thought experiment and concern ourselves with today's questions, many of which are structurally similar to some of the above quotes (either the real ones, or the initial illustrative but fictitious ones). William Shockley, Nobel Prize winner, has urged the government to provide monetary reproductive disincentives for African Americans, in order to encourage the "best genetic elements" to produce more than the "deficient ones." According to Shockley,

[I]f a bonus rate of $1,000 for each point below 100 IQ, $30,000 [were] put in trust for a 70 IQ moron of twenty-child potential, it might return $250,000 to taxpayers in reduced costs of mental retardation care.[2]

As is now well known, in 1969, the psychologist Arthur Jensen published his article claiming to scientifically prove that the gap in IQ scores between European Americans and African Americans was subtantially due to genes.[3] This infamous piece was not only acknowledged by the most prestigious educational journal in the United States, but it was also read in its entirety into the Congressional Record. That the entire analysis was logically flawed (as Jensen himself later admitted), did not seem to faze the politicians who had it read into the Congressional Record.

Richard Herrnstein, again from Harvard, provided the following observation:

[T]he privileged classes of the past were probably not much superior biologically to the downtrodden. . . . By removing artificial barriers between classes, society has encouraged the creation of biological barriers. When people can take their natural level in society, the upper classes will, by definition, have greater [biological] capacity than the lower.[4]

E. O. Wilson, once again from Harvard, writes,

It pays males to be aggressive, hasty, fickle and undiscriminating. In theory it is more profitable for females to be coy, to hold back until they can identify the male with the best genes. . . . Human beings obey this biological principle faithfully.[5]

In Robert Wright's widely read book on "evolutionary psychology," he summarizes:

Evolutionary psychology professes to be the surest path to a complete explanation of human behavior. . . . And to know all is to forgive all. Once you see the forces that govern behavior, it's harder to blame the behaver.[6]

Itzkoff's recent highly-praised analysis notes,

The research of [some] geneticists . . . view[s] the significance of "g"—general intelligence—as constituting the product of a very small number of genes. . . . Because of the quiet but tangible reality of these facts of human nature, what we see around the world as well as in our country is a competitive scramble to secure a high economic, intellectual, educational position. To find and educate these highly intelligent individuals ought now to become the overriding purpose of national policy. . . . For the flood of other humans now being born into a world of diminishing horizons the prognosis is decidedly pessimistic.[7]

Specifically studying the evolutionary explanation of human races, Rushton notes that:

Evolutionary selection pressures are far different in the hot African savanna where Negroids evolved, than in the cold Arctic environment, where Mongoloids evolved. Hence, it was predictable that these geographic races would show genetic differences in numerous traits. . . . It is provocative, to say the least, to treat each of these vast races as a separate human subspecies whose multifarious patterns of behavior are reduced to an average position on a gene-based scale of reproductive strategy. But the question I asked myself repeatedly was: Did the facts fit the theory? . . . I have been persuaded . . . that the races do differ, genetically, in the mechanisms underlying their behavior.[8]

And, some time ago, I received the remarkable *The Dispossessed Majority* by unsolicited mail, and read the following:

The upholders of heredity further substantiate their case by referring to the Negro's political and cultural record. They point out that neither in the Old World nor in the New has the Negro ever produced a system of government that went one step beyond the most elementary form of absolutism; that indigenous Negro societies have left behind no literature, no inscriptions or documents, no body of law, no philosophy, no science—in short no history. Even in those fields of art where Negroes have displayed some creativity and originality, the ultimate effect, at least on the West, has been anticultural— the contorted ugliness of modern painting and sculpture, the jungle screeching of jazz and rock music. . . .[9]

Given all of the above examples, it could be argued in each specific case what is wrong with the thesis. Some of them are obvious (e.g., Jensen's notions about IQ differences between African and European Americans); others may seem reasonable to the average reader, which is what makes them so dangerous. What I hope to show in the rest of this chapter is that there is a fundamental problem with asking the question in the first place. That is, any of the following questions are simply not worth asking.

"Is this behavior genetic?"

"How did this behavior evolve through natural selection?"

"What is the fraction of this behavior that is determined by genes?"

Perhaps other similar questions or rephrasings of these typical questions can be thought of. But the sense of the set of questions is clear. My intent is to suggest that almost all such questions are essentially illegitimate ones, given what we know with certainty about biology and what we are slowly coming to understand about human social behavior.

There is always a danger in suggesting that a seemingly scholarly question should not be asked in the first place, that one will be accused of censorship for not being willing to accept the question itself, even that one is afraid of the answer and therefore wishes that the question would never be asked in the first place. While I appreciate the sentiment, and, indeed, welcome the idea as one that modern society would do well to consider more widely (as, for example, when the true motives of those who rule nation-states are questioned), I reject the accusation in this concrete case. There are certainly legitimate reasons to suggest that a particular question has been formulated, or even simply phrased in such a way that the answer is automatically flawed. The old joke, "Do you still cheat on your boyfriend?" is a rather trivial, yet real, example. More important are the questions that are not dependent on tricks of phraseology, the ones that cannot be properly posed even with a significant change in phraseology.[10] It would not, for example, be regarded as legitimate today to ask the question, "How far is it from Paris to the edge of the Earth?" or, "Exactly how fast does the spinning wheel have to go to get the silk to change to gold?" even though such questions would have had significant meaning to earlier thinkers. There are, it seems, clear situations in which the fundamental question itself ought not to be asked, not because one fears the answer, but, rather, because modern knowledge has rendered the question meaningless.

A clear example is offered by James Burke in the television series *The Day the Universe Changed.* Burke considers the case of the Salem witch trials. Several women had been accused of being witches and, thus, faced death by burning. During the actual trials, several of the women offered vigorous and compelling defenses. Arguments were made as to why they were not witches. The exact nature of those arguments is not important. What strikes us at the close of the twentieth century is the fact that the question was asked in the first place, that it was taken as a serious question even by the accused, and that never was it even suggested that the question itself was a silly one. Hardly any reader today would countenance the question "Is she a witch?" not because he or she fears the answer, but simply because the question is ridiculous, given our frame of reference.[11]

This is the sense in which I argue that the questions themselves are inappropriate when applied to the species *Homo sapiens,* given what we today know about both genetics and human societies. In making that argument, I begin with a refresher course in what we know today about some relevant biology, specifically what we know about how the genotype of an organism is converted into its phenotype, perhaps the most fundamental transformation problem in all of biology.

THE ELUSIVE TRANSFORMATION

The phenotype is the external expression of the genotype. This classic distinction is perhaps the first thing taught in the genetics section of high school biology. It is also frequently the only remnant of formal genetics that lingers in the mind by the time the ten-year reunion rolls around. The blue-eye gene we now know is a segment of DNA, and that segment is the gene while the blue of the eye is the phenotype associated with that gene. The problem is, how does the DNA actually cause the blueness of the eye? How does the blue develop? How does that development happen in different environments? These are the key questions that are understood so well at a conceptual level, yet only recently have come to be known in their specifics.

Conceptually, we have had the story straight for some time now. DNA makes proteins. At the most elementary level, the protein is the phenotype and the DNA the genotype. But most proteins are made by a combination of genes operating in a highly regulated fashion, and most phenotypes of interest are more than a single protein. This undeniable and generally recognized fact has not really affected biological pedagogy very much. It is not, for example, uncommon to hear a biology teacher (myself included) simplifying a bit in suggesting that "these proteins then enter into life's processes," a true enough statement, but with little real content. Indeed, the transformation from genotype to phenotype only begins with the construction of a protein from a strand of DNA, the protein subsequently entering into combinations with other proteins to make larger products, some of which feed back not only to that particular strand of DNA, but also, perhaps, to other segments of DNA, keying in the production of yet other proteins, in a bewildering array of biochemical interactions that we understand well for only a few simple phenotypes. That bewildering array of mutually interactive chemical interactions in all its detail is the transformation process that makes phenotype from genotype. It is what is known in biology as "development," and those who specifically study its details are known as developmental biologists.

The other component of this transformation process is perhaps too obvious to even worry about. People who eat a lot tend to get fat; when you go to the beach your skin gets dark (if it wasn't already); or when you put bleach on your hair it changes color. In short, phenotypic characteristics are strongly sensitive to environmental conditions. The color of one's skin and hair, as well as the portliness of one's body, are all characteristics that are known to be determined by genes. Yet we see how they are also determined by the environment.

This, then, is the subject. It is as if we have a play, the script of which is metaphorically the genotype, the stage and interacting actors the environment, and the developmental process the unfolding of the action. The actors may flub their lines, they may speak them flawlessly, they may purposfully change them. That does not change the fact that a script actually exists. The transformation process is thus akin to the developmental play unfolding on the environmental stage according to a genetic script.

GENETIC AND ENVIRONMENTAL CONTROL IN DEVELOPMENT: THE LAC OPERON AND ACETABULARIUM[12]

We begin with a simple example to demonstrate the operation of genes as a developmental action unfolds. When you drink a glass of milk, the bacterial cells in your stomach are faced with the problem of digesting it. This is a general problem in the sense that these bacterial cells are constantly faced with different kinds and quantities of food during the course of the day and night. Do they simply produce all enzymes necessary to digest all foods all the time? That certainly would be possible, but it would also be "inefficient" in that most of the time they would be producing enzymes that would have no particular function at all. Indeed, the process of digesting food, for a bacterial cell, is a far more complicated affair. Many of the necessary enzymes are produced only if the need for them exists in the environment. Thus, for example, the three enzymes that the bacteria needs to digest milk are produced only when milk is in the environment. They are, in a sense, induced by the presence of milk. They are, thus, members of a large category of enzymes referred to as "inducible enzymes," in contrast to other enzymes that are produced more or less continuously, known as "constitutive enzymes."

A very general problem in the production of proteins from DNA is the question of starting and ending. As messenger RNA is produced on the DNA strand, there must be some sort of punctuation marks that tell it where to start and where to stop. On the DNA there are special regions that function exactly that way—they serve as guideposts, telling the components of mRNA exactly where to start their constructions. These regions are called *promoters*. In the case of the bacterial cell producing the enzymes for digesting milk, the three genes that stipulate the three necessary enzymes are located on the same strand of DNA, and they are preceded by a promoter.

There is another gene, located close to the promoter, that produces another kind of enzyme, known as a *repressor*. The repressor has a particular chemical configuration such that it binds to an area next to the promoter, making the promoter ineffective for initiating the process of mRNA formation, and blocking the formation of the three necessary proteins. The area next to the promoter, to which the repressor binds, is known as the *operator*. The combination of the promoter, the operator, and the three genes that produce the three enzymes is known as the lac (for lactose) *operon*. An operon is a combination of structural genes—that is, genes that code for proteins that have functions outside of the genetic structure of the organisms—and regulatory genes, genes that serve to regluate the process of transforming genotype to phenotype. In the case of the lac operon, there are two regulatory genes (the promoter and the operator) and three structural genes (the three genes that dictate the structure of the mRNA that eventually produces the three enzymes that the bacteria needs to digest the milk).

But what about the repressor? Recall that the repressor is another kind of enzyme, produced by another gene, and it binds with the operator to block the formation of mRNA. That gene is another regulatory gene, and it too has its own promoter, the combination of which is known as the lac I operon. So the lac complex is composed of the lac operon and the lac I operon, all on the same strand of DNA. This strand is diagramatically illustrated in Figure 6.1*a*.

The functioning of the lac operon is also illustrated in Figure 6.1. Before you drank that glass of milk, the lac complex in the bacterial cells was in the condition shown in Figure 6.1*b*. The repressor that had been

Figure 6.1. Schematic of the lac operon. (a) Basic genetic sequences, showing the two distinct operons with various gene types. (b) Normal status in absence of lactose (milk). The repressor molecule is produced by the regulator gene and blocks the functioning of the operator. (c) Status in the presence of lactose. The lactose binds to the repressor and thus releases the operator so that the promoter initiates RNA transcription from the three structural genes that are responsible for coding for the three key proteins involved in the digestion of milk.

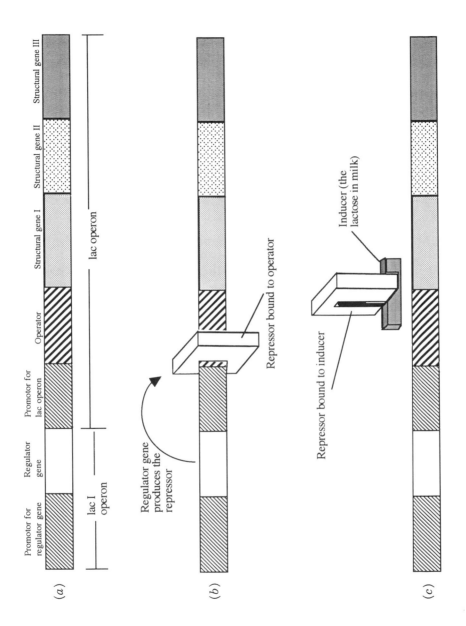

Promotor for regulator gene | Regulator gene | Promotor for lac operon | Operator | Structural gene I | Structural gene II | Structural gene III

lac I operon

lac operon

(a)

Regulator gene produces the repressor

Repressor bound to operator

(b)

Repressor bound to inducer

Inducer (the lactose in milk)

(c)

produced by the regulator gene is bound to the operator in the lac operon. But in the presence of the lactose in the milk you drink, the lactose acts as an inducer, in that it binds with the repressor (Figure 6.1*c*), thus freeing the operator to initiate the process of mRNA transcription, which effectively induces the three structural genes to operate. In a sense, one could use shorthand and say that the lactose in the milk turns the structural genes on and they, in turn, produce the three necessary enzymes.

This system is a very simple system, found in a very simple organism, the common stomach bacterium. For more complicated systems (and most genotype/phenotype transitions are indeed far more complicated) in more complicated organisms, we have only a partial understanding of how they function. About all we know for sure is that they are far more complicated than this. But the reader should realize that this story is indicative of the general sorts of complications that actually underlie the question, "Is it genetically determined?" The regulator "gene" directs the formation of the repressor, which, from the point of view of the operator, is an environmental influence that stops the initiation of the mRNA transcription, until the impact of another environmental factor, lactose, binds with the repressor, thus allowing the operator to initiate the operation of the three structural genes that ultimately result in the phenotypes, the three necessary proteins. Is it genetic or environmental? How much is determined by genes and how much by environment?

An alternative example, somewhat more complicated than the lac operon, is a small green alga known as *Acetabularium,* a small plant that grows in shallow oceans. It is pictured in Figure 6.2. The amazing thing about *Acetabularium* is that it has such a complicated structure, despite the fact that it is a single cell! There are no specialized cells forming tissues and organs, as one would ordinarily expect. The cap, stalk, and rhizoid are all part of the same cell, and the structure of the whole organism somehow is maintained through nothing more than the cytoplasm and cell wall, with the basic instructions for life abiding in the DNA in the nucleus.

Precisely how does this organism develop from its zygote, which is a simple, apparently structureless cell, to the relatively complicated adult form, as pictured in Figure 6.2? To understand this development, we must know more about the structure of the cytoplasm itself. Within the cytoplasm there are long fibrous protein complexes that form a complicated network (referred to as the cytoskeleton). This network is constantly un-

Cap

Stalk

Rhizoid

Figure 6.2. Basic structure of the algae, *Acetabularium*. The dark spot in the rhizoid is the nucleus of the cell.

dergoing chemical change spontaneously, depending on the exact position it occupies within the cytoplasm. The changes in turn create different pressures within the cytoplasm; that is, the exact chemical state of the protein complexes determine whether the cytoplasm is softer or harder at a paricar position.

To see how these spontaneous chemical changes lead to form, we must understand one other factor about the anatomy of *Acetabularium*. The cell wall is "involuted" and the cytoplasm is contained within the two walls that almost touch one another, much like the fingers in a rubber glove as it is half removed from a finger. Thus, the cell of the developing embryo is a hollow shell, the inside of which is called the vacuole, and the outside of which is a double membrane, with the cytoplasm between the two membranes. Through careful study of the turgor pressure in the cytoplasm, it has been possible to demonstrate the development of the general form of *Acetabularium* from nothing more than spontaneous changes in the protein complexes that make up the bulk of the cytoskeleton. As the protein complexes change, they cause dramatic changes in the turgor pressure of the cytoplasm, thus resulting in characteristic changes in the form of the entire organism. The general sequence is illustrated in Figure 6.3. While the overall details are quite complicated, for our purposes it is necessary to note only that once the genes have set up the overall cytoplasmic skeletal configuration, spontaneous chemical changes related to chemical

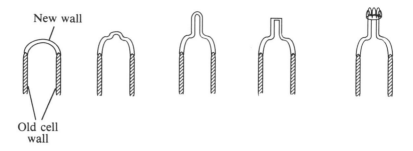

Figure 6.3. The developmental sequence of the stalk of *Acetabularium*, as a function of gradients of turgor pressure in the cytoplasm (see text). (Redrawn from Goodwin, 1994. Reproduced with permission.)

gradients are responsible for generating most of the complicated structure of this organism. It is an example of how particular proteins create environments (different turgor pressures) that generate structure.

The details of either of the above examples illustrate the complexity that is involved in transforming genetic information into real phenotypes. Even if we just consider a protein as the phenotype, the genetic material operates in a complicated interactive fashion to produce the chemical. Furthermore, natural selection may operate at any point in this sequence. A simple change in a base sequence for any of the DNA sequences within the lac operon, for example, could render the entire developmental sequence nonfunctional. On the other hand, it could make no difference at all.[13] Or on those rare occasions, it may make one of the intermediate processes operate faster or slower in particular environments. If that mutation then translates into greater survivorship in that environment or greater production of offspring in that environment, it will spread through the population.

However complicated systems such as the lac operon or *Acetabularium* may seem upon first reading, remember that the phenotypes we usually seek to understand in humans are far more complicated than these. We are interested in races, gender, and various behavioral tendencies such as aggressiveness, kindness, or avariciousness. Unfortunately, our understanding of such complicated phenotypes is far from what it is at the level of the lac operon or the structural development of *Acetabularium*. Perhaps the best understood at present is gender, but even here we face many unknowns and more than a little controversy, as will be discussed in the next chapter.

DEVELOPMENTAL ACCIDENT

If you carefully examine any newborn child, you will discover subtle asymmetries in his or her body: a mole on the left side of the chest that is not on the right side, small tufts of hair on the right but not the left, a discoloring under the right small toenail but not the left. Because of the symmetry of development, physical structures as determined by the genes are usually symmetrical. Yet, the two sides of the baby were in an identical environment, the mother's womb. How, then, would you answer the question, "Is this character (the asymmetry) determined by genes or by the environment?" Clearly, the question really doesn't make any sense. The baby was genetically destined to be symmetrical, yet it came out asymmetrical. However, there was no particular environmental influence that caused the genetic program to be overridden. It was simply an accident. This is what is called a *developmental accident.*

The concept of developmental accident is too frequently ignored when dealing with the relative contribution of genes and environment to phenotypes. This is unfortunate, since it is a universal phenomenon and may very well be crucial in the development of those very phenotypes with which we are so fascinated. While it is not possible to cite a specific example in humans (none has been discovered yet, other than the obvious asymmetries referred to above), it is a simple matter to come up with a plausible story to indicate the potential importance of this phenomenon.

One such plausible story is the development of a particular neural connection. The development of neural tissue is of special interest, since it is where the various characteristics we normally associate with humanness—our capacity to think abstractly, develop language, and so on—are obviously located. But the development of neural tissue also illustrates another exceedingly important aspect of the elusive transformation—the role of developmental accident in the genotype-phenotype transformation.

The basic nerve cell is composed of three structural features: the cell body, the axon, and the dendrites. A nerve impulse normally travels from axon to dendrite, and a given cell, through its multiple dendrites, can recieve as many as 100,000 different inputs. With the billion or so neurons in our brain, there are potentially on the order of 100 trillion connections (if we looked at one single connection per second, for 24 hours, 365 days a year, it would take over 30,000 years to examine all connections).

Exactly how all these connections are made and what they mean is quite beyond our current knowledge, although we assume that the nature of the connections is the underlying basis for human brain function. But the specific way in which particular neurons develop and how they make particular connections is reasonably well understood now. A primordial nerve cell sends out a growth cone, which contains a multitude of finger-like projections that effectively pull the axon along in the proper direction in the developing embryo. The manner in which the proper direction is established is not fully understood, but several mechanisms appear to be involved. In some cases, there are particular cells, known as stepping stones, that act as targets for the developing axon. In other cases, a single neuron makes an initial connection and acts as a guideline for subsequent developing neurons. Such a guiding neuron is known as a pioneer. In other cases, there appear to be chemical gradients that the axons are able to follow as they develop. Nevertheless, in all cases, axons are directed from their point of origin to specific target areas. There is, however, a limit on the ability of a neuron to find its exact final resting place. Through a variety of experimental procedures, developmental biologists have been able to cause axons to come to rest in a variety of incorrect positions. For example, by experimentally distancing the target, an axon normally destined for a particular muscle can easily be convinced to come to rest in the wrong muscle. Even in uninterrupted development, axons routinely make unusual connections, frequently making the study of neural anatomy a somewhat statistical subject.

As neurons develop, the truly critical developmental feature is the ultimate connections that are made from axon to dendrite. An examination of the process at a micro level reveals that axons grow in subtly different directions. It is as if there is a roadway stipulated by the products of the genes (whether cellular stepping stones or chemical gradients), but the particular curves in the roadway are not stipulated exactly. An axon may make a connection with a variety of dendrites from a particular neuron, or even from a variety of different neurons. The developing axon follows the general roadway ultimately stipulated by the genetic program, but the specific pathway finally taken, and the dendrite to which it is finally connected, may be subjected to effectively random forces. In effect, then, the precise connection made by a particular axon is partly an accident of the particular route taken—a developmental accident.

Given that the exact nature of these neural connections stipulates much of brain function, it is not difficult to imagine how a series of developmental accidents may dictate a great deal about that function. Since our knowledge of neural connections and brain function is very primitive, we cannot say anything definite. But the plausibility of developmental accident determining much, or even most, of the difference in brain function among various people is clear. You may be smarter than I am because of your genes, or because of your environment, the two forces usually cited in such cases. Yet, you may be smarter than I am simply because of developmental accident.

POSTPARTUM DEVELOPMENT AND THE FREUDIAN PARADIGM

Almost all of developmental biology concentrates on the early stages of development, from the fertilization of the egg to the emergence of the animal or plant in its final form. In the case of humans, that form is largely taken to be the newborn infant. While all developmental biologists would admit that the biological developmental sequence continues after birth, most active research is concerned with the development that occurs before birth. Those concerned with developmental sequences between birth and adulthood are usually called developmental psychologists. Those concerned with development after the attainment of adulthood are psychologists or sociologists, or, if they study other cultures, anthropologists.

The three stages of human development—prenatal, childhood, and adult—are, without doubt, driven by very different forces. Developmental sequences before birth are largely controlled by gene action within the environment of the mother's womb. Developmental accidents occur, and subtle changes in the environment of the womb also initiate particular sequences, but, by and large, it is a genetic story. At the time of birth, the new human is as different from its endoparasitic forerunner as a butterfly is from a caterpillar. New rules, especially social ones, begin to operate, and whatever genes are doing, they are clearly operating in a new type of environment. Attainment of adulthood implies yet another change, in which the developmental sequences of early childhood are no longer in progress. Yet, development per se does not stop with adulthood. Surprisingly, less is understood of developmental sequences the further we get from the fertilized egg.

From conception to birth, we are clearly dealing with a gene-environment interaction, overlaid with developmental accident, and it makes sense to ask what particular genes are doing to direct the formation of the fetus's body. After birth, it is not so clear that genes are as directly involved. No doubt there are some traits acquired after birth that are strongly influenced by genetic factors operative in the growing child, or even in the adult. The development of language is one such trait. However, it is also clear that other traits acquired after birth are not in the least influenced by genetic factors; an Italian accent, for instance, is one such trait. To a first approximation, most human traits of interest are not currently known to be influenced by genetic factors at all, and it is unlikely that future research will change that fact. It is as if the play that unfolds according to the genetic script suddenly turns into complete improvisation with no script at all after birth, and certainly after adulthood is achieved.[14]

For most human characteristics of interest, there has been insufficient study to really dissect the prepartum and postpartum developmental sequences. Thus, most literature simply asks the question of whether particular traits are influenced by genetic factors, but ignores the question of when the trait emerges in the developmental sequence. Two obvious exceptions are the development of language, as discussed in chapter 4, and the development of gender identity, as discussed in chapter 7. At a more theoretical level, postpartum development is really part of the discipline of psychology. Yet here, too, there is more than a hint of strong biological determinism, some of which is clearly appropriate, but some of which generates a great deal of confusion. An example is the assumption that the newborn is somehow an unadulterated reflection of genetic forces.

Since the classical writings of Freud, there has been a tendency to divide personality into that which is somehow deep and instinctual (the id) from that which is developed in conjunction with the surrounding society (the ego). While these two concepts have undergone a variety of deviations and popularizations, their initial meaning, according to Freud, could not have been clearer.

> . . . the oldest of these psychical provinces . . . we give the name of id. It contains everything that is inherited, that is preset at birth, that is laid down

in the constitution—above all, therefore, the instincts, which originate from the somatic organization and which find a first psychical expression here [in the id] in forms unknown to us.

Under the influence of the real external world around us, one portion of the id has undergone a special development. . . . a special organization has arisen which henceforward acts as an intermediary between the id and the external world. To this region of our mind we have given the name of ego.[15]

The tendency to read into an infant's behavior characteristics that may be as much a figment of our imagination as of reality is well known. But the facts of biological development indicate that even if our reading somehow reflected nothing more than the child's actual behavior, we could not assume that the behavior is representative of some sort of genetic blueprint. It may be. But it also may have nothing whatsoever to do with the child's genes. And it is not generally possible to tell which is which.

Such limitations are extremely important for anyone wishing to speculate about the "nature" of humans as natural selection might have produced particular characteristics, as discussed more fully below. It is popular to interpret the temperament of infants and compare it to that of their parents, the obvious implication being that there is some genetic effect involved. This manner of analysis is simply wrong.

Part of the error is in the assumption that when a baby is born it (1) exhibits certain personality characteristics that will remain with it the rest of its life and (2) those personality characteristics are inherited. The first of these two assumptions has never been examined systematically. Yet it is an important issue in the nature/nurture debate in pop psychology. My own opinion—hardly informed by data, but, then, neither is any one else's—is that as measurement tools become even further refined, it is likely that we will some day discover some personality characteristics that have been more or less fixed by the time of birth. As of now we have no solid evidence for any such characteristics, and the question must remain open.

But whether or not number 1 is true is perhaps less important than the veracity of number 2. Indeed from a social point of view, number 2 is hardly debated and, with the exception of the admission of some prenatal environmental effects, most people assume that it is largely true. But from what we now know of developmental biology, there is no *a priori* reason to expect it to be true. While it certainly might be the case that some, or even all, variability in personality traits exhibited at birth is the direct result of particular gene products, we have no basis on which to judge objectively. It could also very well be that all variability in personality traits observable at birth is due to developmental accidents (or, for that matter, prenatal environmental effects).

Freud's categorization of personality traits into id and ego thus takes on a different meaning. From the point of view of developmental psychology, it may not make much difference. The id may indeed represent some biological framework on which the external environment builds the ego. But "biological" in this sense is not the same as genetic. The baby that is born "fussy," after it becomes a mating adult, will not necessarily provide a gene to make a new fussy baby. Its fussiness may simply be due to an accidental production of a specific protein at some point in neural development, which may or may not occur again in its own offspring. It is incorrect to presume that a newborn's traits are representative of its genetic makeup.

Norms of Reaction and Heritability

If you take a series of cuttings from the same plant and plant them in different environments, they grow differently, depending on the environment. Cuttings from a different plant also grow differently, depending on the environment. However, they may not follow the same pattern as the first plant. For example, the pattern shown in Figure 6.4 is typical. Genotype number one grows tall in the valley, smaller on the slope of the mountain, and smaller still at the top of the mountain. Genotype number two does the opposite—tall on the top of the mountain, smaller on the slope, and smaller still in the valley. In each of the two cases, the three cuttings are from the same plant, so the genetic material is identical in all three localities. But the response, due entirely to the environment, is different in each of the three environments (top of mountain, slope, and valley).

This phenomenon is really quite common. The expression of a gene, its phenotype, is highly dependent on the specific environment in which it develops, and that expression is contradictory for alternative genes. This makes it quite difficult, of course, to even begin answering that normative question, "Which genotype is better?" There is simply no such thing as "better" without the qualifier "in environment x."

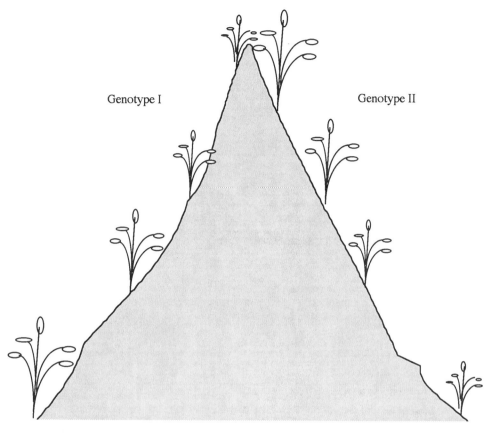

Figure 6.4. Growth response of two different genotypes of plants with respect to an environmental gradient (a mountainside). Note the inverse response to altitude of the two genotypes.

A graph of phenotype over a range of environments, as shown in Figure 6.5 for the plant cuttings, is known as the "norm of reaction." While we have no knowledge of what norms of reaction are for any human social or psychological characteristics, we do have a variety of examples from other animals. Figure 6.5 is typical. Genotype I increases over the defined environmental range, while genotype II decreases over that same range. Given such data, how would one go about determing which is the "best" genotype? It is simply a nonsensical question.

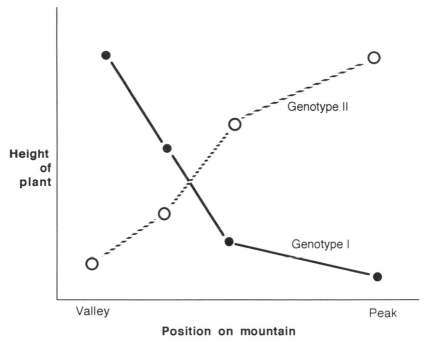

Figure 6.5. Norms of reaction for the plants pictured in Figure 6.4.

One other concept is frequently bandied about, yet misunderstood—heritability. The word heritability has a very specific mathematical meaning in quantitative genetics. In popular culture, however, it has been taken to be more or less equivalent to "genetically determined." It is one of the most misunderstood concepts in the entire nature/nurture debate. Two features of heritability are worth noting here, partly to avoid confusion with much of the literature (much is made, for example, of the idea that IQ is "highly heritable," a questionable fact in the first place, but irrelevant regarding policy even if it were true), but partly to understand the nature of heredity/environment interaction—first, the comparison of two populations with heritability measured within one population, and, second, how heritability changes from environment to environment.

Heritability, formally, is the proportion of variability that is a result of genetics. That is, the total variability of a population can be divided up into that due to genetic differences among individuals in the population and that due to environmentally induced differences among individuals in the population. The proportion of the total variability (genetic plus environmental) that is due to genes alone is the heritability. If all of the differences among individuals in the population are due to genes, the heritability is 100 percent, while if all of the differences are environmentally induced, the heritability is 0 percent.

In Figure 6.6*a,* the plants in the population on the left are all of genotype I (from Figure 6.5) and they are pictured along the mountainside environmental gradient. A population composed of another genotype, number IV, is shown to the right in Figure 6.6a. Genotype IV grows in the same qualitative fashion, tall in the lowlands short in the highlands, but is, on average, larger at all elevations than genotype I. In either the population on the left or the population on the right, the differences among individuals in the population are totally due to the environment (they cannot be a result of genotype, since all individuals in the population are of the same genotype). So the heritability is exactly equal to zero. Yet, as is readily visible, the average difference in stature between the two populations is completely a consequence of genetic difference. So we have a case in which the difference between two populations is totally genetic, but the heritability in each population is zero.

In Figure 6.6*b,* one population is on the leeward side of the mountain and the other is on the windward side of the mountain. In each case, the population is composed of four genetically distinct individuals, and the stature of the plants within each of the two populations is a consequence of genes, and genes alone. But the second population is larger than the first, because it occurs on the windward side of the mountain. Thus, the average difference between these two populations is totally due to the environment, yet the heritability is 100 percent.

From these two examples, we see the futility of trying to relate heritability, as estimated from within a particular population, to the question of genetic determination between two different populations. In one case the difference was totally genetic yet the heritability was 0, while in the other case the difference was totally environmental yet the heritability was 100 percent.

Furthermore, heritability is a concept that applies to a particular population in a particular environment. Consider the two populations in Figure 6.6*c.* The populations are identical genetically. The population on the left is on the leeward side of the island, where the environment is somewhat more harsh than on the windward side, perhaps due to the dryer conditions there. Thus, the performance of the individual plants is dictated by both genes and the environment, one genotype growing large in the lowlands and small in the highlands, another genotype growing small in the lowlands and large in the highlands. The heritability is approximately 50 percent. But now, put exactly the same population on the other side of the mountain, where the lush conditions permit larger growth of all individuals, and the genetic influence disappears. Plants still grow differently from one another, but now the difference is determined by their altitude, not their genetics. The heritability of the population is now zero. And this is a very important aspect of heritability. The concept applies to a particular population in a particular environment. Here we see an example, and it is not at all a particularly fanciful one, in which the same population has a heritability of 50 percent in one environment, and a heritability of zero in another environment. Those seeking to express some "inherent" or "essential" biological qualities of organisms should abandon the use of heritability—it is irrelevant to such questions.

ESTIMATING GENETIC EFFECTS BY STUDYING IDENTICAL TWINS

Any two individuals, human or otherwise, engage in a lifelong process of development, from the time the egg first meets the sperm until death, as

---

Figure 6.6. Example of two populations, each genetically distinct from the other, but with four genetically identical individuals within each. Population on the right is, on average, larger than population on left, and that average difference is a consequence of the genetic difference between the two populations. But within either of the populations, all variability is due to the environment; therefore, the heritability is equal to zero. Example of two populations, each genetically identical with the other, but with four genetically distinct individuals in each population. Population on the right is, on average, larger than population on left, and that average difference is a consequence of the environmental difference between the two populations (one is growing on the leeward side and one on the windward side of the mountain). But within either of the populations, all variability is due to genetics; therefore the heritability is equal to 100%. On leeward side of mountain, size variability is due to both genes and environment, to give a heritability of about 50%. If the same population is moved to the windward side of the mountain, where the environment is generally much better for plant growth, the phenotypic differences among the various indivdiuals disappears entirely and the heritability is 0.

Heritability within populations = 0%, difference between the two populations = 100% genetic.

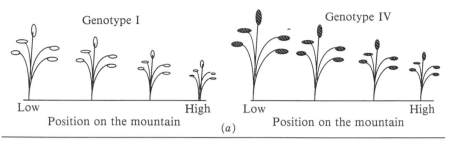

Genotype I

Low　　　　　　　　High
Position on the mountain

Genotype IV

Low　　　　　　　　High
Position on the mountain

(*a*)

Heritability within populations = 100%, difference between the two populations = 100% environmental.

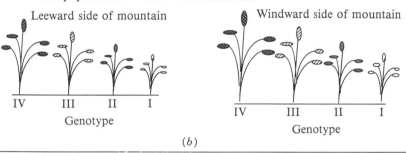

Leeward side of mountain

IV　　III　　II　　I
Genotype

Windward side of mountain

IV　　III　　II　　I
Genotype

(*b*)

Population on the leeward side of mountain. Heritability about 50%.

Same population on windward side of mountain. Heritability = 0%

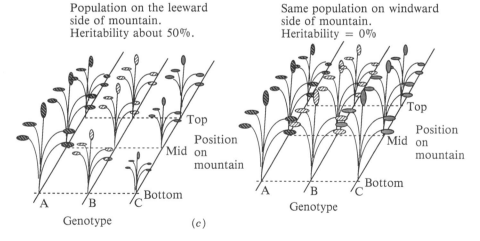

Top

Position on mountain

Mid

Bottom

A　　B　　C
Genotype

Top

Position on mountain

Mid

Bottom

A　　B　　C
Genotype

(*c*)

elucidated in the previous section. Genes interact with environment in a process that unfolds sometimes predictably, sometimes not. For some characteristics—eye color, for example—the genes seem to provide a faithful template on which the external manifestation of the phenotype is unaffected by either the environment or developmental accident. For other characteristics—ability to speak Chinese, for example—the environment seems to provide a faithful template on which the external manifestation of the phenotype is unaffected by either the genes or developmental accident. But for the vast majority of human characteristics, especially those behavioral characteristics that affect us so much, we have no idea of the relative contributions of genes versus environment versus developmental accident. Indeed, in the section that follows I will try to convince the reader that viewing the problem from this perspective is not useful in the first place.

Yet popular literature remains committed to this perhaps anachronistic view. One of the most popular vehicles for studying the problem is the comparison of identical and fraternal twins, reared together and reared apart. It seems like an obvious methodology for getting at the problem. Take two individuals who are genetically identical, put them in different environments, and compare them with two individuals who are genetically different and raised in the same environments as the identical twins. At a superficial level, it is obvious what happens. For some characteristics —eye color, for example—identical genotypes produce identical phenotypes, even though they are raised in different environments. For other characteristics—ability to speak Chinese, for example—dramatically different phenotypes are produced by identical genotypes when raised in different environments. Two identical twins separated at birth, one raised in New York, the other in Beijing, will have the same eye color, but dramatically different abilities in the Chinese tongue.

But this seemingly straightforward experiment works only for such extreme and obvious cases. The critical problem is in our inability to truly assign people to distinct environments. The methodology effectively assumes that twins reared separately have been placed in very distinct environments, or at least that the degree to which environments are correlated is the same for identical as for fraternal twins. Yet we know that a person's social position is, to some extent, determined by his or her appearance. Since identical twins appear more alike than do fraternal twins, their social environments must be more correlated. How much more, we have no idea.

Thus, the correlation in characteristics for identical twins is due partly to their genetic identity and partly to the environmental similarity produced by the society responding to them similarly. And it is not possible to determine the size of the second effect. Thus, there is inevitably an environmental correlation of some unknown size, which might very well determine all of the correlation between identical twins. This effect is explicitly admitted by one of the most well known twin research units in the country: "Infants with different temperaments elicit different parenting responses. Toddlers who are active and adventurous undergo different experiences than their more sedentary or timid siblings."[16]

I would add only that temperaments are not the only characteristics that elicit parenting responses, and, furthermore, "parenting" responses are not provided only by parents. The developing person's phenotype elicits social responses, plain and simple. So if we assume that the "temperaments" are more similar in identical than in fraternal twins, environments of the identical twins are more likely to be similar for them than the same environments would be for fraternal twins. Exactly how much more, we have no idea. Thus, a quantitative estimate of the heritability of this or that characteristic, using identical twins, is simply not valid.

There have been many other critiques of the identical twin studies.[17] For the most part, these critiques are based on a detailed analysis of the case histories of the twins involved in the studies and the fact that the term "raised apart" is frequently a gross exaggeration of the actual fact. Frequently, the twins are raised by family members, are in constant contact with one another, and by no stretch of the imagination could be considered to be growing up in uncorrelated environments. This sort of critique of the methodological details of twin studies, while correct, may leave the impression that if the studies were done more carefully, they would give accurate results. Such is not the case, due to the simple fact elucidated above.

Because of the social nature of human behavior, many characteristics are environmentally influenced in accordance with the appearance of individuals. Since identical twins appear more alike than fraternal twins, they are invariably destined to share a more similar environment with one another. This injects a bias in all estimates of genetic effects, and the size of that bias is impossible to determine. Thus this technique, while superficially seeming perfectly suited for quantifying the role of genes in behavior, is dramatically flawed.

POPULAR MODELS OF DEVELOPMENT: HOW TO THINK ABOUT THE GENOTYPE-PHENOTYPE TRANSITION

Translating the genotype into the phenotype has classically taken the form of the nature/nurture debate. On the one hand is the idea that the phenotype is a faithful representation of the genotype, influenced in some small way by the environment. This is the nature side of the debate. On the other hand is the idea that the phenotype is largely determined by the environment in which it develops, influenced by the underlying genetic constraints contained within the organism. This is the nurture side of the debate. Setting the debate up in this fashion dooms us to misunderstanding. It is true that the naturists are able to provide strong evidence for their point of view, but so can the nurturists. The argument is thus unresolvable, except with a pseudo-quantitative resolution—a percentage of the phenotype is determined by the genes and a percentage by the environment. A fanciful metaphor may help.

Suppose an intelligent alien being, from Mars, let's say, arrives at our planet and is able to observe it from some distance. The Martian arriving in Los Angeles at rush hour will likely characterize life on planet Earth as a fast-moving, hectic assemblage of large metal objects that move around on rubber wheels. Knowing nothing about this assemblage of objects, the Martian must try to understand their collective behavior from simple observation. First, they seem to move together along channels, but there always seems to be a stream going one way and another stream going the other way. But, then, there are a variety of branch channels and sometimes some of the objects go streaming off on one of these branches; sometimes they even stop on the sides of these branches, although occasionally they can stop on one of the main channels also. At relatively regular intervals, there are spots where the objects stop and attach a hose to their rear ends for a short period of time. Furthermore, sometimes when the objects stop, a small particle emerges from the object, and frequently, just before a stationary object moves, one of these small particles enters. Unable to land the spacecraft, the Martian must try to understand the movement patterns of these metal objects from a spacecraft hovering well above the highway.

Certain patterns will seem obvious. Since each of these objects must stop at certain intervals to attach one of those hoses, it is a reasonable hypothesis that the energy necessary for movement of these little metal objects comes from those hoses, and that the size of the metal objects is partially determined by their ability to store the energy material (since the gas stations are positioned at a fixed distance from one another, the cars will have evolved a gas tank exactly the right size to make it from one gas station to the other—or so our clever Martian observers may conclude). The structures on the bottom of the objects (wheels) can easily be observed to move whenever the car is moving, suggesting to one astute Martian observer that these are the agents responsible for the movement of the objects. However, another inventive Martian scientist makes careful measurements of the heat released from these objects and concludes that something under the front part (usually) is converting the energy that is pumped in through the hoses into mechanical energy that is translated to the wheels, thus propelling the objects forward. The movement of the wheels, says this clever Martian, is simply an epiphenomenon of the "real" cause of movement, the mechanism under the hood. A major scientific debate then ensues, with one side arguing that the cause of movement is, the motor, and the other insisting that the wheels cause the movement.

But then a new generation of Martians arrives and is able to steer their spaceships even closer to these moving objects, wherein they find that the small particles that get into and out of the objects are really quite more important than had been realized before. Indeed, they note, it is impossible to find one of these objects moving without at least one small particle inside. They thus conclude that the debate as to whether it is the engine or wheels that cause movement is moot, that their new technology that enables them to see the smaller particles so clearly leaves little doubt as to the real cause of the object's movement—the small particles themselves, which the Martians decide to call people. Yet the old hardliners insist that no one has ever seen an automobile move with its tires stationary nor with its motor not running, and the fact that there happen to be people inside the cars is a secondary consequence of the motor running or the wheels turning. The turning wheels, says one respected Martian scientist from a major Martian university, may very well create a current in the air that draws the particles (the so-called people) into the cars when they are moving, but that the natural tendency is for the people to flee these cars, which they do almost every time the wheels stop turning. Clearly the wheels are the fundamental force, and a mathematical model is even able to demonstrate that there is a balance between the attractive force created by the spinning wheel and the natural repulsive force felt between the cars and the people.

But the new breed of young scientists, with their newfangled spaceships, are able to counter that argument by detailed observation of the particles, the people, under a variety of circumstances. For example, it is noticed that when the people emerge from a particular type of habitat and enter the car, its behavior is frequently quite erratic. They discover that a slight chemical poisoning occurs in these habitats, rendering the people less able to conduct the proper movement of the car, at least for a while. Indeed, sometimes the poisoning is so severe that the car clearly moves contrary to the general flow of the other objects in the channel. They call these habitats bars.

Eventually, all sides in the debate admit that each other side has some validity; the motor/wheel school of thought admits that the people school of thought is partially right, and vice versa. But then they begin the debate about which is "really" more important. Sure, the people are important, says the motor/wheel school, but where would they be without the turning wheels or the heat-producing motor? Of course the motor must be running, says the people school, but where would the car go without the person directing its course of action?

Knowing what we know about cars, highways, gas stations, bars, and the people who frequent all of them, such arguments would seem pretty silly, wouldn't they? Indeed, they would be! But this frivolous metaphor is useful for understanding the current nature/nurture debate. It is now commonplace to "admit" that the debate is passé, that everyone understands that both genes and environment cause human behavior. But this seemingly modern "scientific" approach to the problem is really no different from the Martian scientists admitting that both the motor/wheel and the people schools of thought have their valid arguments. In point of fact, there are certain questions about the behavior of cars on the highway (or people in their societies) that one would be simply foolish to approach from the motor/wheel school of thought. The most careful measurements of the heat given off by the motors or the wind speed created by the wheels will not give you an interesting answer as to why thousands of these vehicles suddenly converged on the parking lot of the football stadium, remained there for approximately three hours, and then all left again simultaneously. The only interesting explanation is that the people all decided to go to a football game.

On the other hand, a single stalled car in the middle of the highway during rush hour creates a major traffic jam, and the people-first school of thought suggests that the smoke rising from the hood is part of a religious ceremony that the people's social constructions have made, and that the people in the other cars slow down as they pass to pay homage to a motor deity. The most detailed observations of the presumedly ceremonial behavior of all the individual people surrounding the stalled car is not likely to provide an interesting explanation for the stalled car. The only interesting explanation is that the car is experiencing vapor lock.

Thus, it is not sufficient to suggest that "it is both motor and people," just as it is not sufficient to suggest that "it is both genes and environment." Some characteristics are clearly not related to genes at all—for example, the particular language one speaks. Other characteristics are clearly not related to the environment at all—for example, the color of one's eyes (at least before colored contact lenses). For some human problems (e.g., cystic fibrosis), it makes a great deal of sense to be concerned with the genes. For other human problems (e.g., the homicide rate in Washington, D.C.), it makes no sense at all. Resolving the nature/nurture debate by allowing that some "percent" of a behavior is due to genes and some "percent" due to environment is not a useful resolution. Indeed, the trendy attitude of placing the problem somewhere along a continuum between "purely genetic, but affected by the environment" to "purely environmental, but affected by the genes," only helps to obscure the true relationship between genes and environment, making the modern interpretation perhaps even more confusing than the old dichotomous debate.

The two extremes in the modern continuum are illustrated in Figure 6.7 for three genotypes producing three phenotypes in an environmental gradient. The genetic determinist (top model in Figure 6.7) sees each of the three genotypes passing through a metaphorical environmental filter. The genotype A stipulates a big phenotype. A hot environment tends also to produce a big phenotype. Genotype C and a cool environment stipulate the opposite. Thus we see the joint effects of genes and environment in that the genes stipulate whether the phenotype will be large or small, and the environmental filter modifies that basic genetic information to create

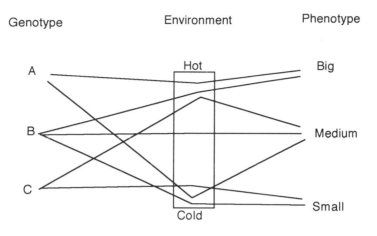

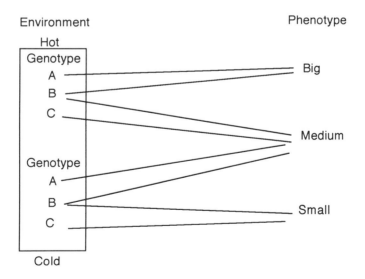

Figure 6.7. Illustrations of the two classic positions on the nature-nurture debate. Top figure illustrates the genetic determinist position; bottom figure illustrates the environmental determinist position.

variance. Genotype A thus produces either big or medium phenotypes, depending on whether it is in a hot or cool environment, and genotype C produces either small or medium phenotypes, depending on whether it is in a cool or hot environment.

The environmental determinist (the bottom model in Figure 6.7) begins by assuming that a hot environment produces large phenotypes, but is influenced by genetic forces. Thus, an organism developing in a hot environment will produce larger phenotypes, big ones if they are of genotype A and medium ones if they are of genotype C. As can be seen in the figure, while genetic forces act to create variability in the system, the underlying rule that a hot environment produces large individuals and a cool one small individuals is not qualitatively altered by the genetic forces.

Both of these viewpoints are incorrect. As discussed more fully later,[18] when two forces are related to one another in a web-like fashion, it is a fundamental epistemological error to assume that they are chain-like. In this case, much like the motor and driver of the automobile, suggesting that the motor is "really" what makes the car go and the drivers just modify what the motor is doing is just as misleading as saying that the drivers are "really" what makes the car go and the motor provides the modifying force. One cannot assign ontogenetic priority to driver or motor, nor can one assign ontogenetic priority to genes or environment. Genes and environment are related to one another in a web-like fashion. They are intimately interconnected, and confusion will follow if you try to assign one or another ontogenetic priority.

The proper focus for understanding development must incorporate (1) the notion that genes and environment are dialectically related, (2) the notion that norms of reaction are not necessarily concordant, and (3) the undeniable fact that developmental accident is a real force in nature. Recalling the earlier examples of the lac operon, the development of *Acetabularium,* and the general pattern of neuronal development, it is possible to begin building a model of genotype-phenotype transition, based on elementary (and well known) transformation processes. For convenience, we can stipulate five elementary processes, as illustrated in Figure 6.8. First, as we saw in the lac operon, environments stimulate the action of genes, just as the presence of lactose in the environment binds the repressor to allow the promoter to stimulate the operator, and thus activate the three structural genes (see Figure 6.1). Second, the genes produce proteins, as the structural genes in the lac operon produce the proteins neces-

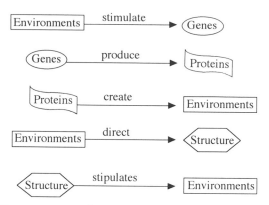

Figure 6.8. Elementary transformations involved in the genotype-phenotype transformation process.

sary to digest the milk that appeared in the environment. Third, proteins create environments. This can be seen in the lac operon, where the proteins produced are the enzymes necessary to digest milk, thus creating anew a lactose-free environment, which activates the repressor to block the action of the promotor on the operator again (see Figure 6.1). It can also be seen in the development of *Acetabularium,* where the protein complexes in the cytoskeleton create gradients of turgor pressure (i.e., an internal environment). Fourth, environments direct structure, as witnessed by the gradient of turgor pressure in *Acetabularium* resulting in the development of surprisingly complex physical structure,[19] or in the development of an axon in a neural field. Environments direct structure in an extremely dynamic way in the case of *Homo sapiens,* as suggested in several chapters in this book (especially chapters 4, 5, 7, 9, 13, 14, and 15). Fifth, structure stipulates environments, as seen in the changing turgor pressure in *Acetabularium* as the cap slowly forms, or when a developing axon follows the structure laid down by a pioneer axon, or when a deranged dictator is allowed to come to power. And remember, in all of these elementary transformations, errors or accidents can happen. It does not always go according to script, which results in the all-important phenomenon of developmental accident.

Given these elementary transformations, a particular developmental sequence may be thought of as a complex network. For example, in Figure 6.9*a,* we see the simple sequence in which environmental factor 1 stimu-

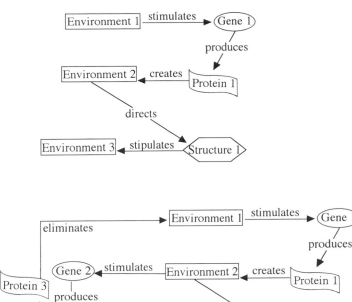

Figure 6.9. Two simple illustrative sequences of genotype-phenotype transition (see text).

lates a gene to produce a protein that creates an environment that directs a structure that creates a new environment. Such simplicity probably never actually occurs in a whole organism. Something more like Figure 6.9*b* might be more realistic—environment 1 stimulates gene 1, which produces protein 1, which creates environment 2, which directs structure 1 but also stimulates gene 2 to produce protein 2, which creates environment 4, which modifies the structure originally directed by environment 2. Meanwhile structure 1 stipulates another environment, number 3, which stimulates gene 3, which produces protein 3 that eliminates the first environment, thus bringing the whole sequence under control. Even this level of complexity is much too simple for what actually happens in nature. However, constructing these webs of causality is far better than asking whether genes or environment (or what proportions thereof) are controlling a phenotype. In particular cases we can stipulate some of the genes, some of the structures, and so on to make a reasonable story of how the developmental sequence actually operates (e.g., the construction of gender roles, as presented in the next chapter). But the most important point is that the web of causality itself is what we seek to understand. With this framework, it makes about as much sense to ask whether a phenotype is controlled more by genes than by environment as it does to ask whether the car is controlled more by the motor or the drivers. Again, there are some phenotypes for which mainly genes are involved, and for which it would be pointless to even consider trying to understand them without understanding those genes. But there are equally some phenotypes for which the vast majority of the developmental sequence has nothing to do with genes, and for which it would be pointless to even wonder about the underlying genetic control. The Salem witches were not innocent of being witches, as there's no such thing as witches, and furthermore, no matter how sophisticated your odometer, you'll never figure out how far it is from Paris to the edge of the earth.

NATURAL SELECTION AND HUMAN BEHAVIOR

A relatively new form of biological determinism has recently evolved, signaled mainly by the publication of E. O. Wilson's *Sociobiology: The New Synthesis*. Sociobiology follows the Haeckelian tradition of interpreting human sociality from an evolutionary perspective. It is an attempt to understand human behavior within the same discourse developed for evolutionary interpretations of other organisms, and has been widely criticized.[20] Yet it remains quite popular among some social scientists— witness the quotes at the beginning of this chapter. Its general form can probably be best understood in historical context.

Since the classic civilizations, and probably before, some people have had a great interest in nature. These naturalists, as they are frequently called, sometimes exhibit almost fanatical urges to observe, collect, and study the various objects we have come to know as "nature." During the modern era, such nature study became common, especially among the richer classes, in part because of the leisure their class position afforded.

Another group that tended to enjoy significant leisure time was the clergy. Consequently, many members of the clergy and significant numbers from the upper classes engaged in, and frequently even dedicated their lives to, the study of nature.

Possibly through the influence of the large number of clergy engaged in nature study, a certain attitude developed among naturalists. Nature took on a religious connotation. The various objects of nature could be seen as the work of the creator, and, thus, their study could be viewed as the closest one could get to studying the creator himself. Consequently, much of nature came to represent the embodiment of the creator, and its study, the study of the wisdom of the creator.

With such attitudes it is not surprising that a sort of informal methodology evolved in which not only the beauties of nature, but also the apparent ugliness, could be viewed as the wisdom of the creator. While it was a simple matter to see the creator's work in the beauty of the butterfly's wing, it was perhaps somewhat disconcerting to note that the disgusting maggots that appeared in rotting meat were also God's creation. But one only had to understand each creature's place in nature to see that God had, in fact, wisely positioned that creature exactly where it was needed for nature to function properly—the maggots were needed to decompose the meat that was no longer usable. A three-part methodology thus evolved: First, make an observation that appears to be at odds with the basic notion that God's creations all have a purpose; second, study the object of that observation in all its detail to understand as much about it as possible; and third, use the knowledge from that study to show how, properly viewed, the original observation indeed did represent an example of the wisdom of the creator.

The publication of and scientific acceptance of Darwin and Wallace's theory of evolution changed the content of nature study, but not necessarily the form. The theory of evolution through natural selection[21] was vigorously attacked, especially by the clergy. Under attack, it became imperative to demonstrate that natural selection could feasibly account for what we, in fact, see in nature. The underlying structure of the attack was frequently in the form of an example from nature that seemed to defy interpretation through natural selection. It then came on the shoulders of the new naturalists, the Darwinian naturalists, to demonstrate how such an example could, in fact, have been the outcome of natural selection. The bright colors of a bird would seem to make it more obvious to predators.

How could natural selection have produced that? If you just look closely, you see that females choose the males with the brighter colors so, despite their obviousness to predators, males with brighter colors tend to pass their genes on to future generations more than males with dull colors.

Such was the nature of the arguments of the Darwinian naturalists. It followed a three-part sequence: First, make an observation that appears to be at odds with the basic notion that all nature is a result of natural selection; second, study the object of that observation in all its detail to understand as much about it as possible; and third, use the knowledge from that study to show how, properly viewed, the original observation indeed did represent an example of the operation of natural selection. In this sense, the form of nature study changed far less than its content. A similar, if not exactly the same, methodology was used by the new Darwinian naturalists as had been used by the religious naturalists before.[22]

No doubt, such a stage of history was essential. Our view of nature as an outcome of evolution was as important a stage in the development of modern intellectual thought as was the notion of a round earth and a heliocentric universe, and, thus, its defense against all challenges was a key intellectual endeavor of the nineteenth century. However, with the rediscovery of Mendel's genetics in 1900, evolution became the underlying basis of modern biology and has not really been seriously challenged since. Political challenges emerge now and then,[23] but a bulwark of intellectual thought in the twentieth century, that evolution has produced the organic world as we see it, is accepted as scientific fact. As in any science the details are continually being debated, but the fact of evolution is not debated by any serious thinker.

Nevertheless, much of the form of nature study has not undergone the same transformation, even though its content has. The content of nature study has gone from (1) how does nature represent the wisdom of the creator, to (2) how does nature represent the operation of natural selection, to (3) nature is clearly the result of natural selection. Yet the form remains stuck in part 2. That is, some of modern biology remains in what might be thought of as an anachronistic methodology. It is no longer necessary to demonstrate that natural selection can account for everything we see. Yet, that is the discourse of many biologists yet today—make an observation that seems at odds with the principle of natural selection, then study that observation carefully to show that indeed it could have been produced by natural selection. This is the context into which the evolutionary interpretation of human behavior has developed, a particular view to which we now turn.

There are three different critiques of this viewpoint: (1) a critique based on scientific methodology that applies to all creatures, not only *Homo sapiens,* (2) a critique that is based on the fact that the human animal is unique because of language and culture, and (3) a critique of the pernicious use of the methodology itself.

As a scientific methodology, the interpretation of various things through evolutionary reasoning, including human behavior, has recently come under severe criticism from evolutionary biologists themselves. Ignoring some of the more biological details, we can summarize this critique with reference to the above history. While the clerics interpreted nature as evidence of the wisdom of the creator, and the early Darwinians were forced to demonstrate how natural selection could be used to interpret life's myriad processes, some modern biologists remain within this methodological paradigm (observe something in nature and tell a story about how it could have evolved through natural selection). Since there is really no reason to defend Darwinism any longer, it might be asked why continue to concern ourselves with whether or not something could be explained by natural selection. Of course it can. But the fact that we can say "of course it can" calls into question the very nature of this intellectual endeavor, at least if it is to be called science in the sense of the modern world. Most biologists know that with the various modes of natural selection that are now known to operate in nature,[24] any feature, be it structural or behavioral, can be rationalized with a story about how it may have evolved. And, as my first wife said,[25] a theory that explains everything is sort of like God.

Being able to rationalize almost any observation that is even theoretically possible creates the epistemological problem that whatever natural selection story is told, the structure of the argument is such that it can rarely be fully tested, at least in a scientifically rigorous fashion. Is the giraffe's neck long because of evolutionary pressure to eat leaves in higher strata of the vegetation, or because an elevated watchpost enabled an efficient sighting of lions? Again we are reminded of Gary Larson's cartoon of a giraffe standing on a chair looking for lions. Since we cannot look into the past to accurately evaluate the selection pressures operative on giraffes as their long necks were evolving, we have little basis on which to differentiate between these two possible adaptive stories. Worse yet, a story that may never occur to us may be the real answer. Since we live in the present, we sometimes tacitly assume that most of nature has always looked pretty much as it does today. That is false. Who knows what selective pressures may have existed in the past? For all we know there may have been a parasitic fly that entered giraffe-like animals through the nostrils, and always hovered below the prevailing vegetation. Giraffes with longer necks were less likely to be infected by this parasite than giraffes with shorter necks. Since the parasite became extinct during the ice ages, we no longer observe its effect, and shall forever live with the false impression that giraffes have long necks to eat high vegetation or sight lions more efficiently.

Since it is always possible to come up with a plausible adaptive story and since alternative stories may never come to mind, as selective pressures are not constant and we cannot use today's environment as a guide to the environments under which natural selection had been acting in the past, most evolutionary biologists have come to eschew this mode of analysis. While it was probably historically significant as a bulwark against the attacks of clerics, and even today it is an enjoyable cocktail party game, it is not likely to remain a centerpiece of evolutionary epistemology. Because of the charm of its simplicity it will probably continue reappearing in the popular literature, much as astrology and parapsychology exhibit remarkable endurance in our supposedly secular world.

While the critique of adaptive storytelling is a general critique of a particular current of evolutionary epistemology, there is a far more important critique when the methodology is applied to the particular animal *Homo sapiens*. It is sometimes suggested that, since humans are animals, they too are subject to nature's laws and thus we should not balk when we come applying evolutionary interpretations to our own species. As a general principle this is valid. Indeed, the entire development in chapter 3 followed the basic principles of evolutionary theory as we know it. However, as noted in that chapter, as we move from *Australopithecus* to *Homo habilis* to *Homo erectus* to *Homo sapiens,* we reach a point in which language and culture come to dominate the species. Because of this domination, whatever evolutionary interpretations may have been valid up to that point become subsumed under a different set of rules—the rules of cultural evolution. And the most important principle, frequently not fully appreciated, is that the rules of cultural evolution are not the same as the rules of organic evolution. Indeed, the strength of Darwinism emerges from the simple constraining fact that genes must be contained within individual organisms. A gene can thus spread through a population only through reproduction of that organism. A cultural gene, or what might be called a meme,[26] is not constrained to exist within individuals, and thus the constraint that makes organic evolution work the way it does no longer exists when we are concerned with the spread of a meme through a population. A "friendlier" mouse is likely to be friendlier because of a gene that makes it so, and thus it makes sense to consider how fast the friendly trait spreads through the population by looking at the reproductive habits of the mouse. A friendlier human is likely to be friendlier because of a cultural history that makes him or her so, and he or she may infect relatives and non-relatives alike with friendliness, thus rapidly diffusing this friendly attitude throughout the population. It makes no sense to interpret that friendliness as if it were something passed on mainly to the offspring of that individual.

The human animal is thus different from all other animals. In no sense does a recognition of this fact represent a rejection of the universality of the theory of evolution. Much as Newton's laws apply when all the assumptions are met, so Darwin's theory applies when all of the assumptions are met. One of the assumptions is that traits are controlled by factors that dwell in the bodies of individuals, and that those individuals are not able to change these factors during their lifetime—i.e., one is born with a set of genes contributed by one's mother and father, and one lives and dies with those same genes. If the factors could be changed during the life of an individual (as some Soviet geneticists of the 1940s and 1950s believed), the basis of the Darwinian theory would be different. Even worse, if the factors are not contained within the bodies of the individuals in the first place, the theory must be thrown out entirely. No one doubts that two objects dropped from the top of a tower will hit the ground at the same time, regardless of their weights. We know this because of Newton's theory and because of experiments that verified the theory, despite the fact that for most people the result seems quite counterintuitive. Yet, if we drop a lead ball and a feather from the top of the Eiffel Tower, they do *not* hit the ground at the same time. Another factor was involved—the atmosphere. Similarly, Darwinian theory says that a trait will spread through a population in accordance with the advantage it affords its bearer with respect to survival and reproduction. Yet we all know that guns do not spread through a population because gunbearers leave more offspring. Another factor is involved—culture.

This general picture has been accepted by most biologists and other scholars interested in human behavior. To those still searching for an evolutionary interpretation of human behavior, two avenues have been taken—first is the insistence that many human behavioral traits in fact are influenced by genetic factors, and thus are indeed within the bodies of the individuals concerned, and second is the assumption that cultural evolution follows the same rules as organic evolution. The first avenue is no longer very common, since the biological evidence of the past quarter-century has left little reason to believe it. For most characters, despite many claims in the popular literature, valiant attempts to demonstrate genetic effects have fallen short.[27] So the vast majority of the characteristics of human behavior that we wish to understand (e.g., friendliness, kindness, aggressiveness, xenophobia, greed, and class solidarity) are simply not amenable to analysis through evolutionary reasoning. Without genes, organic evolution does not happen.

But the argument becomes quite subtle. Clearly, all characteristics have a genetic basis ultimately, since genes do, in fact, control all of life. From time of conception until death, an individual human is a complex interplay of genes, environment, and developmental accident—a genetic script acted by interpretative environmental actors who don't always get their lines right. It is sometimes argued that the genetic effect is small but significant, and thus natural selection could act on it. There is no question that this position may ultimately turn out to be true, but it seems rather unlikely at our present state of knowledge. For natural selection to be an important force, it is not enough that a characteristic have "some" genetic basis; it must have a substantial effect in determining the phenotype. Suppose, for example, that in a given environment a big phenotype carries genotype A with a likelihood of 10 percent. That means that, on average, 10 of every 100 big phenotypes are genotype A. If natural selection acts to eliminate 10 percent of the big phenotypes from the population before they can breed, it will eliminate only a single individual, on average, of genotype A, each generation. Depending on how genotype A is subsequently inherited, the rate at which it becomes fixed in the population could be so small as to be simply insignificant. The story might be different if the likelihood that a big phenotype was genotype A were 99 percent, say. The point is, for natural selection to be a relevant force, the correlation between genotype and phenotype must be substantial. For most human behavioral characteristics of interest, that correlation has not even been shown to exist, let alone be substantial.

The lack of a sufficiently strong genetic basis that would permit natural selection to operate has been, for the most part, accepted among biologists (it does, on the other hand, appear that a variety of social scientists still retain the faith), for most significant human behavioral characteristics. Yet, this acceptance has given birth to a new interpretation. Yes, they agree, human behavioral characteristics are insufficiently correlated with human genetic factors to make natural selection operate in the classic way. But, they note, cultural characteristics also evolve, and natural selection may provide a tool for analyzing the evolution of cultural characteristics. The error in this reasoning was discussed in chapter 4. What gives such remarkable strength to the theory of evolution through natural selection is the simple fact that the transmission of phenotypes is through genes that are contained within individuals and can be transmitted from individual to individual only through the act of biological reproduction, and furthermore that changes in the genetic material (mutuations) are relatively rare. In the case of cultural characteristics, they are not restricted to a location within individuals, nor do they mutate only slowly. Thus the formal theory that biologists use to understand natural selection does not apply to these characteristics.[28] The lead ball really does hit the ground before the feather, simply because the assumptions of the theory that says otherwise are not met.

That we ought to try understanding how cultures evolved is, of course, not under debate. Indeed, that is precisely what the great social thinkers have been doing, from Durkheim to Weber to Marx, from Freud to Jung, from Smith to Veblen to Keynes, from Margaret Mead to Levi-Strauss. Indeed, the intellectual tradition of trying to deal with this problem is rich. The fact that not much progress has been made is not due to the lack of intellectual vigor and brilliant minds that have worked on it in the past and continue their work today, but rather to the immense complexity of the subject matter—a major theme of this book. To relegate all of this complexity to the notion, for example, that Islam spread through the world in the seventh and eighth centuries because those who believed in Mohammed left more offspring that those who didn't, is just a little silly.

There is a final criticism that is always difficult to elaborate since it rings (wrongly) of censorship. In its essence, this criticism is metaphorically the same as crying "fire" in a crowded theater. As is always noted in this particular conundrum, the freedom to say what you want carries with it a certain responsibility to say things that will not cause harm to others. If you wish to yell "fire" in a crowded theater, you ought to be sure that there really is a fire before you cause a stampede. Similarly, when speaking of humans, we should, of course, always tell the truth. But making pronouncements that may cause harm, before the truth of those pronouncements can be assessed with confidence, is irresponsible. The claim that African Americans score lower on IQ tests than European Americans because of genetic factors was an example of such irresponsibility. The claim that women tend not to ascend to executive positions because their genetic makeup suits them to stay at home and take care of the kids is another. Indeed, both statements may in the end turn out to be true (although I rather doubt it, given the current state of overwhelming evidence against them), but until it can be ascertained with a great deal of certainty, making such statements is akin to crying "fire" in the crowded theater.

This is, of course, not a scientific point, but rather a political one. Since the structure of the arguments surrounding the field of evolution and human behavior are all aimed at showing how extant behaviors are the result of natural selecton, there is more than a hint that everything we see is natural. And if it is natural, we shouldn't change it, we should not even want to change it. If God (or natural selection) says that women are not equipped to be corporate executives, who are we to try and go against His will? If God (or natural selection) made blacks dumber than whites, who are we to try and change it? By its very nature, this is a very conservative political philosophy. And whether one is conservative or not, bolstering a poltical philosophy with lies is simply not right.

These, then, are the three criticisms of the use of the theory of natural selection to explain human behavior. First is the general critique that simply telling adaptive stories, while probably important during the times that the concept of organic evolution was under serious attack, is not science and is not likely to lead to any greater understanding of nature. Second is the specific critique that humans, because of the unique feature of language and culture, behave in ways that operate under different rules than other animals, including the tendency to construct socially and form strong discourses. Most of the interesting characteristics of human behavior thus are not under strong enough genetic influence to be available for natural selection to act. While the serious study of how social construction occurs or how discourses form and disintegrate or a variety of other human behavioral traits is of tremendous interest, as indicated in various other parts of this book, formulating such studies in terms of the adaptive question (why would someone exhibiting this behavior tend to leave more offspring?) is thus quite pointless. Third, there is a certain political perniciousness associated with such methodology. Since anything whatsoever that humans do can be rationalized with an adaptive story (that is the structure of the field), all that currently exists can easily come to be seen as nature's unalterable way. Clearly this could be seen as a bulwark for conservative ideology.

Gender and Gender Roles

At the time of this writing, women in the United States remain under-represented in the sciences and math[1] and gays and lesbians must not proclaim their homosexuality aloud if they want to be in the U.S. military. Embedded in the enormous complexity of both of these issues are certain ideas about biology, frequently influenced either explicitly or implicitly by an essentialist philosophy. And here, biological determinism is not the provenance of either the political right or the left, but takes on some very curious forms with various political tendencies claiming not only that their gender or gender orientation is biologically determined but also that it is superior to the biologically determined others. While the biology here is considerably more difficult and unsettled than in the case of race, too often the various positions are not consistent with even the biology that is uncontested. The purpose of this chapter is to provide an overview of this uncontested biology, and explore some of the related sociopolitical questions.

The historical division of labor between the two major genders has been one of the strongest divisions of labor throughout recorded history, ebbing and flowing to some extent, but for the most part forming a central core of social rules in all societies. Furthermore, with few exceptions, the gender role assigned to the male is usually the one that receives the most prestige, at least as the males see it.

Embedded in this history are many remnants of outmoded thinking about gender and gender roles, many conventional assumptions that bear little, if any, relationship to available facts, and the normal assortment of biases that are thought to be bolstered by these assumptions and thinking. It will be the purpose of the present chapter to challenge such biases by challenging the underlying assumptions on which they are based. The assumptions are not necessarily articulable in a compact form, being quite eclectic in both origin and form, but they fall into the general category that I have identified earlier as the natural structures school of thought, or biological essentialism. Generally, women are thought to be the way they are (whatever that may be) because of their genetic makeup, hormonal characteristics, or evolutionary history. To what extent are such thoughts justifiable in light of modern biology?

In a distinct but related way, the biological determination of homosexuality is currently a hotly debated topic. Here, there is a curious turn of events, in that many gays and lesbians seem to be promoting the idea that their orientation is genetically determined, presumably under the assumption that if homosexuality is biologically determined, discrimination against gays and lesbians will make less sense. Later in this chapter, I will argue that first, the biology supporting the claim is, at best, very weak, and second, that the political analysis is extremely flawed. While these questions certainly transcend national boundaries, I begin with an examination of gender roles in U.S. society, and acknowledge from the start that the story might very well be quite different in other societies.

SOME BASIC DEFINITIONS

As elaborated in some detail below, one's identity regarding gender is almost completely formed prior to adolescence.[2] So it makes sense to focus on pre-adolescent children in an exploration of the relevant biological forces. Here things are quite obvious to anyone in the cultures of the industrialized West, where adult gender roles, while currently undergoing revolutionary transformations, have been highly stereotyped for many generations. Children routinely reflect these adult roles, and while the adult roles can be quite variable, the preadolescent child typically reflects a narrower set of behaviors that are readily observable. Little girls are made of sugar and spice, while little boys are somehow fashioned from puppydog tails. Actual testimony from a mother of twins, a boy and a girl, typifies the behaviors we all recognize:

> She [referring to her little girl] likes for me to wipe her face. She doesn't like to be dirty, and yet my son is quite different. I can't wash his face for anything. . . . She seems to be daintier . . . she is so feminine. I've never seen a little girl so neat and tidy as she can be when she wants to be . . . she is very

proud of herself, when she puts on a new dress, or I set her hair. She just loves to have her hair set; she could sit under the drier all day long to have her hair set. She just loves it.[3]

Further testimony punctuates the same basic idea. The mother goes on to describe how her daughter tries to help in cleaning the kitchen while the son could not care less about it, how the girl wanted dolls and "girl toys" for Christmas while the boy wanted cars and "boy toys," how the girl is more sensitive and feeling than the boy. Finally, probably indicating more about the mother than the children (but nevertheless important), the mother goes on to say,

> . . . I would like for both of them to go to college and university, and have some kind of career. That's what I would like for them . . . As long as they get their high school, at least my daughter. My son, it's almost essential, since he will be earning a living for the rest of his life. . . . I found that my son, he chose very masculine things like a fireman or a policeman or something like that. He wanted to do what daddy does, work where daddy does, and carry a lunch kit, and drive a car. And she didn't want any of those things.[4]

The astute reader will undoubtedly note that these expressions not only reflect how a great many people see girls and boys in our society, but also probably indicate a great deal of the mother's prejudices both in how she sees the behaviors and in how she reinforces her son's and daughter's behaviors. Both of these issues are extremely important, and we will return to them below. But for now, the general pattern described for the girl and boy are presented as kind of ideal types: the little girl, neat, tidy, sensitive, and practicing female gender behavior, and the little boy, dirty, rough, and practicing male gender behavior. These are the behavior patterns we seek to understand, from a biological—and otherwise—point of view.

Before examining the details of this issue, it is imperative to understand exactly what is being discussed. The first two concepts that are key to even begin a discussion of the issues are gender role and gender identity. These are concepts first articulated by Money and Ehrhardt in their classic work, *Man and Woman, Boy and Girl* (1972). As stated by Money and Ehrhardt, *gender identity* is

> The sameness, unity, and persistence of one's individuality as male, female, or ambivalent, in greater or lesser degree, especially as it is experienced in

self-awareness and behavior; gender identity is the private experience of gender role, and gender role is the public expression of gender identity.

Gender role is

> Everything that a person says and does, to indicate to others or to the self the degree that one is either male, or female, or ambivalent; it includes but is not restricted to sexual arousal and response; gender role is the public expression of gender identity, and gender identity is the private experience of gender role.

These are the formal definitions. They are difficult definitions to give in a scientifically rigorous way because they are trying to codify something that is inherently difficult to codify. There are generally three different genders: male, female, and ambivalent.[5] Everyone in the society "feels" inside that he or she is one of those genders. Usually the gender identity corresponds to the associated sex of the individual (the "sex" of the individual is not necessarily well defined either, as discussed below), although in a significant number of cases this is not true. Similarly, the gender role usually corresponds to the associated sex of the individual, but not always. The question of homo, hetero, and bisexuality frequently emerges in this discussion. I suggest that this topic is a red herring at this point, and will deal with it in more detail later. For now, accept the fact that the vast majority of gay males have a male gender identity and role and the vast majority of lesbians have a female gender identity and role, while bisexuals most often correspond to the gender identity and role associated with their sex. Thus, in the first part of this chapter, we are talking of identity and role associated with gender, independent of sexual orientation. Indeed, this entire way of looking at the issue is not conducive to the understanding of the question of homo-hetero-bisexuality. Best to think of the latter under a different set of variables, as will be discussed later. For now, we shall be concerned with the sexes, male and female (and ambivalent), and the gender identities and roles, male and female (and ambivalent).

At this point, we must introduce some basic anatomical and other biological facts into the discussion (readers already familiar with the terms chromosome, sex chromosome, hormone, gonad, and genitalia may skip the next three paragraphs). In the nucleus of each cell of the body of each organism on earth,[6] there are small structures that contain most of the DNA of the cell—the chromosomes. In the case of *Homo sapiens,* each cell contains 46 chromosomes, arranged in 23 pairs (see Figure 7.1). One pair in particular is structurally distinct in males versus females (depending, of course, on your definition of male and female), the male containing one member of the pair notably smaller than the other member. This smaller, seemingly deformed, member of the pair is referred to as the y chromosome, and the associated larger member is referred to as the x chromosome. The x and y together are known as the sex chromosomes and usually determine whether a person is male or female, a person with two x's (xx) being a female and a person with an x and a y (xy) being a male. As we will see below, it is not always the case that females are xx nor that males are xy, but it is the most frequent occurrence. Recall the difference between gene and chromosome, genes being sections of DNA[7] and chromosomes being the relatively large structures that contain the DNA.

The human body, like the bodies of all organisms, contains various subunits that must be coordinated in order to make the whole function properly. Such coordination requires some form of communication so that one part of the body knows what another part is doing, so to speak. There are two types of messages that our bodies use for this purpose, nerve impulses and hormones (electrical and chemical messages, respectively). If our body's nervous system is like the electrical system in a typical house, the hormone system would be a system of odors. We can tell if it is a particular holiday if we wake up to the smell of a telltale food being prepared in the kitchen, or we know that someone may have forgotten to take the garbage out for a week even if we do not see the garbage. Hormones are made mainly by glands in the body (collectively referred to as endocrine glands for most hormones, and gonads for the sex hormones), and are carried throughout the body by the blood. Referring to the biology of sex, there are two classes of relevant hormones (known as sex hormones), estrogens and androgens, the former occurring in both male and female, the latter occurring in large concentrations in the male. Thus, estrogens are usually thought of as female hormones and androgens as male hormones, although both types are found in both males and females—it is their relative concentrations at particular times of life that become important. It is extremely important to note the points in development when

---

Figure 7.1. Human chromosomes from blood sample. Top figure is appearance of original preparation, and bottom figure has the chromosomes rearranged in 23 homologous pairs. Note the dimorphism in the xy pair in the lower figure.

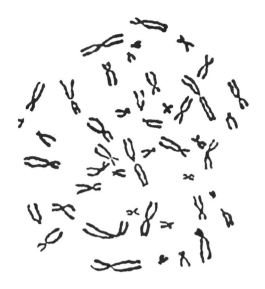

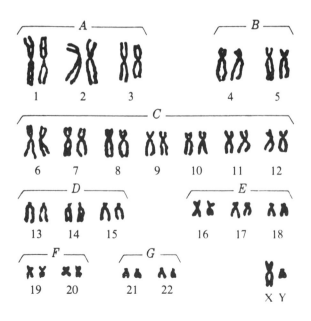

the sex hormones are operative. For all practical purposes, sex hormones are extremely important in fetal development and adult life, being virtually nonexistent in the period between birth and adolescence.

The gonads are the sex organs, referred to as testes and ovaries in animals and ovule and anther in plants. The testes are contained within the scrotum, the scrotum and penis together being the male external genitalia and the vagina, major and minor labia, and clitoris being the female external genitalia. Male and female genitalia develop from identical primordia, as illustrated in Figure 7.2. Remember, the gonads, which produce the sex hormones, are internal (within the scrotum in males and within the body in females) and the genitalia are external.

Proceeding with basic definitions, we are now confronted with the definition of sex itself. Sex may be genetic, chromosomal, hormonal, or social. Almost always, all four definitions are consonant, but in a significant number of cases, they may be discordant in a given individual, representing important information for understanding the relationship between gender and biology. Genetic sex refers to the message given to the individual by the DNA. For some animals it is now well known that a very small piece of the DNA on the sex chromosome (the y chromosome for the male, the x chromosome for the female) determines whether female or male gonads will be formed, and thus, indirectly, whether the individual will be male or female. It is not known for sure, but it is strongly suspected that the same is true for *H. sapiens,* and, if so, it is certainly conceivable to transfer the male genes that occupy only a very small part of the y chromosome to the position of the female genes on the x chromosome, thus creating an individual that has male genes and female chromosomes. We thus must distinguish (although, in practice, this distinction is not really important) between genetic sex and chromosomal sex, the former being the sex that is dictated by the genes, the latter being the sex that is dictated by the chromosomes. In all cases that we know of thus far, the genetic sex and chromosomal sex are always consonant. This is not true for hormonal sex and chromosomal/genetic sex.

The hormonal sex is defined as the sex based on the relative concentrations of sex hormones in the body, and can naturally be distinct from the chromosomal sex, as discussed below.

Finally, social sex is the sex that is assigned to the child by society, beginning with the mother and closest family, through the extended family and other social contacts that may occur. The social sex need not be

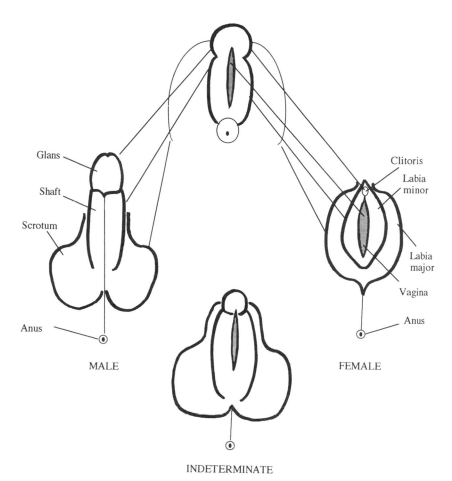

Figure 7.2. Development of male and female genitalia from the same primordia. Lower figure is representative of indeterminate external genitalia.

consistent with either the hormonal nor chromosomal sex, although in the vast majority of cases it is.

In proceeding to a detailed analysis of this problem, it is good to recall the basic terms of the debate that has raged since modern biology emerged at the end of the nineteenth century. It is the old nature-versus-nurture debate, and here, even more than in the case of race, framing the debate in these terms rather obscures the issue. As we shall see in the next section, genes and environment interplay with one another in complex ways during the developmental process, and it is no easier to assign priority to one or the other than it would be to answer the question, "What makes a car go, the motor or the driver?"

THE CONSTRUCTION OF GENDER ROLE AND GENDER IDENTITY[8]

The developmental process from egg to birth, using the elementary transformations explained in the previous chapter, is illustrated in Figure 7.3. We begin with the fertilized egg. As the embryo develops, it reaches a stage in which the gonadal tissue (the part of the embryo that will eventually form the gonads) begins developing, as dictated by the genes in the cells of the developing embryo. Once the cells that are going to become the gonads begin their development as such, genes within those cells direct the formation of hormones. The resulting hormones start circulating through the body of the developing embryo and begin turning on certain genes in those cells that will eventually form the external sexual characteristics, causing them to develop in either the direction of male or female

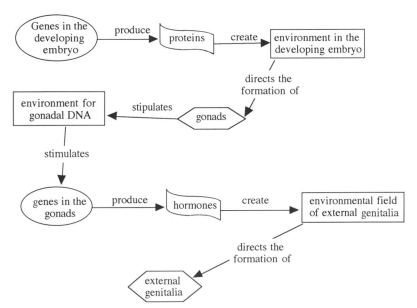

Figure 7.3. Developmental sequence for intrauterine fetal development.

external genitalia and internal sex organs. Thus, there is a three-stage process prior to birth: (1) the genes in the cells of the developing embryo direct the formation of gonads, within which (2) genes direct the formation of hormones, which in turn (3) cause genes in other tissues to be turned on to form either male or female organs, including the external genitalia. At this point, birth occurs.

After birth, sex hormones are no longer produced until the onset of puberty, but significant forces nevertheless act on the developing child, as indicated in Figure 7.4. At the time of birth, the first major event is not directed at the child itself, but rather at the society around it, namely the

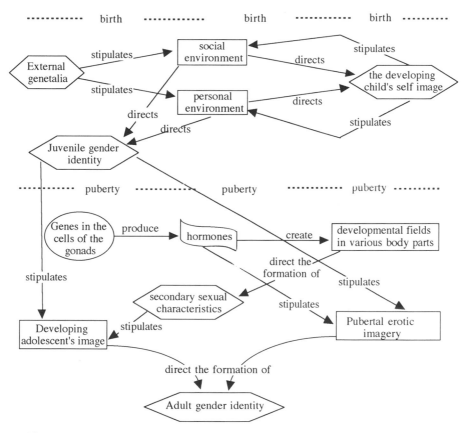

Figure 7.4. Post-parturition developmental sequence (based on Money and Ehrhardt (1972); see text).

mother, midwife (or doctor, nurse, etc.), and, frequently, the father. That is, the newly born child causes a social reaction in its nearby society. The social reaction of the closest relatives causes the child to be presented to the rest of society in a particular way, in turn causing that society to respond in a particular way. If the child has a penis and scrotum it is presented to the society as a boy, and the society responds by interacting with the child in specific ways, some of which are different from the way they interact with girls. In a classic psychological experiment,[9] babies were given to adult subjects to hold and interact with. The subjects were told the child was either a boy or girl, irrespective of its actual sex (the babies were wearing diapers at the time), such that for a given test the subject may have had a boy in his or her hands, but was told that the child was a girl, or vice versa. The subjects were then observed from behind a one-way mirror and the results were spectacular. Individuals who thought the baby was a girl played gently with it, talked about little-girl things, and spoke very softly. Individuals who thought it was a boy interacted accordingly. Clearly, the child had an important effect on the society around it—that is, the subjects who were observed interacting with it—and the society reciprocated by treating the child appropriately to the expectations of its gender.

As the child develops, the social reactions of its family and the more general society around it, along with the child's own experience with its external sexual characteristics, form the developing child's image of him or herself. The child's self image, as well as the continual reactions of others in its world, then direct the formation of the child's juvenile gender identity. The whole process from birth to the end of the juvenile period has been one almost exclusively dominated by the interaction of the growing child with the society around him or her. The process can be thought of in three general steps: (1) the baby's external genitalia cause a social reaction in the parents and closest siblings, which cause the child to be treated in a specific manner; (2) the specific manner in which the child is treated, plus the external genitalia, cause a social reaction in the developing child's image of her or himself; and (3) the developing child's image of her or himself, plus the social reactions of others, cause the juvenile gender identity to be formed.

The next major event is puberty, at which point the hormones begin to kick in again. At the onset of puberty, genes in the cells of the gonads direct the formation of hormones, which in turn cause certain other genes to become active. The active genes in the appropriate body parts direct the formation of secondary sexual characteristics, such as body hair, strategic body fat, lowered voice, mammary glands, and the like. The combination of the newly acquired secondary sexual characteristics plus the juvenile gender identity direct the formation of the developing adolescent's image of him or herself, at the same time as the juvenile gender identity combined with the level of hormones circulating through the body direct the formation of the pubertal erotic imagery. Thus, at this point, the erotic imagery—whether one becomes sexually aroused mainly by males or females—as well as the personal self-image, are both determined in a major way by the juvenile gender identity, although the hormones enter into the picture at least indirectly through the secondary sexual characteristics, and perhaps more directly, although this latter point remains something of a controversy. Finally, the pubertal self-image plus the pubertal erotic imagery direct the formation of the adult gender identity. The role of the pubertal erotic imagery here is somewhat controversial, since it is clearly the case that most gay males and lesbians have either same-sex erotic imagery or ambiguous erotic imagery, yet for the most part develop a gender identity consistent with their sex rather than their erotic imagery.

Thus, the sequence from puberty to adult may be visualized in five interrelated steps: (1) genes in the cells of the gonads direct the formation of hormones, (2) the hormones turn on genes in appropriate body parts to direct the formation of secondary sexual characteristics, (3) the secondary sexual characteristics combined with the juvenile gender identity direct the formation of the self-image, (4) the juvenile gender identity, and perhaps hormone level, direct the formation of erotic imagery, and (5) the juvenile gender identity, along with the self-image and the erotic imagery, direct the formation of the adult gender identity. All of this is illustrated in Figure 7.4.

The final step in this developmental sequence has to do with the transition from adult gender identity to adult gender role. This sequence is somewhat more difficult to describe, since it is not exactly well known, at least not in the sense that the development of gender identity is. Apparently some combination of adult gender identity coupled with certain social rules and political arrangements direct the formation of the adult gender role. Acting out the adult gender role of course leads to the very social rules and political arrangements that direct the formation of the social reactions to babies, thus starting the whole cycle over again. This being

the case, it is fairly obvious that changing social rules and political arrangements would have substantial effects on gender roles in the society at large,
since the cyclic nature of gender identity determination would be changed.
Indeed, throughout the course of history, this is likely how gender roles
have been modified.

RELATIVE IMPACTS OF BIOLOGY AND SOCIETY ON GENDER IDENTITY FORMATION

The above scenario makes it quite evident that the only reasonable vision
of gender identity is one that views genes, hormones, and the social environment as interacting codeterminants of the developmental process (and
do not forget the role of developmental accident). Indeed, in most cases,
the system works very smoothly in that a genetic and chromosomal male
produces testosterone, is treated like a male by society, and develops a
male gender identity and role. But sometimes, alternative pathways are
followed. Recall from the previous chapter how accidents are part and
parcel of the developmental process. In the case of gender, there are sometimes very large and spectacular alternative pathways that the process
follows.

First, there are many cases in which one or another step in the development of gender identity is blocked or distorted in some fashion. When
this happens in the general arena of hormones or genes, it is treated as a
medical problem, and when it happens in the arena of social relations, it is
generally ignored. Second, there are points in history when the political
arrangements in the cycle are challenged by one or another party (usually
the female of the species), frequently resulting in attempts by those opposed to change claiming that the extant system is somehow natural, emphasizing the biological—hormonal and genetic—side of the process.

Both of these exceptional cases are of interest. The second is of special
interest today, since the feminist movement that arose in the 1960s has
been growing and challenging many traditional ideas of sex roles, at least
in most of the developed world. As expected, those who benefit from
maintaining ideas as they were are attempting to emphasize the biological
side of the coin, and traditional family values are vaguely argued to be part
of our genetic and/or hormonal heritage. The first is of special interest in
that it provides us with an enormous amount of solid evidence concerning
the role of the various biological forces. That is, if one is concerned with

the question of whether biology or society is destiny, we are able to say quite a bit about the importance of genes or hormones relative to the social environment, mainly based on those medical cases in which individuals are not consonant for the various types of sex, as defined above. We have many cases in which an individual who is genetically a male turns out to be a hormonal female, due to an accident of development. Or an individual who is a hormonal and genetic female is socially determined to be a male. This is the sort of information that can be used to gain evidence one way or another about the relative importance of biological and social forces in the determination of gender identity.

I caution the reader from the outset that the determination of gender identity is a complex process that involves genes, hormones, and society in a web of interconnectedness, as described above. So, as we proceed to discuss the evidence relevant to the biological determination of sex roles, always keep in mind that the process is ultimately best described as a continual feedback loop between biological and social processes.

Before we look at the accumulated medical evidence, it would make sense to ask what sort of information would be completely convincing—what sort of evidence would be unequivocal? It would be ideal to have genetically identical individuals, one of which is female and the other, male. Naturally, this is impossible, but for the ideal experiment this is what we would require. The two genetically identical individuals should be raised in the same environment in all respects except sex. Considering the developmental sequence as described above, such an experiment would allow us to determine to what extent the genetic messages of the developing child were seeping through the social messages. The children would be raised in the same environment, with the same genes, but with different socialization regarding sex roles. If we see differences between the two, those differences cannot be due to the genes, and must be a consequence of the social part of the above sequence.

Such an experiment was actually done. In an unfortunate medical accident, when a pair of identical twin boys both underwent the ritual of circumcision, the penis of one of the children was cut off. Naturally, this was a grave accident, which was shocking for the parents. After substantial medical and psychological counseling, the parents decided to raise the second child as a girl, and after appropriate constructive plastic surgery (to make the girl's external genitalia appear female), the children began their normal lives. The boy was raised as a boy, the girl as a girl, and neither child knew their genetic sex. So we have here a case where the genetic sex and the assigned sex were different for one of the children (a situation for which we have many other examples, as described below), and we can ask the question, "To what extent does the genetic message 'I am a boy' sneak through the social message 'You are a girl' "?

Fortunately for science, this case was followed fairly closely by medical researchers, and we have a great deal of qualitative information about the childhood of these two children. During their entire preadolescent lives, neither child knew of the background, the boy thus thinking he was a boy, the girl thinking she was a girl (which, of course, was true in the sense of assigned sex for both children). What was the result of this experiment? Take, for example, testimony from the mother:

> She [referring to her little girl] likes for me to wipe her face. She doesn't like to be dirty, and yet my son is quite different. I can't wash his face for anything. . . . She seems to be daintier. . . . One thing that really amazes me is that she is so feminine. I've never seen a little girl so neat and tidy as she can be when she wants to be. . . .[10]

As the reader may recall, this is the testimony I used to introduce the subject of gender role and gender identity. That is, these two children were about as normal a little boy and girl as one could imagine. If the genetic message "I am a boy" was coming through, it certainly was not detectable by either the parents or the children.

The little girl did, in fact, engage in a significant amount of "tomboyish" behavior, but not outside of the range normally exhibited by girls. Furthermore, the experiment was only relevant until the time of puberty, since at that time the gonads would start producing sex hormones again, and the little girl would have to be told about her condition in order to begin appropriate hormone therapy, such that she would not develop male secondary sexual characteristics. But within the confines of the experiment, the results are quite spectacular, and clearly not what had been expected. Apparently, the social forces associated with one's perception of oneself, which derives not only from one's body, but from what friends and acquaintances say, is overwhelmingly important in the formation of juvenile gender identity. The genes, if they play any role at all, appear to be of minor importance at this point in the developmental sequence (the genes are nevertheless quite important in the developing embryo, being ultimately responsible for setting the nature of the external genitalia, which, of course, is the key stimulus that sets off the social sequence in the first place).

One must be cautious in interpreting a single experiment such as this. After all, it is only a single case and it is possible that if it were repeated with a different set of twins, something else would happen. A single example should always be suspect. Furthermore, the mother and father of these children clearly knew that the little girl was a genetic boy and could have unknowingly treated her differently. That difference could have been either in the direction of overcompensating for the fact that she was genetically male, thus emphasizing the social aspect, or it could have been in the direction of subtly treating her more tomboyishly, that being her "natural" state. We have no way of sorting out such subtle effects, and simply have to admit that the experiment was not, after all, perfect. Its results are spectacular and say quite a lot about the role of genes versus socialization during the preadolescent years, but we should nevertheless take those results as tentative.

A variety of related studies are also relevant. These studies have been done with matched pairs of hermaphrodites. Hermaphroditism is a condition in which the external genitalia are ambiguous, for example, an enlarged clitoris (or micro penis), or reduced scrotal sac (or enlarged labia), such that the newborn cannot clearly be labeled a boy or a girl (see Figure 7.2). There are multiple origins of the condition, as one could probably deduce from simply examining the general processes of fetal development. For example, in the developing embryo, the fetal gonads usually secrete sex hormones in a mix appropriate to the sex of the embryo (mainly estrogens for females and mainly androgens for males). At a particular point during the developmental sequence, the hormones produced by the fetal gonads (for example, androgens) direct the formation of the external sexual characteristics (which would be male in the case of androgens). If at that point in time the mother's body contains a high level of some particular hormone (say estrogen, which could be in abnormally high concentrations for a variety of reasons), that hormone may leak across the placenta and become intermingled with the blood of the embryo. If the estrogen leaking from the mother's blood supply overwhelms the androgen produced by the embryo's gonads, the child, who is a genetic and hormonal boy, may be born with genitalia of a girl. More likely, the estrogen is likely to provoke some female development and the androgen some male development and the genitalia come out looking intermediate between the two. This is just one of the possibilities that can produce children whose genitalia are ambiguous—hermaphrodites. It is quite possible to have genetic and hormonal females who are structurally males, or genetic and hormonal males who are structurally females. But the most common form of this sort of ambiguity is hermaphroditism.

The usual way of dealing with hermaphroditism is through plastic surgery and reassignment of sex. That is, the parents of a hermaphrodite make a decision to raise their child as a boy or girl, and having made that decision, they usually elect to have plastic surgery done on their baby to reconstruct it according to the assigned sex. Consequently, there are many cases in which a baby is raised as a female when its genetic and hormonal sex is male, and vice versa. It is not generally thought that the gender assignment of "ambiguous" is healthy for the child, and thus, to my knowledge, there are no individuals in the world who have been intentionally raised ambiguous, although in recent years several examples of people who nevertheless feel quite ambivalent have come forth. Our discussion here will focus on those individuals who have had a definite assignment to either male or female, by far the vast majority of hermaphrodites.

The condition is relatively rare, but common enough to provide a strong data base for the questions at hand. In their pioneering work, *Man and Woman, Boy and Girl,* authors Money and Ehrhardt summarize a number of hermaphrodite studies. Most interesting are a series of studies in which hermaphrodites were match-paired for as many factors as possible, except for assigned sex. That is, for example, two people would be a single matched pair if they were approximately the same age, from the same socioeconomic class, had acquired their hermaphroditism from the same developmental sequence, and so on. The only specifically desired difference between them was their assigned sex. The development of gender identity was then studied for these matched pairs (the matched pairs are as close to the ideal experiment as we are ever likely to get, since the genetic and hormonal sex of the matched pair are identical and as many of the other factors as possible have been made identical, but the assigned sex is distinct).

The interested reader is referred to the Money and Ehrhardt text for the many intriguing details of these studies. But, as a general summary, it can be said, quite unequivocally, that the studies overwhelmingly support the idea that the assigned sex is far more important than the genetic/hormonal sex in determining juvenile gender identity, and sex roles in general. Several lines of evidence suggest that the genetic and hormonal effect may be leaking through at subtle levels, but the overall determination of the gender identity appears to be the social component.

These studies are clearly not the ideal studies. Among their various problems is the likely tendency of parents to choose plastic surgery consistent with the general tendency that appears in the external genitalia. If that general tendency is correlated with the hormonal levels in the fetus (a likely prospect), the possibility that the hormones could have affected some other aspect of the developing embryo (e.g., some aspect of brain development) cannot be discarded. The conclusions from these studies must thus be taken quite tentatively.

In the end, we must come to the conclusion that, taking all the studies together, it would appear that while the socialization process involved in the development of juvenile gender identity appears to be overwhelmingly important, the question remains an open one in a strictly scientific sense. On the other hand, it is abundantly clear that the other side of the coin is completely incorrect. Those who suggest that biology is somehow destiny, and that we risk something negative by changing the various cultural and political forces that direct the behavior patterns associated with gender differences, have nothing scientifically valid supporting their case. If there is a biological force determining gender identity or role, it is sufficiently subtle that it has pretty much escaped detection after many years of serious study.

OPRESSION BASED ON GENDER

At least some of the biological forces involved in gender issues are reasonably clear, as indicated above. Others remain enigmatic. Indeed, even the basic definitions have recently been questioned. Ann Fausto-Sterling[11] has suggested that there are at least five sexes, although two of them are far more common than the other three.

The extreme position taken by some that the female role in society is largely determined by biological forces is wrong. The position that suggests that females are endowed with similar potentials as males seems substantially correct, with some obvious exceptions (e.g., females will probably always be, on average, physically smaller than males). Why, then, do almost all societies in the world have institutions that clearly oppress women? In some New Guinean tribes, women are routinely gang-raped as part of cultural traditions; many African cultures still practice clitoridectomies; women in India are beaten and sometimes killed for failure to meet dowry demands—the list is, unfortunately, long. And the tendency is not that such oppression is sometimes one way and sometimes the other, as we might expect given the lack of significant biological input into the gender identification process. In virtually all cultures, women are regarded as the inferior sex and treated accordingly.

To understand such oppression we must first acknowledge that the actual behaviors constituting gender role are quite variable from culture to culture. In the Western industrialized cultures, women are the sensitive, intuitive, nurturing sex and the males are the "warriors" (although their current battlefields are a bit metaphorical), the breadwinners, rugged and insensitive. In other cultures, such specific behaviors seem almost reversed, with the females taking on the rugged "Marlboro Man" image and the males being more gentle and nurturing. But what seems invariable is, first, the tendency for a strong distinguishing sequence of dual behaviors (i.e., one for males and one for females), and, second, a devaluation of those patterns assigned to the female.

It is beyond the purposes of this book to pursue this topic in much more depth. A great deal of recent work done by feminist scholars has shed some light on the question, but, in my opinion, has mainly served to confirm what many had expected all along—it is an extremely complicated issue. As *Homo sapiens* emerged from *H. erectus,* it is quite possible that gender differences already were in place, and even quite possible that at that time genetic forces were more in play than they are today. By the time modern *Homo sapiens* emerged from archaic *H. sapiens,* language and culture were already dominating human affairs, and it is thus likely that cultural evolution already had begun molding gender differences. The Neolithic revolution coincided with a sedentary life style and, among other things, certainly removed various barriers to the female gender—for example, the probable elimination of spacing children relatively far apart so the migratory habits of the hunting and gathering life style were not impeded. This event alone would have had a strong impact on whatever social forces constructed gender roles. Undoubtedly, many other material changes had similar influence on the cultural evolution of gender role. But deciding exactly what those forces were, how they operated, and what patterns emerged from them, awaits further study.

Specifically in the industrial West, feminist scholarship has made significant inroads into our understanding of these issues, although much much more remains to be done. Recently, Carol Tavris [12] summarized the prevalent ideas that seem to have emerged after the past half century of scholarship and political work on women's issues and the response to them. According to Tavris, one can summarize the variety of viewpoints in three general categories: (1) men are normal, women are "opposite" and deficient; (2) men are normal, women are "opposite" but superior; (3) men are normal, women are (or should be) like them. Her point is relatively clear from her formulation of the problem—that the entire analysis proceeds from the point of view that "men are normal," which automatically implies something about women (something other than "women are normal").

Such misdirected formulation has resulted in a distortion of gender issues in a variety of ways, not just in terms of the direct oppression of women. For example, on political issues society typically thinks in terms of the "important issues" such as drugs, the state of the economy, warfare, and international relations, while a whole series of issues that really ought to be taken just as seriously are thought of as "women's issues," such as day care, birth control, and peace. The way pressing problems are practically faced also bears the scars of this bias. Consider, for example, the presumably uncontroversial question of international violations of human rights. There are legitimate issues, such as freedom of expression, freedom of assembly and organization, and there are "illegitimate" issues, such as denial of women's suffrage, wife-beating, genital mutilation, and forced prostitution. Even the formulation of problems in the first place can be hopelessly corrupted, as reflected, for example, in ready acceptance of newspaper articles talking about the feminization of poverty—I have yet to see an article containing the phrase "the masculinization of wealth."

After examining these issues in some detail, Tavris concludes,

> [Women's] dilemmas will persist as long as we look exclusively inward to their psyches and biology instead of outward to their circumstances, and as long as women are blamed for not measuring up.

The previous discussion of this chapter is perfectly consistent with such an opinion. While I can hardly disagree with Tavris on her programmatic conclusion, a further point ought to be made. Much of the perceptive analysis that Tavris and other feminist writers have been able to present is based on serious studies of gender issues. Such studies are obviously crucially important, given the way societies around the world are changing, and one can at once applaud the efforts of the many women's studies programs that seriously consider such issues and damn the society that refuses to give such programs the support and respect they deserve. It is in this academic setting that some day we will understand more about the genesis, nature, and potential for change on this all-important topic.

THE QUESTION OF HOMOSEXUALITY[13]

Perhaps the only minority group in the United States that remains a target of legalized discrimination is the one associated with some form of same-sex orientation. Gays, lesbians, and bisexuals are constantly reminded of their predicament by many forms of subtle social and political discrimination, extreme violence directed against them, and Jim Crow-like laws that make it legal to discriminate against them. The disorder known as homophobia, whose etiology remains somewhat of a mystery, afflicts many straight people and occasionally results in outbursts of violence, usually directed at gay males. Yet it is the subtle effects of homophobia that are the most pernicious, since they penetrate many aspects of daily personal and professional life, and alter people's behavior in ways that even they find hard to understand. This has resulted in a society that is not exactly pleasant for people engaging in some degree of homosexual orientation, a situation that is not universal, neither across regions nor over time.

The response to this condition by those most directly affected has, to some extent, paralleled the civil rights movement. Political mobilizations to gain civil rights for gays and lesbians began to spread in the industrialized world in the 1960s and have continued to the present. As part of these mobilizations, a degree of pride has replaced much of the guilt that used to be associated with a homosexual orientation, and gays and lesbians have come to view their sexual orientation as normal and healthy, even if homophobia continues to plague the straight society around them. Yet within that newfound and justifiable gay pride, an essentialist trend has begun to emerge, curiously paralleling the earlier arguments of some homophobes who argued that homosexuality was a natural abomination. Naturally, the new essentialism does not regard homosexuality as an abomination, but does regard it as "natural." Some proponents of gay rights have concluded that if there is a biological basis for their sexual orientation, it would be difficult for society to continue its oppression of them. Others have responded that in other circumstances, for example Nazi Germany, it was an underlying assumption that homosexuality was in fact biologically determined, a fact that had little effect on the devastating consequences of homophobia. The notion that gay oppression will somehow be lessened if society can be convinced that it is genetic is unrealistic at best.

But whatever the political ramifications, the biology is still quite controversial. What is the actual evidence for a biological basis to sexual orientation?

Before we even begin asking this question, we must clarify the terms of the debate, beginning with a definition of the term itself. While it seems obvious to members of the Western world that homosexuality is simply the act of engaging in some form of sexual behavior with a same-sex partner, the important thing about the definition is an implied deviance. It is not simply a neutral evaluation of a person to say, "You are a homosexual." The definition of the word (as incorrect as this may be in our modern understanding of the practice) implies a deviation from normalcy. So, when we begin analyzing homosexuality and homophobia, it is important to begin with an understanding of the origin of the concept in the first place. The definition of homosexuality (including the implied deviance) has varied throughout time, and still varies from place to place, as illustrated by the following examples.

In many New Guinean and Australian aboriginal groups it is thought that something of a man's essence is given to another person with the ejaculate. Having sex with a woman is thought to be giving away a small piece of one's manhood, and thus the majority of sexual activity of younger men is with other men, mainly older men. Typically, marriage is culminated with the wife's older brother taking in the new husband, the two men engaging regularly in sexual relations. The wife's brother thus imparts a bit of manhood to the new husband with every sexual act. Taken over an individual's lifetime, it would not be unusual for an individual to have engaged in far more homosexual acts than heterosexual ones; indeed, it is considered quite abnormal and deviant for a male not to engage in homosexual activities. Such a male would probably be thought of as our equivalent of effeminate—after all, he had given so much of his manhood to those scurrilous heterosexual encounters without the reaffirming insertion of manhood from his legitimate male partners. An imagined locker-room conversation might sound like, "I really think Eddie is going queer.

He has been sleeping with nothing but women for the past two months. Imagine how draining [of his manhood] that must be. And with no men to keep him up to speed. Man, that's weird!"

Here, the definition of deviance with regard to sexual orientation has more to do with timing and quantity. It is normal and expected for younger men to become sexually involved with older men, a part of what is thought to give them their manhood. It is expected that they will eventually have sexual relations with women also, but that is somewhat dangerous in that a bit of manhood is taken away with each ejaculation, replenished only by sex with a man. So deviant behavior could be sex with women before the proper manhood-defining homosexual bonds, or perhaps continuing homosexual bonds with no subsequent heterosexual behavior, or improper insertion (the younger male is always the insertee). The concept of a "homosexual" as a deviant category simply does not exist, even though one's normal sexual orientation always includes same-sex activities. It should also be noted that men and women generally develop sex-specific gender identities and roles. Note how the male role in this case includes a great deal of homosexual behavior, and we can presume that the development of juvenile gender identity must include some homosexual eroticism. Thus there remain definite male and female gender identities and roles; it is just that their exact natures are quite different from what they are in modern Western society.

A distinctive situation occurred among almost all North American Indians at the time of the European invasion. Most often occurring with men (although that may, in the end, be a function of biased reporting of early chroniclers), but occasionally with women, the berdaches were people who took on the gender role and presumably identity of the opposite sex. There were a variety of developmental sequences that led to the situation, but according to early explorers it seems to have been quite common throughout the continent (perhaps suggesting a rather old origin). For example, a mother may have decided to raise one of her sons as a girl. The social development sequence then followed the pattern of female gender identity and role, and the sexual male became effeminate, wore women's clothing, engaged in female economic activities, and was excused from usual male social responsibilities. His sexual activities were with non-berdach males, and he was treated much like other women were treated in the society. Males who had sex with berdaches were not thought to be somehow deviant, and it was usually regarded as quite normal to engage in such activities, although some observers report a degree of loss in male status from relationships with berdaches.

Female berdaches also existed, participating in male activities such as hunting and warfare, donning male clothing, and developing sexual relationships with non-berdach women. As with their male counterparts, female berdaches apparently had the gender identity and role of the male, and non-berdach women having relationships with them were not looked down upon.

Homosexuality in ancient Greece was apparently universal. No words nor conceptualizations existed for homo- or heterosexual behavior; it was simply all regarded as sexual behavior. Some individuals—Alexander the Great, for example—were apparently strictly homosexual, and probably there were others who were strictly heterosexual, but by far the norm of the society was bisexuality. Curiously, despite the apparently complete permissiveness and acceptability of bisexual lives, there was a clear definition of deviant behavior. The submissive partner was thought to be inferior. Most of the heterosexual encounters were dominated by the male and seemingly the homosexual encounters were dominated by the older male. For the older male in a homosexual encounter or any male in a heterosexual encounter to play the permissive role was thought to be deviant.

The role of homosexual behavior in the military society of the Celts is noteworthy. According to one observer, Celtic men

> . . . are much keener on their own sex; they lie around on animal skins and enjoy themselves, with a lover on each side. The extraordinary thing is they haven't the smallest regard for their personal dignity or self-respect; they offer themselves to other men without the least compunction. Furthermore, this isn't looked down on, or regarded as in any way disgraceful: on the contrary, if one of them is rejected by another to whom he has offered himself, he takes offence.[14]

Taking all of these, and the many other examples that could be cited, together, it is difficult to avoid some obvious conclusions. First, homosexuality and bisexuality have existed throughout history. Second, it seems relatively unusual to find homosexual behavior thought of as deviant—while there are indeed many examples that do find it so, far more examples can be cited in which homosexual behavior is regarded as normal. Third, that which the society regards as deviant varies enormously, and would seem to be socially constructed.

Given this background, we now return to the problem of defining homosexuality. If we are to simply accept the seemingly simple definition of "someone who has sex with a member of the same sex," we will include virtually all male members of many New Guinean cultures, and the entire male population of ancient Greece. If we incorporate something about gender identity into the definition we will include the Indian berdaches, but the homosexual Celts will be excluded. If one insists that the historical and anthropological data somehow be reasonably incorporated into the definition, it becomes almost like defining a wise man, a good woman, or a friendly encounter. All such phenomena have very specific meanings within our own culture, but their social construction seems to be so plastic that any attempt to define them in a more general sense simply fails the test of minimal objectivity.

The conclusion that seems inevitable is that homosexuality is a social form of behavior that varies in form and social content across time and space.

Nevertheless, it is sometimes felt by both gays and straights that something felt so deeply, as is sexual orientation by most people, must have some sort of deep biological origin. An analogy to see the fault of such reasoning is accent in language. For most people, if their foreign language training begins later in life, they retain an unmistakable remnant of their original language—Maurice Chevalier was clearly a Frenchman, Albert Einstein was obviously German, and we all know people in our personal lives whose original language is clearly discernable when they speak. For all of these people, to speak English without this deviant behavior (i.e., the foreign accent) is simply not possible. The habit goes very deep and, try as they might, they cannot rid themselves of it. Yet no one would ever suggest that an accent in language was biologically determined.

It is worth a moment's reflection as to what sort of genetic system would be involved if it ever turned out that homosexuality is genetically determined. We would have to accommodate, within the same system of genotype/phenotype transformation, the Native American berdachs, the Celts, and the ancient Greeks, as well as the homophobic society of today's United States. What sort of genetic basis could account for all of these patterns? If homosexuality were genetically determined, it would take a very complex genetic system indeed to be able to account for all of these forms. On the other hand, we can say with a great deal of confidence, although rather trivially, that if genes are involved, we all have the gay gene (since several societies are or have been almost completely homosexual in the sense that virtually all of the males regularly engage in homosexual activities, all male members of the society must carry those genes).

This leaves us with the question that started this section. What evidence exists in support of the idea that homosexual or bisexual behavior has some sort of biological basis? The question has not yet been answered, partly because the terms are so difficult to define in the first place. The popular press continually publishes accounts of various studies "discovering" the underlying genetic basis of homosexuality. Later follow the inevitable criticisms of the studies, and, thus far, their discreditation, which is mainly ignored by the media.[15] The long history of this pattern, similar to that of discovering a biological basis for male-female gender differences, should caution all of us to view any new results skeptically. Surely, many other studies will come forth "demonstrating" a biological basis for homosexuality, and just as surely will follow their critics showing what was wrong with the study. In fact, what we have so far is a rather large lack of evidence supporting the biological determination hypothesis. Some day we may find it. But so far it remains elusive.

Those who find this conclusion unsettling because of the supposed aid and comfort it provides for society's homophobes should not fret. Whether or not gays, lesbians, and bisexuals are that way because of genes, hormones, or society has little to do with the way they should be treated, nor with the possible messages they may have for the straight world. As with the above example of language accent, if one becomes gay because of life-style patterns that occur during one's early upbringing, there is nothing whatsoever that is suggested by biology, psychology, or any other science that suggests that the behavior is less legitimate, deeply felt, or impossible to change than if it were determined by hormones or genes. Rejecting civil rights for gays and lesbians based on the fact that their behavior is socially rather than biologically determined is equivalent to jailing anyone who speaks with an accent.

Carbon Cycles and Energy Flows

In short bursts of speed, the cheetah is the fastest animal on earth. For a period of two to three minutes, an immense amount of energy goes into nature's most impressive drag race, where gazelle and cheetah rapidly accelerate to more than 60 mph, almost competitive with street dragsters.[1] The race car functions energetically in a familiar way—a fossil fuel is mixed with air, ignited, and the resultant explosion pushes a piston, which makes the wheels turn. The energy source is fossil fuel. A parallel story for the cheetah is a case history of the movement of material and energy in ecosystems. It is quite an interesting story, and is representative of some very general principles of how ecosystems work.

The cheetah gets the energy to chase the gazelle from the last gazelle it ate. The gazelle is the fuel it must fill up with, first, to get to the next gas station, and second, to perform life's other important function, reproduction. The gazelle provides not only the necessary energy for the cheetah to function, but also the materials it uses to make its own body parts. The stretched cheetah leg muscle, bursting with the energy that will suddenly contract it to create powerful leg movements, is composed of protein, which comes from the gazelle meat last consumed by the cheetah.

Cheetahs are nothing special regarding such transformations. In the same savannah with the cheetah one can find lions eating zebras, weaver birds eating insects, insects being eaten by spiders, tiny mites eating tinier mites (see Figure 8.1).[2] Each of these predatory events is an example of an important generalization—many animals derive material and energy from the consumption of other animals. As in all cases of generalization, some rich and interesting details are lost—the swiftness of the cheetah, the ferociousness of the lion, and the beauty of the weaver bird are all rele-gated to nothing more than transfer of material and energy—but general-ization is one important mode of understanding the world, and certainly an important tool in the bag of scientific methodology. So we proceed with the example of the African savannah and the generalizations that emerge.

If some animals gain from other animals all the material they need to build their bodies and all the energy they need to make them work, from where do those other animals get it? Consider the following proposition. Let us isolate in a closed arena foxes, chickens, beetles, and fleas. The fleas feed off the blood of the foxes, the beetles eat the fleas, the chickens eat the beetles, and the foxes eat the chickens—a perpetual motion ecosystem (see Figure 8.2). What is wrong with this picture? It is not immediately obvious, *a priori,* why such a system could not work. Each day an equiva-lent of 10 calories of fox is converted into 10 calories of fleas, 10 calories of fleas into 10 calories of beetles, 10 calories of beetles into 10 calories of chickens, 10 calories of chicken into 10 calories of fox. Thus each 10 calo-ries lost is replaced by 10 calories gained. Could the system work?

Knowing nothing about energy transfer in ecosystems, we could not say that such a system would not function. However, we must take mind of a very important ecological principle that was empirically established long ago. The principle is that a vast majority of the energy stored in one animal (or plant) is lost or dissipated in the process of consumption. The exact amount varies enormously from animal to animal, but as a rough rule of thumb, one can say that approximately 90 percent of the energy stored in a zebra (say) is lost when the zebra meat is converted to lion flesh. This being the case, we can easily see why the fox-chicken-beetle-flea ecosystem is simply not possible—converting 100 calories of fox to 10 calories of fleas to 1 calorie of beetles to .1 calorie of chicken leaves .01 calorie of fox to replace the 100 calories we started with, and means that we have ever less energy in the system.

This principle of energy loss through consumption leads to an im-portant conclusion, namely, that energy dissipates in ecological systems. But if energy ultimately dissipates, an external source of energy must be fed in, that is, something continues to fill the gas tank while we press on with the drag race. The metaphorical equivalent to the gas station is not what the cheetah or lion eats, but what the gazelle and zebra eat, plants. To understand how plants function as the metaphorical gas station, we

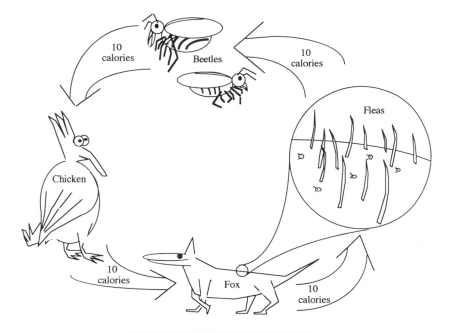

THE PERPETUAL MOTION ECOSYSTEM

Figure 8.2. The theoretical perpetual motion ecosystem.

must take a side trip to some slightly more technical points in order to understand energy transformation in a more physical/chemical sense, specifically at the level of the connections between chemical elements.

ENERGY TRANSFORMATION

Energy, the capacity to do work, is fundamental to life, as most of us realize early in the morning. Interpreting the groggy feeling one has in the

Figure 8.1. Ecosystem dynamics of the African savannah. Top left, impalas graze on the grass of the Serengeti. Top right, Grévy's zebras and reticulated giraffes graze on the herbs and trees of the extremely dry savannah of northern Kenya. Lower left, male lion feeds on young giraffe killed the night before, while hyenas wait in the background for an opportunity to sneak in and grab a bone. The dark coloration on the giraffe carcass is an incredibly dense population of flies. Lower middle, a nest complex of weaver birds, predation at a different level, but the same energy relations as the lion and giraffe. Bottom right, a spider web in Amboselli National Park in southern Kenya, predation at yet another level.

morning as a lack of energy is probably not physically and biologically correct, but nevertheless captures the idea well—energy is the capacity to do something.

Energy in the ecological sense must be understood at a smaller level, at the level of connections between chemical elements. A useful metaphor is an acrobat on the top of a tower, jumping onto a seesaw, thus propelling her coperformer into the air. Standing on the top of the tower, she has the potential to provide energy to propel her comrade to the top of a second tower (see Figure 8.3). But after performing this piece of work, she must climb the tower if she is to do it again. Two types of energy transformations are involved here, first, to propel her colleague into the air, second, to reclimb the ladder. The first happens more or less spontaneously (i.e., she simply has to jump to release the energy necessary to do the job); the second happens only after considerable energy is actively invested in the job of climbing the tower again.

This metaphor relates to how energy is stored in the bonds that hold chemical atoms together, just as it is stored in the acrobat perched on top of the tower (not in the acrobat nor the tower, but in the perching). As those chemical bonds break (as she jumps off the tower), the energy that was holding the atoms together (the tower that kept her from falling to the ground), is released to perform a necessary biological function (propelling her comrade up into the air). But a biological system that did nothing but break chemical bonds would not be around for long, since all the bonds would eventually break and we would have nothing but acrobats standing on a level ground, looking for some place to jump down. The chemical bonds must be built again; the acrobat must climb the tower.

An ecological system must contain both types of energy transformations,[3] the first to make it function, the second to have the energy to do the first. And a fundamental property of energy is that it goes away and does not come back, flowing through the system, never recycled. Acrobats do not spontaneously appear at the tops of the towers. This means that some source of energy must come from the outside, something that provides the acrobat with the energy to climb the tower again.

The general form of the chemical transformation that makes biology function is the breakdown of bonds between atoms. The major atoms of concern in biology (by no means the only ones, but simply the most abundant) are carbon (symbolized by C), oxygen (O), and hydrogen (H). These three elements, along with many others in smaller quantities, are

Figure 8.3. Perched at the top of the tower, the acrobat jumps to release the energy contained in her being perched on top of the tower. After her comrade is propelled into the air to the top of the other tower, she must climb the first tower again before she can release the energy again.

bound together (remember, it takes energy to keep them together—that's the energy we can use later) in huge assemblages, molecules. For convenience we can call those assemblages C-H-O, remembering that such abstract symbolism is for convenience, not to obscure but rather to make life easier.[4]

The breakdown of C-H-O is essentially equivalent to the process commonly called burning. If you bring a piece of C-H-O into contact with enough heat, and in the presence of oxygen, it catches fire. That is fundamentally how the energy is released from the bonds. We could simply say, "C-H-O + O gives energy." But what happens to the atoms? Recall that all of these energy transformations are associated with the connection between the atoms, not the atoms themselves (breaking them apart gives a totally different type of energy, as you probably guessed). So, after the transformation, we will still have the carbon, oxygen, and hydrogen atoms around, but what form will they take?

Because of certain particulars about the elements carbon, oxygen, and hydrogen, there are fixed rules about how they may combine with one another. It is unimportant from our point of view to understand the whys and wherefores of these rules, only to understand that they exist. Thus, we may have two hydrogens connecting with each oxygen to form water (symbolized as H-O-H, or H_2O), two oxygens connecting with a carbon to form carbon dioxide (symbolized as O-C-O or CO_2), and two oxygens connecting with one another, to form molecular oxygen (symbolized as O_2).[5]

Thus, when C-H-O combines with oxygen, it is actually combining with molecular oxygen, so we use the shorthand C-H-O + O_2. And what results? Water and carbon dioxide, H_2O and CO_2, plus, of course, energy. This is perhaps the most basic process of life, and is called respiration (not in the sense of respiring when we breathe, but in a strictly chemical sense). Respiration is the underlying process whereby energy is extracted from the bonds of C-H-O and can be symbolized by the simple chemical equation,

$$\text{C-H-O} + O_2 \rightarrow CO_2 + H_2O + \text{energy}.$$

Understanding respiration as the immediate source of all energy for life's processes leaves us with the question of where the energy-rich chemical bonds come from in the first place—what energy source allows the acrobat to climb the tower again? The answer is the sun, specifically, light from the sun. There are specialized organs in most plants that enable them to convert the small packets of energy that are contained in sunlight into the rich chemical bonds that are eventually mined by the process of respiration to generate the energy needed for life's processes.[6] Because the process uses light to synthesize the necessary chemical bonds, it is called photosynthesis, and is effectively the reverse of respiration. Carbon dioxide and water are the necessary resources, energy from the sun drives the process, and the results are energy stored in the chemical bonds of C-H-O and molecular oxygen. The chemical formula is, thus,

$$CO_2 + H_2O + energy \rightarrow C\text{-}H\text{-}O + O_2.$$

This is life's most fundamental process, the capture of energy from the sun. It happens because plants are able to perform photosynthesis (make energy-rich chemical bonds from the sun) and all organisms, plants and animals, are able to burn those chemical bonds to get energy. It makes life itself possible.

BUFFALO DUNG

Returning to the African savannah, let us refocus on things smaller and not so romantic as lions and gazelles, dung. When I was visiting the Masai-Mara National Park in Kenya, I became something of a tourist attraction myself as I crouched over a piece of buffalo dung, taking pictures and being amazed at the variety of organisms that made dung their home (see Figure 8.4). The most spectacular were the famous scarab beetles that roll a ball of dung and lay an egg in the ball. But what impressed me most was the enormous variety of life in one small patch of dung. In a period of about an hour I counted at least 8 different species of hover flies, 6 species of scarab beetles, one species of rove beetle, and numerous other beetles and flies.

As fascinating as the diversity of life in dung may be to an ecologist, there is a more important observation worth making. If you come back a few months later to look for the same piece of buffalo dung, you will see a spot of especially lush grass, but the dung will be completely gone. Yet, if you had sterilized the buffalo dung before it hit the ground and zapped it with pesticides so that insects and fungi and bacteria could not grow on it, when you came back a couple of months later you would not see a spot

Figure 8.4. Top photograph is of buffalo dung on the Serengeti of southern Kenya. Bottom photograph is close-up showing action of a dung beetle extracting dung to roll up into a ball.

of green grass, you would just see a piece of very dry buffalo dung. This suggests that the myriad of hover flies and beetles have something to do with the disappearance of the dung and with the lush spot of grass that replaced it. The dung, in combination with the flies and beetles and whatever other organisms were there, provided the grasses with something that caused them to grow, or helped them to grow better. That something is called nutrients. Nutrients had to have come from the dung and/or animals living in and on it, but the dung came from the buffalo who got it from the grass in the first place. So the nutrients must be contained in the grass that the buffalo eats and must be released back to the grass by the action of the beetles and flies. Because the grass and the buffalo and its dung appear to be "composed" of these nutrients, the beetles and flies (and other things that we can not see) are called decomposers, since they decompose the leftover grass in the buffalo dung back into a form that the plants can use, the nutrients.

THE FOUR TROPHIC LEVELS

We have now examined, through various examples, the four basic components of all ecosystems, called *trophic levels*. First is the component that is not forced to consume other things, but, rather, uses energy from the sun and nutrients from the soil to construct itself and store energy. At this trophic level is the primary production of the system, accomplished by plants—also called *primary producers*. Second are the things that directly consume plants—buffaloes, zebras, gazelles and such. At this trophic level is the primary consumption of the system, accomplished by animals called *herbivores*. Third are the things that directly consume animals—lions, cheetahs, dragonflies, weaver birds and such (see Figure 8.1). At this trophic level is the secondary consumption of the system, accomplished by animals called *predators* or *carnivores*. Fourth are the things that consume everything else after it is dead—the scarab beetles, hover flies, fungi, bacteria and such. At this trophic level is the decomposition of the system, accomplished by those organisms we call *decomposers*.

The picture is now complete, including the rather important difference between the behavior of energy and matter in an ecosystem. A relatively standard diagram is presented in Figure 8.5. I have presented the carbon and oxygen cycle alongside the energy flow diagram to emphasize the difference between the two—matter cycles, energy flows.

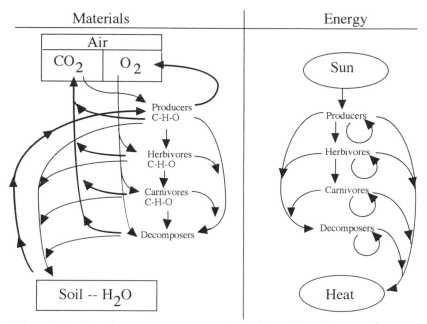

Figure 8.5. The elementary processes of material cycling and energy flow. Note how, in the left graph, all materials are continually cycled into and out of the biological system (i.e., producers, herbivores, carnivores, and decomposers), while in the right graph, the energy from the sun enters the system and is eventually dissipated as heat.

Consider, for example, a single atom of carbon in the system. We begin with the atom attached to two oxygen atoms as carbon dioxide in the air. A plant captures that chunk of carbon dioxide and, through the process of photosynthesis, converts it into C-H-O (the producers in Figure 8.5). The atom, now incorporated into the C-H-O molecule, transfers to a primary consumer (the herbivores in Figure 8.5) as a piece of the plant is consumed. It then is transferred to a carnivore as a piece of the same molecule when the carnivore eats the herbivore, and finally transferred to the decomposer when the carnivore dies. The decomposer uses the piece of C-H-O in respiration, thus returning the carbon atom to the air in the form of carbon dioxide again. Naturally, at any one of the trophic levels, that particular piece of C-H-O could have been used in respiration, thus transferring it back to the atmosphere well before it ever reached the decomposer trophic level. Any of the four cycles is possible (air-producer-air, air-producer-herbivore-air, air-producer-herbivore-carnivore-air, air-producer-herbivore-carnivore-decomposer-air).

Now look at the energy side of the diagram. Energy enters from the sun, is captured by photosynthesis, and is stored in chemical bonds. Respiration occurs inside of the plant's body to release energy to perform life's functions, and part of the plant's body is consumed by a herbivore. During the process of transferring energy from the plant to the herbivore, approximately 90 percent of the energy is lost as heat, with only 10 percent converted to herbivore body. Respiration occurs in the herbivore's body to release energy to perform life's functions, and part of the herbivore's body is consumed by a carnivore, in which respiration releases energy for life's functions. At every transfer of energy from one level to another, approximately 10 percent of the possible energy is actually transferred.

Energy flows and matter cycles; this is perhaps the most fundamental principle of ecology. Many ecologists, the systems ecologists, devote their lives to the detailed determination of exactly how energy flows and matter cycles in particular ecosystems. Much of their work may, at first glance, seem arcane and useless, but recently the world received quite a shock (and is probably due for an even bigger one) regarding what systems ecologists learned about the carbon and oxygen cycles.[7]

CYCLING OF MATTER—THE CARBON AND OXYGEN CYCLES IN HISTORICAL PERSPECTIVE

The cycle of one important nutrient has already been introduced. Referring to Figure 8.5, carbon, in the form of carbon dioxide, is taken from the air by plants during the process of photosynthesis. The complicated organic molecules (symbolized here as C-H-O) that contain the assimilated carbon are transferred to animals. When the animals break down these compounds to obtain energy in the process of respiration, the carbon is released back into the atmosphere as carbon dioxide. Thus, carbon cycles through the system, beginning in the atmosphere, passing through the bodies of plants and animals, and eventually returning to the atmosphere.

The oxygen cycle is a little more complicated than that of carbon. Oxygen, in a form combined with carbon as carbon dioxide, and in a form combined with hydrogen as water, enters the plant, and through the process of photosynthesis is recombined partly into molecular oxygen and released into the atmosphere, and partly into the energy-rich organic compounds (C-H-O). These organic compounds are then transferred to the bodies of animals and converted, through the process of respiration, into carbon dioxide and water (H_2O), thus completing the cycle.

It is of considerable contemporary interest to reflect on the history of the carbon and oxygen cycles. An important phase in the carbon and oxygen cycles occurred some 300 million years ago. This was a period in which plants as we know them today, at least the overall forms—trees and such—evolved, and oceans were rising and falling. Large coastal areas (remember that the continents in those days were not in the same places they are today) were repeatedly flooded, killing the vegetation and most of the decomposers in the ecosystem. So the vegetation, recently killed by the flood, was not subjected to the normal ecological process of decomposition, but rather decomposed extremely slowly, almost as if it were not decomposing at all. Buried by hundreds of thousands of years of accumulation of swamp muck, and then covered by, perhaps, volcanic ash or lava flows, that vegetation retained the bulk of the chemical bonds that contained all that energy. The only difference is that the weak bonds were all broken, and all that eventually remained were the bonds that were somewhat more difficult to break, those that release the most energy. This is the substance we call coal.

The formation of crude oil is somewhat more complicated than coal. From the point of view of ecological systems, oil results from the same process as the formation of coal[8]—the burial of biological material before it runs through the decomposer box in the ecosystem, such that over time it loosens the weaker energy bonds, and consequently provides something that we can burn. Coal and petroleum thus represent a deviation from the normal material cycles and energy flows operating today, and form the basis on which *Homo sapiens* has transformed the world.

Between 1450 and 1550, England experienced an explosive growth in energy-demanding technologies.[9] The source of that energy was biological—that which had been stored in trees during the past hundred or so years, and was found in the form of wood, which was converted to charcoal. As always happens, when the rate of harvest increases and the humans responsible do not care to ensure that the rate of replacement is smaller than the rate of harvest, the resource becomes rapidly depleted, which is what happened in England by the middle of the sixteenth century.

Scattered across the southern half of the island were strange black rocks that had been known for centuries (historical records go back to 1100), rocks that would burn something like charcoal. England faced an energy crisis because of its deforestation. This energy crisis forced the adoption of black-rock utilization for the energy input into the developing industries of the island, thus connecting the biological energy storage of more than 300 million years earlier with the present and ushering in the hydrocarbon age, the end of which now seems to be on the horizon.

When the Western world began using the biological energy stored in coal and petroleum, a qualitative change in the carbon cycle was initiated, the ultimate consequences of which we are just beginning to experience. During the course of a year in the days of *Homo erectus,* a certain amount of CO_2 was absorbed by plants and a certain amount of O_2 was released. There probably never was a perfect balance, and we could speculate that in any particular year an excess of carbon was somehow removed from the system, perhaps as a piece of buffalo dung that was not fully decomposed and became buried under a deep layer of volcanic ash, and thus was no longer available to the organisms that normally act to decompose it. The carbon in that piece of buffalo dung thus was removed from the global carbon cycle. No one knows, but we can speculate that somewhere on the order of one one-thousandth of one percent of the carbon may be lost to the carbon cycle each year. Now, when we begin to think in terms of hundreds of millions of years, one one-thousandth of one percent is actually quite a lot, even though when we think in terms of human life it is quite trivial. All of the limestone formations around the globe represent the very slow removal of carbon from the atmosphere through the formation of calcium carbonate skeletons of marine organisms. Furthermore, on average, the accumulation of carbon in fossils, those tree trunks that got buried in swamps formed by rising seas, for example, was similar to the formation of limestone. While the basic rules have not changed, we must realize that the evolution of *H. sapiens* occurred under conditions more or less as they are today, that the removal of so much carbon from the atmosphere, a biological fact that took hundreds of millions of years, was actually a prerequisite for the evolution of the forms of life that we know today.

Since the English made the decision to use black rocks for their energy source, thus initiating activities that ultimately led to the Industrial Revolution, the quantitative aspects of the carbon cycle changed dramatically. Carbon that had been removed from the atmosphere slowly over perhaps 500 million years was suddenly released back into the atmosphere in less than 500 years. In this light, it does not seem surprising that a crisis was created.

Resource Transformation in Homo sapiens

Transformation of resources is a fundamental component of life, whether speaking of a bacterial cell transforming lactose, a lion transforming zebras, or a chimpanzee transforming a stick to poke into a termite nest. Transforming resources by the species *Homo sapiens,* however, takes on unique forms. To conceptualize these forms even minimally, one must include a series of factors that are unique to the species.[1]

Humanness, then, a good part of which consists of social transformation of resources, abstract representation, language, social construction, and discourse, has conditioned a special pattern of resource utilization. While it makes perfect sense to think of any other animal (or plant) in the world as simply using resources, we must think of *Homo sapiens* as using products, which are the result of applying human labor to resources. Yet, human labor is different from the labor applied by the beaver building its dam. Human labor is directed by human social relations, a consequence of the basic characteristics of human sociality.

In this chapter we take a very "materialist" approach to understanding humans.[2] This is not the only approach available, and some would argue that it is too limited. For example, we treat human social construction and discourse almost as if they were black boxes. We say, "Socially organized labor acts on resources to make products," and then we analyze the process whereby these products are consumed and perhaps made into other resources. It could be argued that the focus ought to be on "socially organized labor" rather than the materialism of the resource/product dichotomy. I am in sympathy with such critics, but I insist that this (perhaps crude) materialist approach is useful, albeit not the only possible, or best, approach, given the task at hand—the human use of resources.

Human resource use may be thought of as a social process in which human labor is applied to resources to generate a product, which is of some use to the humans involved. There are three elements and two processes involved.[3] The elements are (1) resources, (2) labor, and (3) product. The processes are (1) production and (2) consumption. Human labor and resources combine in the process of production, and the humans who provide that labor consume the product of production. This simple idea applies to humans collecting acorns, making acorn bread, and eating it, as much as to humans mining iron ore, transforming it into steel, which later is transformed into automobiles, which are used by those humans who provided all the labor that transformed the resources (see Figure 4.3).

Human resource transformation systems are extremely complicated, yet it is possible to invent meaningful categories. Here we consider three categories. First, there is the sort in which the product of the labor-resource transformation is utilized directly. This is still a common form of resource transformation in hunting and gathering people and traditional agriculturalists. Corn and beans are the product of applying labor to the resource called land, and the corn and beans are directly consumed by the farmer. The system is almost always complicated by the fact that some are able to make certain products more efficiently than others, leading to the exchange of products. But the essential feature is that products are used directly, although they may be directly interchanged with one another before use. This is "simple commodity production."[4]

Second, when money enters into the system, the rules change somewhat. The farmer produces corn and beans, but for the purpose of selling them for money. The money is then used to purchase other products that the farmer needs or wants, but does not produce on the farm. So the product of the labor-resource transformation is exchanged for money, which is exchanged for the product of some other labor-resource transformation system. This is "simple commodity production and exchange."

Third, when money begins to dictate the way the whole system functions, the rules change again. A merchant gets money for the purpose of buying products, for the purpose of selling them again. The whole point of the transformation is to increase the amount of money during the transaction. This is "production for exchange value."

So, in this classification of human resource transformation processes, we have first, production for direct consumption (a product is produced and consumed, or P-C); second, production for exchange and use (a product is produced, exchanged for money, which is exchanged for another product, which is used, or P-M-P-C); and third, production for exchange (money is exchanged for a product, which is exchanged for more money, or M-P-M).

The history of *Homo sapiens* has certainly been dominated by the first form. Money entered the picture only recently, and actually became common only after the invention of agriculture. The absolute *dominance* of production for exchange value is extremely new, although its simple *existence* as a force is probably almost as old as money itself. Nevertheless, today, production for exchange certainly dominates our overall human resource transformation process, even seeming to be, somehow, the only "natural" way to operate.[5] Japanese industrialists do not produce Toyotas for people to use; they invest money in an enterprise to receive more money in return.

It is also not the case that the entire population is involved in M-P-M, nor was it the case earlier that M-P-M did not exist. In feudal England, for example, the dominant mode of resource transformation in the society was commodity production and exchange, P-M-P. But embedded in that society were some people, the merchants, who as individuals were clearly operating according to the M-P-M mode—recall the fate of Shylock as a person operating this way in a society dominated by another form of production.[6] Today, perhaps the vast majority of people produce for the sake of getting money in order to buy things they use (P-M-P), but that is not the mode of resource transformation that drives our society. The driving force is the investor, the person who "gets money, buys products, sells products for a profit"—the M-P-M mode. It is a characteristic of the system usually referred to as industrial capitalism.[7]

INDUSTRIAL CAPITALISM

Farmers produce food and fiber to sell on the market, weavers produce cloth to sell on the market, woodworkers produce cabinets to sell on the market—this is the P-M-P system. But in the modern world, a vast number of people (the majority, if we look only at the developed world) are not farmers, weavers, or woodworkers. They do not engage in resource transformation to produce a product that they can exchange. Rather, they enter into an overall system of production that is dominated by those people and institutions who are engaged in the M-P-M mode of resource transformation. This vast number of people have no products that they are able to sell. The only thing they have to sell is their willingness and ability to participate in the resource transformation processes that are operating in the society. That willingness and ability is called labor power, and a whole class of people is characterized as not having anything to sell except their labor power. So, instead of the craftsperson making a violin to sell for money, which is then used to buy the cloth that the weaver made, the former craftsperson gets a job in a violin factory and receives money, not for violins made, but for hours worked.

Generally, in the modern industrial system, the people who provide the labor in the resource transformation systems are not the same people who provide the tools, machines, and factories that are used to transform the resources. The former are the workers in the factories; the latter are the owners of the factories.[8] The owners are the ones who directly make the management decisions about all production processes. Their mode of operation is M-P-M, and their goal is to minimize the first M and maximize the second M; that is, to maximize the profit of their production operation. The money invested in the operation, the first M, includes the money needed to buy the raw materials, upkeep on the machines and tools in the factory, and labor costs. A good manager tries to minimize all of these costs, including the cost of labor.[9]

But, here, the manager faces a complicated and contradictory task. While the workers in the factory constitute a cost of production that is to be minimized, they also participate, along with the multitudes of other workers in the society, in the consumption of the society's products. In trying to maximize profits, the manager is concerned that the factory's products sell for a high price, which can happen only if the workers, in general, are making a lot of money. In contradistinction to what is desired at the level of the factory (for the workers to make as little as possible), at the level of the society a totally opposite goal is sought (for the workers to make as much as possible).

So the owner of the factory effectively has to wear two hats, one as owner of the factory and one as a member of a social class that wishes to sell products at a high price. As owner of the factory, he or she wishes the laborers to receive as little as possible, but as a member of the social class, he or she wishes the laborers in general to receive as much as possible (to purchase the products produced in the factory).

This fundamental contradiction is the probable cause (or at least it was in the earlier days of the industrial capitalist system) of alternating phases of economic expansion and recession. As various factories compete with one another, labor, being one of the major costs of production, is always a target for reduction. Competition forces individual factories to mechanize processes whenever possible, thus giving them the competitive edge, at least for a while, over those factories that have not mechanized. Unfortunately, mechanization overall means unemployment, which means lowered general consumption power, which means economic recession. But economic recession means a reserve of laborers ready to take up new employment, at low wages, which stimulates the opening of new economic sectors, and economic recovery. Since the new economic sectors are composed of individual competing factories, the whole process starts over.

Phases of economic expansion and contraction are not exactly desirable. Economic contraction is classically associated with political instability, something that the factory owners and their political representatives naturally wish to avoid. Furthermore, and probably more importantly, economic contraction means that profits are lowered and generally more difficult to come by. Lowered profits mean less money for investment and, thus, less chance of opening up new economic sectors to generate an economic revival. If new economic sectors do not appear, the general process of economic contraction will continue unabated. Thus, the factory owners (as well as the general population) view such economic contraction as a crisis. It is a crisis at the general level in that it could lead to the demise of the entire economic system, but, more importantly, it is a crisis for individual factory owners in that their entire purpose in life, to make a profit on investment, is threatened. Just how such crises are resolved is an important part of the history of the development of the industrial capitalist system.[10]

FORCING OTHERS TO BEAR THE REAL COSTS OF PRODUCTION

Reducing labor's reward is the most obvious and most analyzed form of minimizing the overall cost of resource transformation processes. A second mechanism almost always operates, and deserves much more attention than it normally receives: the political/social/cultural assumption that some real costs of production are to be borne by individuals outside of the resource transformation process. Since primitive resource transformation systems likely made no computations of inputs in the first place, it is understandable how socially bearable costs of production were automatically assumed to be borne by others.[11] In the modern resource transformation system called industrial capitalism, or, equally, in the former command economies of eastern Europe and the Soviet Union, the owner or manager of a production facility would be inefficient not to at least try to get others to pay for pieces of the production process. Thus, for example, in the United States, warehoused goods are transformed into items for sale in retail outlets by trucks that haul the goods from warehouse to store. Those trucks travel along the interstate highway system that was built by funds from general tax revenues. One cost of production, the cost of building the interstate highway system, was not borne by those who engage most directly in the production process. In this case, the argument is that the general good, meaning the general economic good, is enhanced by this large transportation system, and that its enormous cost could never be borne by any single group of producers who may immediately benefit from its existence. Yet, those very producers are involved in producing products that are used by the general population, so it makes sense to require the general population to bear the costs of this piece of the production process.

This is a general phenomenon that occurs not only under industrial capitalism, but also in almost all reasonably complex socioeconomic systems, past and present.[12] Certain production processes are socially desirable, but they contain elements that cannot bear the cost of such production, so a social contract is established in which someone else (a slave population, a religious caste, a social class, an unpowerful social grouping) is assumed to pay for that piece of the production process. For example, a hundred industries would prosper and make products used by the whole population if they only had access to number 47 screws. But present conditions make the production of number 47 screws unfeasible by any individual production facility. If possible, it would obviously make sense to develop a social contract in which the population in general subsidizes the production of these screws, to promote the flourishing of those hundred industries and the desired and useful products they will produce.[13]

The ready acceptance of this basic and seemingly universal economic principle perhaps explains the curious willingness, at least until recently, to accept other arrangements that seem patently unfair according to a variety of ethical systems. When a local manufacturer discharges waste into a local waterway, the cleanup of that waterway is borne by the local community, not by the manufacturer.[14] When Union Carbide leaked poison into the air of Bhopal, India, the poor residents of the shantytowns around the plant died, not the families of Union Carbide executives or shareholders.[15] Such cases are similar to the interstate highway system. A major cost of production (cleanup of waterways, death caused by leaking poison) is not borne by the producer.[16]

When accounting for the production process, such costs are set at zero; that is, they are regarded as external to the system—what ecologists refer to as externalities. Unfortunately, the parallel with the interstate highway system only goes so far. For the most part, society in general agrees that the negative impact on people's lives from the interstate highways is trivial compared to the enormous benefit the system brings them. But are the people of Bhopal willing to accept the risk of death to receive the benefits of the Union Carbide factory in their town? Do they have much choice in the matter? Clearly, Union Carbide is capable of making the calculations and it will most naturally choose to locate its plant in an area in which as much as possible of the production process is regarded as an externality.

What makes it so difficult to deal with externalities is that the definition of what constitutes an externality is a complicated social question, involving political ideology far more than economic or ecological factors. The primitive hunter set fire to a grassland so that the new grass provided forage for small mammals that could then be captured. That the fire extracted a cost from the society—altering the vegetation, making the area unsuitable for some other sorts of economic activities—was never questioned. The hunter was not required to return the altered piece of nature to its original form. When the Standard Fruit Company in Costa Rica sprayed DBCP (a pesticide) on its bananas, it simultaneously sterilized hundreds of banana workers.[17] Who pays the price of the sterilization? Clearly, neither the executives nor the stockholders of the Standard Fruit Company lack offspring. A social contract in Costa Rica stated that the chance of sterilization was a risk the workers had to assume if they wished the benefits of a job (although the workers themselves were not informed of this risk ahead of time). This pattern is quite general. One of the ways of minimizing production costs is to pass on some of those costs to other members of society, who will not or cannot refuse to bear them. These are called externalities.

THE TRAGEDY OF EXTERNALITIES—THE CASE OF THE PRIVATELY-OWNED SHEEP

The existence of externalities is an important feature of environmental politics. It makes obvious and intuitive sense to most people that those involved in the production process should have to pay for the inputs if they expect to reap the benefits. To note that a real cost is being diverted to someone else's sphere of responsibility invokes a sense of unfairness, at least, and sometimes of outrage. Yet the use of externalities in real-world economics has an important place in the history of human resource transformation systems. Two general spheres of production are most often treated as externalities: waste receptacles and renovation of natural resources.

Waste is probably the most obvious. Probably every small community in the developed world can tell of a factory that polluted the local stream, poisoned the wells, or somehow left its waste for someone else to take care of.

Renovation of natural resources is perhaps a more subtle externality, but nevertheless plays a significant role in many production processes. Tropical rain forest destruction would likely not exist at all if wood sold for its "real" price; that is, including the cost of replacing it.[18] With the logic of today's world economic system, the cost of replacement is assumed to be zero.

But the whole idea of externalities becomes a great deal more complex when the suite of actions and interactions collectively known as human social organization is brought into the picture yet further. The phenomenon known as the "tragedy of the commons" has been an influential metaphor in ecology and remains an insightful analogy.[19]

The commons in preindustrial England were the lands that were owned by all, in common. They were used for a variety of purposes, among which was the grazing of sheep. This arrangement provided the ecologist Garret Hardin with material for one of the more influential analogies ever invented in the environmental sciences—the tragedy of the commons. According to the analogy, ownership is a critical issue. Sheep are owned by individual people, and the commons is owned by all. Since the commons is owned by all, it is easy to assume that no one individual will care for it, but since each farmer owns sheep, he or she will tend them well. Furthermore, it will be advantageous to each farmer to increase the flock whenever possible, that is, whenever funds are available to buy another sheep. So each individual farmer, as personal owner of a flock of sheep, attempts to extract as much grass from the commons as possible. It is fairly obvious that such an arrangement could easily lead to overgrazing of the commons, and tragedy for all. Behavior for individual gain thus spells disaster for the society—the tragedy of the commons.

The tragedy of the commons is a popular metaphor for what is more technically called the economics of common property resources.[20] Many natural resources are considered to be common property, owned by no one but exploitable by all, usually because of their nature. Fisheries are prime examples. It would be difficult to parcel off a physical part of the ocean and sell it to particular fishers (although it may have appeared equally difficult to do the same with land under earlier ideological systems—for example, many Native American groups). Managing such resources when the means of production are privately owned is a distinct subdiscipline of economics, the economics of common property resources.

This metaphor is also used in a more general sense (e.g., the world as a commons and people's lives as the privately-owned productive forces, city streets as commons and trash as result of private production practices, and so forth). It carries with it an ideological assumption about (1) what is common and what is private and (2) the behavior toward common goods. First, although it always seems natural and obvious, the things a society regards as common property, are as variable as societies themselves.[21] The right to free health care is regarded as a commons in most parts of the world, but not in the United States. The right to border crossing is assumed between subunits within a nation-state, but not between nations. The system of land enclosures used by the modern industrial world are regarded as barbaric by many indigenous peoples.[22] The ideological nature of the entire idea of the tragedy of the commons is best expressed in the one-liner of Murdoch and Oaten when they renamed the phenomenon the "tragedy of the privately-owned sheep."[23]

Second, it is also a questionable assumption that behavior toward common goods is always irresponsible. While this appears to be true in many cases, it is certainly not inevitable. Public parks in U.S. cities tend to be mistreated by the individuals using them, and public monuments are frequently defaced when unprotected, but religious monuments are almost always spared. Popular art on the sides of buildings in the ghettos of major U.S. cities is rarely defaced, unlike official civic art. Land held in common by indigenous people is frequently, if not usually, venerated.[24] At a more abstract level, one's cultural heritage is a commons that almost always is respected (at least by those in that culture). It is clear that treatment of a commons by individuals depends on underlying ideological assumptions.

The basic structure of the argument can be applied to any situation in which some sort of "reservoir" of resource can be tapped by potential consumers of that resource. Examples abound. The oil field in Pithole, Pennsylvania (described in detail in chapter 10) is an excellent example. Although the oil field was large, so many prospectors poked so many wellheads into the ground that the oil field ran dry in a couple of years—the tragedy of the commons.

But let us not be so analytically restrictive. Resources for *H. sapiens* are not simply pastures or petroleum and such. They include all sorts of social constructs. In the case of Pithole, for example, the fact that the oil was drained so rapidly was a tragedy for the investors, to be sure. But tragedy struck before the wells went dry in that overproduction drove prices down so low that most producers were losing their shirts anyway. That is, the metaphorical reservoir was not the oil, but, rather, the pool of consumers and the oil producers were tapping the consumer's money. One producer would have put only a small amount of oil on the market and the law of supply and demand would have given him (they were all men) a good return from the consumers anxious to purchase. But a large number of producers actually put a large amount of oil on the market, the law of supply and demand drove the price down dramatically, and the producers went broke—a tragedy indeed. But here the commons was the free market and the operating principle was free-market competition— a tragedy!

Punditry and academics aside, this tragedy-of-the-commons structure of the free-market system has long been recognized by anyone who cares. Indeed, much detail about the function of the modern corporation might be usefully analyzed as a struggle to avoid the tragedy of the commons that is dictated by free-market economics.

In a similar vein, the metaphor of privately-owned sheep grazing on a publicly-owned commons is directly applicable to the debate about privatization, although confusion about definitions continue to plague that debate. Casting the problem as a debate between private and public ownership is probably doomed to misunderstanding from the start. We in the West have peculiar notions of private and public, stemming at least in part from the Industrial Revolution and maturation of the modern industrial model. As in all societies, we live within a discourse, which is to say we abide by certain rules without even thinking about what those rules are. Two important rules in our case are (1) competition among productive units is good and inevitable, and (2) certain components of the productive process can be "externalized." The second rule, of course, takes its *raison d'être* from the first, since there would be no need to externalize in the first place if a competitive edge were not needed. The reason for the tragedy is, thus, either that we view commons as externalizable (which we shouldn't) or that we agree that our system ought to be based on private property and economic competitiveness (which we need not). The potential solutions, theoretically, are to (1) develop a social contract in which the commons are not externalizable (in the context of the present U.S. system, this would likely be called regulation), (2) privatize the commons (so that individual owners would responsibly manage their piece of what was formerly the commons), or (3) eliminate or drastically reduce the system of competition and private property (i.e., private property in the sense of production units, not in the sense of personal property). There is no *a priori* reason to suspect that any one of these solutions is better than the others. But it is reasonably clear (I hope) that the so-called tragedy of the commons (or tragedy of the privately-owned sheep) *could* be solved by any of the three.[25]

The tragedy of the commons is, thus, if properly cast, an excellent metaphor for understanding the operation of all sorts of externalities. Human labor converts sheep and pasture into wool, which is sold on the market. Obviously, the person involved in the process should try to minimize (1) how much labor must be invested, (2) how much money is paid for the sheep, and (3) how much it costs to return the pasture to its original state after using it. The critical idea of the tragedy of the commons is that the third factor, pasture renovation, is assumed to have a zero cost. This may be quite a rational assumption under normal conditions.[26] It becomes a tragedy when use is so high that the pasture becomes overgrazed (and, thus, the recuperative process is set back significantly), yet the assumption remains that renovation is costless. The economic calculations required if the system as a whole were to be sustainable would have to include the cost of pasture renovation after overgrazing. And such calculations would be made if the system were changed in any of the three ways outlined above: (1) develop a social contract to preserve the commons, (2) privatize the commons, or (3) eliminate the system that requires externalization. As always, each of these three ways carries other costs with it.[27]

ENVIRONMENTAL DEMOCRACY IN THE THIRD WORLD (OR THE LACK THEREOF)

I was raised in a working-class neighborhood on the northwest side of Chicago. My father was a machinist, my mother an order clerk for a grocery store chain, and all my friends had parents who worked in factories or stayed at home. I never knew anyone whose parents were lawyers or executives or junk-bond traders. I also never knew how those other families lived. Relatively speaking, my family was poor. Major purchases, such as a bicycle or a portable radio, were consciously saved for, and I recall going to a restaurant approximately once a year. Other, more intangible poverty was perhaps more important to me. I recall one event that sticks with me to this very day (and is actually the source of an occasional nightmare). I must have been 4 or 5 years old at the time, and I awoke one morning to find my father sitting in the living room. He was normally at work at that time, so I asked him what he was doing at home. Looking up from his newspaper, he responded, "I was fired and have to look for a new job." I asked him what that meant and, I assume out of a certain frustration with his current position, he snapped back at me, "That means that I'm not sure we can eat dinner tonight." I can understand his frustration at just having lost his job, and obviously he was talking metaphorically about dinner that evening, but for a 4- or 5-year-old kid, the evening's dinner was a very real thing, and the threat of not having it was scary.

Another event is even more vivid in my mind. I recall the terror my family experienced every summer in Chicago during the polio epidemics of the 1950s. No one was sure where polio came from, but we knew that it was just chance whether one contracted that dreaded disease or not. Later in life, I was talking with a colleague who also was raised in Chicago, but in one of the wealthy suburbs. She also recalled the fear of polio and talked of the inconvenience every summer of her family having to move to their summer home to escape the polio season. Some people had to be inconvenienced by moving to their summer home to escape the polio season, while others just had to live with the probabilities. Relatively speaking, that social class that includes auto workers, textile workers, and the like, has a life style that is different from the class that includes the owners of the textile mills, auto factories, and the like. And it is not a question of income or savings alone; it is a question of very basic qualities of life, such as security.

But these differences become almost trivial when we begin examining how the average person in a similar social class position lives in the Third World. I lived briefly in southern Mexico, in a little town called Cárdenas in the state of Tabasco. My neighbors lived in a house made of cardboard, corrugated tin, and an old political banner from the ruling party. Two families lived in a house that measured at most 20 feet on a side, sleeping in hammocks or on pieces of cardboard on the dirt floor. One of the mothers, Maria, had had five children, two of whom were still alive. The other, Magnolia, had had seven, two of whom were alive. Their water source was a broken water line on the street in front of their house; they had no electricity, no sewage. Their yearly income came from an avocado tree in their backyard, from the ice pops the oldest boy, Lorenzo, occasionally sold at the second-class bus station, and, I presume, from any handouts they could gather in the streets (although I never saw anyone in the family begging). The main food was tortillas or bread, occasionally spread with some lard, avocados in season, and any vegetable matter the kids could muster up from garbage dumps and empty lots. During my stay there, one of the little boys in the family died—proximately of diarrhea, ultimately of hunger. I only rarely saw the men of the family; they apparently did not live there, and certainly contributed nothing in the form of income to the families.

Little Elena was 7 and one of the brightest children I have ever known. I taught her how to write her name, a feat of which she was quite proud. I gave her a pencil and piece of paper to practice at home, but her brother tore up the paper and a local pig ate the pencil. René, her brother, was wild, not at all like Elena, and never did learn how to even make an "r," let alone write his name. Lorenzo was 11 and was the most quiet of all the children.

I visited the same family 10 years later, only to find, depressingly, that their lot had not changed significantly. Their house still is made of old scraps of wood and corrugated metal, the floor still of dirt. Elena (now 17) only finished the third grade. Had she been born in Ann Arbor, Michigan, I have no doubt she would have been an outstanding student, probably one of the best. René never went to school at all, and ran away from home, or at least disappeared one day, and no one knows his whereabouts (he is now 17, if he is still alive). Lorenzo, the older brother who sold ice pops, is now a carpenter's helper and, in fact, contributes considerable income to the family. Indeed, the family's situation, according to them, has improved over the last ten years, although from my point of view it seems depressingly the same as before. Elena occasionally does some domestic work, which brings some income into the family, and Lorenzo's job brings a regular, if small, income to the family for the first time. On the other hand, there are more people living in the house, although the house is slightly bigger and some of the cardboard has been replaced by wood.

While Elena and her family represent an extreme of poverty, they also represent the way many people live in the Third World—substantially different from the working classes in the developed world, although the underclass in U.S. inner cities continues to see its situation deteriorate and, according to some measures, approaches Third World conditions.[28] As difficult as life may be for some citizens of the United States or other developed nations, one can hardly fail to notice a dramatic difference in conditions of life in the Third World. It is in the Third World that agricultural production has seemingly not been able to keep up with population growth (actually, this is only an illusion),[29] where dangerous production processes are located, where raw materials and labor are supplied to certain industries at ridiculously low cost, where air and water pollution run rampant, where people live in desperation, where talk of bettering the state of the environment is frequently met with astonishment—"How can you expect me to worry about tropical deforestation when I must spend all my worry time on where I will find the next meal for myself and my children?"

Analysts of the late nineteenth and early twentieth centuries generally agreed on the basic mechanism causing such a pattern. It was thought that the Third World was simply behind, and that the nations of the Third World would develop in time, just as the developed countries had done before. Karl Marx was probably originally responsible for this point of view, typified by the following quote: "The country that is more developed industrially only shows, to the less developed, the image of its own future."[30] Lenin added to this view by noting that when industrialized countries became imperial powers, they inevitably transferred capital to their underdeveloped colonies and thus accelerated the industrialization process. This "time" hypothesis was the accepted wisdom for quite a long period. But, gradually, it became obvious to even casual observers that something was dramatically wrong with this interpretation. Had it been correct, one should have been able to observe the industrialization of the Third World. Yet by the end of World War II, it became evident that the expected development was not occurring. The grinding poverty and stagnated economies of Third World countries seemed to be more persistent than the time hypothesis predicted.

This very simple and obvious observation led to a great deal of analysis, beginning in the 1950s, but with most vigorous discussion and debate during the 1960s and 1970s. The general field of analysis is now known as "dependency theory," and, in its most general form, it holds that the underdevelopment of the Third World is not an accident of history or a product of bad real estate, but an organic outgrowth of the development of the developed world. Development in the Third World was seen as being dependent on events in the First World, and somehow maintained at a lower level in order to benefit that First World. A variety of flavors of dependency theorists have seen the light of day, and literally hundreds of books have been written, representing various, sometimes contentious, debating positions within the general idea of dependency. The one, and I think only, point on which they agree is that the underdevelopment of the Third World occurs because of the development of the First World.

It would be folly even to attempt to summarize the complex and historically conditioned debates within this vigorous field of political economy. Rather, let me summarize what appears to be the most recent and lucid explanation of the phenomenon, one that more or less summarizes what others have said earlier and condenses the arguments into a series of very simple and powerful ideas.[31]

Recall the heuristic characterization of the early industrial system as consisting of two classes of people, the owners and the workers.[32] The owners have to wear two hats in making decisions, first, as owners of the factories, and second, as members of the social class that wants to sell products. On the one hand, they want to pay their workers as little as possible; on the other hand, they want workers in general to make as much as possible. This contradictory position represents the "engine" of economic growth in an advanced economy. The situation today in much of the Third World appears similar. For the most part, we are dealing with agrarian economies in which there are two obvious social classes: those who produce cotton, coffee, tea, rubber, bananas, chocolate, beef, sugar, and many other crops for export, and those who produce food for their own consumption on their own small farms and, when necessary, provide the labor for those who produce export crops. Consider, for example, a Costa Rican farmer I used to know, Carlos. Carlos had worked for the United Fruit Company for more than 10 years, when, because of a temporary drop in the price of bananas on the international market, United Fruit decided to scale back production and Carlos lost his job. The only employer in the area was United, so Carlos and his family were forced to either migrate to another area where a job might be found, or find a piece of land and carve out a farm. They did the latter. Their farm is approximately two hectares in size and they grow cassava and taro and have several small fruit trees that are not bearing yet, a small herd of chickens, and a cow. Carlos feeds his family on the root crops, some basic grains he buys with the small amount of cassava he can sell, the eggs from his chickens, and the milk from his cow. Recently, a German company started an ornamental plant farm up the road, and Carlos got a job there as a night watchman. He told me, "At least I won't forget what money looks like." His salary is about $3.00 a day, but it probably won't last very long. I suspect he soon will once again have only his farm.

Another friend of mine in Costa Rica, Bruce (not his real name), is the chief executive in an international corporation involved in export crop production. After I sat in his living room listening to him close a million-dollar deal on the telephone, he recounted to me how his company was relocating much of its operation in Honduras, where the military "knew how to control the unions," unlike Costa Rica, where strong democratic traditions maintained workers' rights to organize. His main concern at that time, however, was with the threat of recession in the United States, since his company exports luxury products there. That the Costa Rican unions would have made wages higher for Costa Rican workers and thus would eventually promote the growth of the economy was obviously of no concern whatsoever to him (except, of course, in the negative sense that his company would have had to pay them more).

Superficially, these people appear similar to the factory owner and worker of the First World system. But the similarity is skin deep. Yes, Bruce runs a "factory," and Carlos works (or worked) in a "factory." But Bruce is concerned with selling the products of his production process, not to Carlos and people like him, but rather to people in the First World. The export producer of the Third World does not wear two hats with regard to the laborers on his or her farm, since the concern is not to sell the products to those laborers, but rather to the First World. This means that the dynamo of economic growth represented by the contradictory goals of the factory owner in the First World, wishing for richer customers and cheaper laborers, simply do not exist in the Third World. The First World factory owner must be concerned with the general economic health of the working class, and thus there is social pressure to maintain consumption power in that class. There is general agreement that while such an arrangement tends to produce economic cycles of boom and bust, it also represents the mechanism of economic growth, and is therefore the base of development. That very base of development does not exist, to a significant extent, in the Third World. Bruce could not care less whether Carlos can buy cotton or bananas or sugar. Bruce's concern is whether Detroit auto workers and San Francisco yuppies can buy his products.

In Figure 9.1, the basic idea is represented as a flowchart, assuming the First World country produces only automobiles and blue jeans and the Third World country produces cotton and bananas. Just follow the arrows (for example, the auto workers and textile workers "pay money for cars to" the owner of the auto factory, who "pays money for labor to" the auto workers). What I hope is obvious from the diagram is that in the developed world, the money that goes to labor eventually goes to purchase the products, thus providing the machinery of economic growth. The Third World does not include an arrow that connects the export producers (the factory owners) to the traditional farmers (the workers) in the process of consumption. The workers and factory owners of the developed world are the consumers of the products of the Third World.

The normal word used to describe such a situation as pictured in the First World in Figure 9.1 is "articulated" (not articulated in the sense of a speech, but rather in the sense of an elbow or knee). Thus, the typical arrangement in the developed world is referred to as an articulated economy, while that in the Third World is disarticulated (in the sense that the two main sectors of the economy are not connected—articulated—with one another). Furthermore, since the resource transformation systems of

First (Developed) World

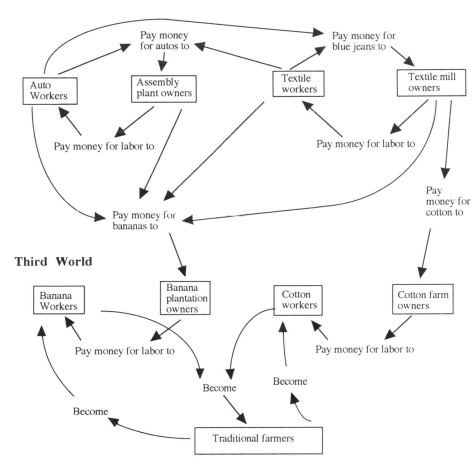

Third World

Figure 9.1. Simplified flowchart of the world resource transformation system. By the action of each entity in a box (e.g., auto workers or textile mile owners), there is a flow from one box to another (e.g., pay money for autos to, or pay money for labor to). The action of the entire dynamic web can be stated as a flow from one boxed entry to another boxed entry. For example, auto workers (a boxed entry) pay money for autos to (the action of a flow) the assembly plant owners (a boxed entry).

the traditional agriculturalists and the export agriculturalists are not connected (at least not in the way the similar processes are connected in the developed world), the economy is dual—the traditional part operates relatively independently from the export part.

This dualism goes a long way toward explaining the differences between the similar classes in the First and Third Worlds. Factory owners in Mexico, whether they be the private farms that produce export crops or the government company that exports petroleum to the United States, do not concern themselves over the fact that Maria's son died of hunger, or that Elena could receive only a third-grade education despite her obvious mental agility, or that René may have had a learning disability and needed special education, or especially that the entire family does not even realize that a different way of life is possible. Maria and her family don't buy oil, they don't buy beef, they don't buy any of the multitude of other export products that make the factory owners' profits. On the other hand, they do work in those factories (sometimes) and the incentive to pay them as little as possible in return for their labor remains.

On the other hand, the factory owners in the United States, whether they be private factories or government-owned and/or -subsidized industries (e.g., all the defense contractors in the United States), care quite a lot that my dad saved money to buy me a bicycle (they make the bicycles) or that my mom worked overtime to buy my sister a special doll (they made the dolls). They even would have been pleased if my mom and dad had worked extra hard to save money for a summer home to escape polio. Sure, they try to pay my folks as little as possible, but that desire is balanced by their wish for the workers in general to be good consumers. So the different structures of economies (articulated in the developed world, disarticulated or dual in the Third World) go a long way toward explaining the relative conditions of the lower classes in those areas of the world. What remains to be explained—and this is a somewhat more difficult concept—is how this dualism in the Third World is maintained.

At this point, I am not sure who expressed the mechanism more clearly, academic economists, or the president of Castle and Cook.[33] Referring to Castle and Cook's investments in the Third World, its president said, "Without overseas investment your entire economic structure collapses in on you." His point is ultimately the same as that of many economists, perhaps a bit more down-to-earth. He simply said that the climate for investment is variable in the developed world, and that the Third

World opportunities for investment are needed for a company like Castle and Cook to ride out the storm, so to speak, when investment opportunities in the First World are limited. Without those opportunities, "your entire economic structure collapses in on you."

Putting it slightly more analytically, the developed world, because of its basic structure, tends to go through cycles of boom and bust, sometimes severe, other times just annoying. During those low economic times, where is an investor supposed to invest? Clearly, without the presence of a Third World, the crisis would be of a qualitatively different sort, in that the Third World provides a sink for those investments during rough times in the First World.[34]

Thus, the dualism of the Third World is functional. It functions to provide an escape valve for investors from the developed world. The West German entrepreneur who started the ornamental plant farm on which Carlos worked as a night watchman invested his money in Costa Rica because opportunities in his native Germany were a bit scarce at the time. What would he have done had there been no Carlos willing to work for practically nothing, or no Costa Rica willing to accept his investments at very low taxation? Clearly, Costa Rica is, for him, a place to make his capital work until the situation clears up in Germany. Union Carbide located its plant in Bhopal, India, not Great Neck, New York. U.S. pesticide companies export insecticides banned in the United States to Third World countries. U.S. pharmaceutical companies pollute the groundwater in Puerto Rico because they could not regard the groundwater as a commons in the United States (or the court costs would have been too great). In all cases, the Third World people must accept such arrangements, largely because of their extreme underdeveloped nature. Underdevelopment simply does not permit democracy, from an environmental standpoint.

Thus, it seems that the developed world has been so successful at economic development, first, because it has an articulated economy, and second, because it is able to weather the storm of economic crisis by looking for investment opportunities in the Third World. The Third World, in contrast, has been so unsuccessful because its economy is disarticulated, and thus dual, lacking the connection that would make it grow in the same way as the developed world. Yet at a more macro scale, the dualism of the Third World is quite functional, in that it maintains the situation in which investors from the developed world can use the Third World as an escape valve in times of crisis. Indeed, it does appear to be the case that the developed world is developed, at least in part, specifically because the underdeveloped world is underdeveloped.

This picture is very general, and certainly does not strictly apply across the board. Many countries simply do not fit into the picture. For example, Taiwan and South Korea are Third World countries that have experienced remarkable levels of economic growth, Hong Kong and Singapore have few peasant farmers, Finland's capitalists have few investments in the Third World, and none of the command economies (the eastern European countries) have significant investments in the Third World. Each of these examples has particular exceptional circumstances associated with it. Far more common are El Salvador, Guatemala, Nicaragua, Costa Rica, the Philippines, Thailand, Vietnam, Mozambique, Zaire, Egypt, and similarly underdeveloped countries. The general pattern seems to be there.

On the other hand, the basic structure seems to be decaying for internal reasons. The wars in Vietnam, Cambodia, Guatemala, Nicaragua, El Salvador, Colombia, Peru, Mozambique, and Angola; the ouster of Duvalier, and later of Aristide in Haiti; a peasant rebellion in Mexico; the Latin American debt crisis; and a variety of other recent events are understandable in terms of the breakdown of the fundamental functional dualism that has characterized much, if not most, of the Third World for the past several centuries. Furthermore, the breakup of the Soviet Union and eastern Europe signifies further complicating effects. Those stories, however, are a bit beyond the intended scope of this chapter.

SUMMARY AND CONCLUSIONS

This chapter is effectively a continuation of a subject begun in chapter 4. In listing the features of *Homo sapiens* that make this species unique, social resource transformation is included as a characteristic on equal footing with tool manufacture, language, abstract thought, and so forth. This chapter is an elaboration of that specific feature of humanness. It began by situating various forms of resource transformation in the general categories evoked by considering the relationships among the elements resources, labor, and product, along with the processes of production and consumption, noting that today's world is dominated by the mode money-product-money (M-P-M), where the second "money" is supposed to be larger than the first. This is the underlying structure of industrial capitalism.

The functioning of the social resource transformation system known as industrial capitalism was then outlined from the point of view of one of its key internal contradictory elements, the need for individual firms to reduce labor costs while, at the same time, hoping to face large consumer demand (laborers also being consumers). The need to reduce labor costs is conditioned by the competitive marketplace, which also drives firms to try to get others to pay for their production costs, the tendency to externalize whatever production costs possible, another tendency of the industrial capitalist system.

One of the most powerful metaphors ever developed in the environmental movement was the so-called tragedy of the commons, which has as its centerpiece the dangers associated with externalizing real production costs. This metaphor was presented and analyzed in great detail, explicitly noting that while the externalities referred to in the original statement of the metaphor were all assumed to be environmental, the basic structure of the argument includes all effective externalities, and is indeed related to the tendency of industrial capitalism to force others to bear the costs of production.

This set the stage for the elaboration of structures that perhaps represent the largest metaphorical externalities in the world today, the Third World. Taking the point of view that the modern industrial capitalist system is a worldwide system, the Third World is seen as part and parcel of that system. Its disarticulated nature, effectively imposed by the developed world, is a clear example of one of the world's largest externalities. When Japanese companies export tropical hardwoods from Indonesia or when United States companies open maquiladoras in Mexico, real costs are partially externalized, and the reason they can be externalized is because of the basic First World-Third World dichotomy that has evolved since industrialization. Just as the pasture of the traditional commons was expected to be renovated either by nature or by someone else, the tropical timbers of Indonesia are expected to be replaced by someone else and the social services required by workers in the maquiladoras are expected to be paid for by someone else. It is a tragedy.

Energy and the Evolution of the Hydrocarbon Society

As the post–Cold War world continues its evolution, ominous events cloud the same horizon that was filled with joy only a few years ago. In addition to the well-known and seemingly intractable political and economic problems that dog our planet from Bosnia to Mexico, modern industrial society seems to have run into an environmental roadblock. Politicians sometimes seem oblivious to such problems. Conservatives argue that further expansion of the economy is necessary so that those who currently own the most wealth will be encouraged to invest more, thus creating more jobs and government revenue. Liberals argue that we need the sort of economic expansion that solves people's problems and provides them with hope for the future. Conservatives feel the only way to accomplish the liberal agenda is through the conservative program, whereas liberals feel the conservative agenda is self-serving and hypocritical, promising little for the majority. Yet, within all of this debate, there is little serious concern for the environmental roadblock. It is possible that neither the liberal nor the conservative agenda is viable.

If economic expansion—be it liberal or conservative—involves the same sort of assumptions that have evolved about how an industrial society must run, it may be that we have run the course. The production of solid waste in cities has reached proportions that are clearly unsustainable. Toxic wastes are making us sick in ways that we are just beginning to understand. The accelerated emission of carbon dioxide and other greenhouse gases into the atmosphere portends possible catastrophic consequences for the future. The list could go on.

Furthermore, the Gulf war of 1991 signaled the world's acknowledgment that ecological forces are as important as economic and political ones in international affairs. As so eloquently put by Andrew Ross (1994, p. 160),

> . . . the Gulf War . . . was the first *explicitly* ecological war in modern history. In this war, ecological concerns were a preeminent feature from first to last, from the OPEC oil-pricing imbroglio that impelled Saddam Hussein to invade Kuwait, to the use of the environment as a weapon by both sides, to the monumental ecological consequences, for refugee populations and for the physical environment, of the destructive forces unleashed during the forty-three days of combat.

The environment, broadly conceived, was the ultimate basis on which the first post–Cold War war—the first ecological war in modern history—was fought.

So the signs of trouble are seen by some to outweigh whatever spoils of war we were to have been bequeathed by "winning" the Cold War, be they new political forms (e.g., ethnic cleansing in Bosnia or Rwanda), or recalcitrant environmental problems (only brave souls or innocents eat much fish from the southern Great Lakes anymore), or confusing economic structures (homeless Russians are beginning to ask the same questions as homeless residents of Washington, D.C.), or "ecological" wars. Where did they all come from, why are they persisting, and what do they mean for the future?

The short answer is that they are simply a consequence of the industrial model, that we have reached a point in the evolution of that model which requires us to rethink some of its assumptions. In order to do so, we need to know something of how we got here. The following brief historical narrative intends to do just that.

ORIGINS

The emergence of *Homo erectus* marks the beginning of the use of concentrated energy—fire.[1] Fire was used most certainly for cooking and protection (from wild animals, for example), and probably for hunting as well. This marks the first major revolution in resource transformation[2] and, in a sense, is as important as language and culture when defining the species. From a biological point of view, it enabled this species to utilize biologically fixed energy hundreds or thousands of times more efficiently then it had before.[3]

As *Homo sapiens* evolved, a wide variety of energy sources other than simply burning wood came into use. Windmills and water wheels were employed early on, mainly for grinding grain. Animals were used very early as beasts of burden (at least as early as 10,000 B.C.), and agriculture, as it developed in the Middle East, would never have taken the form it did had it not been for animals pulling the plows.[4] Perhaps most important of all was the use of wind to fill sails to take first the Muslim traders, and then the European colonists, around the world.

All of these forms of energy come from the same source, the sun, whether it be the animals who eat the grass that photosynthesized its material from the energy of the sun, or the wind filling Columbus's sails, which comes from the sun heating the earth's surface. Recall the basic energy processes involved in life. In photosynthesis, carbon dioxide combines with water, using the sun's energy, to produce energy-rich compounds (ERCs) and oxygen. Those energy-rich compounds are used later when energy is needed. The process that makes the energy available to be used to do work is called respiration and is effectively the reverse of photosynthesis, the combination of the ERCs with oxygen (basically the same thing as burning), to produce carbon dioxide and water, plus energy.

A most direct concentrated energy use system can still be seen in India (see Figure 10.1). Cows are sacred there. They can be seen not only in rural villages, but even in the streets of the largest cities, where they frequently cause great traffic jams. They eat plants—they are herbivores—and after their partial digestion of the plant matter, they produce feces, which contain partial residues of that plant matter, just as the buffalo dung in chapter 8. But when the dung is produced, it is not just left to the decomposers. Members of India's lowest castes gather up the dung, form it into patties, and dry it in the sun. Dried patties are then sold as a fuel source, mainly for cooking fires. In this way, the energy that had been fixed by plants is concentrated by the cows and processed by a socially organized human population, to be usable for the production of heat.

One might initially ask, why use the cow at all? Why not directly burn the plant material that the cow eats? This brings up an important issue: the quality of the ERCs. Why not, for example, use the cow's food, grass, as fuel rather than the partially digested plant matter that the cow leaves

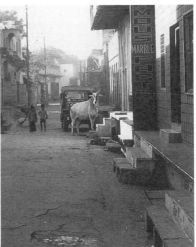

Figure 10.1. Elementary energy transformation in northern India. Top left, a typical food stall in New Delhi. Thousands of such small fires are fueled by a very special energy source. Top right, a sacred cow making her rounds in Agra. Shortly after this picture was taken, a local resident appeared out of the doorway in front of the cow and dumped garbage on the stoop for the cow to eat. Lower left, a mother and her son whose job it is to collect the cow dung, make it into patties, and set it out to dry in the sun, as it is doing on the bank in back of them. Lower right, a vendor takes the dried cow patties to market.

behind? That would be inefficient because the grass contains many different ERCs, some of which give off a great deal of heat when burned, others
of which give off very little. Through the process of digestion, the cow
effectively eliminates the low-energy ERCs, and leaves a relatively concentrated mass of high-energy ERCs.

Concentrating the high-energy ERCs is the underlying principle of
charcoal production. Undoubtedly, our early ancestors noted that a log
placed on the fire late at night and later extinguished by covering with dirt
could be removed and used to fuel a fire again later. It would soon become
obvious that such a partially burned log was lighter than it had been when
first put on the fire, yet it burned almost as long as the original log would
have. Indeed, when charcoal is made, about 50 percent of the wood's
potential energy is used up in the process, but its weight is reduced by 70
percent to 80 percent. It is really quite the same, in principle, as the cow
digesting the grass. The cow breaks down the low-energy ERCs and leaves
the high-energy ones in its dung. The process of charcoal-making does the
same. If one must transport firewood for long distances, it thus makes a
great deal of sense to reduce the weight, even if some of the potential
energy in the wood has to be sacrificed. If a load of firewood on your back
would be enough to cook three meals, a load of the same weight of charcoal would be enough to cook seven or eight meals.

Nature performed the same process when it made coal. Trees that
lived more than 300 million years ago, in the particularly lush vegetation
of the Carboniferous Era, were buried at the bottom of acidic swamps and
were thus not decomposed by the decomposers in the normal trophic cycle. But they did "burn," if ever so slowly. For all practical purposes, nature made charcoal, for during those 300 million years of lying buried in
the swamp (which later was covered over with oceans, sand dunes, volcanic ash, lava flows, and suburban malls) the low-energy ERCs burned
away, leaving only the high-energy ERCs. Thus, these very old trees,
which have been converted by nature to the equivalent of charcoal, represent an excellent energy source, containing an immense amount of energy
in a small volume. We call them "coal."

When we use coal, we are simply completing a process that started in
the past. More than 300 million years ago, the trees died and decomposers
started decomposing them (breaking down the ERCs contained therein).
The decomposition process was interrupted by burial in the swamp. Today, we dig up the remains of those trees and burn them for energy, thus

completing a process that began long ago. But note that we are simply making use of the fact that nature made some excellent charcoal for us.

COAL AND SOCIETY

The historical trajectory experienced by England in the era approximately corresponding to the 100-year period from 1450 to 1550 saw a time of intense economic expansion requiring enormous increases in energy use. During this period, the main source of energy was charcoal (originally wood, but as forests were chopped down, the nearest source of wood became too far away and it became rational to make charcoal).[5] Forests had already been devastated by the need for construction of houses and ships. The increasing demand for energy required by rapidly developing technology, necessitated ever greater quantities of charcoal which caused yet more forests to fall. The result was eventually an almost complete deforestation of the British Isles. It was what we today call an "energy crisis."

Recall the basic equations of resource use, in which a resource can be conceived of as renewable if its rate of exploitation is smaller than its rate of recuperation. Before 1400, the English feudal system was probably using wood resources in a renewable fashion, although forests were already scarce. Charcoal was made in faraway places and carted to the centers of use. But energy was mainly used for heating and cooking, and the rate of forest growth across the whole island was probably quite sufficient to make up for the rate of charcoal making and use.[6]

The technological advances that began around 1450 changed all of that and made the rate of charcoal-making much larger than the forest's rate of recuperation, thus converting a renewable resource into a nonrenewable one.[7] This point underscores the important fact that our form of socio-politico-economic organization dictates whether a resource will be renewable or not. It is not the resource that determines its renewability, but, rather, our use of it. Also note that the perception of a resource's renewability is highly dependent on one's time horizon.

England's response to the energy crisis was quite predictable. It certainly was obvious that by 1400, England was headed toward an immense problem with energy resources. Furthermore, the existence of the so-called black rocks was well known to the world. As early as 1100 A.D., surface coal seams had been discovered, and local peasants regularly used the black rocks as sources of energy—i.e., 450 to 500 years before the energy crisis, coal, the material that would solve the crisis, was well known.[8] It warrants considerable reflection that a very clear alternative to the use of charcoal was well known to the English people and perhaps only needed a bit of technological improvement to become practical. Yet it was ignored until the crisis was upon them.

The energy crisis stimulated the use of coal dramatically, and the next fifty years (from about 1550 to 1600) saw a dramatic rise in coal-based energy use. Further advances in metallurgy and warfare, a new technology of construction with baked brick, and the generalization of space heating all contributed to a dramatic increase in energy use. Also, for probably the first time in history, air pollution became a human health hazard, with London having the dirtiest air in the world at the turn of the seventeenth century.[9]

The next 100 years saw new technological problems arise with the dramatic increase in coal use, especially in the mining of the coal itself. As miners went ever deeper following the natural seams of coal, the problem of flooding in the mines became progressively more severe. In response to this problem, Thomas Newcomen built the first functional steam engine (1712), which enabled the mines to go much deeper than before.[10] But the steam engine's significance was not simply that it permitted more efficient mining of coal, but rather that it ushered in a totally new mode of production. Energy was "harnessed" in the sense that heat energy, which was now abundant, could be turned directly into mechanical energy. This was an historic event without precedent, for it gave rise, only 50 years later, to an enormous and rapid expansion of the textile industry.[11]

The textile industry already existed, of course, but the transformation of the *resource* cotton into the *product* cloth was an extraordinarily labor-intensive feat.[12] Cotton had to be spun into thread and the thread woven into cloth. Both spinning and weaving were labor-intensive operations and employed a large fraction of Britain's working class. Then, in the last half of the eighteenth century, both of these operations were mechanized, taking advantage of the amazing change wrought by Newcomen's steam engine—the spinning jenny (first built by James Hargreaves in 1764) and the power loom (introduced in 1785 by Edmund Cartwright) revolutionized the textile industry.

THE AGE OF OIL

Petroleum is, energetically, the same thing as coal, but its ultimate origin and formation are quite different. Millions of years ago, small organisms, mainly in oceans, died and sank to the bottom. At the very bottom of the deep oceans, the rate of decomposition can be exceedingly slow, and these partially-decayed organisms accumulated in local areas. As the sea dried up (over a period of millions of years, oceans dried up and reformed many times in a given area), these partially decomposed organisms became covered with sediments, similar to the carboniferous tree trunks that formed coal. But, in this case, organisms became entrapped in the cracks of the rocks that were forming under the immense sediment loads, and the resulting pressure caused them to move through these cracks and eventually come to rest in large underground reservoirs. These reservoirs became the oil fields we battle over today. Ultimately it became for the United States what coal was for Britain—the resource on which the country rode to world dominance.[13]

Much as it may be difficult to imagine today, one of the main technical issues of the nineteenth century (and before) was lighting. Especially in the northern winters, it was impossible to sleep 13 or 14 hours a night, and the human animal is not particularly adapted to engage in activities through lunar illumination. The ability to control fire, of course, provided the first lighting for *H. sapiens*. Yet, while hauling firewood for cooking or warmth seemed obviously worthwhile, one hardly needed a roaring fireplace just for the small amount of illumination needed to see one another for talking, or for reading later on. Thus, various types of lamps were invented to supplement the age-old candle (Figure 10.2). Among the best of the lamps were those that used whale oil. But the price of whale oil soon became prohibitive for all but the wealthy. Near the turn of the nineteenth century, an English coal mine operator devised a product called coal oil, or what we know today as kerosene. Kerosene rapidly began to replace whale oil, since it could be made quite cheaply from the world's abundant coal sources. Throughout the nineteenth century, kerosene became dominant as lighting fuel, and the growing U.S. population represented an insatiable market for this fuel.

Attention rapidly focused on the fact that this new product strongly resembled what had come to be known as rock oil or Seneca oil, a naturally-occurring material that was well known throughout the Appala-

Figure 10.2. Whale oil and kerosene lamps (From the collection of Henry Ford Museum and Greenfield Village).

chians.[14] Seeing great potential by combining the new growth in kerosene use with the apparently substitutable rock oil, an adventurous entrepreneur formed the Pennsylvania Rock Oil Company and began the long process of learning how to convert the raw material (petroleum) into a consumable product as much like kerosene as possible.

At this time, the use of petroleum on a world scale was well known and the discovery of rock oil in Appalachia was not particularly important. As early as 100 A.D. in Burma and 400 B.C. in the islands of the Ionian Sea, substantiated reports of the use of petroleum as fuel were well known. The proverbial burning desert sands were not a consequence of the sun's rays, but rather, the surface oil of the Arabian peninsula that caught fire and burned for years. What was prescient for the Pennsylvania Rock Oil Company was seeing the similarity between rock oil and kerosene and the possibility of manufacturing the latter from the former. If that could be done, the tremendously growing demand for kerosene could be tapped into.

Only six years after its founding, the company produced 500,000 gallons of kerosene and increased that production to more than 2 million gallons by 1870. While almost all of the production was, as would be expected, kerosene, several by-products (wastes) were an inevitable consequence of the production process. As is always the case, enterprising people sought to turn the waste products into something useful, and by the late nineteenth century, a variety of minor products were being produced by the industry, including lubricants and fuel oils. But there was one waste product that no one could find a use for, and it was produced in large quantities by the process of making kerosene. That useless product was gasoline.

The early success of the Pennsylvania Rock Oil Company did not go unnoticed by the rest of the entrepreneurial world. In particular, John D. Rockefeller and his Standard Oil Company emerged at this time. By the turn of the century, Standard Oil was effectively the only oil company in the country (Figure 10.3), with the exception of several smaller companies in California.

Petroleum was well known throughout the world well before the United States wanted more of it for making kerosene. But it was a resource in short supply. The only crude oil that was known was that which leaked onto the ground or into streams, such as what leaked into the Pennsylvania creek near Titusville, which became known as Oil Creek. The problem was that it never occurred to anyone that oil could be "mined" the way coal could.

Finally, a group of investors in the Pennsylvania Rock Oil Company struck on the idea of drilling. They reasoned that a technique already in use for mining underground salt (known as "boring") might be used to

Figure 10.3. An early horse-drawn delivery vehicle for the newly formed Standard Oil of Indiana (From the collections of Henry Ford Museum and Greenfield Village).

see if the underground sources from which the surface leakages derived could be tapped. It seemed like a far-fetched idea at the time, but with the stakes so high, with the demand for kerosene seen as limitless, it was worth a try.

Colonel Edwin Drake was contracted by the investors to travel to Titusville and try his hand at drilling. Teaming up with a blacksmith known locally as Uncle Billy, Drake began drilling with the same technology commonly used to drill for salt water. Setting up the derrick and actually getting the drilling done was not an easy task, and the colonel's funding gradually ran out, with all but one of the original investors jumping ship. Just as the last investor sent Drake a letter ordering him to cease work, Uncle Billy reported to the colonel that oil was seeping up through the drill hole. They attached a common water pump to the hole and began pumping oil out of the ground, something thought to be impossible just days before. Effectively, Uncle Billy and Colonel Drake made the discovery that made the oil industry possible.

Refining companies sprang up, and land claims were made throughout the oil creek basin; the rush of entrepreneurs into the area created a gold-rush mentality. The technology was quite simple, and anyone with the slightest bit of ingenuity could easily drill for oil, given the rights to the land. And the competitive marketplace did what it was supposed to do—it reduced the price of crude oil very rapidly as the "gold" rush proceeded. In one year alone, during the rush, the price of a barrel of oil went from 10 dollars to 10 cents. This was not the first time that producers saw the need for supply management,[15] but it was one of the most dramatic.

But the clear economic lessons of unbridled competition were not as important as the lessons that should have been learned about common property resources. Oil occurs in interconnected fields under the ground, and is effectively a common property resource, which is certainly not renewable, especially on a local level. While it may have seemed to the individual entrepreneurs that their particular piece of property held their oil, the fact was that they were all drilling a large number of holes into a single source. The result was what any reasonable person would expect, as exemplified by the brief history of Pithole, Pennsylvania. Oil was struck there in January 1865. Land speculation began immediately, and by September of that year, a location that had been too small to place on a state map had become a town of 15,000 people, and oil was flowing at a rate of 6,000 barrels a day. Then, in November of the same year, the well stopped flowing, pumped dry by individual entrepreneurs frantically trying to pump out more oil than their neighbors, just as good entrepreneurs are supposed to do. By January 1866, just a year after the original discovery, Pithole had begun its decline into obscurity, and a short time later, it was little more than a ghost town. One piece of land that was purchased for $2 million in 1865 sold at auction for less than $5 in 1878.[16]

AUTOMOBILES AND THE RISE OF THE MODERN SYSTEM

Henry Ford provided the world with perhaps one of the most important inventions of the Industrial Revolution—the mass production system.[17] Ford began his automobile production in an atmosphere of growing consumer potential and the new availability of that previously useless substance called gasoline. One can hardly overemphasize the transformation of the world that was wrought by the introduction of this transportation device. Indeed, it was seen as soon as it was produced as potentially revolutionary in its transformation of society. An early analyst predicted (much to the ridicule of his audience, who thought he was exaggerating) that some day we would find "hundreds" of these vehicles in every major U.S. city. What an exaggeration!

World War I was a watershed for automobiles, especially for their equivalent in warfare. In one historically crucial event, all the taxis in Paris were commandeered by the French military to transport troops to the front. The famous Paris Taxi Brigade was put into operation and transported thousands of French troops to the battle front—the birth of modern mechanized warfare.[18]

Just prior to the outbreak of World War I, an important antitrust case was brought against Standard Oil, fueled to a great extent by the influential articles of Ida Tarbell. The decision was against the company and Standard Oil was forced to break up into several companies, each of which was considerably weakened, and forced into healthy competition with each other.[19] While the antitrust suit was clearly a step in the right direction to demonopolizing the oil industry, it also opened the door to another threat. Shell's famous leader, Henry Detering, began buying up oil leases in the United States, recognizing the debilitation of the formerly all-powerful Standard Oil.

Detering himself realized that too much competition was bad for the major companies, and, in 1928, he convened a top-secret meeting in Achnacarry, Scotland. He claimed that the meeting was simply a sporting event, at which he and his friends were going to get together for a weekend of shooting, but his "friends" included representatives of all the major oil companies in the world. The signing of the Achnacarry agreement was a key event in the development of the modern hydrocarbon society. In an effort to cut costs for all companies in one fell swoop, Detering devised an arrangement in which transportation costs for any oil delivery would be assessed to a buyer based on the longest transport possible, yet be delivered thorough the shortest route possible. For example, if Shell had a tanker in the Caribbean and was to deliver a load to Corpus Christi, Shell billed the buyer as if the oil were coming from the Persian Gulf. All companies signed this agreement (there were other, more complicated aspects of the agreement), which represents the first organized effort on the part of the world's largest oil companies to set prices. Indeed, even though the Achnacarry agreement never functioned well in practice, it was a watershed in that it set the tone and underlying assumptions of the entire indus-try—the major oil companies shall be responsible to set prices to ensure the largest profits possible.

THIRD WORLD NATIONALISM

Perhaps the major event related to the hydrocarbon society between the two world wars was the action of the Mexican government between 1917 and 1938. The Mexican Revolution resulted in a new constitution, which retained national sovereignty over all subsoil wealth, resulting in a clear contradiction to the previous assumptions that a foreign company could own rights to such wealth. The ensuing argument raged for more than 10 years and was particularly important because of substantial holdings of Standard Oil of New Jersey (one of the products of the breakup of Stan-dard Oil in 1911), and Gulf, to say nothing of significant properties of the Royal Dutch Shell Group. The Mexican government was trying to set a dangerous precedent, maintaining subsoil rights regardless of who owned the surface. In 1927, the U.S. government threatened to invade Mexico to protect U.S. oil companies, and the Mexican government sent in its own army with a promise to set the oil fields on fire in case of an invasion. While that confrontation was eventually defused, the general debate con-tinued. In the 1930s, Mexican nationalism and its desire to control its own resources grew, and resentment against foreign ownership of Mexican re-sources grew concomitantly. Finally, in 1938, president Lazaro Cárdenas nationalized the oil industry, forming PEMEX, the Mexican petroleum company. The worldwide significance of Mexico's action was that it set the stage for the rebellion of the Third World. For the first time in modern history, an ex-colony took control of some of its own resources. It would have repercussions that we still feel today. As the Cold War emerged from the ashes of World War II, the Third World became an important arena of conflict, and Mexico's action with regard to petroleum set much of the stage for that arena.

At a more general level, the nature of World War II would have been different had it not been for petroleum. Indeed, it is commonly acknowl-edged that oil won the war for the Allied powers. But more important for an understanding of the nature of the hydrocarbon society were the politi-cal and ecological factors that were born in the ashes of World War II. First, major centers of economic and military power were destroyed and the United States emerged virtually unscathed by the war, in a world with little economic or political opposition. It was thus a time of enormous competitive advantage for the United States. Second, a host of petrochemical products (such as plastics, pesticides, fuels, and textiles) took center stage in the developing world economic system. Third, the United States took up the position of world leader in a new world order, where battle lines were drawn between the U.S. on one hand and the Soviet Union on the other. The Soviet Union, of course, may have shared the victory with the Allied powers, but it also suffered material destruction on a large scale.

A major World War II event that set the stage for much of the world's politics occurred in modern Iran immediately following the war. Throughout Iran's modern history, its oil had been dominated by Anglo-Persian. In post-war Iran, a western educated nationalist, Mohammed Mossadegh, began political activities that were reminiscent of what had happened in Mexico 20 years earlier. In 1951, Mossadegh was elected to lead the country and began a process that appeared similar to the Mexican example. The First World countries, especially Britain, became concerned, since it appeared to be a threat to their domination of oil supplies. Anglo-Persian dominated the oil business there and finally called on the British government to do something about Mossadegh. Britain was still quite weak after the war, so the British intelligence agency M16 called on the CIA to coordinate an effort to eliminate Mossadegh. The M16/CIA plan called for the organization of street demonstrations, teams of thugs to terrorize Mossadegh supporters, and a propaganda campaign to discredit Mossadegh. The campaign was successful, and, in 1953, Mossadegh was overthrown and the Shah of Iran installed as the leader, hand-picked by M16 and the CIA.

The CIA's actions in Iran in 1953 predated similar actions in the Third World, apparently aimed at breaking any spirit of independence that Third World people may have gleaned from the lessons of the French, American, and Mexican Revolutions. It would be repeated throughout the world.[20]

THE HYDROCARBON AGE

Since World War II, we have seen the growth of a society that is almost fully dependent on oil. The traditional use of petroleum—energy—has continued and expanded considerably. Fossil fuels fire electrical generating plants throughout the world, and gasoline powers the ubiquitous automobile. Industry and transportation are fully dependent on oil, and even the mere suggestion that there will be some problem with the supply line can cause major crises, including war.

But perhaps even more important was a sequence of events that began much earlier, with the need for lighting. While kerosene had become the standard fuel in the United States, a different solution to the lighting problem was in the works in Europe. Acetylene gas seemed to be a perfect substitute for the coal gas that provided only dim light. Throughout Europe, acetylene gas production facilities were set up, and the dawn of the acetylene age seemed on the horizon. But it was not to be. Several factors, the most important of which was the new availability of cheap electricity, drove the demand for acetylene gas to near zero.

But in the wake of the failure of almost all acetylene companies, a discovery was to be made that changed the world almost as much as the Industrial Revolution itself. The airplane was a general part of war preparations in the early twentieth century. In 1912, as part of this war effort, a German chemist mixed acetylene with two other chemicals in an attempt to find a chemical that could be used to treat airplane wings to make them impervious to various weather conditions. When he mixed them together and left them in the sunlight, a thick milky substance formed, and eventually solidified. At the time the substance was thought to be useless and was ignored for the next 20 years. But in the 1930s, renewed interest developed in this material. It was a chemical variant of polyvinyl chloride, PVC. It was the grandparent of plastics.

From this accidental invention arose an entire life style based on plastic substitutes, or what have come to be viewed by some as "fake" products. We now have fake cloth, fake wood, fake metal. It is nothing less than a new view of the nature of the species, the plastic society. Indeed, it is difficult to imagine what our society might look like if plastics were suddenly removed.

Furthermore, the very nature of the world agricultural system was dramatically transformed during this same time period. The use of petrochemicals (pesticides and fertilizers) in agriculture is virtually the definition of the "modern" agricultural system.[21] The United States has the most productive agricultural system in the world (based on amount produced per acre), popularly attributed to the use of the chemicals developed during and after World War II.

But, naturally, there has been quite a down side to this revolution. First, the production of hazardous waste represents a new form of production. In all other production processes, the concern is with the rate of production of waste and how it balances with the rate of decomposition of that waste.[22] For the first time in history, we produce wastes that decompose slowly if at all, and indeed some of which are toxic. Furthermore, many side products of production processes are dangerously toxic, such that industrial accidents carry a far higher potential for doing great harm than they have in the past.[23]

Finally, the same pollution that filled London's air in the sixteenth century continues to be produced, in a far more complicated and perhaps less noxious form, but certainly much more rapidly. While its effects on human health are the same as they were in London, they now have created problems that appear to be worldwide and extremely dangerous—we have just begun to understand the depths of those problems.

Among the major global problems already identified are prospects for the warming of the earth's atmosphere in the future. There is considerable debate on many aspects of global warming. What is known for sure is that (1) carbon dioxide and other greenhouse gasses are increasing in the atmosphere (this is simply a consequence of applying the chemical process that releases energy stored by biological processes, but using material that was biologically stored over a period of perhaps 50 million years and releasing the carbon dioxide from that storage in a period of 500 years); (2) if all else remains constant, the world will become warmer, on average; and (3) if the world warms up, some grain-producing areas will receive less rain, seas will rise and inundate many coastal areas, the frequency of violent storms will increase, and a host of other secondary consequences will occur; and (4) if we cut emissions of carbon dioxide and other greenhouse gases now, the world will warm up more slowly.[24] Thus far these ideas remain uncontroversial, although a great deal of controversy remains about the details. The biggest controversy centers on how fast all of this will happen. Some feel we must act immediately; others feel no great harm will be done if we wait. From a scientific point of view, it is not possible to judge the time element. It might be that predicted changes will arrive as soon as 40 or 50 years from now, or it might be that more than 100 years will pass before they arrive. But it must be fully appreciated that there is little, if any, controversy on the ultimate effects.

On the other hand, there is considerable cause for immediate concern regarding ozone. Several chemicals used in our hydrocarbon society ascend to great heights in the atmosphere and chemically interact with ozone to break it apart. Yet, it is actually the ozone layer that makes terrestrial life possible in the first place.[25] Ultraviolet light causes cancer, and perhaps other problems as well. The ozone layer in the upper atmosphere acts as a shield against incoming ultraviolet radiation, thus making life itself possible on land. Most recently, the seasonal hole in the ozone layer that develops over Antarctica has been expanding at an alarming rate. Residents in the southern third of Chile, the populated country closest to the ozone hole, have already begun reporting abnormalities, including cancers and cataracts, in themselves and their farm animals.[26] Whether these are due to the reduced ozone is not possible to say for sure, but they certainly should be cause for great alarm.

THE MODERN ERA OF THE HYDROCARBON SOCIETY

The modern era can be dated more or less with the formation of the Organization of Petroleum Exporting Countries (OPEC) in 1959. While OPEC never did function very efficiently, it represented a challenge to the hegemony of the so-called seven sisters, the seven oil companies that dominated world oil trade at that time. They were Standard Oil, or Esso (later Exxon), Mobil, and Chevron (all of which resulted from the 1911 antitrust suit against Standard Oil), Gulf and Texaco (born of the Spindletop strike in Texas), British Petroleum, and Shell (from the Royal Dutch Shell Group).[27] To some extent, the seven sisters functioned similarly to the way Henry Detering had envisioned in the Achnacarry agreement, setting prices cooperatively to maximize profits of all oil companies. The formation of OPEC, at least initially, challenged this function.

The Yom Kippur War broke out in Israel in 1973 and created the energy crisis that alerted many formerly complacent people to the reality of our dependence on oil. The reduction in the flow of oil, because of the Arab boycott, created lines of cars at gas stations and many other secondary effects in the developed world. The energy crisis led, first, to an acknowledgment on the part of the First World that it had become totally dependent on this one basic resource, petroleum, and, second, to a realization on the part of major oil companies that they, too, were vulnerable to the vicissitudes of the political winds. Thus, a new contract was established, in which OPEC and the seven sisters negotiated all aspects of the oil trade (i.e., OPEC and the major oil companies would come to cooperate in setting oil prices and production goals).

The final chapter in the story could be thought of as the defining moment of the post-Cold War era. In 1989, the Soviet Union fell, and the primary political alignments of the post-World War II world came to an end. While we are still reeling from this turn of events, and still struggling to find the next political course, certain arrangements have become obvious. The most critical event to date of the post-Cold War world was the Persian Gulf war, a war still only vaguely understood by all parties. To understand that war one must begin somewhat earlier,[28] with the formation of the Ba'ath party.

In 1930s Paris, a group of Syrian students in the Arab Students Union devised a strategy for an anti-colonial campaign in the Arabian countries. A decade later the Ba'ath party grew out of this tendency and was formally inaugurated in Damascus. The party sought to speak for the entire Arab world and had two characteristic features that seemed to drive its operations, a denunciation of the values of Western consumerism, and a contempt of all rivals, Arab and non-Arab alike. By the 1950s the Ba'ath party had divided into two factions, one Syrian, the other Iraqi.

Saddam Hussein first came to world attention when he was forced to flee to Egypt after an aborted attempt on the ruler of Iraq in 1959. He returned to Iraq four years later to organize the Ba'ath underground militia. His efforts were highly successful, and in 1968 the party seized power in Iraq. He continued working his way up the party hierarchy and, in 1979, he was appointed leader of the party and consequently leader of Iraq.

Iraq is an invention of the post-World War II breakup of the Ottoman Empire. It contains three ethnic groups, defined geographically. In the north of Iraq are the Kurds, fully 20 percent of the population. The Kurds represent an ethnic group spread out over Iraq, Turkey, and part of Iran, in a contiguous territory some of them refer to as Kurdistan. (A movement among the Kurds for the establishment of an independent Kurdistan has been resisted most actively by both Turkey and Iraq, and remains an important piece of the political landscape yet today.) The southern marshes of Iraq are home to the Shiite Muslims, mainly farmers who could be thought of as allied religiously with Iran (although, of course, the Iraqi Shiites are Arabs while the Iranians are Persians). The Shiites comprise 50 percent of the Iraqi population. In the center of Iraq are the Sunni Muslims, less than 30 percent of the population, but the core of the Ba'ath party.

One must also understand the events in Iran in the late 1970s. The CIA's Shah of Iran, placed in power after the successful ouster of Mossadegh in 1953 (see above), had very little popular support. His regime had been corrupt and in many ways brutal, eventually leading to his overthrow by the Ayatollah Khomeini and his deeply religious followers, the Shiite Muslims who constituted a vast majority of the population of Iran. The enthusiasm of the Iranian revolution of 1979 sparked two watershed events, the taking of U.S. hostages in the U.S. embassy in Tehran and an increase in propaganda aimed at Iraq's Shiite population, effectively calling on the Shiites to join in a holy war against all Islam's enemies, which, of course, included Saddam Hussein and the Ba'ath party, fully controlled by Iraqi Sunnis (but, don't forget, the Ba'ath party itself had subdivided in the 1950s into the Syrian and Iraqi factions). Finally, recall that the southwestern lowland of Iran, known as Khuzistan, contains 90 percent of Iran's oil production, and also hosts an almost 50 percent Arab population (Iraq frequently refers to Khuzistan as "Arabstan").

The first event of the Iraq-Iran war was probably the execution of the most prominent religious leader of southern Iraq, a Shiite, of course. Saddam then attacked the Iranian oil fields in Khuzistan, expecting a victory in two or three weeks. Saddam's reasons for starting the war were complex and multiple. He wished to gain control of the southern Shatt-al-Arab waterway, since Iraq never had (and still lacks) convenient access to the Persian Gulf. He felt it crucial to stave off the revolutionary threat felt from the Shiite south, a threat openly promoted by the new theocracy in Tehran. He probably thought he could gain control over Khuzistan, thus incorporating 90 percent of Iran's oil into Iraqi territory. He also had designs on becoming the recognized leader of the Arab world, a goal to which a victory over the Persians would certainly contribute. Finally, and most definitely important from a tactical point of view, Iran was weak at the time.

But the expected two- or three-week victory was not to be had. Iran proved to be far more capable of defending itself than had been expected, and, within weeks, engaged in retaliatory bombing raids against Iraqi oil fields. Furthermore, Syria (which is ruled by the other faction of the Ba'ath party) shut down the pipeline that carries Iraqi oil for export. The result was seven years of a stalemated war between Iraq and Iran, in which many people died, but no territory or political concessions were gained by either side.

Then, in 1987, the war seemed to change course. Iran, with new military might (supplied in part by the weapons sent to it by the United States as part of the Iran/Contra scandal), captured the Fao Peninsula in southern Iraq and launched an attack on Kuwait, in retaliation for its support of Iraq. Suddenly, Iran was clearly winning the war.

Faced with a potential Iranian victory, and still scarred by the Iranian hostage affair, the United States quickly went to the aid of Saddam Hussein, supplying him with considerable military intelligence, and perhaps even weaponry. The United States also shot down an Iranian civilian airliner, killing 290 civilians, an act that the Iranians are convinced was a premeditated action designed to help Saddam (an assertion denied by the U.S. government). At about the same time, Iraq also began the extensive use of chemical weapons. So the combination of U.S. support and extensive use of chemical weapons put the war back on its stalemated footing. The Saddam Hussein who appeared to be on the verge of defeat in 1987 was back in power by 1989, in part due to the efforts of the U.S. government.

This background set the stage for Saddam Hussein's invasion of Kuwait in 1990, and the first major international conflict in the post-Cold War world. Saddam's reasons for invading are fairly clear. As before, Iraq has always needed access to the Persian Gulf, which he would have gained with the annexation of Kuwait. Furthermore, the Rumaila oil fields lie on the border with Kuwait, and it had long been thought (probably with some truth) that Kuwait had been "slant drilling" (drilling from the Kuwaiti surface on an angle to get into oil that was really under Iraq). Control of the Rumaila oil fields was clearly another goal of the war. Also, Kuwait had been involved in what appeared to be a coalition with the major oil companies against OPEC, in that Kuwait had been overproducing oil (against its agreed-upon limit within the OPEC accords), thus lowering the price on world markets. Iraq had complained about this, but Kuwait remained intransigent on the issue. Finally, Iraq had long considered Kuwait part of Iraqi territory,[29] and its capture would clearly propel Saddam to the height of leadership of the Arab world.

The U.S. role in Saddam's invasion of Kuwait is highly controversial. There appear to be three opinions on that role, any one of which could be true. First, some claim that the U.S. ambassador to Iraq, when approached by Saddam's agents about the potential invasion, informed Iraq that the United States had "no problem" with it. Such a response would have seemed logical to Saddam, since the United States had been his staunch supporter only two years earlier. Second, some claim that the U.S. ambassador meant to give support only to the capture of the Rumaila oil fields, and Iraq misinterpreted the response to signify a go-ahead to invade all of Kuwait. Third, the Bush administration maintained that the U.S. ambassador gave a clear signal not to invade at all. It would be impossible to determine, with current available evidence, which of these three is actually true. Perhaps future historians will clarify it, but, as of now, all seem fairly plausible. What is clear is that Saddam somehow got the message that it was all right to invade, and Desert Storm resulted.

The fallout of Desert Storm is still taking shape. What is clear, as former President Bush has so frequently enunciated, is that we are living in a New World Order. The Allied attack on Iraq could hardly have been more successful. Even after subtracting the hyperbole of wartime press reporting,[30] the victory of U.S.-led forces was overwhelming. And it is important to acknowledge what this means to Third World nations. No matter how evil you have come to believe Saddam Hussein is, it is a fact that he commanded the world's fourth largest army, clearly the largest military in the Third World. Such a complete, and utterly humiliating, defeat of the largest army in the Third World certainly gives pause to any Third World leader who might have designs on building his or her own military might as a way of gaining independence from the First World. Furthermore, the idea, spawned by Mexico in 1938, defeated by the CIA in Iran in 1953, reignited by Iran in 1979, that a Third World nation can assert independent control over its petroleum resources, was defeated again in Iraq by Desert Storm.

Thus have we constructed the New World Order in the hydrocarbon society. We remain dependent on petroleum as the basis of our industrial society, the waste products thus produced are poisoning us, and the international order thought necessary to maintain order in the system is seemingly etched in stone. And the future? Not much is clear.

ELEVEN

Component Interactions
(Population Ecology)

America used to have lions. For a long time, parts of America probably looked a lot like Africa, with big herbivorous mammals, lions and other predators, scavengers and decomposers, and so on. However, during the famous ice ages, all the large mammals became extinct, making the Western Hemisphere look quite different, ecologically, from Africa. Some similarities remain, however. One of the most dramatic for nature lovers is America's equivalent of the African leopard, the jaguar.

I first visited the tropics in 1968, traveling the length and breadth of Costa Rica, sampling the impressive diversity of tropical life that country has to offer. One of my goals on that trip was to see a jaguar in the wild. In retrospect, such an expectation derives from inexperience, jaguars being quite shy and retiring. Yet, at the time, I felt that if I was going to be in jaguar habitat for approximately 10 weeks, the chances of spotting one were quite good. Since that time I have logged at least 200 weeks in jaguar habitat, and the most I can boast is several tracks in the mud, and some very characteristic feces.

Tracks and feces are not exactly what would have made Stewart Granger or Richard Chamberlain excited (you may recall, they are the old and less-old actors who played the legendary Quartermain in the classic *King Solomon's Mines*), but it turns out that jaguar feces can provide some rather interesting information. The biologist Harry Greene, of the University of California at Berkeley, has been studying the feeding habits of jaguars in a rain forest in Costa Rica by examining the contents of their feces (it is very difficult to even see a jaguar, let alone watch one eat, but it is somewhat easier to collect their droppings). He finds that, of all the possi-

255

ble sources of food available to these large cats, by far their favorite item is sloths. The sloth is a very slow-moving, tree-dwelling animal that hardly anyone thought was a normal diet item of jaguars until a clever biologist began examining feces and noticed a very characteristic type of hair that was almost always present. It is fairly easy to spot a sloth's hair, because each piece of hair has a little groove that goes along its entire length, and that groove, curiously enough, explains why sloths always seem to have a green cast to them, and always smell moldy. Living in that long ridge on each hair in the sloth's coat, is a particular species of algae that lives nowhere else in the world.

The jaguar is a carnivore, and the sloth is an herbivore.[1] One of the sloth's foods are the leaves of a particular type of tropical tree, the *Cecropia* tree. If you wish to spot a sloth in the rain forest, seek out the *Cecropia* trees—that is where most sloths are spotted. Since they are so frequently seen in these trees, ecologists for years had assumed that that is one of their favored foods. However, the fact that sloths are most frequently seen in *Cecropia* trees turns out to have nothing to do with their relishing the leaves (which are actually quite dry and coarse).

Cecropia trees are unusual in the tropical forest in that they are virtually devoid of the vines and epiphytes (plants that live on other plants) that so characteristically cover almost all other species of tropical trees. Why? An interesting exercise can be performed on one of these trees by anyone with a little curiosity. Find a *Cecropia* tree, preferably a small one, and then find a nearby vine. Take the vine and carefully pry it loose from the surrounding vegetation and wrap it around the tree, making sure that the leading tendril is touching the trunk. Then return that night to see what is happening.

The *Cecropia* tree is a very unlikely candidate for anyone to choose to eat, not only because its leaves are very tough and unappetizing, but because there are terribly aggressive stinging ants that live inside of the trunks, and one would think that the sloth would be quite deterred by them. But for some reason, these stinging ants do not bother the sloths; they do not even seem to recognize them as living organisms.

That the sloths are not bothered by these stinging ants is surprising, since the whole point of having the ants there in the first place seems to be to deter herbivores. Indeed, a whole slew of herbivores is standing in the wings waiting to chomp down on their leaves, however undesirable they may seem to us. A variety of beetles and moths (caterpillars) are known to enjoy a meal of *Cecropia* leaves, but are not permitted to do so because of the stinging ants that live inside of the trunk and swarm all over the leaves.

But perhaps even more important, one of the biggest problems a tropical plant faces in its environment is the growth of vines. The ivy vines growing on the sides of university buildings may be aesthetically pleasing to students and alumni, but if the buildings on which they were growing were trying to photosynthesize, the story would be different. For plants living in the type of environment in which *Cecropia* lives, one of the biggest hazards is vines. Growing more rapidly than the *Cecropia* can, they are an ever-present threat. If they attach to the trunk of a growing tree, within a few months they will likely reach its canopy and begin shading its leaves from the sun. Which brings us back to the little exercise described above. When you return to look at the vine tendril you put on the *Cecropia* tree, you will discover that the ants have discovered it and are not taking kindly to it. In fact, they will be lined up on both sides of the leading tip of the tendril, chewing on it. By chewing on the tip of the tendril, in a matter of hours the growing part of the tip is destroyed. Indeed, a *Cecropia* tree without ants usually becomes covered by vines in a matter of months, has its capacity to photosynthesize dramatically reduced, and frequently dies. And this explains why people thought for so long that sloths preferred to eat the leaves of *Cecropia* trees—that was the place you usually saw them. Now we know that was simply because the vines that covered other trees, making sloths difficult to see in the mass of foliage, could not grow on *Cecropia*s because of the stinging ants inside.

So the ants obviously are quite beneficial to the *Cecropia* tree, but what is it, if anything, that the *Cecropia* tree provides for the ants? It is clear that the ants have a place to put their nests inside of the hollow trunk of the *Cecropia* tree; indeed, this could very well be the reason the trunk is hollow in the first place. But, additionally, the *Cecropia* has small glands on the base of its leaves, and these small glands produce energy-rich food bodies that the ants consume with relish. Furthermore, the ants have a habit of physically placing, and then caring for, small insects called mealybugs on the inside of the trunk. The mealybugs have long pointed snouts that they use to penetrate the tissue of the tree and suck out its juices. They are herbivores, and they clearly have a negative effect on the tree. The ants later eat the mealybugs, thus effectively getting energy and matter from the *Cecropia* by using the mealybugs to do so. For the ants, the mealybugs are cattle and the *Cecropia* tree is a pasture.

So we have the jaguar that eats the sloths, which eat the leaves of the *Cecropia* tree. The sloth hair is grooved, providing living quarters for algae, and the *Cecropia* trunk is hollow, providing living quarters for an ant that protects the tree from herbivores and vines. But the ant also grazes mealybugs, herbivores, on the inside of the trunks. Thus, centered on this one species of tree, the *Cecropia*, we have a relatively complex set of interactions (see Figure 11.1). How shall the knowledge we have about this system (the complex set of interactions) be represented to provide the most insight about the system? We could simply represent it as a diagram of energy flow and material cycles, much as has been done in Figure 11.2*a*. The *Cecropia* is the producer, the beetles and caterpillars, sloths, and mealybugs are the herbivores, and the jaguar and ants are the carnivores, the fundamental information of the systems ecologist. But isn't it obvious that a great deal of interesting and important information about what we actually know about the system is left out of such a representation? And that is precisely why we have an alternative representation, in the style of population and community ecologists.

Figure 11.2*b* is a diagram of the same system, more along the lines of population ecology. The elements are connected by short lines, on the end of which is indicated either a negative effect by a small circle, or a positive effect by an arrowhead. Thus, the jaguar has a negative effect on the sloth and the *Cecropia* has a positive effect on the ants. The population ecologist is interested in, first, the way in which populations change in time and space, and second, the way in which various populations interact with one another. The first topic includes questions of exponential growth and density dependence, as described below; the second usually includes three qualitatively different forms of interactions, negative/negative interactions

---

Figure 11.1. The *Cecropia*-sloth system. Top left, a *Cecropia* tree with a sloth in evidence. Top right, sloth (photo by Doug Gill). Bottom right, mullarian body at the base of the leaf of the *Cecropia* tree. Small white bodies are the energy-rich food sources eaten by the ants. Bottom middle, cutaway view of the stem of the *Cecropia*, illustrating its hollow nature, where the ant nest is located. Bottom right, a *Cecropia* tree that has lost its ant colony. Note the heavy vine growth on the trunk.

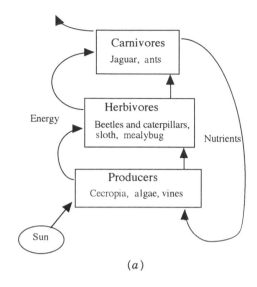

(a)

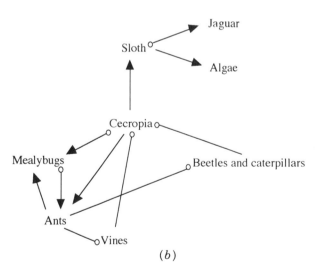

(b)

Figure 11.2. Diagrams of the *Cecropia*-sloth system. (a) Forcing the system into a traditional trophic level diagram. (b) An interaction diagram of the same system.

(usually called competition), positive/positive interactions (usually called facilitation or mutualism), and positive/negative interactions (predation, parasitism, herbivory). In the sections that follow we shall examine first, the way in which single populations change in time; second, the way in which various populations interact with one another; and finally, what might be said about a larger number of populations interacting with one another.

SINGLE POPULATIONS IN TIME— EXPONENTIAL GROWTH[2]

If we begin with a population of just two individuals, and in a particular unit of time those two individuals produce exactly two other individuals, and no one dies, we will expect the following population sizes through time: 2, 4, 8, 16, 32, and so on. This is the famous exponential sequence, and is true for any population that reproduces at some rate, with no mortality associated with its density. It is sometimes surprising when one first takes note of the particularities of exponential growth. For example, in the above example, the population increased by 16 individuals in the fourth time interval. Without thinking too carefully about it, take a quick guess at how many individuals the population will add in the eighth time interval. Or, if you consider a population of water lilies that doubles itself each week, if it takes 32 weeks to cover exactly half of the pond, how long will it take to cover the rest? Of course everyone tends to quickly think that if it took so long to get half way, it will take that long to get the rest of the way, but the fact is that it will only take one more week to cover the rest of the pond. The basic qualitative form of exponential growth is illustrated in Figure 11.3.

A useful way to characterize an exponentially-growing population is simply with a single number, its per-capita rate of growth. In the above example, the population grew with a per-capita rate of growth of 1.00 (for each individual in the population, a single individual was produced). But the actual rate of growth could be any other value. Suppose, for example, that instead of each pair of individuals producing two new individuals in a time period, they produced three. This would make the per-capita rate of growth 1.5. If they produced five, the per-capita rate would be 2.5. If they produced just one, the rate would be .5. This basic per-capita rate is known as the *intrinsic rate of natural increase*.

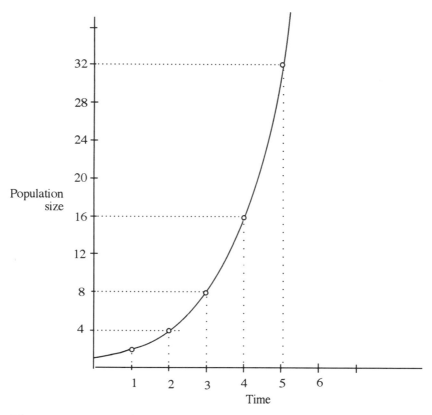

Figure 11.3. Graph of population size over time, illustrating the basic form of exponential growth.

POSITION AND VELOCITY—SOME GENERAL CONCEPTS

This kind of analysis, when first encountered, can be a bit confusing and warrants some further explanation. The reader who is already familiar with rates of change and their analysis (i.e., calculus) may conveniently skip the present section, which is intended as an aid to those not yet familiar with the basic concepts.

Suppose we have a petri dish containing a nutrient medium, and we inoculate it with a single bacterial cell. Suppose further that the petri dish can contain a maximum of 1 million cells. We thus expect that at any future time we will be able to characterize the bacterial population as a number somewhere between 0 and 1 million (presuming that the entire population could die out, in which case its number would be 0). So we could, if we wanted, mark the size of the population as a tick mark on a vertical line that had markings ranging from 0 at the bottom to 1 million at the top. The representation of the size of the population thus becomes a *position* on the vertical line, somewhere between the 0 on the bottom and the 1 million on the top.

It would be the same, for example, as a 1,000-meter drag race. Your position on the race track could be expressed as how far you are from the start, and could be placed on a vertical line scaled from 0 at its bottom to 1,000 at its top. When you start the race your position is at 0, and when you finish the race your position is 1,000. At any time during the race your car will be somewhere between 0 and 1,000. A graph of the race could be made by plotting the position of the car on the vertical line for each second of the race, plotting the time on a horizontal axis. Looking at a point on the horizontal axis tells you how far into the race you are, and the corresponding point on the vertical axis tells you where you are at that time (i.e., where you are between the 0 and 1,000 meter marks). Your position on the vertical axis at any particular time on the horizontal axis is frequently referred to as your "state" at that particular time. So if we refer to the state of a system at some particular time, we usually are referring to its position on the vertical axis at that time. These concepts are summarized in Figure 11.4.

If you are in the car during the drag race, you can look at the speedometer whenever you please and tell what your velocity is. So, in addition to knowing where you are between the 0 and 1,000-meter marks (the state of the system), you can also stipulate how fast the state is changing, that is, how fast your position is changing. This you do by looking at the speedometer and recording the velocity. For many problems in science, we approach understanding through a careful stipulation of the state and rate of change of the system. Indeed, for the vast majority of problems in engineering, the usual approach is to begin with the question, "How does the rate of change vary?" After asking that simple question, the engineer usually brings some very sophisticated mathematical techniques to bear on the problem (the techniques are those one learns in courses in calculus and differential equations), but, conceptually, almost all such problems are similar to looking at the speedometer during the drag race.

The bacterial population is no different. To understand the popula-

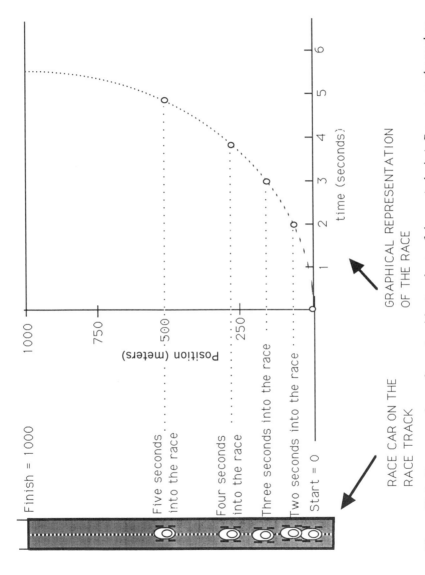

Figure 11.4. Race car analogy of state (position) and rate of change (velocity). Race car on the track at left begins its race, and its position (state) at any given time into the race is shown on a graph of position against time.

tion, we concern ourselves with its state and rate of change. Its state is represented as some position on the vertical line between 0 and 1 million and we could easily determine this position by simply counting the bacterial cells at the relevant point in time. The rate of growth is somewhat more difficult to calculate, but, in principle, we simply seek to look at the population's "speedometer." Again, the method used to calculate the rate of growth is quite sophisticated in practice, but conceptually quite simple. How rapidly is the population growing at a particular point in time? The best way of conceptualizing this is to imagine that we have a device that measures the velocity in the same way the speedometer on a car does. This device tells us how fast the population is going, in the same way the speedometer tells us how fast the car is going.

It is perfectly natural and probably quite obvious to think of these problems as a graph of position (state) versus time, as we did in Figure 11.4. Reading charts in the newspapers often requires interpretations of exactly this kind of graph. But frequently, to gain a deeper understanding of a process, it is useful to think of the problem also as a graph of the rate of change (velocity) graphed against the position. In the drag race, suppose you glance at the speedometer as you pass each 10-meter mark on the drag strip—as you pass the first 10-meter mark, how fast are your going? as you pass the second 10-meter mark, how fast are you going? and so on. You have effectively constructed a graph of velocity versus position (or what the engineer would call rate of change versus state). As we will see below, understanding populations frequently requires us to think in terms of rates of change of the population and how those rates of change vary depending on the size of the population. It may be useful to continue thinking of the problem in terms of the drag race, where the rate of change of the population is the velocity of the car and the size of the population is the position on the drag strip.

SINGLE POPULATIONS IN TIME— LOGISTIC GROWTH

As described above, a population is normally expected to grow exponentially if its rate of birth and death are perfectly constant. Qualitatively, exponential growth looks like the graph presented in Figure 11.3. However, there is an alternative way of looking at population growth. Rather than constructing a graph of the state of the system over time (as was done in Figure 11.3), we gain different sorts of insights by looking at the rate of change versus the population density (recall the above example of glancing at the speedometer at each 10-meter mark). A population that changes from 2 to 4 to 8 to 16 increases by 2, 4, and 8, respectively (i.e., its rate of change is 2, 4, and 8). This rate of growth is known as the *absolute growth rate*. If you make a graph of the absolute growth rate versus the population size (that is plot 2 versus 2, 4 versus 4, etc. . .) the result will be a 45-degree line (i.e., it will have a slope of 1). For another population that changes from 2 to 5 to 12.5 (i.e., for each individual you add 1.5 individuals, the intrinsic rate of 1.5 we had above), you would plot 3 against 2 (since when the population contained 2 individuals it added 3 individuals), 7.5 against 5, and so forth. The result is again a straight line, this time with a slope of 1.5. These two examples are presented in Figure 11.5. Note that representing the population in this fashion, the slope of the line is equal to the intrinsic rate of natural increase. (As an exercise, sketch in on Figure 11.5 a population with an intrinsic rate of 2.5, and another with an intrinsic rate of .5).

Exponential population growth rate is a theoretical construct for natural populations. It assumes from the start a constant production of individuals per capita. No population in nature actually does this. Rather, the production of new individuals is conditioned by the number of individuals already in the population (the population growth rate is said to be "depen-

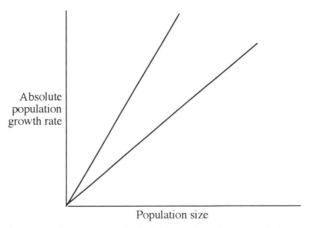

Figure 11.5. Rate of growth (velocity) plotted against population size, for the exponential equation.

dent" on the density of the population—or simply, the population is density dependent). So, for example, rather than having a population that grows like this—2, 4, 8, 16, 32, 64, 128, 264, 528, the population would more likely grow like this—2, 4, 8, 15, 28, 52, 95, 120, 124, 125, 125. This pattern, initially looking something like exponential growth (2, 4, 8), but eventually levelling off to some constant value (124, 125, 125) is known as *logistic growth,* and to a first approximation, most populations in nature follow this sort of pattern. In Figure 11.6, a population growing logistically is shown, along with the original example of an exponentially growing population.

If we now make a graph of the actual rate of growth versus the population density in a logistic population, we see something quite different from before. Using the example of logistic growth, when the population changes from 2 to 4, its growth rate is 2, when it changes from 4 to 8 its growth rate is 4, and so on. Plotting 2 (the growth rate) versus 2 (the initial population size), 4 versus 4, 7 versus 8, and 13 versus 15 (from the above example of logistic growth), we no longer have a simple line, but we have a "humped" curve. The difference between this humped curve and the straight line of exponential growth is the difference between logistic and exponential growth, and is illustrated in Figure 11.7.

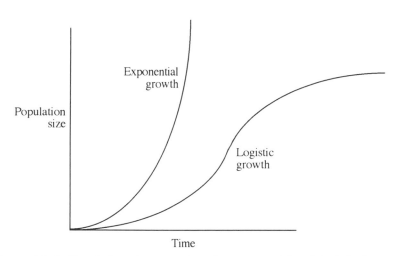

Figure 11.6. Population size over time for exponential and logistic forms of growth.

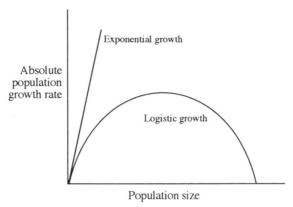

Figure 11.7. Rate of growth plotted against population size, for an exponential and a logistic growth pattern.

POPULATIONS INTERACTING—PREDATION, PARASITISM, HERBIVORY[3]

The first population interaction type we shall consider is perhaps the most basic, when one population has a negative impact on another and receives a benefit from that other, the most common examples of which are predation, parasitism, and herbivory. Whether speaking of cattle production (basically a case of herbivory) or lobster production (a case of predation— us on them), or AIDS (a case of a parasite on us), a great variety of human affairs are associated with this fundamental type of interaction.

Some time ago, Israeli ecologist Emanuel Noy-Meir noticed a curious pattern of production in Australian pastures. In a series of nine pastures, all of which appeared to be identical, a particular number of sheep was introduced. At the end of the grazing season, the amount of meat from the sheep in each pasture was carefully measured. Taking the amount of sheep meat as roughly proportional to the grazing rate (it's not quite the same, but is a relative measurement), we can thus plot the grazing rate on the vertical axis and the amoung of grass on the horizontal axis. Since the grazing rate is the rate at which grass is leaving the system, this graph is similar to a velocity versus state of the system graph as introduced in the last section.

What a range manager might expect from such a system is a group of points, with an identifiable center located at the mean value of grazing rate

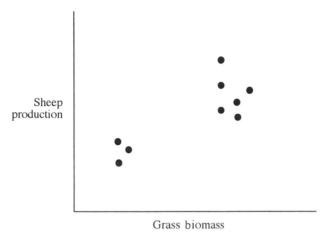

Figure 11.8. Sheep production on nine different pastures. The position on the *x* axis is inferred from the context of this experiment, so as to have maximal heuristic impact—it is not really known. Data from Noy-Meir (1975).

on the vertical axis and the mean value of the amount of grass on the horizontal axis. Interestingly, that is not what was encountered. The actual results of the experiment are shown in Figure 11.8. Rather than the expected cluster of points, two distinct clusters were observed, one at low meat production, the other at a relatively high level of meat production. These two distinct outcomes of the experiment were obtained despite the fact that all the pastures were seemingly identical and exactly the same number of sheep, all presumably of the same general physical health, had been introduced into each of the pastures. How can we account for this dichotomous result?

Let us suppose that a fixed number of predators (the sheep) is in the environment, and that the rate of finding and eating prey (the grass) is constant. Assume, for the moment, that 25 percent of the prey population is eaten each time unit. So if there are 4 prey units (e.g., 4 kilos of grass), 1 will be eaten in the first time unit, if there are 12, 3 will be eaten, and so on. We can presume that the 25 percent rule is true up to a point. If the prey become very abundant, and the predators are constant, we must reach a point at which the predators become saturated, and cannot eat more than a particular number of prey items, no matter how many are presented to them. So, for example, we might be dealing with a predator population that eats 25 percent of the prey per time unit, until the prey reaches a density of 100, at which point the predator population can no longer increase its capacity to eat, and continues to eat 25 percent of 100 (25 prey units) no matter how high the prey population goes. Thus a new graph can be made, in which the predation rate (number of prey units eaten during a particular time unit) is plotted as a function of the number of prey units in the population. Such a plot is shown in Figure 11.9. Note also that this predation curve changes in an obvious fashion as the number of predators in the system increases.

If we return to the above logistic example in which the population exhibited the pattern 2, 4, 8, 15, 28, 52, 95, 120, 124, 125, 125, recall that the rate of change of this population when plotted against its own density resulted in a humped curve, as in Figure 11.7. Now we take the predator curve (Figure 11.9), and combine it with the prey curve (Figure 11.7), and obtain the combined curves, as presented in Figure 11.10. The critical point of this graph is that the predator curve indicates prey individuals removed from the population (the rate of predation is actually the rate of removal from the prey population), while the prey curve indicates

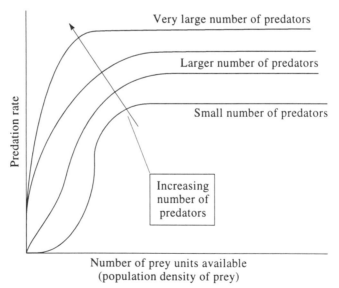

Figure 11.9. Predation rate as a function of number of prey units available. Note the general manner in which the curve of predation rate changes depending on the number of predators in the system.

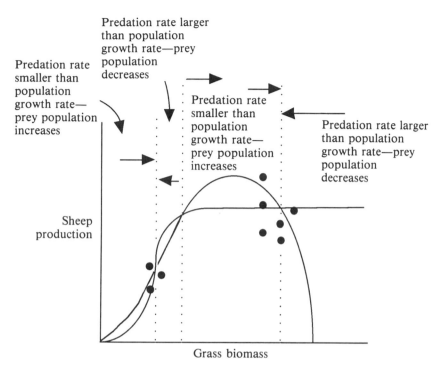

Figure 11.10. The prey population growth rate and the predation rate plotted together. Every place the two curves cross the prey population growth rate is equal to the predation rate, which means there is an exact balance between the rate at which prey units are added through population growth and the rate at which they are subtracted through predation. The stability of these equilibrium points is deduced by looking at the predation rate and population growth rates near that equilibrium point. Note that of the three equilibrium points, the middle one is unstable in the sense that any system near it will tend to move away from it. This kind of equilibrium is known as a "break point." Note that this particular example has three equilibrium points. If either of the two curves were shaped differently, the number of equilibrium points could also change. Of special interest is when the lower equilibrium point does not exist (see, for example, the middle predation rate curve in Figure 11.11), and the break point thus divides the prey density into two regions, one in which the prey increases to an ultimate equilibrium number, and another in which the prey decreases to zero (the lower equilibrim point in this figure effectively moves to the zero point). Data points as in Figure 8.

prey individuals being added to the population. So at any point where the curves cross, the rate of adding prey items through population growth will be exactly equal to the rate of removing prey items through predation, and thus the prey population will be unchanging (since those lost to predation will be exactly replenished through birth). The most general case is shown in Figure 11.10. There are three points at which the rate of predation is equal to the reproduction rate (i.e., where the curves cross), one of which divides the prey population between those densities that decrease from those that increase, the other two of which indicate a stable point at which the prey will have a constant density. The original data for the Australian sheep are also plotted in Figure 11.10, illustrating Noy-Meir's elegant explanation of the originally perplexing result—some of the pastures correspond to the lower equilibrium point, some to the upper one.

Figure 11.10 also indicates a very important structural feature of predator/prey interactions (also of interactions involving parasites and herbivory). There is a critical density below which the prey population declines, since it is eaten too rapidly by its predator to maintain its numbers (this is sometimes referred to as a "break point"). Examples of such break points are suggested by historical literature. For example, when European diseases were introduced to the Americas, the rate of attack (of the disease) was so large that it pushed many native human populations effectively to zero, which is to say that at the time the diseases arrived, the populations were likely below a break point.[4] When predators such as domestic cats are introduced onto islands with bird populations that have existed for thousands of years without effective predators, the cats' rate of predation soon becomes so large, that the bird populations fall below the break point, and the birds become locally extinct or reach a much lower population density. Many other examples could be cited.

This formulation of predation dynamics is also convenient for understanding the tragedy of the commons, as explained in chapter 9. Suppose, for example, that the prey population is a commercial fish population and the predator curves represent the fishing effort of a human population. Then we have the prey curve of Figure 11.7 combined with the predator curves of Figure 11.9, where instead of the number of predators stipulating which of the three curves are operative, the number of fishing boats (or efficiency of fishing technology) becomes the relevant variable. As we see in Figure 11.11, with just a small number of fishing boats, the fish population stabilizes at a relatively high population density and fishing

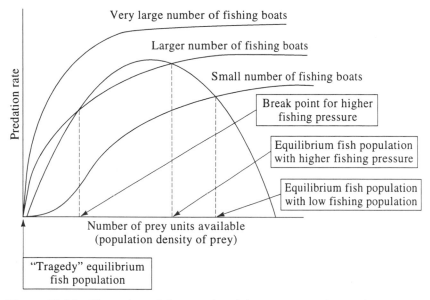

Figure 11.11. Illustration of the tragedy of the commons using predation rates and prey population growth curves.

success (project the point at which the two curves cross to the vertical axis) is relatively high. When more fishing boats enter the water, the equilibrium fish population goes down, but the fishing success goes up, and, furthermore, a break point appears, suggesting the possibility that over-fishing of the population could drive the fish population to zero. Finally, when a large number of fishing boats enters the commons, the fish population is brought down to its "tragedy" level (i.e., zero).

PREDATOR/PREY DYNAMICS

In the above analysis, we presumed that for a given equilibrium state, the number of predators remained constant. The predators may have been sheep (preying on grass) or fishing boats (preying on fish), but in each case, a single predator curve implied a constant number of predators. The classical ecological theory of predator and prey does not make this assumption, but rather allows the predators to increase their population density in response to the prey that they eat. In other words, if the prey population is very large (say, above some critical threshold) the predator population will increase, while if the prey population is very small (say, below that same critical threshold) the predators will be dying of starvation and their population will thus decrease. Similarly, we expect that if the predator population is very large, the prey population will tend to decrease (since the prey are being eaten very rapidly by the predators), while if the predator population is very small, the prey population will tend to increase. Thus we can imagine two critical values, one for the predator and one for the prey, that stipulate whether the populations of each will increase or decrease.

The dynamics (the way these two populations change over time) can be easily visualized on a graph of predator population size versus prey population size, as presented in Figure 11.12. The two populations will tend to oscillate with respect to one another, which will appear as a circular or elliptical motion on a graph of one population's density plotted against the other's. If the system were to start at exactly the point where the two critical lines cross, it would stay exactly there, but anywhere else, it would form a circular or elliptical orbit around that point, much like the planets around the sun. But such a situation is highly dependent on the predator/prey system being exactly in balance, something that we suspect rarely happens in the real world. It is similar to trying to balance a marble on the top of an overturned bowl. If balanced exactly perfectly on the top of the bowl, it will stay there forever. But the slightest deviation from that exact position and it will fall to one side of the bowl or the other.

Consider, for example, our initial assumption about the ability of the prey to increase its population. We assumed that below some critical predator density the prey could increase, while above that density the prey would necessarily succumb to the effects of the predator, and decline. This was the assumption that led to the balancing act of the predator/prey system maintaining itself exactly on the point where the two critical values crossed (see Figure 11.12). But a glance at real-world predators will convince anyone that this is a situation that is almost impossible. My dog chases squirrels in my backyard all the time. He is surprisingly efficient, and if I did not intervene, I suspect he would catch a couple of squirrels a week. Supposing this to be true, is it likely that the ability of the squirrel population to increase is simply a function of whether there are more than or less than a certain number of dogs hunting in my backyard? Obviously, if the squirrel population is very small, a single dog (if permitted to catch as many squirrels as he wishes and is able to) is likely to be able to reduce

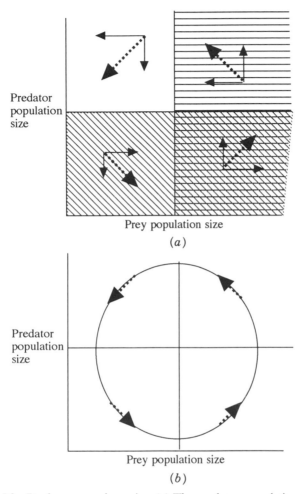

Figure 11.12. Predator-prey dynamics. (a) The predator population size plotted against the prey population size, and the space divided up into four regions, defining the unique behavior of the system within each region. Area shaded by horizontal lines indicates where the predator population will increase. Area shaded by diagonal lines indicates where the prey population will increase. Area cross-hatched indicates where both species increase. Large vectors (arrows) are simply the sum of the action of the two associated smaller ones. (b) Qualitative behavior of the overall system as deduced by the arrows in part a.

the squirrel population, perhaps even drive it to extinction. But if the squirrel population is somewhat larger, it would likely take two or three dogs to do the same job. And if the squirrel population was very large, only a pack of dogs would be able to cause it to decline.

In other words, in the real world, the actual number of prey in the population is an important variable in determining the "critical value" of the predator population that will cause it to begin a population decline. This means that we cannot simply draw a horizontal line and suggest that below it the prey population increases and above it declines. Rather, that line must be a sloping line, reflecting that at lower prey densities the critical predator density is lower than at higher prey densities, as pictured in Figure 11.13a.

But this arrangement implies something very important about the supposed balance point where the two critical values cross. It is no longer a balance point. As illustrated in Figure 11.13a, part of the space that used to push the predator to decline and the prey to increase (the lightly shaded arrow) in the neutrally balanced case is changed so that it points away from the balance point. This creates an unstable effect, and drives the ellipses away from the crossing point, as illustrated by the trajectory in Figure 11.13b. It is as if a planet in an elliptical orbit suddenly gained enough speed to fly away from its center sun and continued orbiting, but at ever-increasing distances from the sun. This is what is known as an unstable focus, the focus being the theoretical stable point in the center, and the unstable appellation indicating that the state of the system is forever spiraling away from the center.

It should be noted that the particular argument offered here for the instability of the equilbrium point is not the only possibility. Other, more complicated, scenarios yield the same result, but are well beyond the scope of this book. The only important point is to note that the neutral stability stipulating that the system will remain fixed at the center point if it is placed exactly there is not likely to ever happen in nature. Rather, nature frequently arranges things such that the center point is fundamentally unstable.

On the other hand, nature also arranges things such that biological systems do not blow up—we are, after all, not knee-deep in bacteria or fungi all the time. Either the prey or the predator eventually reaches some upper value above which it cannot climb, which puts the brakes on the expanding spiral. Thus, no matter where the system starts, it eventually winds up on a particular trajectory, once again orbiting around a theoretical equilibrium point. This special trajectory is known as a *limit cycle,* as pictured in Figure 11.13*b.*

Actually, the most interesting aspect of predator/prey behavior is not the limit cycle itself; that is simply another form of "equilibrium" behavior, the equilibrium is just an elliptical trajectory rather than a single point. The most interesting thing is suggested simply by the two operative forces. If one force pushes the system away from its theoretical equilibrium point, and another force pushes it toward its equilibrium, we have countervailing forces operating. A limit cycle is certainly one possible result of these two countervailing forces. But is it the only possible result?

In Figures 11.13*c* and *d* we see diagrams of a more general statement of these countervailing forces. There is an area between the two forces where we expect the system to eventually arrive and be maintained. Certainly a single limit cycle would fit in this area (the shaded area in Figure 11.13*c*). But a great many other trajectories could fit in also. The new science of nonlinear dynamics (some of which goes by the popular title of chaos theory) suggests that a sort of whirlwind of trajectories might fit into the shadow zone quite well. This whirlwind would be highly unpredictable on a micro scale, but its overall structure would be easily seen simply from a knowledge of the two opposing forces.

Perhaps a more physical model will help clarify this idea. Consider the model in Figure 11.14*a,* an inverted cone with a marble spiraling down to a circular trough at the bottom. The marble is analogous to the point in the predator/prey space, the inverted cone on which the marble spirals down is analogous to the instability forcing the point away from its theoretical equilibrium, and the circular trough is analogous to the upper bound nature puts on either the prey or predator, or both. As long as these physical parts are arranged as in Figure 11.14*a,* the system behaves well, with the marble spiraling down the inverted cone and eventually spiraling around the trough again and again. But what if the upper-bound force is much stronger? What if the trough is reflected upward, such that it causes the marble to jump back to the face of the inverted cone every time it winds down to the bottom? This is illustrated in Figure 11.14*b.* The marble at the top of the cone starts its winding descent, winds downward toward the bottom trough, just as before, but as it spins down to the trough it overshoots the bottom and is reflected back to the surface of the cone. As the marble is repeatedly thrown back to the face of the cone,

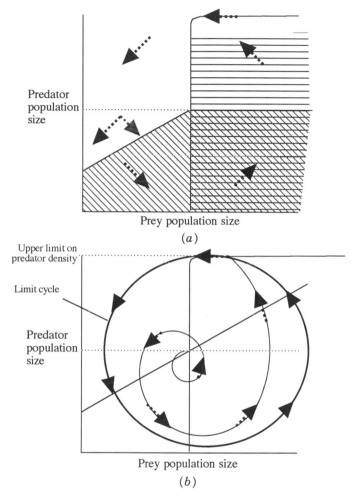

Figure 11.13. Putting the "non-linearities" into the basic predator-prey system. (a) The formerly horizontal line that separated regions of prey increase from prey decrease is now a sloping line at low prey population sizes (see text). The consequence is that part of the space in which the predator decreased while the prey increased (lightly shaded arrow) has become space in which both predator and prey decrease. Thus, the formerly stable point where the two lines crossed (as in Figure 11.12a) is no longer stable, and the oscillations of predator and prey are expected to spiral out, like a planet revolving too rapidly to be maintained within the gravitational force of its sun. The predator is, on the other hand, limited by some other force, which means the line separating the increasing from decreasing

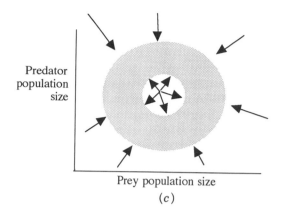

Prey population size

(*c*)

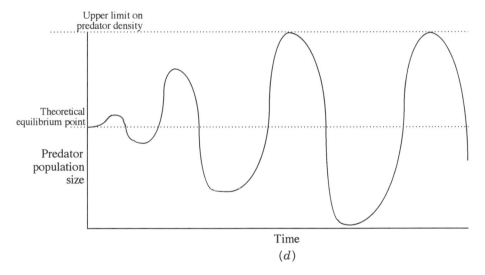

Time

(*d*)

predator population is "bent" at the top, which is to say that the predator simply cannot increase its population size forever (Rosenzweig and MacArthur, 1963). (b) The consequences of these additional features are that the originally stable point is no longer stable but the system will tend to spiral away from it, but the constraint of not allowing the predator to increase will cause the system to enter a permanent cycle, called a limit cycle. (c) The basic idea suggests that a predator-prey system will have two force fields acting on it, one an unstable field forcing the system away from its equilibrium, and the other a stabilizing field, forcing the system back toward the center. The result is some region in which the system will inevitably wind up because of the joint action of these two forces. (d) A simple predator population, obeying the rules suggested in parts a, b, and c.

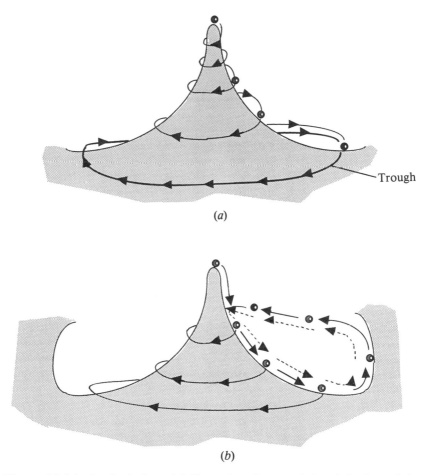

(a)

(b)

Figure 11.14. A physical model illustrating the population behavior of the predator-prey system of Figure 11.13 (see text for explanation).

it begins the spiral down the cone from an unpredictable point on that cone, a point determined by where the exaggerated trough has actually thrown it back. The overall result is that the system continues its spiraling motion, but is strongly constrained to almost always lie within a particular subset of the overall predator/prey space (again, like the shaded area in Figure 11.13*c*). It is, formally speaking, chaotic, but the chaos is what gives it its form—something like a tornado in which any two particles within the tornado will rapidly become randomized with respect to one another within the tornado (in chaos theory, this is the famous sensitive dependence on initial conditions), but the tornado itself has a well-defined and well-known form (in chaos theory, this is the increasingly acknowledged form within chaos).

A variety of mathematical models of ecological systems have provided some spectacular examples of chaos and highly structured form.[5] Such examples are now common where three or more species are interacting with one another, at least when one of the species is a predator. However, just because mathematical models are able to generate a pattern does not in any way suggest that the pattern really exists in the natural world. And here we are really just beginning to explore the possibilities.

POPULATIONS INTERACTING—COMPETITION, MUTUALISM

The most frequently studied of the various population interactions is competition. When one population seeks to use resources that are similarly claimed by another population, we have a competition for those resources. It is generally believed[6] that the process of biological competition is one of the main driving forces determining how ecosystems are structured. It is thus not surprising that so much attention has been given to the phenomenon.

In the example of jaguars and sloths, the vines compete with the *Cecropia* tree to see which can get the most light energy from incoming radiation. The sloth competes with the beetles and caterpillars for *Cecropia* leaves. The mealybugs compete with both the sloth and the caterpillars and beetles for *Cecropia* leaves. The competition may not be strong (i.e., it may not affect the populations very much), but simply because of the structure of who uses what resources, we begin with the assumption that competition is operating, at least potentially.

The assumed importance of competition is actually not all that old an idea. Early ecologists presumed it was happening, but never put it all that much at center stage with regard to nature's basic principles. To the extent it was specifically acknowledged at all, it was usually thought of as something like a sporting event, with two teams competing with one another on the soccer field or basketball court, or two individuals running down the track. With this metaphor in mind, the fundamental question was simply, "Who will win?"

This essential attitude was dramatically altered in the early decades of the present century by two mathematical analyses and a critical experiment. The mathematical analyses were identical formulations undertaken almost simultaneously, but independently, by Alfred Lotka, an insurance man in England, and Vito Volterra, an Italian mathematician.[7] The critical experiment was undertaken with small one-celled animals called *Paramecium,* by the Russian physiologist G. F. Gause.[8] The details of neither the mathematical analysis nor the critical experiments but rather the principal conclusion, are important for us here. Both the theory and the experiment concluded that when biological competition occurs it is not always a case of winners and losers, but, rather, under certain conditions, persistence of both populations in a no-win state. Thus the metaphor of a soccer or basketball game was not as appropriate as would have been a chess game, in which both checkmate and stalemate are possible. If the intensity of the competition was very large, one or the other population would win (and the other would become locally extinct), but if the intensity of competition was relatively small, neither species would win, and both would remain in a perpetual state of stalemate. The basic idea that when competition is very intense one or the other population must become extinct is known as the *competitive exclusion principle,* or Gause's principle.

This basic idea has become a key focus for much of the research done by population ecologists. The sports metaphor prejudice remains, and when two distinct populations are seen using the same resource, it is normally expected that one or the other should "win," driving the other to extinction. When both persist, the search begins for some sort of mechanism that allows the two to persist, tacitly assuming that the usual condition should be extinction of one population or the other. Much of what we think we know about the structure of ecosystems (e.g., how many species are there, what is the distribution of individuals among those species) is ultimately tied up in one way or another with this basic idea.

Competition between species has a variety of important practical consequences, many of which are associated with agriculture. Weed problems in crop production, for example, are clear examples of the operation of ecological competition. How fast a tree plantation becomes available for harvest, what is the average catch size of halibut, how does the migratory locust affect tribal herdspeople in Africa: these and many other similar questions are all questions about ecological competition.

Despite the presumed importance of competition, there is little doubt that most interactions between populations are positive interactions, or facilitations. The ants that protect the *Cecropia* trees from herbivores and the sloth that provides little grooves in its hairs for the algae to live are two examples. Our digestive tracts would not function without bacterial populations that do much of our digesting for us, and many plants could not reproduce if they did not have animals to pollinate their flowers, nor could they disperse if animals did not carry their seeds around. The world's coral reefs would look quite different if the many corals that contained algae within their bodies did not exist, and the organisms we call lichens are combinations of fungi and algae, mutually facilitating one another's lives. The currently accepted theory of the origin of the eucaryotic cell in the first place is a theory involving mutual facilitation of two microorganisms. No matter how you look at it, facilitation is the most common of the basic interactions (mutual facilitation is called, simply, mutualism).[9]

But despite the fact that facilitations are unquestionably the champions of the interactions, they receive a trivial amount of attention from population biologists when compared to competition and predation. For example, in a survey of several major ecology textbooks, about 48 percent of the space was devoted to each of predation and competition, and less than 5 percent devoted to facilitation.[10] Why? The answer will be left as an exercise for the reader.

Because ecologists have devoted so little attention to facilitation, not much can be said in a very general way about it. It turns out to be somewhat more complicated at a theoretical level than either predation or competition, and it is difficult to summarize its basic ideas. Facilitation can include either extinction or persistence, and adds yet another twist to the qualitative outcomes possible in that both species can become extinct (i.e., in some cases there is a "joint" break point, such that if both populations ever go below that point, they will both become extinct).

It would not be appropriate here to dwell on the details of facilitation, since they are quite complicated and not yet fully understood. But it does make sense to distinguish between two forms that are quite different and have substantially different consequences. A particular facilitative action may be either obligate or non-obligate.[11] For example, most orchids must have a particular species of bee attracted to their flowers to pick up the pollen and take it to another plant, otherwise the plant would not reproduce at all. The bee facilitates the reproduction of the orchid in an obligate fashion, in that the orchid population would eventually become extinct if the bee population were not there, which means the orchid is obligated to be facilitated by the bee—obligate facilitation. On the other hand, the ants in the *Cecropia* tree certainly help the tree by removing vines and scaring away herbivores, but if we remove the ants the *Cecropia* population would not become extinct, it would just become more restricted in the types of habitat it could occupy (i.e., those habitats with fewer vines and caterpillars), which means that it is not obliged to be facilitated by the ants—nonobligate facilitation.

COMMUNITIES AND ECOSYSTEMS

The holy grail of population ecology has always been to understand not just these simple interactions, but also what happens when they are all put together. That is, two competing plant species may coexist or not, a predator and prey may oscillate forever, or a mutualistic pair may disappear without a trace. But what happens when five competitors are eaten by four predators, three of which are mutualistic with one another? This has been the real challenge of population ecology, and it is a difficult challenge indeed.

One of the more interesting aspects of this challenge is trying to understand the indirect connections among the various components. For example, when the jaguar eats a sloth, it is actually eliminating one of the enemies of the *Cecropia* tree. Thus, the jaguar has a positive effect, albeit indirect, on the *Cecropia* tree. The basic idea is simply that "an enemy of my enemy is my friend." This concern for indirect effects in trophic webs has had many significant practical applications.[12]

Competition and mutualism, in a sense, are both fundamentally indirect processes from the start. Two species are in competition for a resource, for instance, which means that one species modifies the resource in such a way that the other is not able to get as much of it or utilize it as efficiently as if the competitor were not there. Consider, for example, the lion and the cheetah of chapter 8. They both eat herbivores, so we can say they are in competition with one another. But the most direct effects in their population dynamics derive from their eating habits, while the competition they experience from one another is mainly through eating each other's food. One could say, then, that competition between lions and cheetahs is an indirect consequence of both of them modifying the potential environment of each other—eating each other's food.[13]

Some forms of mutualism are, likewise, a consequence of indirect effects, although this is not as easy to see as the case of competition. For example, lions eat mainly antelope, and cheetahs eat mainly gazelles. If gazelles and antelope are in competition with one another for pasture that is in short supply, the fact that lions effectively reduce the competitive effect of antelopes on gazelles (by eating them) means that lions are, indirectly, facilitating the food source of cheetahs.[14]

It is in this area of multiple interactions that population ecology touches base with popular ecology. Since ecology began to fire the popular imagination, two major ideas about the nature of ecosystems have resurfaced with remarkable regularity. A striking feature about these two ideas is that they are in fundamental opposition to one another, a point that frequently escapes notice. On the one hand, ecosystems are thought to be fragile creatures that can easily be damaged by the careless hand of man and woman. On the other hand, ecosystems are stable organisms, honed by the hand of evolution to be "harmonious"—the "balance of nature." If an ecosystem is going to be a stable balance, it is obviously not likely to be fragile. Yet, both of these ideas seem to resurface repeatedly in the popular ecology movement.

Perhaps nowhere are these two ideas applied more vigorously than in the debate about the size of an ecosystem, that is, the number of interacting components, the biodiversity. Curiously, both the fragility and the stability of ecosystems are thought to be correlated with biodiversity. Two common metaphors could help explain the rationale behind this idea. On the one hand, a large amount of biodiversity may be thought of as the connections in a spider web—the more connections, the stronger the web. Thus, because a rain forest (for example) has so many connections, it must be very stable. On the other hand, the immense biodiversity may represent a house of cards, with many cards interacting with one another to keep the house standing. It may indeed be balanced because of the large number of cards, but removing just one of them could very well cause the entire house to come tumbling down. So which metaphor makes sense in fact? Are highly diverse systems like highly connected webs that gain their strength and stability from the multiplicity of connections? Or are they like a house of cards, balanced precariously on the edges of those mutually dependent cards, subject to a total collapse if a single critical card is removed?

Recent developments in the field of nonlinear dynamics suggest that ecosystems might be structured in a totally different way, as suggested above in the case of predator prey dynamics. It may be that most ecosystems are "unstable" in the sense that the central tendency is to oscillate or deviate away from theoretical equilibria, but to be bounded in such a way that the system continues to be thrown back toward that unstable equilibrium—what might be referred to as chaotic structure. At this point, we can only conjecture on this idea, although several arguments from theoretical ecology point to its feasibility. Even more intriguing is the idea that periodic disturbance (to be discussed in more detail in the following chapter) may provide the "controlling" factor that limits the basically unstable underlying nature of the ecosystem, thus providing what is effectively a chaotic structure, but a chaotic structure that is driven by an outside force. The tropical rain forest, as well as the coral reef, nature's two most diverse ecosystems, may very well be driven by such dynamics.[15]

Ecosystems in Space and Time

Standing on the equator in the Western Hemisphere very likely puts you in the middle of the Amazon rain forest. The feeling is characteristic—it is hot, it is humid, and in all likelihood it is raining. Were you to fly for an hour or so from this point directly west, you would encounter the Peruvian desert. The feeling is again characteristic—it is hot, it is dry, and almost certainly it is not raining (Figure 12.1).

The look and feel of these two ecosystems, of the animals and plants that you can see, could not be more different. The rain forest is lush, green, filled with life. Trees tower and vines climb, insects buzz and birds call, life itself appears to dominate what can sometimes be a claustrophobic environment. The desert is dry, yellow, with life only sparsely present. Indeed, one has to look closely to see evidence of life at all—a piece of lichen here, a spider there, an occasional clump of moss-like vegetation, all dried up. How can a short flight bring one to such different ecosystems? That is the question of ecosystems in space. How is it that different points on the planet contain such different ecosystems?

A similar phenomenon can happen with respect to time. Outside of Mombasa in Kenya, there is a farm called the Baobab Farm. It has been in existence for about 20 years, and if you walk through it you see large trees, vegetation surrounding you, soil on the ground; in short nothing that would seem out of the ordinary to a lay person. But if you could go back 20 years and stand on the same spot, as its owner and founder R. D. Haller did in 1971, you would be standing on bare rock. The farm is the site of an old limestone quarry.[1] The difference between its appearance now and its appearance 20 years ago is no less than staggering, and is quite similar to the difference between the Amazon rain forest and the Peruvian desert. How can it be that only 20 years can bring one to such

Figure 12.1. Top photo is of a flooded Amazon rain forest, about 100 miles north of Manaus, Brazil, on the Rio Negro. Bottom photo is the Peruvian desert, about 100 miles north of Lima. Both photos were taken at approximately the same latitude.

different ecosystems? That is the question of ecosystems in time. How is it that different points in time contain such different ecosystems?

ECOSYSTEMS IN SPACE

All life requires water, so it is no surprise to learn that availability of water is one of the two critical factors for understanding ecosystems in space. Anyone raised in the northern climates can easily appreciate the other factor—there is not a lot of green to be seen in the northern winter. Indeed, animals and plants are extremely sensitive to temperature.

These are the two factors that determine whether a point on the globe will have a rain forest or a desert, a hardwood forest or a boreal forest, a Mediterranean scrub or a pine scrub. At this level, there is nothing mysterious. A large amount of rain in a very hot climate will normally produce a rain forest, and a very small amount of rain anywhere will normally produce a desert. A large amount of rain in a cool climate will produce a northern deciduous forest. What about savannahs and grasslands? The famous east African grasslands that gave rise to our own lovable species is blessed with a warm climate with abundant rainfall. Should it not be a rain forest?

While many factors are involved, heat and water are of central importance. So, in order to understand, minimally, the distribution of ecosystems in space, we need to understand how temperature and precipitation are distributed over the globe. Once the general distribution of these two factors is understood, we will proceed to some of the other factors involved.

In the mid-nineteenth century the British meteorologist Hadley described a model of the earth's atmosphere that seemed to make a lot of sense.[2] Since the sun shines most strongly on the equator, he reasoned, the air near the surface of the earth would tend to heat up more rapidly near the equator than on other parts of the globe. Because hot air tends to rise, there would be a tendency for the air near the equator to rise. That much is indisputable. But Hadley took his observation much further and set the stage for our modern understanding of global patterns of atmospheric circulation. He reasoned that if air near the equator was rising, it had to go somewhere. It was kept within the vicinity of the earth by the force of gravity, and thus could not keep rising forever. Furthermore, the air that had risen from the surface of the earth near the equator would have to be replaced by some other air, and, he asked, where would that air come from? It does not take much deductive power to see where he was headed. If air rises at the equator, it must eventually move toward the poles after it ascends to the upper level of the atmosphere. The air rising at the equator must be replaced by air to the north and south of it, so we see a general pattern of air rising at the equator, moving high in the atmosphere, dispersing poleward, falling at the poles, and moving toward the equator near the ground, to start the process over again. The earth, according to Hadley's primitive model, had two cellular circulations, one in the northern hemisphere and one in the southern hemisphere. Air falls at the poles, travels along the surface of the earth toward the equator, where it rises high into the atmosphere, where it is dispersed to the north and south poles. That was Hadley's model, but it turned out to be wrong.

The critical fact that Hadley failed to include in his model was that the earth turns on its axis. As the earth turns, the air above it lags behind, such that the mass of air near the equator that began to rise veers off to the west (since the earth beneath it moves toward the east). So as the rising air moves upward and poleward, it also moves westward. The earth spins so fast that the westward movement of the air causes turbulence before the air can reach the pole, and this turbulence creates a kind of barrier to the air coming from the equator "trying" to get to the pole. Consequently, at approximately 30 degrees north and south latitude, the air moving poleward runs into this zone of turbulence and is forced downward. This is the pattern that dominates the equatorial and lower latitudes of the earth, rising air at the equator and falling air at about 30 degrees. This basic pattern of circulation is diagrammed in Figure 12.2.

An important characteristic of rising air is changing temperature. As you climb a mountain, you can easily sense the change in temperature, with the air cooling as you ascend. As air rises, it cools. If the air contains some water vapor, the rising air eventually cools enough so that the water vapor condenses, creating rain. We thus have a fairly robust rule of thumb—rising air causes rain (but, as you will see below, this is not always true). This is exactly what happens at the equator. Most of the air near the equator tends to rise, because that is where the sun's rays are most concentrated, and that rising air drops most of its water in the form of rain. Thus, by the time the air reaches the upper layers of the atmosphere, it has lost all of its water, and has no place to gain water again before it

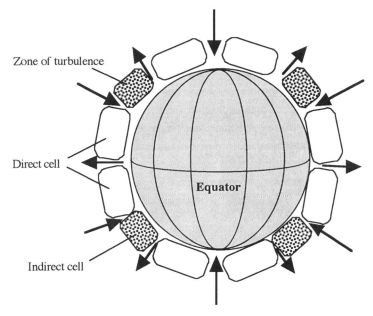

Figure 12.2. Formation of the elementary cellular circulation in the atmosphere. The indirect cell is simply a result of the average flow of air throughout the turbulent zone.

encounters the turbulent zone and begins to fall. So the falling air near 30 degrees is virtually devoid of water.

Two of the world's great ecosystem formations are thus created. Where the air is rising, and thus it is raining a lot, is where the rain forests of the globe are concentrated, and under the dry falling air is the location of the planet's deserts. The map in Figure 12.3 illustrates the approximate position of the world's deserts and rain forests. As you can see, they tend to be found more or less in those belts caused by this global climate phenomenon.

A second dominating feature of climate is its seasonality. Anyone raised in the northern climate appreciates this fact, especially on those frigid February mornings. Because of the earth's tilt with respect to the sun, we have winter when the sun follows a path across only the southern third of the sky. Since the sun never gets very close to overhead, and since its rays strike the ground at a very oblique angle, it never is able to heat

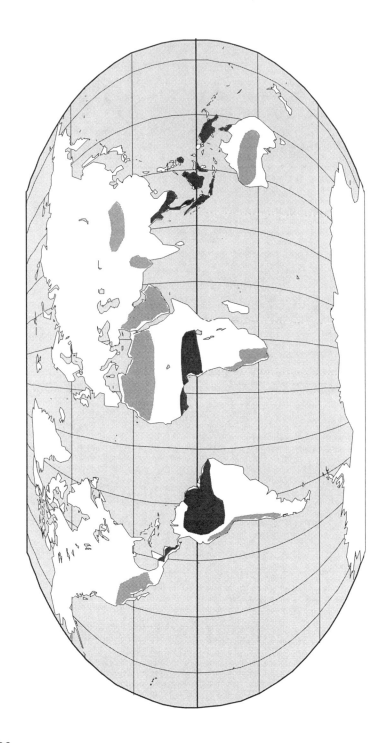

292

up the ground very much, and we are reminded of the knife-edge of existence we occupy on this planet as most life shuts down for half the year. When the sun's path across the sky brings it more nearly overhead, its rays more directly strike the earth (i.e., they do not go through nearly as much atmosphere) and we are warmed, sometimes beyond our desires—summer. These zones of the earth are known as temperate zones (really not a good choice of phrase—better we should say, simply, higher latitudes), and are characterized by a cool or cold season. This is the climatic zone in which the temperate forests, dominated by trees that drop their leaves in the cold season, are to be found (Figure 12.4).

For much of the world's population, the winter/summer dichotomy is not based on hot and cold nearly as much as it is based on wet and dry. While what causes cold and warm seasons is fairly obvious, what causes wet and dry ones is not nearly so obvious, but in the final analysis, that also has to do with the position of the sun. The sun beating down on the equator, as described above, actually shines on what should be called an "effective" equator. The location of the band around the earth that experiences the sun directly overhead changes seasonally. In the middle of the northern winter, the "effective" equator is actually quite far south of the physical equator, while in the midst of the northern summer the effective equator is quite far north of the physical equator. What, then, happens at the exact physical equator? When the sun is directly overhead at noon at the vernal equinox (March 21) the rising air drops its rain, but when the sun is at its southern solstice (December 21) the rising air mass is significantly to the south of the physical equator, indeed, far enough that the air high up in the atmosphere encounters the turbulent zone somewhere around the physical equator. The belt of falling air mass has effectively migrated south, and the area of the actual equator is suddenly dry. This is the origin of the wet and dry seasons in tropical climates.

Thus, we see how it is possible to account for several general ecosystem types merely from speculating about global weather patterns. When the climate is hot and wet, as it is near the equator, we have tropical rain forests. If its seasonality includes a significant dry season we have tropical dry forests. When the climate is dry, as it is in the belt of falling air (i.e.,

---

Figure 12.3. Approximate distribution of the major rain forests (dark shading), and deserts (diagonal hatching) of the world.

Figure 12.4. The temperate forest. Top left, summer in the Smoky Mountains National Park. Top right, the signs of fall, a nutrient pulse from falling leaves, near Ann Arbor, Michigan. Lower left, winter, the only season where life is effectively shut off entirely, near Ann Arbor, Michigan. Lower right, reinvigoration of spring, near Ann Arbor, Michigan.

high pressure), we have deserts. When seasonality includes a winter, we have temperate forests.

However regular these global patterns may be, there is a great deal of variability caused by local effects. An illustration of this can be seen in a single day's travel in most countries of the Central American isthmus, for example. If you begin near the Pacific Ocean in Nicaragua or Costa Rica, about March, you will encounter vegetation that is very dry in appearance, trees without leaves, thorny leafless bushes, dry grass. It is the dry season, and one need not be a botanist or climatologist to sense it. About a two-hour drive eastward first takes you up through mountains, and then down towards the Caribbean coast. By the time you begin descending the mountains toward the Caribbean you notice that the vegetation changes remarkably. It is suddenly lush and green, and it is probably raining (Figure 12.5). In this short trip you have experienced two phenomena that are basic to climate formation (and thus to the understanding of why ecosystems are where they are)—a rain shadow and orographic lifting.

The air moving westward (because the earth on which we stand is moving eastward) picks up water that evaporates from the surface of the Caribbean. When that air encounters the land mass of Central America, it is forced to rise because of its encounter with the land mass. This type of air movement is technically known as *orographic lifting,* and results in the same physical processes as when it rises because of surface heating—it cools as it rises. Thus, because of orographic lifting, the rising and cooling air will drop whatever water it contains, as illustrated in Figure 12.6. What, then, will happen as this air mass passes over the mountains and enters the Pacific side of the isthmus? The mountains will have created a metaphorical shadow in that the air will be relatively dry, having dropped its water on the eastern side of the mountains. Such a metaphorical shadow is called a *rain shadow.* So the dryness we saw on the Pacific side was due to the rain shadow effect of the central mountain mass of the isthmus, and the wet rain-forest vegetation we saw on the Caribbean side was due to orographic lifting imposed by that same mountain mass.

One of the world's wonders has to be the Himalayan mountains. I recall that on a plane flight from New Delhi to Calcutta, I had been staring out the window at a cloud bank for some time before I realized that the cloud bank wasn't composed of clouds at all, but of a virtually continuous line of snow-covered peaks. This imposing structure had been created 45 million years ago, when the isolated land mass we now call India crashed

Figure 12.5. Comparison of vegetation on both sides of the Central American isthmus. Top figure is lowland tropical rain forest of the eastern slope (Costa Rica); bottom figure is dry tropical forest of the western coast (Nicaragua).

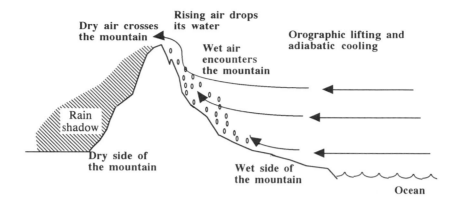

Figure 12.6. Orographic lifting and adiabatic cooling on a mountain slope.

into the Asian land mass, thus pushing the land up and creating the Himalayan mountains. To the north of these mountains one finds the Tibetan plateau, an immense area of relatively great altitude and, consequently, sparsely vegetated. During the northern summer, the sun beats down on this large expanse of land and, partly because of its sparse vegetation, heats it up considerably. The Tibetan plateau thus acts as a heat source for the air near it, which consequently tends to rise. But the Tibetan plateau is immense in size, so it results in an immense amount of air being lifted in the later weeks of the northern summer. This mass of rising air must be replaced, which is done by drawing in air from the south (also, to some extent, from the north), which means it is drawing air from the Himalayas and their foothills. Air being drawn out of the foothills must be replaced.[3] The replacement air comes in off the Indian Ocean. It is laden with moisture from that ocean, and as it replaces air drawn from the Himalayas, it encounters those same mountains and is orographically lifted, which means it cools, which means it drops its water, which means it rains torrentially. These are the summer monsoons.

Another special effect is illustrated by the opening lines of this chapter. Remaining at exactly the same latitude, one can go from one of the wettest places in the world, the Amazon rain forest, to one of the driest places in the world, the Peruvian desert. If rain forests and deserts are caused by the equatorial rising of air and later falling of dry air as described above, how can this be true? One clue to this mystery can be gained by a swim in the Pacific Ocean off of the Peruvian desert. I was never able to get into the water there—it is unbelievably cold, and that is the explanation (Figure 12.7). An ocean current moves from the Antarctic up the coast of South America, and it is very cold indeed. The offshore breezes that hit land are thus cooled by these cold Pacific waters, and as they are orographically lifted, a strange thing happens. The sun beating on the desert sands creates a great heat source and as orographic lifting proceeds, the air is actually warmed rather than cooled (because the cold air coming off the Pacific Ocean encounters the warm sands of the desert). Thus, the water vapor contained in the air remains there as the air proceeds up the Andes. In other words, there is no lack of water in the Peruvian desert, but it is all contained in the air that is being warmed as it rises and thus cannot make rain. Here we see the importance of ocean currents, which are capable of turning a piece of the earth that ought to be rain forest into desert, about as big a change as could be imagined.

Ocean currents are important worldwide as modifiers of the climate.

Figure 12.7. Pacific coast of Peru, illustrating the cause of the Peruvian desert. The towel is protection against a very cold breeze, and the mollusks on the beach and in the hand are similar to those that can be found in northern North America.

The entire western side of Europe is as benign as it is because of an ocean current arising near the equator, carrying its warm water all the way to northern Europe. Granted, residents of Great Britain may find it unusual to call the climate there benign, but compared to what one would expect from just the direct effects of sunlight, it is benign indeed, as is the climate of all of Scandinavia (Figure 12.8).

Almost all of the above discussion has been concerned with tropical rain forest, tropical dry forest, temperate forest, and desert. Yet there is another ecosystem that has arguably been much more important to *Homo sapiens* than any of these others, the ecosystem where we originated, the ecosystem that gives us the great corn belts of the United States, Argentina, and the former Soviet Union, the ecosystem that looms large in our legends of westward expansion in the United States. The great grasslands represent perhaps the largest ecosystem in the world, in physical extent. Yet their existence cannot be explained with reference to heat, water, and seasonality, as can the others. We must include time in the analysis of ecosystems if we are to understand where grasslands come from.

Figure 12.8. Vegetation near Rovaniemi, Finland, very close to the Arctic Circle.

ECOSYSTEMS IN TIME

That old empty lot is really overgrown. The crabgrass is really taking over the lawn. There is not much more to say than that. If you leave an area alone, after it has been disturbed, the biology changes. An empty lot becomes choked with weeds, a lawn first gets loaded with crabgrass, and, if you leave it alone much longer, gets more and bigger weeds, eventually choking out the grass altogether. There has been a succession of different forms of vegetation, a process that is known appropriately as *ecological succession*. It always occurs after a disturbance, may not occur in a totally predictable fashion, occurs for various reasons in various places, and has eluded our attempts at finding a general mechanism to explain it—Darwin gave us natural selection to explain evolution, we await _____ to give us _____ to explain succession.[4]

But certain patterns of succession are well known. The first distinction of critical importance is the difference between primary succession and secondary succession. *Primary succession* is the same thing as soil formation (in terrestrial ecosystems), and occurs on what is usually referred to as "parent material," things such as a lava flow, a field of volcanic ash, the bare rock left after a retreated glacier, a dune of sand blown up in back of a beach, and many other examples. The combination of biology and climate causes changes in the parent material in such a way that it becomes recognizable as a soil. There are usually recognizable stages involved in the process, varying dramatically from place to place on the globe. Primary succession on a lava flow in Central America takes a totally different form from the same process on a lava flow in the desert of Arizona, although certain forces are consistent from place to place.

Far more important for practical questions (e.g., sustainable development, land reclamation, restoration of natural areas, agriculture) is the concept of secondary succession, that which happens in an empty lot in downtown Detroit, a golf course in Grosse Pointe, or an abandoned farm in Sri Lanka. When a large disturbance comes into an area, such as a hurricane, earthquake, or construction of a shopping mall, the original vegetation may be severely altered. After that alteration, a sequence of vegetation types successively occupy the site in a relatively predictable manner; this is what is known as *secondary succession*.

The first plants to arrive are appropriately termed pioneers, and are typically sun-loving fast growing species, things like grasses, vines, and some fast-growing trees, and they form a vegetative community frequently called "pioneer vegetation." As the pioneers grow, other species begin to arrive, often becoming established because of facilitation by the pioneers, but sometimes simply arriving later because of a different sort of dispersal mechanism. These species are called secondary species and are less sun-loving, usually grow more slowly than the pioneers, but have the capability of strongly competing against those pioneers. Since competition is strong,[5] the secondary species tend to displace the pioneers, and we have what is frequently called "secondary vegetation" (the distinction between pioneer vegetation and secondary vegetation is not hard and fast, however). Subsequently, other secondary species come into the area ("late successional species") and act on the original secondary vegetation in the same way that the latter acted on the pioneer vegetation. Ultimately, a group of species arrives and stops the process. That is, eventually the vegetation stops changing, the various plant species stop succeeding one another, and we have a plant assemblage that stays constant, at least with respect to the actual composition of species. This final stage is called the "climax" stage.

An abandoned cornfield outside Ann Arbor, Michigan, provides an example. After abandonment, the vegetation is composed of the same weeds, usually a lot of grasses, that originally plagued the farmer when he or she was trying to grow corn. These plants, the pioneers, are especially good at getting to a site quickly (frequently their seeds are carried by the wind, sometimes by birds who fly from field to field), and are able to grow extremely rapidly in bright sunlight. Other, more slowly growing species also come into the old field, but are not seen at first, because they appear as small seedlings among the primary vegetation. But, indeed, they are there. They are species you ordinarily think of as shrubs plus some trees that are especially good at growing fast in high-light conditions (for example, aspens in Michigan). These secondary species do not grow quite as rapidly as the pioneers, but are able to survive the lower-light conditions that exist among the pioneers. As the shrubs and secondary trees get taller, about the second or third year after abandonment, the area closer to the ground becomes partially shaded, and those grasses and other pioneers that originally came into the field have a more difficult time growing— they are able to respond with very rapid growth when light conditions are high, but are not able to survive very well when light conditions become lower. So the secondary vegetation (the shrubs and secondary tree species) competes with, and kills, the primary vegetation. While this is happening, the ground beneath the secondary vegetation becomes relatively open, even though it is shaded above by the secondary shrubs and trees, and the seedlings of the later secondary forest are able to invade (typically, species like hickory and oak trees).

These forests, in Michigan usually composed of oaks and hickories, may last for a long time, perhaps hundreds of years, or they may be quite transient, replaced within a century; it really depends on the underlying soil. A sandy soil is very porous and dries out easily, while a soil with more clay content tends to hold moisture. If the soil is slightly more clayey, the understory of the oak-hickory forest is invaded by seedlings of maple and beech, which eventually take over the forest, although the process usually takes over a hundred years. If the soil is more sandy, the maple and beech may never be able to get started, because they cannot stand the dry summer. Thus the climax ecosystem around Ann Arbor, Michigan, is either oak-hickory forest or beech-maple forest, depending on the clay content of the soil.[6]

Ecological succession is also usually characterized by a dominance of indirect interactions, as discussed in the previous chapter. The pioneering vegetation that originally invaded the abandoned field in Michigan would have continued to choke out the forest trees were it not for the shrubs that invaded and shaded it. Thus, the shrubs had an indirect positive effect on the trees, since the latter could not have survived in competition with the pioneer vegetation (the shrubs were the enemy of the pioneer species, which were the enemy of the trees). Vegetative succession appears to operate with this fundamental indirect effect quite frequently.

The process of vegetative succession is usually presented as above—that which happens to an old abandoned field after agriculture. However, the process is always occurring in nature as a consequence of various disturbances, and the details of vegetative succession may very well depend on the type of disturbance. Perhaps the most well-studied natural disturbance, after which vegetative succession proceeds in a regular fashion, is the formation of a light gap in a forest.[7] Old forests typically have old trees, and old trees do not live forever. A sudden gust of wind will bring an old tree down, creating a hole in the forest canopy (known as a light gap), and bathing the understory with light. Succession follows in which light-gap pioneers enter the gap first, followed by secondary species, and eventually a climax tree grows up to take the place of the tree that fell. The process of replacing a fallen tree with a new tree takes on the order of 30 to 100 years, depending on the type of forest.

Recently a great deal of attention has been given to succession following large storms (Figure 12.9).[8] A large storm may create an exceedingly large light gap in the forest, and the question arises whether post-storm succession is just like a very big light gap, or whether something qualitatively different happens because of the immense size of the damage done by the hurricane. While the answer to that question is still elusive—many studies are currently under way[9]—it is easy to see why it is an important question. A storm's damage to the forest is similar in many respects to that done by a logging operation. Understanding the natural process of succession might very well provide insight for designing methods of forestry that are more ecologically rational than those in current use.

Figure 12.9. Central American tropical rain forest before and after hurricane damage. Photo on left is forest on the eastern slope of Costa Rica, typical of forest along the entire eastern slope of Central America. Photo on right is similar forest on the eastern slope of Nicaragua four months after having been struck by Hurricane Joan in 1988. While the damage is severe, regrowth has already begun.

Figure 12.10. The grasslands of North America. Top left is the short grass prairie of South Dakota. Top right is subsequent to the passage of a cool fire in Idaho. Lower left, the sod of the prairie was so heavy that it was frequently used in construction. Here is a shed, the roof of which is made from prairie sod. Lower right, the steel plow was a necessary invention for the hard work of sod-busting to prepare farms in the grasslands.

Figure 12.11. Tropical savannas in Africa. Top photo is of the Serengeti plain in southern Kenya. Lower photo is near Samburu, in northern Kenya.

There is one extremely important aspect of succession that could be predicted from a knowledge of the successional pattern in a given area. For example, imagine what would happen in an area of frequent landslides if the rate of landslides was greater than the rate of succession, which is to say, if the time between landslides was smaller than the time necessary to reach the climax vegetation. Obviously, one would expect the disappearance of the climax species from the area, and the area would be expected to be a patchwork of different secondary stages of succession, depending on when the last landslide occurred. This type of vegetation is known as a "disclimax."

One situation where a disclimax is extremely important occurs when the force of disturbance is fire.[10] For example, what would happen in the above example of an abandoned Michigan cornfield if we set fire to the field every 20 years? We would kill all the secondary species (the shrubs and secondary trees) that have grown in the area, and open up the field to be invaded again by the grasses and other pioneers. At any specific point in time we would see some vegetation between zero and 20 years old, depending on the time of the last fire. What if we burned the field every one or two years? At any random point in time we would see nothing but pioneer vegetation, but that vegetation would remain the same for ever (assuming we continue our burning cycle). It would be a disclimax.

This is the origin of the world's grasslands (see Figures 12.10 and 12.11), the distribution of which is approximately shown in figure 12.12. If, at a given location, one of the aspects of seasonality is dryness, and the soil is such that moisture is not held well, we expect fires to occur naturally (from lightning) with some regularity. So the grasslands of the western United States, Central Asia, Argentina, East Africa, and everywhere else, are products of this phenomenon—they are all fire disclimaxes.

But there is another complication. The presence of large herbivores sets the stage for this disclimax to occur. Large herbivores—the mammalian types, such as antelope, bison, and zebras—eat the vegetation, thus keeping back the shrubby vegetation that might create a slight shade, which might maintain enough moisture to stop the fires. The herbivores

---

Figure 12.12. Approximate location of the world's grassland ecosystems. Dark shading represents tropical savannah. Diagonal hatching indicates temperate grassland.

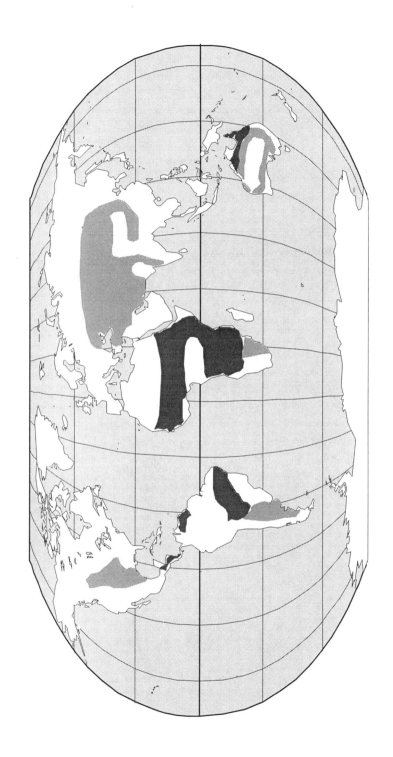

307

thus keep the habitat in a state where the sun can penetrate to ground level and dry out the vegetation.

A great variety of well-known disclimaxes exist in the world (e.g., California redwoods, New England pine forests, Mediterranean scrub) and many others may actually be disclimaxes even though we have no way of really knowing. The one that is most widespread, however, and accounts for the distribution of the most common vegetation type in the world, is the one that is created by the combination of large herbivores and fire, the world's grasslands.[11]

In sum, we have seen how, at a most general and simplified level, the five main world ecosystem types (tropical rain forest, tropical dry forest, temperate forest, grassland, and desert) are distributed, and what causes that distribution. Rising air at the equator caused by excessive heating at the earth's surface creates the conditions for tropical rain forest, while that same air dropping at higher latitudes creates the conditions for deserts. The yearly movement of the sun creates seasonality, which creates tropical dry forest in tropical latitudes and temperate forest in higher latitudes. Finally, the existence of large herbivores and a dry season strong enough to permit regular fire creates the conditions for grasslands, the only major ecosystem type that is a true disclimax—as far as we know. Obviously, this is only a summary of what is actually a very complex topic. Many other categories and subcategories are usually recognized,[12] but for purposes of introduction and overview, with a sense of dynamic origin, the categorization into these five types is of great use, and is as far as we will go.

THIRTEEN

Agriculture, The Most Basic Resource Transformation

As you read this chapter, about 50 hectares (1 hectare = 2.47 acres) of tropical rain forest will be cut down, and several million hectares of land will be sprayed with poisons. With those two actions, several species of animals and plants may disappear forever, the culture of some forest-dwelling people will be destroyed forever, some farmers and farm laborers will be killed or severely injured, and part of the environment will be rendered useless for future production. Yet agriculture, the cause of these problems, is the basis for the evolution of modern human societies, and undoubtedly the most important system of resource transformation ever invented by the species. Human life as we know it in the modern world would certainly disappear if agriculture ceased to exist.

So, we confront two faces of agriculture—the most basic and important of all human resource transformation processes and the major cause of some of the planet's most troublesome problems. How can we resolve this apparent dilemma? First we must understand some elementary concepts about agriculture, where it came from, how it evolved, and how it functions in today's society. This is the purpose of this chapter.

AGRICULTURE AND HUNTING AND GATHERING AS SIMPLE RESOURCE UTILIZATION SYSTEMS

Before agriculture, the basic resource utilization method of *Homo sapiens* was hunting and gathering (which includes fishing). Most resources, be they wild grains or buffalo or whitefish, behave qualitatively like the populations described in chapter 11. If we plot the rate of resource increase against its density (or, equivalently, the rate of increase of harvestable material such as seeds, as a function of the quantity of that harvestable material), we get a characteristic humped curve.[1] If a human population is harvesting this resource, that human population becomes something like a predator or herbivore, and we can plot the rate of harvesting on the same graph (just like the rate of predation was plotted before). A possible configuration of these two rates is shown in Figure 13.1.

In Figure 13.1, we see a basic fact of nature. Given a particular relationship between rate of increase of a plant or animal and its human consumer, the resource (the plant or animal) increases at a rate that is normally much higher than the rate of harvest of the human population, and consequently, humans harvest at what might be called a sustainable rate.[2] Viewing human resource use from this point of view places *Homo sapiens* in the position of almost any other predator or herbivore. However, as argued in earlier chapters, the human species is quite different from other organisms and it would be foolish not to incorporate those differences into a model of human behavior.

In the minimal model of resource transformation presented in chapter 4 and elaborated further in chapter 9, humans involve themselves in socially organized labor to engage in production of products. Socially organized labor is itself affected by the various resources available, and those available resources are always changing, which is another way of saying

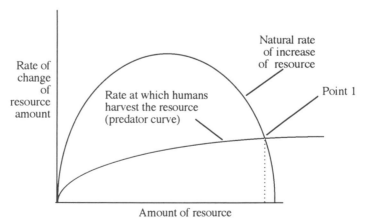

Figure 13.1. The balance of the natural rate of change with harvest rate for a natural resource.

that technology has a way of evolving. As time passes, harvesting the wild plants or animals by hunters and gatherers changes as a function of the changing nature of socially organized labor. One of the consequences of this change may be an increase in the efficiency of harvesting the resource (although by no means does this absolutely have to happen). For example, socially organized labor may come to produce spear points, thus increasing hunting efficiency tremendously, or the use of digging sticks may make the harvest of some tubers much easier, or the invention of a net may make fish harvesting magnitudes more efficient. These are all examples of the production of a product that will be consumed as a resource in the harvesting operation, and all have the general effect of increasing the harvesting rate. The basic system changes when the technology of harvesting increases, as illustrated in Figure 13.2. As the rate of harvesting increases with better technology, we move from predator curve A to predator curve B, and from a situation that was sustainable (in the sense that a balance would be reached between the harvest rate and the replenishment rate), to a system that is fundamentally unsustainable (in the sense that the harvest rate is always larger than the replenishment rate). The process is formally equivalent to the tragedy of the commons. This basic transformation was undoubtedly important when *Homo sapiens* was a hunter and gatherer, and remains an essential feature of natural resource use yet today.

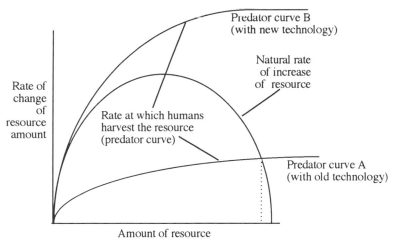

Figure 13.2. Diagrammatic representation of how changing technology changes the amount of resource available.

Perhaps the most dramatic illustration of technological changes leading to unsustainability are reflected in the early Americans. Arriving in America about 12,000 years ago, the technological advances associated with fire, stone tools and probably changing social organization raised the efficiency of harvesting the large herbivorous mammals that for thousands of years had made the grasslands of the Americas look much like Africa. While it is still a debatable interpretation, most anthropologists now agree that the hunting activities of the early Americans drove the large mammals to extinction.[3] Apparently the predator curve looked something like curve B in Figure 13.2.

Technological developments that changed socially organized labor very frequently led to a system that was unsustainable, at least on a local level and for a short period of time, tempting us to suggest that just such a pattern could account for the development of agriculture. It is easy to see what agriculture does in such a natural resource system. If it becomes a "cared-for" resource like corn or wheat, its rate of production is higher at all amounts, and it will be kept producing at much higher levels than in its predomesticated state. The consequences are illustrated in Figure 13.3.

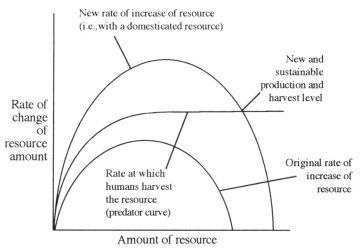

Figure 13.3. Impact of domestication on resource availability. Lower rate of increase curve associated with the "wild" (undomesticated) resource, leading to a depletion of the resource (i.e., the equilibrium point is at zero). Upper rate of increase curve associated with the domesticated resource, leading to a new and sustainable production and harvest level.

What had become an unsustainable system because of advancing technology could become a sustainable system again through the invention of agriculture.

This is a very simple picture of how agriculture may have transformed what had become an unsustainable system into a sustainable one. It is a useful conceptual framework for visualizing the difference between hunting and gathering and agriculture, but ultimately it probably fails as an accurate description of what really drove the invention of agriculture. From archaeological evidence, we know the pattern was much more complicated than anything that could be captured on such a simple graph.

AGRICULTURE'S MULTIPLE ORIGINS

It is actually quite a remarkable bit of history. The basic resource transformation process we call agriculture arose at least three independent times, probably more: first, in the fertile crescent at the eastern end of the Mediterranean, associated with the domestication of wheat; second, somewhere in eastern Asia, associated with the domestication of rice; and third, in southern Mexico, associated with the domestication of corn. And, not only is the surprising fact that agriculture had multiple origins now well-known, but more recently we have also come to appreciate that it developed in at least two distinct patterns, for at least two distinct reasons. Flannery has done a most extensive analysis of the best known origin sites, the eastern Mediterranean and Mexico,[4] both of which will be briefly described.

Extending from the shores of the Mediterranean in Lebanon and Israel east to the Zagros Mountains in Iran, northward to the southern half of Turkey, and southward to the Sinai peninsula is an area characterized by rugged relief and a corresponding diversity of vegetation zones. Across the northern boundary a mountain chain forms an arching backbone that extends from Anatolia to Mesopotamia. Before recent deforestation, these mountain slopes supported an open deciduous woodland. Paralleling this arc is another of rolling foothills and low mountains known as the "hilly flanks," covered by open savannah. These hills in turn flank the Fertile Crescent, formed by the broad valley of the Tigris and Euphrates rivers, and the well-watered Mediterranean region of the coastal Levant (today's Israel, Gaza, Lebanon, and parts of Jordan and Syria) containing open woodlands. The close proximity of diverse habitats and the rich flora and fauna of these regions played an important role in the development of agricultural systems.

At the close of the Pleistocene Era (about 12,000 years ago), a changing climate (warmer and wetter) coincided with a change in the foraging strategies of the hunter-gatherers of the Levant. Rather than relying almost exclusively on large game, they began using a variety of resources, both plants and animals. Thus, a pattern of hunting wild sheep, deer, gazelle, and wild cattle gave way to a pattern of "hunting" fish, turtles, shrimp, birds, acorns, almonds, pistachios, field peas, and wild cereals. These new patterns, though still not agricultural, coincided with the establishment of permanent settlements. Thus, the nomadic hunter-gatherer became settled hunter-gatherer, but was not yet the agriculturalist. Such was the pattern of resource acquisition in the Levant (note that, contrary to older interpretations of agricultural origins, settled village life came before agriculture here).

The Zagros Mountains further east, bordering today's eastern Iraq and western Iran, had a very different environment from that of the Levant, with a unique distribution of plant and animal resources. The wild cereals, although present, did not form dense stands on the limestone-derived soils of this region as they did on the richer soils of the Levant. On balance, however, the limestone hills provided abundant, high-quality forage for wild sheep and goats, two important domesticable animal species. In this distinct environmental setting, developments roughly parallel to those of the Levant occurred, but with several important differences that reflect adaptations to the lower density of plant resources and higher density of herd animals.

In contrast with the sedentary communities of the Levant, the pre-agricultural sites in this region indicate an early orientation toward mobile herding and animal husbandry. The economic focus of these mobile populations appears to have been hunting combined with incipient animal husbandry. Although these sites contain stone tools for processing plant materials, most of the tools appear to be for hunting.

Based on the data from these early village sites, several generalizations can be made. First, in areas of high natural productivity and diversity such as the Levant, sedentary villages preceded plant cultivation and domestication by several thousand years. The subsistence of these early villagers appears to have been a broad-based one, combining intensive collection of wild cereals, nuts, and legumes with fishing, hunting large mammals, and collecting snails and shrimp. It was in the context of this intensive and consistent harvesting of wild cereals that important genetic changes (i.e., evolution) were imposed on these cereals. These changes decreased natural seed dispersal and increased harvestabilility, and by about 9,000 years ago domesticated cereals first appeared in these villages.

By contrast, in areas of lower natural productivity, such as the Zagros Mountains, subsistence settlement systems continued to be highly mobile until a much later date, relying on the mobile resources of both hunted and herded animals. It was only after the development and introduction of reliable, harvestable grains that fully sedentary villages were established in these more marginal regions. Thus, even within the Near East, two distinct paths to agriculture can be traced. In the Levant, an early stage of sedentary intensive hunting and gathering developed directly into one of sedentary cereal cultivation. In the Zagros, mobile intensive hunting and gathering led to an intermediate stage of mobile animal husbandry, and then to sedentary agriculture.

The full-fledged agriculture we see developed in Egypt, Mesopotamia, and the Indus valley some two thousand years later (see Figure 13.4), bears the mark of this dual development, one emphasizing animal husbandry and the domestication of animals, and the other emphasizing permanent settlement and domestication of plants. Draft animals, domesticated animal products such as milk and meat, and plant products, especially cereals, thus form the human-modified resources on which the agricultural habits of the people of Egypt, Mesopotamia, and the Indus valley were formed.

Patterns of agricultural evolution in Mexico could not have been more different. The tropical highlands of Mexico are formed by the confluence of two major mountain chains, the Sierra Madre Occidental (a southern extension of the Rocky Mountains) and the Sierra Madre Oriental, and their southward extension, the Sierra Madre del Sur. This rugged mountain mass creates a topography with relatively little level land. In terms of human habitation, therefore, the most significant features of this mountainous terrain are the flat basins occurring between ranges. Most of the area has a semiarid climate, with rainfall limited to the summer months.

During the early pre-agricultural hunting and gathering phase (from about 9,000 to about 4,000 years ago), human occupations were of two types: either very small camps representing the microbands (or individual

families) of the dry season, or much larger sites, representing the mac-robands (or groups of families) that gathered together in the wet season. The degree of group aggregation was a direct function of resource abundance, which depended on seasonal rainfall. With the post-ice age climatic changes, one resource habitat expanded greatly, that of the thorn-scrub-cactus forest.

Subsequent to this change, maize appeared in the diet, and it is thought that incipient agriculture was begun. Yet, overall, life continued much the same as earlier, with microbands in the dry season and mac-robands in the wet season. The macroband encampments became larger than those of the earlier phase, however, indicating that the groups may have stayed together longer, possibly due to their changing subsistence base. Although they were still mainly plant collectors who also hunted and trapped, it was during this period that they began acquiring domesti-cated plants.

Then, about 4,000 years ago, the settlement pattern seems to have changed. Macroband settlements, consisting of 5 to 10 houses, were es-tablished along river terraces adjacent to agricultural resources, and ag-ricultural output now provided a significant proportion of the diet, with a slow but continuous increase in productivity through time. Although some of the houses may have been occupied year-round, a portion of in-habitants moved to specialized hunting camps during the dry season, sug-gesting that the population was still only semi-sedentary.

Finally, about 3,000 years ago, full-time agriculturalists became evi-dent. These people lived in small villages of 100 to 300 inhabitants and depended on corn, several species of squash, gourds, beans, chili peppers, avocados, and other fruits for much of their subsistence.

Note how this sequence differs substantially from the Middle East, in which two very distinct forms of resource transformation—one migratory

---

Figure 13.4. Agricultural production led to the evolution of complex societies. Top photo, from Abu Simbel in upper Egypt (note the people on lower left for scale). Such monumental structures are testament to the social complexity that could evolve after agriculture became the dominant mode of food acquisition. Lower photo, from the Negev desert in Israel. The row of rocks is the remains of an old Israelite agricultural system in which small dams were constructed in dry creek beds to impede the flow of water, making it available for agricultural produc-tion. Even in some of the most difficult environments in the world, *H. sapiens* has been able to modify the environment for agricultural production.

and based on domesticated animals, and the other sedentary and based on domesticated plants—came together to form the full-fledged agriculture that eventually spread to the three major river valleys: the Nile, Tigris-Euphrates, and Indus. The Mexican history shows no significant domesticated animals, but indicates a gradual settling into sedentary life evolving along with the gradual adoption of agriculture as the main form of resource transformation.

WHY AGRICULTURE?

The older literature on the origin of agriculture presumed agriculture to be a far more efficient resource transformation system than hunting and gathering, and the interesting question became, what stood in the way of plant domestication and the invention of agriculture for such a long period of time? More recently, detailed studies of extant hunter-and-gatherer societies have turned that question on its head.[5] If one follows hunters and gatherers during the day and carefully examines what they do, one finds that the majority of their time is leisure. On average, this kind of society engages in just a few hours of daily work devoted to maintenance activities (i.e., gathering and preparing food and the like). For example, even in the harsh desert environment of South Africa's !Kung, in one six-hour day a single person can gather enough plant material to feed the family for three days. Primitive agriculturists, on the other hand, spend more than half their waking day engaged in sustenance activities, with a great deal of uncertainty about production added. So, the fundamental question becomes not what prevented people from inventing agriculture, but rather, what coerced them into a form of production that required such hard work when a well-known alternative, hunting and gathering, was clearly available?

Most pre-agricultural societies were well aware of the potential of agriculture and even engaged in some informal agricultural activities during the course of their normal seasonal cycle,[6] perhaps scattering some seeds in an area to which they knew they would return, perhaps eliminating some unwanted plants from an area in which desired plants were growing. But the socio-economic activity called agriculture, with its necessity of preparing land, sowing seed, husbanding plants, harvesting plants, and storing the harvest, was something they may have known, but for a long time chose not to do. And it is not hard to see why. If hunting and gathering was so easy (as it apparently was), why switch the basic resource transformation system to something that was harder? What, in fact, caused the switch?

As indicated above, the switch seems to have been caused by different factors in different places. But there seem to be three general forces, various combinations of which were involved at different times and in different places—increased human population, technological change in harvesting, and a changed environment. An increased human population means that the rate of harvesting of the products of hunting and gathering would have to be increased, leading to exactly the same changes described earlier for changed technology (see Figure 13.3). A change in hunting and gathering technology was already described above, and from the point of view of rates of harvest and rates of resource increase, could easily have led to the adoption of agriculture as a way of life (see Figure 13.3). A general deterioration in the environment, perhaps caused by a change in weather or perhaps by the activities of the hunters and gatherers themselves, caused a decrease in the capacity of the resources to replenish themselves, leading to the same general problem, a rate of harvest that exceeded the rate of replenishment. The way in which these three forces create resource depletion is illustrated in Figure 13.5.

SLASH-AND-BURN AGRICULTURE

The most common form of primitive agriculture, and one still practiced in many places in the world today, involves the use of fire and a reliance on the ecological process of succession.[7] In principle, it represents the easiest solution of two ecological problems that are inherent in agricultural production, the problem of plant competition (weeds) and the problem of nutrient cycling (recall the discussions of these topics in chapters 6 and 9). In the informal agricultural systems of the past, it is likely that hunter-and-gatherer bands scattered seeds into native grasslands. What would have happened to most of those seeds? The seeds would germinate, but they would rapidly become shaded by the already extant grasses. A very simple way of solving this problem would be to burn the native grasses before scattering the seeds, thus forcing the nondesirable species to at least begin at the same level with the desired plants (Figure 13.6).

The second ecological problem generated by the invention of agriculture is that of nutrient cycling. Recall from chapter 6 that ecological sys-

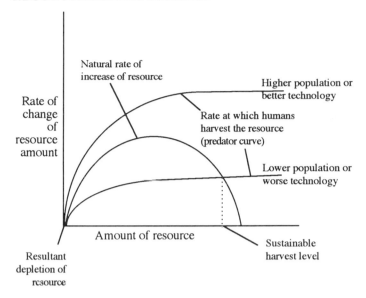

Natural rate of
increase of resource

Rate of
change
of
resource
amount

Higher population or
better technology

Rate at which humans
harvest the resource
(predator curve)

Lower population or
worse technology

Amount of resource

Resultant
depletion of
resource

Sustainable
harvest level

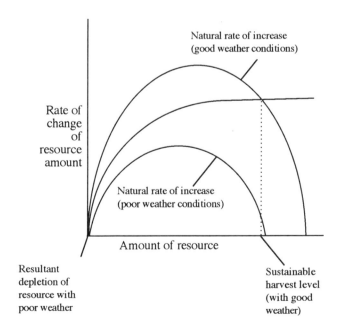

Natural rate of increase
(good weather conditions)

Rate of
change
of
resource
amount

Natural rate of increase
(poor weather conditions)

Amount of resource

Resultant
depletion of
resource with
poor weather

Sustainable
harvest level
(with good
weather)

tems recycle their nutrients. All the nutrients in a forest or grassland are recycled as dead leaves decompose, releasing nutrients into the soil, to be later picked up by the roots of other plants and reused. We have reason to believe that most systems unperturbed by *Homo sapiens* are fairly much in balance regarding nutrient flow—the amount of nitrogen, for example, released into the soil from the decomposing leaves that drop in the fall is exactly equal to the amount of nitrogen picked up by the trees in the spring as they put on their new leaves.[8]

But consider what happens when agriculture is imposed on the system. Harvesting some of the biological material removes it from the system so it cannot be available for recycling. Burning exacerbates this problem tremendously, in that nutrients normally stored in plant material, and, thus, held quite securely in the system, are released en masse by the burning process. The crops utilize much of this nutrient material, but much of the rest may be taken out of the system through running water, depending on certain details of the particular soil and climate involved. Thus, the land must be abandoned after a while, since the nutrient cycling process has been interrupted and there is a net export of nutrients out of the system. After the land is abandoned the process of ecological succession takes over, and a succession of various plant and animal species occupy the abandoned agricultural land, slowly bringing it back into a relatively stable nutrient cycling system, at which time the farmer may come back, burn the new vegetation, and start the cycle over again. The cycle may be as short as 10 years or as long as 50, depending on the nature of the soil and the successional process that takes over after the land is left idle. So, in a sense, the process of ecological succession "solves" the problem of disrupting the nutrient cycling system with agriculture.

The slash-and-burn system then can be seen as applying fire to natural vegetation to release the desired plants (the crops) from the process of

Figure 13.5. Summary of three of the forces creating resource depletion. In the top graph, the lower resource harvest rate is associated with a lower population density or a poor technology and leads to a relatively high sustainable harvest level. If the technology of harvest improves or the population becomes larger, the higher resource harvest rate (predator curve) is expected, leading to a depletion of the resource. In the lower graph, the change in weather conditions causes a change in the natural rate of increase of the resource, such that a high sustainable harvest level under good weather conditions is converted to a depleted condition with poor weather condition.

Figure 13.6. The slash-and-burn agricultural system. Top left, the forest has been cut and the resulting slash allowed to dry. The dried slash was then burned. Top right shows a corn seedling growing out of the ash that resulted from the burning. Bottom photo shows a typical slash-and-burn farm in early stages of production. Three crops (maize, squash, and beans) are clearly visible.

biological competition, but, in the process of doing so, creating a problem of net nutrient loss from the system. It thus requires abandonment of a particular site after a short period of time to allow the process of ecological succession to bring the system close to its original level of nutrient cycling. More than anything else, it represents a complex change in the social organization of energy in the resource transformation process which convert land and seed to food.

THE INTENSIFICATION OF AGRICULTURE

As with almost all systems involving human resource transformation, the slash-and-burn system is in continual evolution, the details of which depend on where and when one observes it. One of its rules that appears to remain consistent from place to place is a tendency to shorten the fallow cycle, to return to a piece of land more frequently. Thus, what was a 20-year cycle eventually turns into a 16-year cycle and then to a 10-year cycle, and so on. This process is usually known as the "intensification" of agriculture, in the sense that the "extensive" system involving leaving large amounts of land fallow (i.e., not under cultivation) gradually gives way to an "intensive" one in which all land is simultaneously under cultivation.

Earlier analysts had emphasized a sort of Malthusian approach to this topic, suggesting that as family size (or the size of whatever local population was involved in agricultural production grew), it was necessary to put more land into cultivation in order to feed the ever-growing population, eventually leading to the shortening of the fallow cycle. The sequence then was thought to be a simple relationship between agriculture and population growth, the increased productivity of agricultural production enabling the population to grow and, thus, requiring more land. Population growth was the underlying driving force, and agricultural production allowed it to reach its more or less natural high level.

This view was challenged some time ago by the geographer Ester Boserup,[9] who proposed that the situation was, at least sometimes, quite the reverse. The amount of labor required for making a piece of land agriculturally productive was relatively large, and frequently it was the fact of agricultural production itself that promoted a faster rate of population growth, precisely the opposite of what had been generally assumed before. If a farmer sees that a certain number of acres must be planted to feed the family, he or she understands that a certain number of work days are required to make that piece of land productive. If the number of work days is excessively large, it is natural to hope for sons and daughters to help fill those hours, thus promoting population growth. That the extra sons and daughters will some day require yet more land (to produce more food) is not likely to come to mind during those long hours of backbreaking work in the field.

On the other hand, it is almost certain that the other extreme occurs at least occasionally. The production necessary to feed the family is small (because of a small family or a very productive soil, for example), so the farmer is not required to work very many hours. The tendency will be in the general direction of overproduction, and a surplus of food will be felt. The surplus of food will suggest that so much land in production is not necessary, and the land in production will be reduced the next year.

Effectively, what we have is a pair of countervailing tendencies. First is the tendency to promote more children or migrants to the area to help work the land deemed necessary to cultivate to support the local population. This means that the population will increase and require more land to be put into production, which, in turn, will require a greater amount of labor to work the extra land just put into cultivation—a continual cycle. Second, there is a tendency to take land out of production when it appears that a surplus of food is being produced. A surplus may arise for various reasons, perhaps because the climate changed to allow higher production, or some of the population emigrated to make general food requirements less. These two countervailing tendencies can produce either a slowly increasing population, a slowly decreasing population, or a stable population, as well as a slowly increasing amount of land in production, a slowly decreasing amount of land in production, or a stable amount of land in production. The conditions for each of these outcomes is fairly easy to establish,[10] but are beyond the intentions of the present text. The point to be appreciated here is that there is no necessary tendency for a population to grow and thus require an ever-increasing amount of food and thus land under cultivation. That may be the case under some conditions, but other conditions may provoke exactly the opposite, or even a stable population balanced between the desire for a larger population to help work the land and the tendency toward a smaller population due to a deficit of production.

SETTLED AGRICULTURE VERSUS NOMADISM

Early settled agriculture coexisted with a nomadic lifestyle, whether the settled farmers of the Middle East interacting with the camel-based nomads of the surrounding desert, or the settled farmers of southwestern North America interacting with the hunting and gathering people further north, or one of the many other examples that could be cited. The interaction between settled people and nomadic people was one of the major features that influenced the evolution of culture.

To see how this may have worked, it is useful to imagine the general discourse of these two groups with regard to the resource transformation process. Both groups use socially organized labor to transform natural resources into usable products, but the nature of the natural resource itself is very distinct. At one extreme, the hunter and gatherer, or nomad, views land and the vegetation on it as the basic resource from which resources are to be gathered, either directly as in the gathering of acorns from oak forests or indirectly in the grazing of livestock. The social organization of labor is aimed at organizing the collection of the resources that exist on the land and transforming them into acorn bread, milk, or whatever other product the culture dictates.

At the other extreme, the settled agriculturalist also begins with land as the basic resource, but in a totally different context. Socially organized labor is applied to the land to transform it, not simply to harvest from it. The land is changed, through labor, from a grassland to a productive field, and the field then becomes an intermediate product, which goes into a somewhat separate resource transformation process. These differences are illustrated in the resource transformation diagram of Figure 13.7.

Referring to Figure 13.7, it is obvious how the hunter and gatherer views an agricultural field quite differently from the farmer who cultivated it. From the hunter and gatherer's point of view, the field is a piece of nature ready for the taking. From the farmer's point of view, it is a product of socially organized energy applied to the natural resource known as land. The hunter and gatherers that invade the farmer's cornfield and pick the ears of corn are, from their point of view, doing what they have always done, gathering nature's bounty. What they are doing, from the farmer's point of view, is stealing part of his or her production. Of course, both are right, both are moral, both are ethical. By carrying out their normal resource transformation activities, however, they come into conflict. The

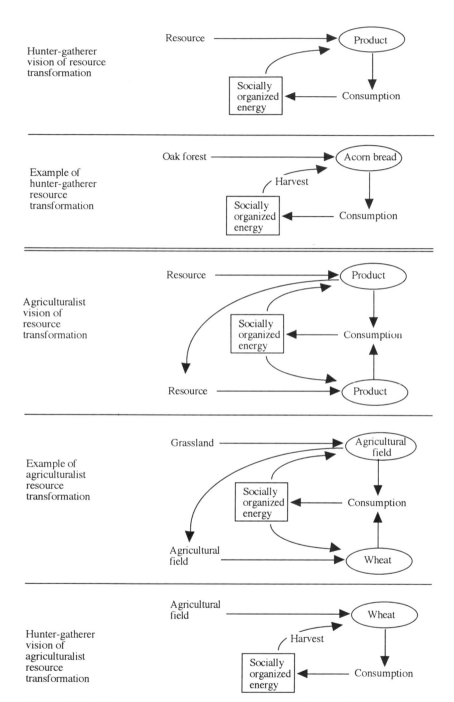

Figure 13.7. Diagrammatic representation of various forms of resource transformation (see text for explanation).

resolution of this sort of conflict clearly must have had a great influence on the early evolution of culture, whether by building walls around the city, or developing trade relationships between the two groups, or slowly merging the two processes.

Consider an imaginary example. Imagine a population of nomadic herders coming in contact seasonally with a settled agricultural people. At first, the agricultural fields appear as nothing more than pasture and the nomads herd their goats or cows onto the fields. The farmers respond by attacking and killing some of the goats. The herdspeople respond by killing the farmers. That is one, admittedly rather simple, scenario. But an alternative scenario, also rather simple, would involve a sort of negotiation in which the farmers would agree to make some of the harvest available to the herdspeople in exchange for their keeping their goats off of the fields, the herdspeople would agree to provide the farmers with some goat's milk in exchange for more of the harvest. What would be created is a totally different form of resource acquisition, in which both cultures benefit by having a more varied diet (the farmers get goat's milk, while the herders get grain). But most importantly, both cultures dramatically alter their resource acquisition processes. Rather than transforming the basic resources to products for consumption, part of the purpose of producing the product is for exchange. The product has changed from something whose value is embodied in the utility it gives to the producer, to something whose value is embodied partly in its ability to be exchanged for other products. It has become, at least partly, a commodity. Recalling the analysis of human production systems presented in chapter 9, we would still be dealing with a system of "simple commodity production," since money is not yet involved. However, the change involved in viewing the product of one's labor not in terms of what it will be used for, but rather, in terms of what it will be exchanged for, is obviously a revolutionary change in consciousness about the resource transformation process.

THE FIRST STEP IN THE MODERNIZATION OF AGRICULTURE

Once the full intensification of agriculture occurred, a variety of new tendencies began to appear. It is fairly obvious that under a slash-and-burn system, the easiest way of responding to social and biological events would be to either put more land in fallow or take more land out of fallow, giving rise to the sorts of changes Boserup analyzed. But what would one expect if all the available land had already been taken out of fallow? The same pressures would be felt, but the solution of modifying the fallow period would no longer be available.

Recall that burning the field was the major form of land preparation, the main purpose of which was to remove other vegetation, weeds. But much of the weedy material would have underground stems that would immediately send up shoots again. Burning certainly removed weeds, but not completely. Probably in response to the continual problem of weeds, the idea occurred to someone to dig up the underground parts of the weeds, effectively ushering in the era of the plow (Figure 13.8).

The plow would not have been of much use without draft animals to pull it, and likely, for this reason, the plow never evolved in America.[11] And the plow was one of the major innovations that generated other innovations, especially those involved with metallurgy. The Bronze Age and the Iron Age of the Old World never materialized in the Americas, possibly due in part to the lack of this all-important technological innovation.

Figure 13.8. The plow still in use in many places in the Third World (here in central India) is almost identical to the original plow of Old World agriculture.

AGRICULTURE IN THE MODERN WORLD

The changes induced by the Columbian interchange were among the most spectacular in the history of humanity. The structure of the world as we know it today was established at that time. We have already seen, in part, how slavery and agriculture evolved together, mainly associated with sugar production.[12] In a more general sense, the European merchant societies took control of the world from the Chinese/Arab monopoly through the vehicle of international trade, incorporating colonial outposts that supplied raw materials to fuel their industrial development. These raw materials included luxury products (e.g., sugar, spices), drugs (coffee, tea), or industrial inputs (wood, cotton, indigo and other dyes), most of which were agricultural products.

Thus was set up the basic form of the world as we see today, with the Third World a consequence of those early colonies, and industrial capitalism the dominant form of resource transformation in the developed world. Today the world is a single economic entity, and the notion of industrial capitalism existing in the First World and some more primitive form of capitalism existing in the Third World is an outmoded form of thought. The globe is one world system, the developed world one part of it and the Third World another part of it, all connected in a complicated network.[13]

While this view is accurate, it nevertheless makes sense to treat the developed world as different from the Third World in some contexts. Understanding agriculture in a developed country like the United States is sometimes hindered by an overly romantic notion of the farm. As part of the original expansion of European America and the development of something of a centerpiece of democracy "American style," the rugged farmer carving a homestead out of the wilderness looms large in our legend. While the yeoman farmer may have been important in both the Europeanization of America and the establishment of the particular form of democracy practiced earlier in our history, the farm and farmer of today bear as much resemblance to this romantic vision as Beltway brokering does to Athenian democracy.

One of the key barriers to analyzing the current agricultural situation in the United States is a confusion between farming and agriculture. Farming is the resource transformation process in which land, seed, and labor are converted into peanuts. It is Farmer Brown cultivating the land, sowing the seed, and harvesting the peanuts. Agriculture, contrarily, is the decision to invest a certain amount of money in this year's production; the application of the tractor and cultivator/automatic seeder to the real estate; application of herbicides, insecticides, fungicides, nematocides, and bacteriocides to the growing crop; automatic harvest of the commodity; sale of the commodity to a processor; grinding up the products and adding emulsifiers, taste enhancers, stabilizers and preservatives, packing in convenient and "pleasing-to-the-consumer" jars; and marketing the trade name of Skippy or Dippy. In short, while farming was the production of peanuts from the land, agriculture is the production of peanut butter from petroleum.

This transformation of farming to agriculture happened in two recognizable waves, the first beginning at the end of the Civil War and culminating with the emergence of the hydrocarbon society earlier in this century, and the second starting toward the end of World War II and still evolving. It was actually before the outbreak of the Civil War that Cyrus McCormick built his revolutionary reaper, a device that could be attached to a team of horses and pulled through the field to harvest automatically.[14] One of the surprising facts of mechanization history is that McCormick's machine did not come into use until well after the Civil War had begun, despite the fact that it was well known some 20 years earlier. It was not some subtle cynicism that farmers had about "new-fangled devices," it was, in fact, quite a rational assessment of economic facts that caused them to remain with a technology that required five people per acre at harvest time, when they were well aware of this new technology that required only one person per acre.[15]

The all-important factor was availability of labor. The westward expansion of agriculture, which had populated the Ohio valley and was in the process of populating lands further west at the time the Civil War broke out, required a supply of harvest labor that was easily met by the comparatively large population of potential workers. The many men who were looking to establish homesteads or in some other way articulate with the agrarian economy provided a ready source of cheap harvest labor. With all that cheap labor available, it simply made no sense to invest a large amount of money in an automatic harvester, and the McCormick reaper remained an underutilized "new-fangled" device for almost two decades. The device that revolutionized agriculture and even strongly contributed to the making of the industrial revolution in the United States was ignored for years, not because of unreasonable or backward farmers, but because of logical and correct economic calculations.

With the outbreak of the Civil War labor became scarce, and McCormick's reaper was widely adopted, initiating a change in the mentality of farmers. Machines in the fields was to be the future of agriculture, and a host of automation devices followed McCormick's reaper, ranging from corn harvesters to threshers to automatic seeders and many others. At this point, one of the limiting factors was power. The horse team was replaced by the steam engine for certain processes, but many processes could not conveniently utilize steam engines.

The next great event occurred in the early parts of the twentieth century. The internal combustion engine made all of the automated devices that had already been invented even more efficient. The introduction of the internal combustion engine, effectively, the introduction of fossil fuel-based traction power, completed the first major transformation of farming to agriculture.[16]

Finally, in conjunction with chemical research that was aimed at the development of weapons and the control of tropical diseases during World War II, a miracle seemed to emerge. Agriculture had always been limited by pests, mainly insects. The miracle was a chemical, dichlorodiphenyl-trichloroethane, or DDT. Pests could be killed by DDT much as enemies could be killed in war, and indeed, the warring metaphor was skillfully used to transform American agriculture again.[17] Soon, agriculture became fully dependent on chemicals formulated from petroleum, thus completing the transformation of agriculture to what we see today. A farm is a technologically sophisticated factory that uses, first, fossil fuels to drive large machinery, and, second, products derived from fossil fuels to eliminate unwanted pieces of the biology (i.e., pests).

In conjunction with this massive technological transformation, the social structure of resource transformation underwent a major structural change.[18] This social transformation had to do with the way in which critical agricultural commodities were bought and sold. Of course, it had been quite usual that agricultural products were traded—indeed, quite usual that middle persons of various sorts were involved, as far back in history as one can go. But at the close of the eighteenth century, a food crisis loomed in western Europe that must have seemed something like the energy crisis of the sixteenth century. Wheat had been a staple crop as long as anyone cared to remember, but the form in which it was eaten was class-dependent. The lower classes ate mainly porridge or gruel, soup-like preparations that required very little grain to fill a stomach. The upper classes ate a more elegant product—bread. For this the wheat had to be ground into flour, and the flour mixed with water and yeast, made into a dough, allowed to rise, and finally baked. Such an immense input of labor could only be afforded by the well-to-do, and the peasant class continued to be satisfied with its porridge.[19]

During this period, long-distance trade in agricultural products was largely restricted to luxury goods such a chocolate, tea, coffee, and sugar. The main agricultural goods that fed the Industrial Revolution—cotton and wheat—were hardly traded at all internationally before the late eighteenth century. There was simply not enough demand, since cloth was made mainly from wool, and local production of wheat for porridge and bread fully satisfied all needs.

Toward the end of the eighteenth century, two factors combined to change this pattern dramatically. First was the evolution of improved technology in milling of grain, and second was a change in the social organization of work. The improved milling technology caused the price of bread to decline, making it more available to the masses, and, more importantly, it was certainly inconvenient for factory workers to bring gruel or porridge in their lunch buckets. The result was a dramatic increase in consumption of bread and a concomitant increase in demand for wheat. In almost all European countries, local agricultural production simply could not keep pace, leading to a dramatic increase in international trade in wheat.

This led to the first important international wheat-trading business complex the world had ever known, including key points at Liverpool, Constantinople, and Odessa (Figure 13.9). Odessa had been an important center for grain trade since Catherine the Great made it a point of consolidation of the Russian empire in 1774.[20] Colonists were given land in exchange for settling in southern Russia (in what is today Ukraine and Moldova). Unbeknownst to Catherine or the nobles or serfs who colonized the area, they inherited one of the finest pieces of agricultural real estate in the world, on par with the rich soils of the U.S. Great Plains and the pampas of Argentina.[21] Odessa became the market for the hundreds of thousands of farms that eventually dotted the surrounding countryside.

The grain trade was then a chaotic business with little predictability about supplies. Clever grain merchants developed a system to take samples of grain from ships at Constantinople, carry those samples quickly over-

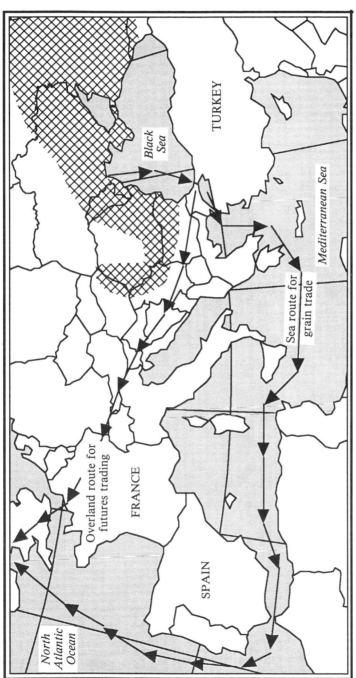

Figure 13.9. Basic trade patterns in the evolution of the grain trade. The hatched area is the approximate location of European and Asian grassland soils, the source of incredible agricultural wealth. Ships normally set out from Odessa on the Black Sea. Upon traveling through the very narrow straits at Constantinople (now Istanbul), speculators were able to assess the quantity and quality of ships' cargos. As the ships slowly made their way through the Mediterranean and around the Iberian peninsula, the rapid ground travel brought news to Liverpool and other European ports long before the shipments actually arrived. This arrangement thus allowed, and even promoted, the trading of "future" deliveries.

land to the trading houses of Europe, and sell a future shipment based on that sample. This was the beginning of "futures trading." Agreements to buy and sell grain shipments were made in well-known centers, usually clubs or informal gathering places such as coffee houses. Liverpool became the center for buying grain destined for the mills of England.

So, by the end of the eighteenth century in the industrially burgeoning Europe, we had the beginnings of a grain trade that involved (1) a serf farmer who sold grain (or gave tribute) to (2) a landowner (usually nobility in Russia), who sold it to (3) a transporter who transported it to Odessa, where (4) a shipper bought it and sailed to Constantinople, where (5) a representative of the shipper took a sample of it and brought it overland to (6) Liverpool and other European trading centers to (7) a primitive commodity exchange center, where (8) another merchant bought it to be sold to (9) the miller.

Into this system stepped a former French peasant farmer by the name of Leopold Louis-Dreyfus. At the age of seventeen Louis-Dreyfus left his family's farm in Sierentz, crossed the Swiss border, and sold his share of the season's wheat harvest in Basel. His hands would never touch farming dirt again. He spent several years in the stream of wandering merchants involved in the grain trade all over Europe, established his own grain business in Basel, and took out large loans aimed at enlarging his business. He arrived in Odessa in the 1860s and purchased the bulk of the grain elevators in the city. He then sent out his own agents, not to buy grain from farmers, but to sign contracts to purchase grain in the future from farmers. At the other end of his enterprise, in western Europe, he sold those contracts for future delivery. By the 1870s, he was contracting for wheat from the Russian hinterland, shipping by rail to his grain elevators in Odessa, shipping the grain on his freighters, and selling futures and grain to buyers in Hamburg, Bremen, Berlin, Mannheim, Duisburg, and Paris. The Louis-Dreyfus Company had become the first giant grain company in the world. Similar stories could be told for four other giants, Bunge of Argentina, Continental of New York, Cargill of Minneapolis, and André of Switzerland. These five giants dominate the world grain trade much like the seven sisters (now six) dominate the world petroleum trade.

While this pattern is most highly developed specifically in the grain trade, similar patterns developed in other sectors of the food industry, such as canned vegetables and processed foods. Beginning with the Industrial Revolution and continuing with only minor variation today, buyers of agricultural products tend to become large, and most financial decisions tend to be made far from the source of it all, the farmer. By the time Louis-Dreyfus arrived in Odessa, the serf farmers of Russia had little knowledge of or control over what happened to their grain after it left their farms. But those who purchased it were involved in high finance throughout the industrial world.

This historical development has created a particular model that we might refer to as the modern agricultural system. Recalling the minimal model for human resource transformation systems, we can represent the changes in agriculture as in Figure 13.10. Figure 13.10*a* shows farming the way it used to be, with basic resources combined in the production facility (the farm) to produce the products (food) that were consumed as part of the regenerating process for socially organized labor. In Figure 13.10*b* are the structural relationships after the technological developments referred to above. In the resource transformation process of modern agriculture we have three units: the unit that supplies the inputs to the farmer, the unit that is the farm itself, and the unit to which the farmer supplies the products. And we immediately see some problems from the very nature of this structural arrangement.

In Figure 13.10*c,* this relationship is illustrated in a more streamlined fashion, showing the transfer of money (horizontal arrows) and the rational economic desires of all three components (the vertical arrows). The suppliers obviously wish to get the most money possible for their products, while the farmer wants to pay as little as possible for those same products. Similarly, the buyers want to pay as little as possible for the supplies they buy from the farmer, while the farmer wants them to pay as much as possible. Clearly, there are tensions here, and in that never-neverland called perfect competition and free trade, one might expect that these tensions would resolve themselves to produce fair prices and terms of exchange among the various parties involved in this three-part resource transformation process. But such a world usually exists only in textbooks. In the real world, various forms of political power are exerted to alter that theoretical free market.

The average U.S. farmer of the post-World War II era was a relatively small entrepreneur, owner of the so-called family farm. Granted, he or she had long before made the transition from simple commodity production (producing food for the family to eat or to exchange for other food) to a full-scale M-P-M (money to product to money) mode, but the scale of

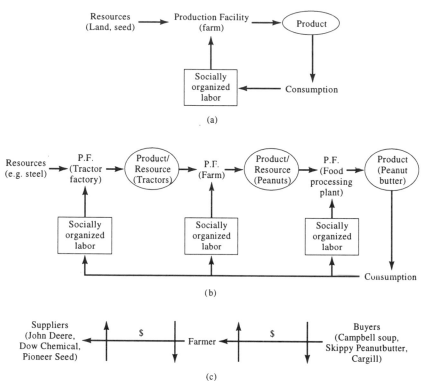

Figure 13.10. Diagrammatic representation of the modern agricultural system. (a) Idealized representation of the "farming" operation, where the production facility is simply the farm and resources are mainly those found on the farm. (b) Representation of the whole modern system of "agriculture," in which three production facilities are intimately interconnected and products from some are resources for others. (c) The "money trail" in modern agriculture.

operation remained exceedingly small compared to the suppliers and buyers (to some extent this is not generally true of farms in the far western states, nor in Florida, but for most of the rest of the United States it is at least approximately true). Suppliers like Dow Chemical or John Deere are giant corporations with monopoly-like control over the markets in which they participate, as are buyers like CPC International (makers of Skippy Peanut Butter) or the Cargill Grain Company. It does not take a Ph.D. in economics to predict what is likely to happen, given such an arrangement. Farmers, with little economic leverage because of their isolated condition and relatively small size, were constantly being squeezed on both sides of the resource transformation system. The way the farmer saw it, suppliers extorted large sums of money for necessary inputs, and buyers refused to pay fair prices for the products, leaving the poor farmer in the middle. This is the fundamental structure of agriculture in the United States and much of the rest of the developed world. It is part of the reason why we have a persistent farm crisis.

CRISIS IN THE MODERN AGRICULTURAL SYSTEM—THE PESTICIDE TREADMILL

The post–World War II agricultural system has been a technical marvel. Production is up; profits are up. In less than a century, the United States has changed from a system in which 70 percent of the population was engaged in agriculture to one in which less than 3 percent of the population is so engaged. And productivity per acre is much larger than before the postwar technological agricultural revolution. It was all a part of the hydrocarbon society and was based on (1) biocides,[22] an indirect consequence of chemical warfare research of World War II; (2) traction power, made possible by the internal combustion engine, fueled by petroleum; and (3) chemical fertilizers. But, as so frequently happens, the miracle also has a downside.

The first indication that something was amiss was the publication of Rachel Carson's *Silent Spring* in 1962.[23] In a book that was as poetic as it was scientifically rigorous, Carson suggested that the massive use of pesticides was having a dramatic negative effect on the environment. Previously, there had been much popular commentary about the human health effects of pesticides, a concern shared even by the pesticide manufacturers. But *Silent Spring* was the first popular account of the environmental consequences of pesticides, contributing not only to concern about environmental poisons, but also providing a springboard for the entire subsequent environmental movement.

What Carson said is now well appreciated. The themes of her book were that pesticides kill not only the targets, but also many species that are not targeted. Pesticides may concentrate in the higher trophic levels (depending on the pesticide), thus making nonlethal doses at lower trophic levels quite dangerous at higher levels. Pests develop resistence to pesticides. The poisonous effects of pesticides and their residues (again, depending on the pesticide) may persist for a long time in the environment.

Silent Spring was an extremely well-documented book. Despite a Herculean effort, mainly by representatives of the pesticide manufacturers, at finding errors, only the most trivial errors were eventually encountered.[24] Nevertheless, an immense and coordinated attack against the book was orchestrated by the pesticide manufacturers, including an attempt by Velsicol to pressure Houghton-Mifflin not to publish the book. Book reviews were generally harsh, and, we later discover, were frequently written by scientists receiving monetary rewards from the chemical industry. As carefully documented in subsequent works,[25] most independent scientists received *Silent Spring* positively, and rereading the book even today suggests understatement was its actual problem.

A less acknowledged, but perhaps even more important, book, *The Pesticide Conspiracy*, by Robert van den Bosch, was published in 1978. This book accomplished three things simultaneously. First, it reinforced all of the analysis of Rachel Carson, with 16 years of more and better data. Second, it made explicit what Carson had only left for the reader to conclude, that pesticides were generating enormous profits for those who manufacture them, and that the "conspiracy" involved government and university scientists receiving direct and indirect financial rewards from this industry. Third, it elaborated a generalized scheme as to how, ecologically, pesticides came to be such a problem. This scheme was called the "pesticide treadmill," and has since become part of the general discourse of the environmental movement (Figure 13.11).

Figure 13.11. Images of the pesticide treadmill in Central America. Top left is an advertisement in the Spanish language edition of Life magazine from 1954, noting that all problems with the cotton boll weevil can be solved with Shell's product Aldrin. A boll weevil is pinned with an insect pin on a map of Central America. Top right, a roadside billboard outside Guatemala City in 1964 has basically the same message ("Put an end to your problems with bollworms by using Sevin"). The difference is that a new pest is the problem (the bollworm never had been a problem before insecticide spraying began), and a new miracle product is offered to solve the new problem—Union Carbide's Sevin. Lower photo shows a billboard outside of Managua, Nicaragua, in 1984. The message is the same, except the pest is now simply referred to as "the pests" (las plagas), since there are so many pests in cotton now (again, most likely a consequence of insecticide spraying), and the product is, of course, new again.

The pesticide treadmill includes three forces operating simultaneously: (1) pest resurgence, (2) pesticide resistance, and (3) secondary pest outbreak. Each of these forces had been well-known even before *Silent Spring,* but they were first put together as a coherent theory in van den Bosch's book.

Pest resurgence is illustrated by the response of the cotton bollworm (see Figure 13.11) to the application of the insecticide monocrotophos. In an experiment performed in 1965, some cotton fields were treated with the insecticide, and others were left alone. After the first treatment, all the fields were sampled and it was discovered, as expected, that there were about 50 percent fewer bollworms in the treated fields. So far, so good. But, seven days later, more samples were taken. Not only were the treated fields newly infested with bollworms, but they actually had more bollworms than the untreated fields. One week later, the treated fields had over 400 percent more bollworms than the untreated fields! After two more treatments with the insecticides, the dramatic 400 percent disparity was reduced, but in all future samplings, the insecticide-treated fields had more bollworms than the others. How could such a thing happen?

Unfortunately, the scientific testing of insecticides focuses on their ability to kill insects, seemingly the obvious and correct thing to do. But, as so frequently happens in ecology,[26] one does not necessarily do what one sets out to do in a complicated ecosystem. Consider, for example, the interaction diagram presented in Figure 13.12. In Figure 13.12*a* is the diagram of what the pesticide engineers originally thought was the problem—bollworms eat cotton. The solution was obvious: Find a poison that kills bollworms. If you have some bollworms in the laboratory and you spray them with monocrotophos, they die. The negative effect of bollworms on cotton, as pictured in Figure 13.12*a,* is thus cancelled by spraying monocrotophos. Right? Unfortunately, Figure 13.12*a* is not complete, and the complications necessary to make it more realistic include the predators of the bollworm, as depicted in Figure 13.12*b*. Note how, by having a negative effect on the bollworms, the wasps, predators of the bollworms, have a consequent positive effect on the cotton.[27] Looking at the diagram in Figure 13.12*b,* one might ask the pesticide engineer how he or she knows that the ultimate effect of applying the insecticide will damage the bollworm more than the wasps, for any child knows that if an action designed to hurt an enemy hurts a friend more, that action is counterproductive.

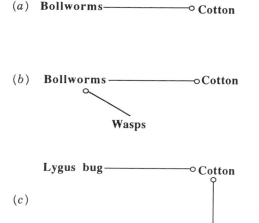

Figure 13.12. Some of the population interactions involved in the cotton pesticide treadmill (see text for explanation).

Failure to examine the problem ecologically (see it as at least the three-factor problem presented in Figure 13.12*b*), rather than economically (the desired product and the impediment to that product as presented in Figure 13.12a), led to the resurgence of the bollworm. Application of the pesticide indeed did kill the target pest, but it also killed the non-target wasps. The result was that the bollworm, now free of its normal predatory control, was able to resurge after the pesticide use.[28] This phenomenon has been observed repeatedly in pesticide applications.

Pesticide resistence is actually a very old phenomenon, and was anticipated long ago.[29] It is one of the most well-documented cases we have of the operation of evolution through natural selection.[30] Most insect pests are herbivores. Since most plants have evolved the ability to produce toxins to protect themselves from herbivores, it is not surprising that insect herbivores have a variety of methods of detoxifying poisons. For example, the production of a particular enzyme may chemically bind a poison, rendering it ineffective. An insect capable of producing that enzyme would obviously be immune to the effects of the poison. An enzyme that operates in this fashion is usually referred to as a detoxifying enzyme, and can operate against a human-produced insecticide as well as a poison produced by a plant.

If a detoxifying enzyme is under genetic control, and there is genetic variability associated with it, we normally expect evolution to result from the application of selective pressure.[31] Let us say, for example, that the gene contains two alleles, A and a, and that the dominant gene is the DNA sequence that codes for the detoxifying enzyme. Thus, all individuals with genotype AA or Aa will be able to produce the detoxifying enzyme and thus be immune to the poison. If we begin with a population in which 90 percent of the population is aa (that is, not capable of detoxifying the enzyme), and we spray a very efficient pesticide, we will kill 90 percent of the population. But the remaining individuals will be of genotypes Aa and AA, corresponding to the resistant phenotype.

Suppose that of the surviving individuals about half are Aa and half AA. The next generation then will result from three types of matings (AA with AA, AA with Aa, and Aa with Aa), resulting in all three genotypes. The relative frequencies of the three will be, AA = 56 percent, Aa = 38 percent, and aa = 6 percent.[32] So in the next application of pesticides, only 6 percent of the individuals will be killed. And, if the cycle is continued, fewer and fewer individuals will be of the aa genotype, and, thus, fewer and fewer individuals will be killed by the pesticide. The population is evolving into a resistant one.

The third component of the pesticide treadmill is secondary pest outbreak. It is nicely illustrated in an experiment examining control of the lygus bug in cotton.[33] Some cotton fields were treated with a mixture of toxaphene and DDT, and others were left as controls. After spraying, the treated fields had no lygus bugs, while the control fields had a significant number. But the interesting part of the experiment is not the lygus bug, but rather the army worm (the caterpillar of a moth), another insect pest of cotton. When the experiment started, there were a very small number of army worms in both control and experimental fields. A week after spraying, a few were encountered in the control fields, and none in the experimentals. Yet another week passed, and the number of army worms in the experimental plots were ten times the number in the control plots. At this point, the army worm had become a very significant pest. A month later, after another treatment with the insecticide mixture, the army worm population in the controls was the same as before, but had more than quadrupled in the experimental fields, making it not only a problem, but a disaster.

What had happened was that the spraying of an insecticide for one pest, the lygus bug, caused another insect that had not previously been a pest (because it was too rare to do any damage) to become one—a secondary pest. Just how such a phenomenon occurs is no mystery, and was anticipated even before the new hydrocarbon-based insecticides were ever invented.[34] A glance at Figure 13.12c makes it clear. The pesticide was aimed at the lygus bug but actually killed the predators, releasing the army worms from their natural predatory control.

Putting these three forces together—resurgence, resistance, and secondary outbreaks—we have a pattern that is devastating in the long run for farmers. A resurgent pest suggests to the farmer that more pesticide is needed, since the problem is worse. Because of the resistance, the pesticide is no longer as potent as it once was, suggesting to the farmer that more pesticide or stronger pesticide is needed, and the new pests that mysteriously appear suggest once again that more pesticide is needed. It seems much like a drug addiction story. The more pesticide you use, the more you need—the pesticide treadmill.

Most scientists now acknowledge the reality of the pesticide treadmill, and a variety of mechanisms for dealing with it have been devised.[35] In the context of the present discussion, the pesticide treadmill is just one component of a much larger crisis in modern agriculture. It is the best known and most well publicized, but, nevertheless, it is only one of a host of ecological problems. Problems with soil erosion, loss of soil productivity, chemical contamination of wells and waterways, overproduction, depletion of genetic stock, and a variety of others suggest that the modern system has run its course and is due for an overhaul. In response to this general feeling, a movement for an alternative agriculture has emerged. It is small and politically weak, but it is worldwide and growing.

AGRICULTURE IN THE CONTEXT OF HUMAN EVOLUTION

The production process called agriculture fits into the evolutionary trajectory of *Homo sapiens* in two distinct ways, as discussed above. First, in a variety of places and at different times, the practice of planting plants and tending them until harvest became the dominant form of food acquisition. This innovation allowed, or propelled, massive changes in the way humans lived. Second, the need to fertilize plants, prepare the land, and control pests became part of the fodder of the hydrocarbon revolution, leading to the massive use of chemical pesticides and fertilizers, as well as the mechanization of almost all agricultural activities. This innovation was an integral part of the final maturation of the "modern" system, and its criticism forms part of the postmodern criticism more generally, albeit subtly.

FOURTEEN

Neo-Malthusianism, Agriculture, and Natural Resources

That the human species faces crucial problems with its environment has long ago ceased to be a debatable issue. The historical evolution of these problems has been outlined in previous chapters (especially chapters 2, 10, and 13), and something of their causes and effects treated in these and other chapters. It should be clear by now that there are many details in a complex web of causation, ranging across a vast conceptual and ideological landscape. It does not take much imagination to visualize, at one extreme, a charismatic Christian evangelist suggesting that the breakdown in family values is at the core of all environmental problems, and, at the other extreme, the suggestion that the avariciousness of the capitalist system is the real problem. While both the loss of tradition and the inefficiencies of capitalism may indeed be involved in environmental degradation, the error here is an epistemological one, in which cause and effect are first imposed on the problem, and then various components falsely infused with ontological priority.

When dealing with cause-and-effect arguments, there is an implicit assumption that effects will cease if causes are stopped. If diseases are "caused" by germs, eliminating the germs will eliminate the diseases. If an acceleration is caused by a force, eliminating the force will eliminate the acceleration. If crime is caused by poverty, eliminating poverty will eliminate crime. If crime is caused by criminals, eliminating criminals will eliminate crime. All such statements have the basic structure, if A causes B, then eliminating A will eliminate B.

In the above four examples, the reader will immediately recognize that two are fairly good approximations to reality, while the other two are at least questionable. Forces and germs do, for all practical purposes, cause acceleration and disease. But there is considerable debate as to the cause of crime. And here is the critical issue—crime is a result of multiple causes. When multiple causality is overlooked or intentionally ignored, it can sabotage even the strongest expectations about the consequences of particular actions. So, if crime is caused both by criminals and poverty, the liberal reformist will be surprised when rising affluence does not bring with it an elimination of crime, and the law-and-order police captain will be perplexed at the failure of the crime rate to go down proportionally with the number of incarcerations.

Furthermore, in assessing problems and their causative factors, regardless of their possible multiple causality, it is important to be clear about what is the problem and what is the cause. According to some, the existence of a large population of people is the problem, and the causative factors are poor access to health care, poverty, unavailability of contraceptives, and the like. According to others, the existence of hunger, poverty, and environmental degradation are the problems and population density is the causative factor. Given that such disparate views seem to coexist in the current political environment, it is no wonder that debate emerges over what should be done. If one sees poverty and environmental degradation as the problem and population as the cause, one naturally concludes that stemming population growth will partially alleviate poverty and environmental degradation. If one sees population density as the problem, one naturally concludes that providing equitable social forces and available contraception will reduce population growth.

Most analysts today reject this simple linear approach and admit to a more interactive and nuanced analysis. Clearly, there is a relationship between population density and these critical sociopolitical factors. But it is not useful to say that one is the problem and the other the cause. Rather, there is an intimate interconnection between the two. When dealing with an issue that is structured in this fashion, it is rather easy to become embroiled in a chicken-or-egg argument when the proper focus should be on the interaction itself.

But even this level of analysis is not sufficient to deal with the complexity of the issue. For example, a growing population may put pressure on local resources, thus promoting technological innovation, which in turn may force a concentration of wealth, which may increase birth rates of the resulting poorer sectors, which may exacerbate the problems of waste disposal, which may create new opportunities for entrepreneurs, which may concentrate wealth further, thus leading to yet higher birth rates, and so on. We do not have a situation of simple cause and effect, but rather a multifactored problem, with a multitude of interactive causative agents.

Despite the seemingly obvious observation that most significant human problems have this multicausal structure, it nevertheless seems to be a passion of the modern world to ignore multiple causality. Yes, we say, "Problem X has multiple causes. However, once we understand those that are proximate and those that are ultimate, we can look for the ultimate *one*." Multiple causality thus is seen as a problem of perception. We force a simple cause-and-effect mentality as we pursue our analysis. Unfortunately, many of the problems we face today are not legitimately amenable to a simple cause-and-effect analysis. Sometimes A causes B, which, in turn, causes C. But more often than not, A and B together codetermine C, which, in combination with B, changes A, which then forces a change on B, and so forth. Causal agents do not necessarily occur in chain-like events (A causes B causes C causes D), but, rather, are connected to one another in a web-like fashion (the interaction of A and B is transformed by the effect of C, which, in turn, was determined partly by the interaction of B with D, which ultimately was caused by the influence of A over D).

When a problem is caused by a set of factors that are connected to one another in a web-like fashion, it is simply wrong to presume they are connected as a chain. Forcing them into a conceptual chain-like sequence may make political pundits comfortable, but confusion will inevitably arise when crime stays the same no matter how many criminals are incarcerated.

One can hardly find a better example of this confusion than in the contemporary debate about human numbers and the environment. Some say that the number of humans is the problem and social and environmental factors the cause, while others say that the social and environmental factors are the problem and population is the cause. But both points of view are flawed for the reasons outlined above—human population is related to a myriad of social and environmental factors in a web-like fashion, and attempts to force it into a chain-like sequence are misleading at best.

To be sure, the planet is a finite place, and there is some upper limit on the number of human beings, or anything else, that it can house. This is a relatively simple mathematical fact and one that is, to my knowledge, noncontroversial. It is also true that the size of the human population must be above a certain level to be able to survive over the long term, if only because of the need for finding mates (there is generally a lower limit for any population). Naturally, we should be concerned that we stay between those limits.

But this concern does not translate automatically into a need to reduce the size of populations. Population size is neither the problem nor the cause of the problem, but, rather, one component in a complex of interconnecting causality—a web-like structure that will not succumb to chain-like causality analysis. This is part of the tragedy of a focus on population as a key issue. It is not, as some people continue to think, an important link in a chain of causality. If it were, programs to control population would surely make sense. But the size of the population is not a link in a chain, but, rather, a component in a web. Cut the population of New York by a million people today, and the effect on the air of tomorrow would be negligible. Eliminate all the people from Gary, Indiana, and the steel industry would continue to belch its sulfur into the air. Cut the population of Acre, Brazil, in half and the remaining cattle ranchers would likely *increase* their rate of pasture expansion and deforestation. The problems of New York, Gary, and Acre are complicated, and population enters the analysis as one of the variables, simultaneously determined by and determining the web of causality that generates the significant social and environmental problems so well known in those three localities.

Despite some vociferous concern over the global nature of the population problem, most visible evidence of the effect of human population density is not to be found at the global scale, but rather at subunits of the globe. Focusing on these subunits, we can frequently identify areas that seem to be either above or below some sort of critical values. For example, in Las Lagunas, Mexico, a traditional land-use system had evolved that was, by all estimates, quite sustainable and environmentally benign. Suddenly, industrial employment opportunities were made available outside the region, and a dramatic decline in the population resulted. The land-use system was dependent on a certain number of people, and when the number fell below the critical value, the sustainable system failed. Thus, a decrease in the population caused severe environmental degradation.[1] If the Penan of Sarawak, Malasia, were suddenly eliminated, the only visible block against the Malasian government cutting down the Sarawak forest would be eliminated.[2] The highland Maya of Chiapas, Mexico, although presumably living in a sustainable manner before the arrival of the Spanish, were immediately converted into an "overpopulated" culture by the introduction of sheep. The sheep overgrazed the fallow lands, thus breaking up the normal slash-and-burn cycle, and generated massive and seemingly irreversible soil erosion, perhaps even creating a zero carrying capacity for this land now.[3] Most residents of large megalopolises in the Third World feel that the pressure of too many people, a product of the massive rural-to-urban migration of the past decade, is a major contributor to both environmental and social decay. Yet, in many depressed, rural towns of North America, the unemployment that resulted from plant closings has led to intense social problems, despite the fact that populations in those towns decreased dramatically.

Examining the population question in specific regions leads to the conclusion that concern with the population density per se is not going to be very helpful in solving either social or environmental problems. As I travel to my sister's house in DuQuoin, Illinois, I go through Gary, Indiana, and the south side of Chicago, where I am impressed with the pressure of enormous numbers of people living in a very small space indeed. The evident environmental and social problems are most certainly partly a function of this immense population density. But then I arrive in DuQuoin, where there are more stores closed than open, for lack of clientele; the mining economy is in ruins, with the remaining unemployed miners trying to figure out where the next payment on their bass boat is going to come from; and I cannot help but see the need for economic recovery, something that will not happen with the dwindling number of people that call the place home.

But the slightest attention to historical detail clarifies what has been happening. It is not useful to note that there are too many people in Chicago, and too few in DuQuoin. The distribution of people in North America is such that some areas might be considered to be effectively overpopulated, others underpopulated. Rural economies have been generally disastrous for the past 15 years, culminating a century-long decline. If you are an investor, would you like to invest in my new venture to open a department store in DuQuoin? If you are a worker, would you move to DuQuoin to look for a job? On the other hand, if the government decided to open a military base there, thus doubling the local population overnight, might your answer be different?

On the other hand, Chicago, with its industrial system drawing European immigrants in the late nineteenth century, its stockyard magnet drawing massive migration from the south earlier in this century, and its general industrial base drawing yet further immigration from Latin America most recently, does not present a population density that I feel comfortable with, and the crush of humanity is certainly part of the explanation for some of Chicago's social and environmental ills. However, does anyone really believe that kicking a million people out of the city would cause a decrease in drug-related crime? In the grinding poverty observable every day in Cabrini Green? In the drive-by shootings, the children rejected, the desperate and disabled living on the street?

In a similar vein, I recall my most recent trip to Mexico. Traveling through the sprawling shantytowns on the city's outskirts reminded me that demographic changes are not simple processes of birth and death rates. Just ten years earlier, those shantytowns were far less extensive. This burgeoning population was not really the result of high birth rates, but rather mainly the consequence of rural-to-urban migration, which itself was fueled by economic and political policies of the Mexican government. I must admit that if I did not take the time to think through the web of causality, my Western-trained mind would undoubtedly have created that common chain linkage (problem: social decay; cause: overpopulation). And as representative of some international aid organization, I might have been moved, through sincere humanitarian considerations, to promote birth control programs in Mexico City. But I ask the reader to seriously contemplate the question—would Mexico City's problems disappear with a lower birth rate, if the rural-to-urban migration continued at its current rate?

THE ORIGINAL QUANTITATIVE ARGUMENT

Malthus's original analysis initially followed along the lines of the developments in chapter 11. Since humans reproduce themselves, there should be an exponential growth of human numbers. A graph of population size over time will take the form already discussed (see Figure 11.2). That the form of growth of the population should be exponential was not original with Malthus, although he popularized the notion.

It was the second part of Malthus's argument that was his unique contribution. He asserted that the rate of production of food would increase at only a linear rate. Thus, if the curve of population were curved upward and the curve of food increase were a straight line, eventually the population curve would have to be larger than the food curve. This simple idea is presented in Figure 14.1. The force of this argument is apparent. It says that no matter what the rate of food production, population will inevitably outgrow its food supply.

The key problem with this apparently elegant argument is that there is not, nor has there ever been, any reason to assume that food production should be linear. Indeed, in all cases of which we are aware, the rate of increase in food production has been either greater or equal to that of population growth. Naturally, this fact says nothing about what might happen in the future, nor does it necessarily argue that the Malthusian vision will not ultimately be true. But it must be admitted that the original vision of an exponential population growth to be compared to linear food growth was simply wrong.

Modern Malthusianists are not so crude, and generally admit that Malthus's position was oversimplified. Their argument, with regard to food production, is simply that food production cannot keep up with population forever, no matter how fast new technology develops. If the inexorable growth of the human population is taken as the "ultimate" cause of

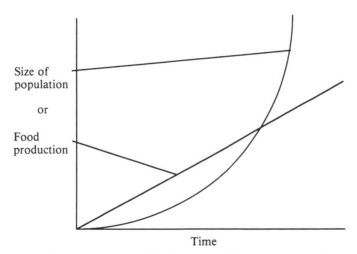

Figure 14.1. The elementary Malthusian idea. If food production increases linearly and population increases exponentially, the population eventually must outstrip the food supply.

various social and environmental problems, and since the nature of reproduction is exponential, they argue, so long as population growth is positive, eventually these problems will come to be, if they already have not actually materialized. Thus, no matter whether overpopulation is now causing problems, it eventually will, and we must thus stop population growth.

Their opponents generally see population density as a single variable in a complex of variables. People generally produce the amount of food and other resources they need, thus explaining the historical fact that food and other resource production has always kept up with population growth. Rather than focusing on population as an issue in and of itself, the focus should be on the socioeconomic forces that cause people to have children.

A VARIETY OF POSITIONS AND SUPPORTING EVIDENCE—A LOOK AT THE CONTEMPORARY STATISTICS

The population issue is most frequently presented as a debate between two extremes. Here, as elsewhere, the real world is somewhat more textured. The recent analysis of Buttel and Raynolds[4] treats some of this complexity. While it is true that the neo-Malthusian position (the size and/or growth rate of the human population is the most critical factor causing environmental degradation) and non-Malthusian position (human population is only one, and not necessarily the most important, factor causing environmental degradation) are contrasting and opposing ends of the spectrum, another factor is now acknowledged as being of considerable importance—food production.[5] On the one hand, there are those who emphasize the role of increased production in alleviating relevant problems; on the other hand, there are those who deny that increased production itself will have much of an effect—the productionists versus the nonproductionists. The former feel that the key to solving relevant problems is to increase production (which frequently is a euphemism for economic growth, although in this analysis it strictly refers to food production), while the latter feel that the amount of production is a relatively unimportant variable. Of course, even here we will find subtle differences as we read accounts of various authors, but most will conveniently fit into one of the four categories defined by crossing the productionist axis with the Malthusian axis.

Thus we can think of the debate as having four camps: productionist non-Malthusians, productionist Malthusians, nonproductionist non-Malthusians, and nonproductionist Malthusians.

The *productionist non-Malthusians*[6] feel that there are no ecological limits to economic growth (e.g., much economic growth may be in service-type economies, in which more economic activity does not automatically imply more resource use, and those forms of economic growth that require increased use of natural resources will be "naturally" limited when resources begin to be scarce and thus the price of obtaining them goes up) and that population growth can play a positive role in development (through increased demand for products and infrastructure, provisioning of a larger labor pool, and certain economies of scale—as Boserup has noted, the more people, the more chance for innovative solutions to environmental problems). The *productionist Malthusians*[7] agree that increased production is the key to relevant problems, but they see population growth as the main factor limiting the ability to increase production adequately (as agricultural scientists continue to provide more efficient crop varieties, they argue, rapid population growth continues to stifle their efforts by creating an ever increasing target to which they must aspire), thus viewing population growth as the main underlying factor limiting the effectiveness of increased production. The *nonproductionist non-Malthusians*[8] regard the distribution of resources as the most important factor (if production is increased, but only the elites are able to take advantage of that increased production, how can the production help solve the problems of any but the elite?), and view increases in population growth rates as consequences of, rather than causes of, poverty and underdevelopment. The *nonproductionist Malthusians*[9] retain much of Malthus's original argument and feel that either the size of the population or its rate of growth is the underlying force causing relevant problems.

Buttel and Raynolds present data aimed at asking how much evidence can be mustered in support of each of these positions (recalling that it would not be surprising to find some evidence in support of all four, since the issue is one of multiple causality to start with). Using a data set representing conditions in most of the world's underdeveloped nations, they asked, what might be expected from these four positions? A key variable is the rate of change in food consumption—the amount of food eaten by an average person this year compared to the amount eaten last year. Generally, if conditions are improving, we would expect this rate to be positive, while if conditions are worsening, it will be negative. This rate of change in food consumption ought to be correlated with various other factors, depending on one's position regarding the Malthusian issue. Each of the four positions expects a particularly large correlation between the rate of change in food consumption and some particular variable. The *productionist non-Malthusian* position expects that the correlation is with growth in gross domestic product. That correlation is .35, as expected. The *productionist neo-Malthusian* position expects the correlation to be directly with agricultural growth rate, and indeed it is, but only modestly so—.29. The *nonproductionist non-Malthusian* position expects that the correlation is positive with equality of income. Using the percentage of income received by the lowest 20th percentile as an estimate of inequality, the correlation is .43, as expected. The *nonproductionist neo-Malthusian* position expects that its correlation with rate of population growth will be negative (since their argument is that population numbers *per se* cause the problem, when populations grow particularly fast the rate of change in food consumption should be large and negative). In fact, Buttel and Reynolds found, that correlation is .136, a statistically insignificant result and actually in the wrong direction. These expectations and observations are summarized in Table 14.1.

While one can find some support for all but the nonproductionist Malthusians in these data, it is clear that the strongest support is with the non-Malthusian position most generally. Buttel and Raynolds present a variety of other data that generally support this conclusion. The bulk of

Table 14.1. Correlations between rate of change in caloric input and key variables for four schools of thought on food and population

Position	Key Variable	Expectation	Observation
Productionist non-Malthusian	domestic product growth	+	.350
Productionist neo-Malthusian	agricultural growth	+	.290
Nonproductionist non-Malthusian	income inequality	+	.429
Nonproductionist neo-Malthusian	population growth	−	.136

the evidence appears to be on the side of the nonproductionist non-Malthusian side, although if one wishes, one can find threads of support for any of the four positions. Indeed, some of the polemics surrounding this issue stem from a reading of the available data from only one point of view. Buttel and Raynolds are the first to examine all sides of the issue asking for evidence of support for the various positions, using a consistent data set. Their conclusion is quite simply that the least supportable position is that of the nonproductionist Malthusians, and the most supportable one is that of the nonproductionist non-Malthusians.

The above analysis was restricted to a sampling of countries of the Third World. A related, but in some ways more obvious, view can be obtained from an examination of worldwide statistics. Statistics from 58 countries, ordered according to gross national product (per person), are shown in Table 14.2.

A variety of insights can be gained from a careful examination of these data. First, note the striking difference between Third-World and developed-world GNP. South Korea has the highest GNP for the Third-World, with 38.7 percent of the GNP of the United States (that is, if there were perfectly even distribution of the country's production, each individual in South Korea would receive 38.7 percent of what each individual in the US receives), and Spain has the lowest for the developed world, with 57 percent. There is a clear break between South Korea and Spain. However, we do not see an evident relationship between that break and population density. While it is true that the two most highly populated countries in the world (Bangladesh and South Korea) are in the Third World, the First World has its share of highly populated countries also (e.g., the Netherlands, Japan, and Belgium), and while Australia has only 2.27 people per 100 hectares, Mauritania has 2.05. As a whole, the average population density for the Third World is 107 (90, if Bangladesh is excluded), and that for the developed world is 140, a difference that is not statistically significant. But in terms of birth rates, a clear and obvious difference is seen, with the Third World averaging 33 births per 1,000 people per year and the developed world 14 births per 1,000 per year; the birth rate in the Third World is more than twice as large as that of the developed world. Parallel with birth rates, we see the pattern of distribution of wealth dramatically different between the Third World and the developed world (although not so clear as GNP itself). In the Third World, the richest 20 percent of the people have more than ten times the wealth of the

Table 14.2. Basic statistics for 58 countries*

Country	Year	Population density	Birth rate	GNP	Gini	Poorest 20%	Richest 20%
Ethiopia	1981–82	44.84	51	1.5	0.3116	8.6	41.3
Tanzania	1991	27.41	45	2.7	0.54	2.4	62.7
Guinea-Bissau	1991	27.78	46	3	0.5142	2.1	58.9
Rwanda	1983–85	280.77	40	3.3	0.287	9.7	38.9
Uganda	1989–90	74.15	54	4.6	0.3218	8.5	41.9
Nepal	1984–85	141.13	38	4.8	0.297	9.1	39.5
India	1989–90	268.73	29	5.2	0.312	8.8	41.3
Bangladesh	1988–89	794.44	31	5.3	0.2838	9.5	38.7
Kenya	1992	44.31	37	5.9	0.5172	3.4	61.8
Mauritania	1987–88	2.05	50	6	0.3998	3.5	46.3
Côte d'Ivoire	1988	40.06	45	7.1	0.3354	7.3	42.2
Senegal	1991–92	39.59	41	7.6	0.497	3.5	58.6
Lesotho	1986–87	63.33	33	7.7	0.5142	2.9	60
Ghana	1988–89	66.11	41	8.2	0.3528	7	44.1
Honduras	1989	48.21	37	8.3	0.5382	2.7	63.5
Zimbabwe	1990–91	26.60	34	8.5	0.5188	4	62.3
China	1990	121.56	19	9.1	0.3496	6.4	41.8
Pakistan	1991	149.87	40	9.2	0.3036	8.4	39.7
Bolivia	1990–91	6.82	36	9.8	0.4012	5.6	48.2
Philippines	1988	214.33	32	10.7	0.3878	6.5	47.8
Sri Lanka	1990	263.64	21	12.2	0.2962	8.9	39.3
Indonesia	1990	96.75	25	12.8	0.3214	8.7	42.3
Peru	1985–86	17.43	27	13.3	0.4274	4.9	51.4
Morocco	1990–91	58.61	28	14.1	0.3748	6.6	46.3
Dominican Republic	1989	148.98	26	14.5	0.4676	4.2	55.6
Guatemala	1989	88.99	37	14.6	0.5426	2.1	63
Jamaica	1990	218.18	25	16.3	0.396	6	48.4
Jordan	1991	38.73	38	18.3	0.385	6.5	47.7
Tunisia	1990	51.22	30	22.2	0.3818	5.9	46.3
Botswana	1985–86	2.41	36	22.4	0.4988	3.6	58.9
Brazil	1989	18.08	23	22.7	0.5734	2.1	67.5
Panama	1989	32.47	25	23.5	0.5224	2	59.8
Costa Rica	1989	62.75	26	24	0.4328	4	50.8
Algeria	1988	11.04	30	24.8	0.3694	6.9	46.5
Colombia	1991	29.32	24	24.9	0.476	3.6	55.8
Thailand	1988	113.06	20	25.5	0.4126	6.1	50.7
Mexico	1984	43.41	28	32.4	0.471	4.1	55.9
Malaysia	1989	56.36	28	34.8	0.5304	4.6	53.7
Chile	1989	17.97	23	35	0.5194	3.7	62.9
South Korea	1988	441.41	16	38.7	0.3312	7.4	42.2

Table 14.2. (*Continued*)

Country	Year	Population density	Birth rate	GNP	Gini	Poorest 20%	Richest 20%
Spain	1988	77.43	10	57	0.281	8.3	36.6
New Zeland	1981–82	12.55	17	62.3	0.3766	5.1	44.7
Israel	1979	242.86	21	63.1	0.3304	6	39.6
Finland	1981	14.84	13	69.1	0.3174	6.3	37.6
U.K.	1988	235.92	14	72.4	0.384	4.6	44.3
Australia	1985	2.27	15	75	0.366	4.4	42.2
Netherlands	1988	410.81	13	76	0.2884	8.2	36.9
Sweden	1981	19.33	14	76.2	0.2924	8	36.9
Italy	1986	192.03	10	76.7	0.3332	6.8	41
Norway	1979	13.27	14	78	0.3072	6.2	36.7
Belgium	1978–79	322.58	12	78.5	0.281	7.9	36
Denmark	1981	120.93	13	80.7	0.3308	5.4	38.6
France	1989	103.99	13	83	0.3484	5.6	41.9
Canada	1987	2.75	15	85.3	0.3386	5.7	40.2
Japan	1979	329.37	11	87.2	0.2874	8.7	37.5
W. Germany	1988	225.77	10	89.1	0.328	7	40.3
Switzerland	1982	168.29	13	95.6	0.3672	5.2	44.6
U.S.	1985	27.25	16	100	0.363	4.7	41.9

*Population density is thousands of people per 100 hectares in the year indicated in column 2. GNP is per capita and is measured according to purchasing power parities (World Bank, 1994, pp. 244–246), and presented as percent of U.S. GNP. The Gini coefficient is estimated from World Bank figures (World Bank, 1994), and is an estimate of the relative concentration of wealth, 1.0 for a completely concentrated system, 0.0 for a perfectly equitable one. As a first approximation, one can think of the Gini coefficient as "percent concentrated." So, for example, Brazil is 57 percent concentrated, whereas Spain is 28 percent concentrated. Birth rate is live births/year per 1000 people. Poorest 20 percent and richest 20 percent refer to the percentage of wealth held by the poorest and richest segments of the country. Countries whose economies are based strictly on nonproductive activities (Hong Kong, Singapore, Malta) were also excluded. Otherwise, the only criterion for inclusion in this data set was the availability of the data to calculate the Gini coefficient.

poorest 20 percent (on average), while in the developed world, that privileged class has only about 7 times more than the lower 20 percent. In the distributional data there are many complexities that we cannot deal with here (e.g., several developed world countries, such as the the United Kingdom and its former colonies, have distributional data that are almost as bad as those of the Third World), but as far as the overall pattern is concerned, inequality is smaller in the First World. This general picture of equality (relatively speaking) correlating with population growth rates is what would be expected by the non-Malthusian model. This is not to suggest that equality in income distribution is a magic bullet, as can easily be seen in the case of Bangladesh. Equal distribution in a country so poor is not likely to have much of an effect on alleviating the conditions that cause high birth rates.

All of these data suggest that the neo-Malthusian position is not very well supported, while the various forms of non-Malthusian positions are, relatively speaking, consistent with available data. Country-by-country analyses[10] and problem-by-problem analyses[11] invariably suggest similar conclusions. It is difficult, empirically, to sustain the Malthusian position, although it could always be argued that the system is so complex that the various indirect connections among various factors obscures the true underlying relationship. Perhaps we can gain further insights about birth rates and population densities if we examine the overall patterns of these aggregated data.

The relationship between vital statistics and economic development has long been acknowledged. The classic formulation of the demographic transition is a simple statement of the fact that as development procedes,

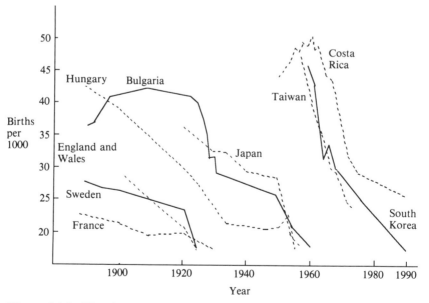

Figure 14.2. The demographic transition in various countries. (Adapted from Murdoch, 1980, with permission.)

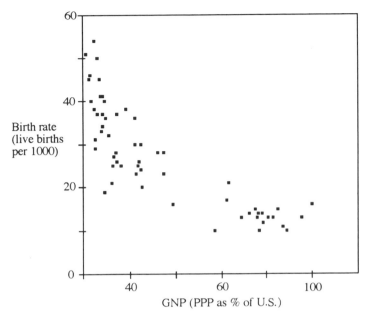

Figure 14.3. Birth rates as a function of GNP (PPP refers to "purchasing power parity"—World Bank, 1994) for the 58 countries of Table 14.2. Countries tend to cluster around the developed-Third World axis, with the points on the upper left representing the Third World and the points on the lower right representing the developed World.

first death rates fall (due to higher standards of living and better medical care) and then birth rates fall (due to lowered desire for having children). That this pattern has been true in the past for what is today the developed world is well known, and the evidence that it is still true for the underdeveloped world is at least circumstantial. The demographic transition of birth rates for various countries is shown in Figure 14.2.

That this transition is related to general economic indicators is also hardly debatable. As shown in Figure 14.3, there is a clear relationship between birth rate and gross national product (even though the latter is not the best estimate of development). The points clustered on the upper left of the graph in Figure 14.3 represent the Third World, while those clustered on the lower right represent the developed world. The United States has the highest GNP in the world and a birth rate typical of developed countries, although this is a point worthy of further analysis. The graph presented in Figure 14.3 might be interpreted quite optimistically in the sense that as development procedes, birth rates decline, and we might expect the demographic transitions that have occurred in the past (see Figure 14.2) to repeat themselves for the rest of the underdeveloped world. But a more pessimistic interpretation is also possible. What if the development process does not proceed? We must, then, ask some simple questions about the development process itself.

In the modern industrial world, development has had a particular trajectory thus far in the countries we today call developed, and we might expect that trajectory to repeat itself for other societies in the near future. Indeed, countries such as South Korea, Malaysia, and Mexico seem, superficially, to be following that very pattern. Competitive firms enter a free market and compete for consumers. The process of competition forces increases in production efficiency, thus lowering prices, making more goods and services available to more people. At least that is the way the idealized story goes. As the average citizen of this world knows, the real picture is not always so rosy. Indeed, many have noted some contradictory aspects of the model, not the least of which is the countervailing tendencies of trying to reduce the cost of labor (for production efficiency) while at the same time trying to ensure that consumers have enough money to buy products.[12] When consumers are workers, and when workers are fired, the will and ability to consume—effective demand—naturally declines, and economic expansion is stifled.

Of particular importance is today's Third World. While the developed world of today had the distinct advantage of economic arrangements we would not countenance today (slavery, colonialism, neocolonialism, and the like), the countries seeking to develop today do not have such advantages. Worse, they are forced into competition with countries that have already gone through the development process, if they seek to expand their economies beyond the traditional export bases they have so long used to promote economic growth. An economy dominated by the production of goods for export will have its economic growth stifled, as Henry Ford realized many years ago. If the citizens of your country cannot purchase the goods your capitalists produce, true economic development is never likely to occur.

One of the legacies of neocolonialism is a dramatic inequality of income. This has its historical roots in the nature of a "peripheral" economy, in that when products are almost always being exported elsewhere, there is no social pressure to increase the well-being of local workers, and thus a local demand for locally produced products is difficult to generate. Whatever one's political ideology, there appears to be general agreement that an economy must be "articulated," which is to say, consumers must make enough money to be able to purchase what they produce. This is the central problem is most underdeveloped countries today. They face a chronic "underconsumption" crisis, in that their general populace is not economically viable enough to create sufficient aggregate demand to promote economic development. This point is really rather obvious, as articulated by John Kenneth Galbraith:

> When viewed as a social concern, a reasonably equitable distribution of income is traditionally urged; it contributes to a sense of fairness and is a manifestation of social justice. Such a thought is, however, strongly condemned and righteously resisted by those of more conservative, politically cautious belief. For them it assails the principle that what one receives is either a human right or a needed incentive; it invades and sets aside one of the high principles of the market system.
>
> Not mentioned in this continuing and often ardent debate is the possibility that a highly unequal distribution of income can be dysfunctional as regards the performance of the economic system. That may well have been the case in the United States in recent years.
>
> Specifically, when income is equitably distributed, there is little question as to its ultimate disposition. It is spent or it is saved, invested and thus spent. There are no large pools of funds that are held in idleness because no one, or not many, have sufficient income to support such accumulations.[13]

It had always been thought that export-led growth would lead to more equitable distribution of wealth and generate economic growth. Capital generated from exports was to be reinvested locally, thus providing more jobs for local people, providing them with higher wages, and thus creating a consuming class that will provide enough effective demand to generate economic growth. That has not happened in recent years, primarily because a small class of the very wealthy have managed to maintain sufficient political power to accumulate even vaster wealth, at the expense of the poor, whose economic condition has stagnated in the past 20 years. Yet it is exactly those poor who are needed to form the consuming backbone of an articulated economy. Indeed, it is not surprising to find a general correlation between income distribution and development, as suggested in Figure 14.4.

With regard to the data in Figure 14.4, note that there are generally two clumps of points, one to the upper left and one to the lower right,

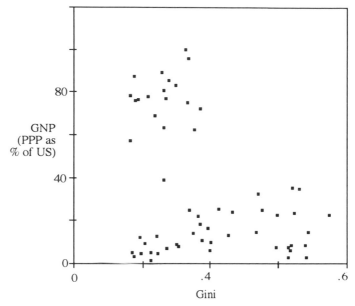

Figure 14.4. Gross national product as a function of the inequality of wealth (Gini coefficient).

corresponding roughly to the developed world and the Third World. The developed world is characterized not only by a relatively high GNP, but also by a relatively equitable distribution of income, compared to the Third World. Also note the one point apparently between the two clumps of points (at a GNP of 39 and a Gini coefficient of .33). That is South Korea. Furthermore, there are nine countries that are characterized by very high inequality and very low GNP—Guinea-Bissau, Kenya, Zimbabwe, Honduras, Lesotho, Guatemala, Dominican Republic, Senegal, and Brazil—what we might call the "stagnant societies." In Figure 14.5, the same data are presented with some further interpretative information. The developed world and the Third World are encircled, as is the zone of stagnant societies. Also, the approximate trajectory of South Korea during the past 25 years is indicated. Finally, the zone of "normal" development is indicated approximately as a hatched area. With this schema, we can imagine a variety of pathways that "development" might follow in the future.

The normal pathway assumes that increasing equality in income will

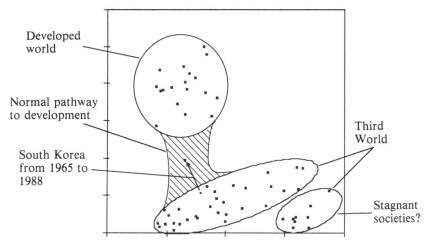

Figure 14.5. Same data as Figure 14.4, with interpretations of various groups of data points (see text for explanation).

tend to promote the development of a demand-based economy, which will spur economic growth. Judging from the extant data on Third World economies at the present time, it may even be the case that some loss in GNP will have to be tolerated as incomes are redistributed, since in the mainline Third World economies today, there is a small but significant trend to increase GNP with an increase in inequality (note how the ellipse containing the data points of the Third World is tilted upward). To be sure, there are other possibilities. The form of development that appears to be in the minds of most developmental experts today assumes that with proper capital investment, one may avoid the question of inequality altogether. This may indeed be possible, but note how it will require crossing a region in which no country currently exists, and one that has never been crossed before—high levels of both inequality and GNP. This sort of development may very well require some new and currently unknown modes of economic planning.

Finally, it is possible that new forms of economy might actually evolve. With the recent increase in inequality in some developed countries (e.g., the United States), the continued stagnation of others (those in the "stagnated societies" group), and the increased inequality associated with modest gains in GNP of many Third World countries, this new form may be on the horizon. Indeed, the recent trend to globalize markets and production, without attendance to distribution factors, as typified by the new globaliztion treaties (NAFTA, GATT), is perhaps the first warning sign of such a tendency. If this form of economy is, in fact, currently evolving, the consequences could be appocalyptic. Not since European feudalism will we have seen such economic disparity as will evolve when First and Third Worlds alike will be typified by a small ruling economic elite in the midst of impoverished masses. Certainly, new forms of politics and economics will have to evolve, for the economic model currently being marketed to the world will not be able to withstand such an arrangement (when the whole world works for General Motors, but only the executives make enough to buy cars).

No one can say with certainty what the demographic consequences of any of these patterns might be. While we are relatively certain that small changes tomorrow will have the same effects as they had yesterday, once uncharted terrain is entered, the rules that created the correlations in the past may very well change also. Thus, while we can be relatively sure that a developmental sequence that follows the usual pathway will generate lowered birth rates as it has in the past (e.g., Figure 14.2), new pathways may generate new patterns of change in vital statistics.

THINKING ABOUT POPULATION ECOLOGICALLY

Beginning with a biological focus, it is easy to see human populations as the same as all other animal populations, with a rate of increase and a fixed carrying capacity, and thus with a clear potential for exceeding their carrying capacity. But might we form a different analysis if we begin from a different point of view?

As any other population, humans consume resources and modify their environment. In the case of this very special species, however, exactly what they do seems to be far more important than how many of them do it, and the human species is unique in having a complex social organization that links how many of them are doing something to exactly what it is that they are doing. The social organization of resource transformation,[14] perhaps from the times of *H. erectus,* certainly from the times of the dawn of *H. sapiens,* makes it especially difficult to disentangle the size of the human population from the things those humans do.

Consider for example, a renewable resource of some sort. Development of that resource can be conceived of as a rate of extraction, to be balanced against a rate of replenishment. This problem may be envisioned as a graph of the rate (either rate of extraction or rate of replenishment) against the amount of resource. The traditional way of conceptualizing this issue is shown in Figure 14.6.[15] To the left of the sustainable extraction level, the rate of replenishment (i.e., the natural rate at which the resource increases) is greater than the rate of extraction, and the amount of resource increases. To the right of the sustainable extraction level, the rate of replenishment is less than the rate of extraction, and the amount of resource decreases. Since below the sustainable level the resource increases and above it the resource decreases, the sustainable level itself is a stable point.

What happens if the human population grows? It is customary to think of growth of the human population in terms of an increase in the extraction rate. As shown in Figure 14.7, the extraction rate curve is expected to be ever larger as the human population increases. Eventually the resource is overexploited and goes to zero (as illustrated by the last exploitation curve in the figure). So with a higher population, the sustainable extraction level of the resource decreases, up to a point at which it suddenly declines to zero. This is the simple model that is frequently used to demonstrate the effects of population on resources.

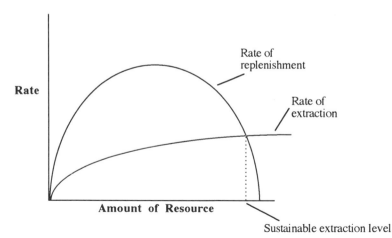

Figure 14.6. Comparing rate of extraction with the rate of replenishment to show how a stable equilibrium forms where the two curves intersect (see chapter 11 for an explanation of these dynamics).

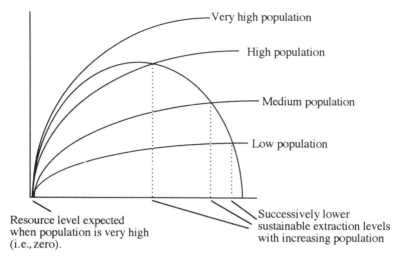

Figure 14.7. Effect of different population sizes on the sustainable extraction levels of a natural resource, the Malthusian vision.

A closer examination of what actually happens with resources and human populations reveals a somewhat more complicated picture. If an elevated population is associated with changes in the resource transformation system, as most often happens, it is just as likely that the extraction curve will be lower with increased population. For example, in the agrarian society of the first half of the twentieth century in Puerto Rico, forested land was converted to agriculture at a rate that undoubtedly was greater than the rate at which agricultural land reverted to forests, thus looking much like the picture presented in Figure 14.7. But then, associated with a major industrialization program, people began moving away from the countryside to take jobs in the expanding industrial sector, and eventually many people simply emigrated to the United States.[16] So, if one were to reconstruct the graph of Figure 14.7 for the last half of the twentieth century for Puerto Rico, it might look something like that in Figure 14.8. As the population density of Puerto Rican people increased, their consumption and work habits changed dramatically, and it is those changes in consumption and work habits that changed the rate of exploitation in such a way that there is actually a negative correlation between amount of forest cover and overall population (counting the population of Puerto Ricans as a whole).[17]

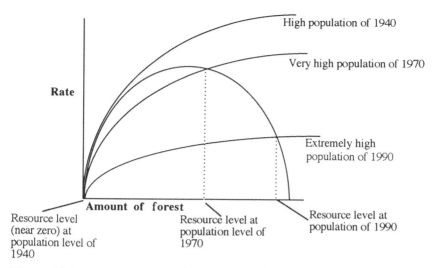

Figure 14.8. Comparing rate of extraction with the rate of replenishment to show how contradictory results can emerge when mode of resource extraction changes with population density. Example is of tropical forest cutting in Puerto Rico, where the people were mainly farmers in 1940, but by 1990 were almost entirely urbanized.

Alternatively, changes in human resource transformation systems (which may accompany change in population size) may change the rate of replenishment of the natural resource itself. When hunting and gathering people gathered the wild grains that occurred naturally in the Levant, one might have seen a pattern similar to that of Figure 14.7, with ever smaller stocks of grain resources over the years as populations increased. But what actually happened was that the resource curve itself changed through the invention of agriculture, leading to an increase in grain availability with the higher population, as shown in Figure 14.9.[18]

In these examples, as well as innumerable others that could be provided, the relationship between population and environment (in the above examples, "environment" is the resources) is always an indirect one. The size of the human population determines, to some extent, the nature of the resource transformation system and the latter determines, to some extent, the size of the human population, or at least the rate at which it grows. This principle has been stated many times before and in many different ways.[19] If you put a single family in the desert they will starve, but

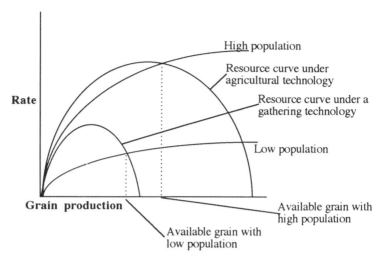

Figure 14.9. Effect of different resource curves and population densities on the sustainable extraction levels of grain.

if you put a hundred families in the desert they will build a canal to irrigate their crops. A small population will overgraze a hillside in a desperate attempt to get resources out of poor soils, whereas a larger population will build a series of terraces to produce agricultural products. In all of these examples, it would be misleading at best to try and understand the relationship between humans and their resources by focusing on the size of the human population. Twelve million people living on a small island trying to eke out a living with primitive rain-fed farming may very well be "overpopulated" in terms of the resources available to them, yet ten times that many people living on a smaller island making their living with factories, banks, and stock markets may be the center of the most powerful country in the world and not even think about the question of overpopulation.[20]

These simple examples are meant to illustrate the elementary idea that what people do matters at least as much as how many of them are doing it. A large population living in an ecologically sustainable way is likely to provide a better future all around than a small population living in an ecologically damaging way.

There are those, of course, who retain a religious fervor about the population issue. Granted all of the above, they say, but the bottom line is that the world is finite and every new human means one more mouth to feed. Damn the evidence that, frequently, larger populations are better fed and live more in harmony with their environment than smaller populations. Ignore the fact that, time and again, a declining population has had worse effects on the environment than before it was in its decline. As one population crusader told me (this is a real example), "I don't want to hear the facts, they just confuse me—there are just too many people in the world." If one's senses say the world is flat and the sun revolves around the earth, and no concrete evidence to the contrary will be admitted, there is not much left to argue about.

It is of some interest to ask why the ideology of overpopulation retains its popularity. While the psychological aspects of this question are beyond the intended scope of this book, there is a political side implicit in overpopulation ideology that is frequently at the heart of the matter. And that political side is pernicious, to say the least, as suggested in chapter 2.

THE PERNICIOUSNESS OF OVERPOPULATION IDEOLOGY

It was horrifying to many in the developed world that there was a self-conscious decision to exclude discussion of the overpopulation issue at the United Nations Conference on the Environment and Development—the Rio Summit of 1992.[21] Not just a few from the major environmental organizations of the United States and Europe were shocked, to say the least, that what they had thought and preached as the ultimate cause of all human misery, but especially of environmental deterioration, was not even to be discussed at the first major international meeting on the environment. What might be the significance of such a momentous decision?

The obvious (and wrong) interpretation was quick to emerge from U.S. and European mainstream environmental groups: The Third World simply has not gotten the message. They keep looking at proximate factors such as underdevelopment, equity, unfair terms of trade, and the like, and fail to see the ultimate cause, population pressure. But those from the Third World have, in fact, considered the arguments of the neo-Malthusians and generally have found them to be lacking in merit, something that is apparently difficult for some developed world environmentalists to appreciate. Indeed, some Third World environmentalists go further than just to note that overpopulation is not the important issue. They go on to cite various cases in which neo-Malthusian ideology has had pernicious effects in the Third World.

One of those examples is Puerto Rico, as captured eloquently in the film *La Operación*.[22] The "operation" is the sterilization operation that was performed on thousands of Puerto Rican women during the 1960s and 1970s. It was a program that was developed specifically in response to the supposed overpopulation of the island. Women coming to hospitals for delivery were targeted for sterilization. On a massive scale, the operation was performed on women of child-bearing age, who were sometimes only vaguely informed about the consequences of the operation, very rarely given the opportunity to reflect seriously over its gravity. By 1980, fully one-third of Puerto Rican women of child-bearing age had been sterilized, all because Puerto Rico had an "overpopulation problem."

The irony of the program is that the problems of Puerto Rico became progressively worse even as outmigration actually lowered the population.[23] If population had been the cause, certainly the outmigration of the 1950s and 1960s would have helped solve some of the problems,[24] but, in fact, it apparently did not. That the problems remain even today is not really surprising. But the importance of the episode is the example it provides of the potential perniciousness of overpopulation ideology.

Perhaps the most often-cited political use of overpopulation is the infamous analysis of Garrett Hardin.[25] Hardin likened the world situation today to a lifeboat. We in the developed world are in a lifeboat, and the people in the underdeveloped world are swimming in the ocean all around us. They can be saved only if we let them in our lifeboat. But our lifeboat is not big enough to accommodate them, and if we let them in, we will all sink. Thus, any humanitarian gestures on our part would only spell disaster for all, and we are better off concentrating our efforts on our own lifeboat rather than worrying about the poor people drowning in the ocean around us. This seeming ethical dilemma is called "lifeboat ethics," and has been given new life recently as the "stretch limousine" ethics model.[26]

It does not take much familiarity with either politics or history to see how the lifeboat metaphor is either wrong or unfair (perhaps both). The relationship between the First World and the Third World is less reminiscent of a lifeboat than a gunboat. We in the First World are in a gunboat and have been sinking all the other boats in the ocean. Every time the drowning people fashion a raft out of the scraps of their former lifeboats, our gunboat comes around and smashes their raft. The drowning people in the ocean are the ones who have to make the decision. Should they just keep swimming and hope some day the gunboats of the First World will let them start building rafts, or should they get together and tip those gunboats over? While it will not be popular in the developed world, gunboat ethics might soon come to dominate the discourse of people in the Third World.

Even though it would be nearly impossible to understand anything without metaphor, we must also remember that metaphors are, by their very nature, approximate. Reality is never a metaphor; a famous person once said that the price of metaphor is eternal vigilance. Neither the lifeboat nor the gunboat reflects the world accurately, although a fair reading of history would probably give more of a nod to the gunboat metaphor. Reality is more complicated.

But what is especially pernicious about the lifeboat ethics argument is the way it sets out the framework for debate and, by doing so, limits the possible outcomes of those debates. For example, in a recent, supposedly politically neutral, textbook relating biology to human affairs, a special box presented the issue as follows:

> Garrett Hardin presents the metaphor that the United States and other economically advanced nations constitute a lifeboat that contains comparatively affluent individuals. The peoples of the impoverished countries of the world are struggling in the water outside, hoping to be admitted to the prosperous lifeboat. Hardin concludes that, to preserve the safety (prosperity) of the lifeboat that is already limited in capacity, the affluent passengers must prevent others from boarding. In essence, the economically advanced countries should take an isolationist attitude and repel boarders, primarily by curtailing immigration and restricting the export of foods.[27]

Having presented the issue in this way, it doesn't really matter much how the ethical quandary is resolved. The problem is formulated so that one group of people will win—in this case, the ones in the First World. Note that by the nature of the problem setup, the only possible outcomes are to either not let people in the lifeboat, or cause the entire world to perish. Dr. Hardin has effectively said that either you agree with his position or you shall cause the demise of the entire world. Now that we have framed the debate in this unbiased fashion, let us go on to argue whether we should agree with Dr. Hardin or cause the world to end. Yes, quite a fair debate.

What if the presentation of the issue were made as follows:

> Stats Grobkin presents the metaphor that the United States and other economically advanced nations constitute a gunboat that contains comparatively affluent individuals. The peoples of the impoverished countries of the world are struggling in the water outside, trying to construct life rafts but being continually blown out of the water by this gunboat every time they get close to building a raft. Dr. Grobkin concludes that, to be able to construct life rafts and, therefore, save themselves from drowning, the peoples of the impoverished countries must find a way of eliminating those gunboats. In essence, the economically depressed countries should take an aggressive attitude and destroy the gunboats that are preventing them from building life rafts, primarily by promoting revolutions both within their own countries and in the developed countries.

Of course, the actual data of concern, the existence of a First World and a Third World, and the environmental problems are the same in each scenario. And the childlike conclusions we are expected to draw are obvious in each scenario. But the second has a dramatically different programmatic content than the first: Either you drown or you help me tip over the gunboat. Now that I have framed the debate in this unbiased fashion, let us go on to argue whether you agree with Dr. Grobkin or prefer to drown. Yes, an equally fair debate. If I may paraphrase Boss Tweed, I don't care who wins the debate as long as I'm the one who sets its terms.

The United States, with about 6 percent of the world's population, uses more than 20 percent of the world's resources. We are hardly in a lifeboat. When countries of the Third World try to take control over their resources, from Mossadegh in Iran, to Arbenz in Guatemala, to Allende in Chile, to Vietnam, Nicaragua, Angola, Mozambique, Puerto Rico, Cuba, Dominican Republic, El Salvador, Guatemala again, Indonesia, Malaysia, and others,[28] the U.S. and its First World allies have been quick to intervene and make the world safe. Exactly what the world is being made safe for is understandably viewed with some cynicism by people in the Third World, when rhetoric about human rights, freedom, and democracy gives way to blatant concerns about control over resources and markets. If the gunboat or lifeboat are the only competing metaphors, it seems to me that the gunboat wins hands down.

CASE STUDY—THE OVERPOPULATION PROBLEM IN CENTRAL AMERICA

At one time or another, all of the countries in Central America have been cited as having an overpopulation problem. Taking the analysis to something of an extreme, the United Nations actually declared that the 1969 war between El Salvador and Honduras was a result of overpopulation.[29] Several years ago, when I was giving a lecture on Nicaragua, the least densely populated country in the region, a professor of geography suggested that Nicaragua's problems were really caused by overpopulation, since most of the population was concentrated in the western third of the country—it appears that for some neo-Malthusians there is no lower value that population density can attain without being "overpopulated." That the problems normally associated with overpopulation exist, to one extent or another, in each of these countries cannot be denied, but if one wishes to understand these problems, one must deal with the complexity of human resource transformation, and its historical development, both internally and internationally. As a partial antidote to essentialist thinking about the population problem, I offer this section as a brief introduction to the historical, political, economic, and ecological complexities that must be considered if one is to understand issues of hunger, poverty, natural resource misuse, resource depletion, and the like—hopefully convincing the reader that the simple story of "overpopulation is the underlying cause" is untenable with a little understanding of the complexity. I begin with some ecological and historical background, and follow with brief country-specific stories about Guatemala and El Salvador.

The Ecological and Historical Background

All countries in Central America have basically agrarian economies, and perhaps the most important underlying feature of agriculture is the soil. While the soils of the region are diverse and their exact location unpredictable at a fine scale,[30] some simple generalizations are possible and quite useful. There are basically four soil types: volcanic, rain forest, alluvial, and hillside.

The chain of volcanoes that extends from central Costa Rica to the northwest corner of Guatemala has been spouting volcanic ash for the last 100,000 years, providing a base on which soils are formed. Soils formed in the recent past (i.e., in the past few thousand years) from those volcanic materials tend to be very rich and potentially productive for agriculture. Thus, associated with the long volcanic chain that forms the backbone of Central America's Pacific seaboard, is a belt of rich volcanic soils that provide the base for coffee production in the mountains of all five countries and cotton in the Pacific lowlands of Guatemala, El Salvador, and Nicaragua.

On the eastern side of the isthmus, the predominantly north-south orientation of the major mountain masses catches the trade winds after they have accumulated moisture from their trip across the Caribbean, and drive them upward, causing the accumulated moisture to fall and creating a belt of rainy climate throughout the Caribbean seaboard of the isthmus. This belt of rainy climate is the location of Central America's rain forests. These major mountain masses are generally much older than the volcanic chain of the Pacific seaboard (on the order of 20 to 40 million years versus a few thousand). Their age, combined with continued high temperature and rainfall, have created a soil that is famous for its lack of productivity, the classic "bad" soils of rain forest areas, characterized by high acidity, low nutrient content, high iron and aluminum content, and extremely low capacity for storing nutrients.

Crisscrossing both the poor rain forest soils in the east and the rich volcanic soils of the west are soils formed from the material deposited by flooding, both historic and prehistoric. These soils are referred to as alluvial soils (which simply means they were deposited by water), and are frequently quite good for agriculture, depending generally on when they were deposited (a rule of thumb is, the newer the better) and what they contained when they were deposited. The alluvial soils represent the most coveted soils on the Caribbean seaboard, and effectively represent long strips of good soils in a sea of poor soil, the strips corresponding to the flood plains of the major rivers in the area.

Finally, throughout the isthmus, there are mountainous areas, typically characterized by high slopes surrounding valley lowlands. As a general rule, the valleys contain alluvial soils, while the surrounding slopes contain a variety of soil types, but are all characterized as unsuitable for agriculture simply because of their slope. Agricultural activity usually results in unacceptable soil erosion, and thus cannot be sustained.

Thus, the soils of Central America consist of just these four major categories (in reality, of course, there are many others). Their distribution

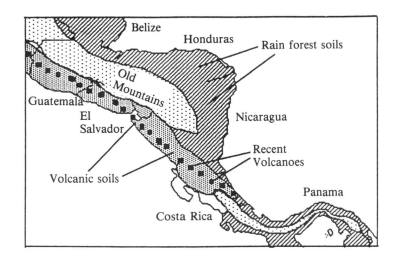

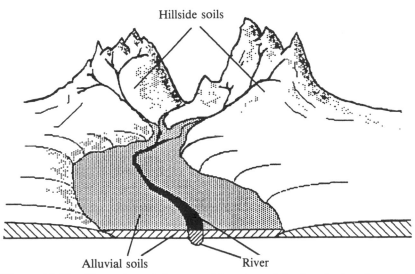

Figure 14.10. Illustration of the general location of the four basic soil types in Central America.

in Central America is summarized in Figure 14.10. The first two (volcanic and alluvial) are typically rich and can be excellent for agriculture, while the latter two (rain forest and hillside) are typically very poor and probably best used for forestry or just left alone.

This soil pattern in the isthmus provides the backdrop for the distribution of agriculture and population. At the time of the European invasion, the volcanic soils of the Pacific seaboard were the most densely populated with agriculturalists.[31] Especially notable was the watershed of the Lempa River, which is a combination of alluvial and volcanic soils, and which effectively became the definition of the state of El Salvador. The Caribbean seaboard, on the other hand, was characterized by small groups of humans, making their living off of agriculture (probably mainly restricted to the bands of alluvial soils) and diverse utilization of rain forest products (e.g. hunting, fruit gathering).

With the expansion of export agriculture, beginning with (1) the English producing sugar on the Caribbean coast of Belize, Honduras, Nicaragua, and Costa Rica, and the Spanish extending their control over the Pacific seaboard through the cattle-based hacienda system, through (2) the days of liberal reform and independence, when coffee production formed the basis of today's oligarchies, through (3) the expansion of banana production by the United Fruit Company in Guatemala, Honduras, and Costa Rica, through (4) the modern export system based on cotton in Guatemala, El Salvador, and Nicaragua, and cattle in El Salvador, Nicaragua, and Costa Rica,[32] and finally with (5) the most recent expansion of "nontraditional" export agriculture,[33] the story for the peasant farmer has been monotonous—agriculture for export gradually expands throughout the good soils, leaving the poor soils for the peasants.

Peasant agriculture that has been pushed onto the poor soils of the hillsides or rain forests must face a certainty—the soil's productive capacity will erode, sometimes quite rapidly. On the rain forest soils, if agriculture is practiced immediately after clearing the forests, the nutrients that were contained in the living vegetation form a natural fertilizer, and very high crop yields are frequently obtained. But, because the soil structure does not permit the storage of nutrients, those that were not used immediately in the process of crop growth typically leak out of the system, either in the region's abundant surface water runoff or down to the deeper layers of the soil. The hillside soils literally wash away after the natural vegetation is cleared.

A second ecological factor—pests—is of great importance to peasant agriculture. While not restricted to peasant agriculture, pests have two properties that make them particularly difficult for peasant agriculturalists. First, many insect pests in Central America are secondary pests, having emerged from a state of insignificance to achieve problem status from a combination of the expansion of the crop (that is their food and it is only natural that pests should expand as their food source does), and the use of pesticides (recall the operation of the pesticide treadmill).[34]

Before export agriculture became dominant, peasants saw a much larger land base, with soils that did not lose productivity, or did so much more slowly, with the clear possibility of moving on to a different location if weed problems became too severe or soil fertility declined, and with the effective absence of insect pests (the majority of insect pests that peasants face today are likely the result of excessive pesticide spraying in export crops). In such a premodern state, peasant agriculture was frequently abandoned at specific sites, to start the process of ecological succession, resulting in secondary forest and eventually, if no further incursions occur, old-growth forest.

This general picture of peasant agriculture has created essentially two schools of thought about how to solve the problem of "peasant production." While there is admittedly a continuum between the two schools of thought, it is useful to distinguish the two, if only as ends on a continuum. The first school of thought sees the problem in its historical perspective, that peasant production is currently on marginal lands because of the politics of export agriculture expansion and domination, both past and present. It sees the disarticulated economy and associated imperialism located in the United States as the main problem, and seeks political solutions through social reforms, such as agrarian reform, and national liberation. The second school of thought sees the problem as a contemporary real-world problem, eschews the political problems stemming from past inequities, and attempts to solve problems within the seemingly unalterable political constraints that exist today. The proposed strategies of these two positions are, not surprisingly, quite distinct, the first emphasizing change in political structures, and the second emphasizing technical solutions to extant problems; the first accusing the second of pandering to and actually making possible unjust social arrangements, the second accusing the first of just being politically motivated; the first accusing the second of trying to apply a bandage to a cancer, the second accusing the first of simply being unrealistic about what is possible in today's world. The first corresponds more or less to the nonproductionist non-Malthusian, and the second to the productionist neo-Malthusian, as described above.

We now turn our attention to modern agricultural production in Central America. From an ecological perspective, modern export agriculture faces a series of problems that are superficially the same as peasant agriculture, yet has an effect on the environment that is magnitudes more severe. In other terms, one might say that modern agriculture erodes the conditions of production, sometimes quite spectacularly. Consider briefly two particular crops, bananas and cotton, both of which are critical to the history of Central America.

To establish a modern banana plantation, it is necessary to construct a sophisticated system of hydrological control, such that the physical nature of the soil is significantly altered—leveled, crisscrossed with drainage channels, and so forth. To avert fungal diseases a heavy use of fungicides is required, and because of the large scale of the operation there is little opportunity for modern integrated pest management.[35] Thus, the soil may become saturated with such pesticides. The banana plants create an almost complete shade cover and thus replace all residual vegetation.

Politically and economically, modern banana plantations inherit their structure from English tea plantations in India. A First World company typically owns and operates all aspects of the production facility, a form of economic organization known as "enclave" production. Local labor is contracted, but the vast majority of produce and capital are exported from the country.

A large amount of labor is required for banana production. However, most of the work is not typically "farming" type work, but rather factory-like tasks. Workers are concentrated in packing houses, where they work in a production-line atmosphere, dramatically different from what one normally thinks of for rural labor. Yet, workers in banana plantations originally come from farming families and frequently return to farming (or try to) when they lose their jobs in the banana operation.

Perhaps the most significant assault on the conditions of Central American agricultural production came from the expansion of cotton in the region in the 1950s. At the time of its introduction, pesticides were virtually unknown. By the 1980s, however, not only was cotton production dramatically overloaded with pesticides, but it was also difficult to find any crops that were produced without pesticides. It is probably the most cited case of the "pesticide treadmill" in the world.[36] Such an intense utilization of pesticides has taken its toll on both human health and the environment. Former cotton fields in the northwest of Nicaragua, for example, are biological deserts, with the only apparent life being pests that have evolved resistant to the pesticides.

While cotton production was mainly concentrated on the Pacific seaboard of Guatemala, El Salvador, and Nicaragua, its ecological effects may have had much larger consequences. Currently, tomato farmers in the Sebaco valley of Nicaragua, at least 100 km east of the main cotton growing areas, are being decimated by whiteflies, which are resistant to all known pesticides and reproduce extremely rapidly. The resistance and high reproductive rate are, arguably, consequences of the operation of the pesticide treadmill in cotton production. Cotton production on the Pacific seaboard thus may have had an effect on peasant tomato production in a valley more than 100 km away.[37]

Politically and economically, cotton production is quite different from banana production. While both are designated for export, cotton production facilities are rarely owned by international concerns. Rather, a local bourgeoisie evolved, and in all countries concerned, it dominated all aspects of cotton production. Typically, such producers were small in comparison to the large banana companies, but large with respect to national land ownership. From the point of view of the labor force, there is little difference between cotton and bananas—both occupy the best lands and drive the small producers to ever more marginal soils, and both offer temporary employment to landless and land-poor peasants. The nature of the work is quite different, however, with cotton employing people mainly for harvesting.

The above two examples represent only a sampling of the general structure of modern agriculture, and I hope they suffice to convince the reader that modern agriculture in the Third World is quite different ecologically than its peasant counterpart. Modern agriculture significantly alters the conditions of production, while peasant agriculture does so to much less of an extent, yet peasant producers are linked as temporary workers to the modern agricultural enterprise.

But in addition to, and related to, the direct ecological effects, modern agriculture has had important secondary effects on peasant agriculture itself. First and foremost has been a dramatic transformation of the land tenure system. As modern agriculture has expanded, peasants have been displaced to marginal lands, a fact of both past and present.[38] Second, modern agriculture appears to create ecological problems that peasant agriculture is then left to solve. When the banana companies left the south-western corner of Costa Rica, they left a legacy of environmental degrada-tion, including contaminated soils and drainage systems that no longer function. Peasant farmers trying to farm tomatoes in the Sebaco valley of Nicaragua are plagued by the whitefly, a devastating pest likely created by the indiscriminate use of pesticides in cotton for the past 30 years. Many other examples could be cited.

The structure of agriculture in Central America reflects the picture outlined in chapter 9. The peasant farmer is self-sufficient, or at least can be. This self-sufficiency means that he or she need not have a job, that basic social security is to be found on the plot of land where the family can be fed. But the national economies of all Central American countries have been fueled by export agriculture—bananas in Costa Rica, Honduras and Guatemala; cattle in Honduras, Nicaragua, and Costa Rica; coffee and sugar cane in all five countries; cotton in Guatemala, El Salvador, and Nicaragua. In all cases, the export sector, which dominates the national economy, utilizes a large amount of labor; indeed, it operates a system of agriculture that in earlier times probably would have been operated with a slave system. During good times for a particular crop, much is planted and many workers are hired. During bad times, workers have no jobs, but are not called "unemployed"; rather, they are called peasants. This is the classic disarticulated economy described in chapter 9.

This fundamental structure is quite functional for the developed world in that investment opportunities are far more diverse and flexible if its companies are allowed a large number of openings, with little local competition, to invest strategically. The ex-colonies of the European pow-ers thus provide an important service to the investors of the developed world: the United States, with its peripheral countries of Latin America; France, with its peripheral countries in Africa and Southeast Asia; En-gland, with its peripheral countries in Africa and the Caribbean, and so on. The relationship is most obvious in the case of the United States, but others participate in the same structure, inherited quite directly from the days of colonialism. When the going gets tough at home, look to invest-ment opportunities abroad, especially in areas with little competition ei-ther from other developed countries or from local capitalists.[39]

Given this background, it is quite apparent how a quick look at condi-tions as they actually exist at any one point in time could easily give the impression of overpopulation. The peasants currently trying to reclaim land from a German export farmer in the Sarapiqui valley of Costa Rica are doing so because they have no land of their own. One might easily conclude that if there just weren't so many of those peasants they wouldn't be putting the pressure on that land. Indeed, it is much easier to think that way than to have to grapple with the complexities that the peasants were mainly attracted to the region to work for the banana companies, whose purchase of the bulk of peasant agricultural land was mainly for speculative purposes in the first place, that the German exporter arrived in Costa Rica largely because of inadequate economic opportunities in Germany at the time, that export agriculture generally occupies all the good soils, and so forth. Reality is complex, overpopulation is simple.

Guatemala: Bananas and the Threat of an Example[40]

Late in the nineteenth century, Lorenzo Dow Baker, a ship captain, picked up a small load of a curious yellow fruit on a stop in Jamaica. Upon arrival in Boston, he sold the load so rapidly that he immediately got the banana fever and teamed up with his entrepreneurial friend Andrew Preston to form the Boston Fruit Company. Preston took charge of marketing on the home front and Baker took care of finding fruit to bring to Boston. The company flourished.

About the same time, a certain Minor C. Keith was looking to fulfill his destiny. Keith was from a railroad family. Toward the end of the nineteenth century, there was a dramatic lull in the demand for new rail transport in the United States, and a railroad man like Keith was facing the possible failure to fulfill his mission in life, which was to build railroads. He moved to Costa Rica, where he easily obtained government concession to build a railroad from the central city of San José to the port town of Limon. Having built the railroad, he soon found that Costa Rica's economy was not exactly dynamic, and there was really very little to transport on his new railroad. Just about at that time, however, he heard of the remarkable success of Baker and Preston with their Boston Fruit Company, and realized that Costa Rica had a perfect climate for banana production. Keith's new banana plantations thus gave his railroad its needed *raison d'être*.

The banana trade grew rapidly, with Guatemala and Honduras joining Costa Rica as major production sites, and as many as 10 companies producing bananas and 8 shipping them. Then, in 1898, the Boston Fruit Co. teamed up with Keith's operation, purchased the major shipping and production companies involved in the banana business, and formed what they called the United Fruit Company. Guatemala, Honduras, and Costa Rica haven't been the same since.

The United Fruit Company grew by leaps and bounds over the next half century, and by the early 1950s it was the largest landowner in Guatemala and one of the largest in both Honduras and Costa Rica. Not only did it have a huge amount of land in production, but it was also holding an equally large amount of land in reserve, perhaps for speculative purposes, or perhaps for future banana production. Nonetheless, it was true that the largest landowner in Guatemala was sitting on a large amount of idle land,[41] while most peasant farmers had either very small plots or no land at all.

One immediately sees two ways of interpreting this situation—the few large landowners have too much land, or there are too many peasants. If one does not assume the latter neo-Malthusian position, one is forced to ask questions about land distribution. Why is it the way it is? How did it get that way? Is there another way to do it?

Recall the dynamics of peasant agriculture. Large export agriculturalists purchase (or sometimes steal) the peasant lands that are on the good soils (in this case, the alluvial soils of the rain forest areas for the most part—refer to Figure 14.10), forcing the farmers onto the poorer soils on the hillsides or in the rain forests. So, while the United Fruit Company was owner of 565,000 acres of land, the largest landholders in the country, 75 percent of the peasant families were either without land at all, or had small plots of land that were marginal at best. Such an arrangement was clearly tinder for a social explosion.

The social explosion came not as a violent outburst, but, rather, in a sophisticated and civilized political campaign. In 1950, one candidate ran on a ticket of agrarian reform, in which he promised to purchase land held by large landowners and redistribute it to small peasant farmers. His name was Jacobo Arbenz, and he won the election on that platform.

The agrarian reform program of Arbenz was rapidly put into action after the election. Land that was not being used for production on farms of more than 90 hectares was targeted for expropriation. The expropriations consisted of lands taken from 1,059 farms with an average size of

1,740 hectares. Approximately 100,000 peasants received title to the land thus expropriated. It was not difficult to see why Arbenz was popular.

His undoing probably was the expropriation of United Fruit Company land. While the United Fruit Company was the largest landholder in Guatemala, only 9 percent of its land was actually being used. Consequently, about 97,000 hectares on the Pacific Coast and 70,000 hectares on the Atlantic coast were expropriated, for which the company was compensated with $6 million, based on its own stated value of the land.

What Arbenz had done was to challenge the basic arrangement of the disarticulated economy of Guatemala. Such a challenge seemed a harbinger of things to come, perhaps, and caused a great deal of consternation in the halls of the politicians and their clients in the United States. If it was true that "without overseas investment your entire economic infrastructure collapses in on you," as the president of Castle and Cook put it, Guatemala, in taking charge of its own resources, was certainly a threat to the free-wheeling investment opportunities available in the Third World.[42] And if Guatemala, as one of several dozen countries that performed the same function, was not particularly important in and of itself, what might happen in Costa Rica or Nicaragua or Honduras if Guatemala were to be successful? Indeed, shortly after Arbenz's victory and initial confrontations with the United Fruit Company, both Costa Rica and Honduras began making demands of the United Fruit Company, presumably buoyed by Arbenz's success.

The United Fruit Company itself was a powerful entity, not only in Guatemala, but in the United States itself. As the owner of over 300 million acres of land, 2,000 miles of railroads, and 100 steamships in Central America, the United Fruit Company was obviously an influential player in international politics. Furthermore, Secretary of State Dulles was a senior partner in the Sullivan and Cromwell law firm, which was the principal legal agent for the United Fruit Company. His brother was, of course, the head of the CIA.

Finally, and most importantly, the Cold War was becoming a defining feature of U.S. politics at just about this time. The Eisenhower administration (especially Vice President Nixon) was to set the stage for the cold warrior.[43] The international Communist movement claimed quite a theoretical package for the oppressed, and it was not difficult to see Communists behind every threat against a capitalist venture wherever it occurred.

Despite the evident non-Communist nature of Arbenz himself, the fact that his legislature contained several deputies that were members of the Communist party, and the simple fact that he promoted agrarian reform, either led the cold warriors to believe there was a Communist conspiracy afoot, or enabled them to justify their actions based on the threat of such a conspiracy.

In 1954, the Eisenhower administration went into action.[44] A lesser colonel in the Guatemalan army, Castillo Armas, was chosen by the CIA to "lead" the revolution against the Guatemalan government. The plan had been hatched at the upper levels of the U.S. government, almost a year earlier. The CIA knew that neither the Guatemalan people nor the Guatemalan military would rally to the cause of overthrowing Arbenz, so they had to rely on a strategy of causing Arbenz to surrender without a true military threat. This meant that they had to create the impression of a real threat to the extent that Arbenz would be convinced that he had no other way of avoiding a bloodbath other than resigning. Through some duplicitous diplomacy and a great deal of propaganda, the Arbenz government was led to believe that Castillo Armas had a large force poised to engage the Guatemalan Army (he never actually had more than 300 troops) and that the U.S. armed forces were ready to enter the fray in support of the overthrow. Most spectacular was the bombing of Guatemala City by CIA planes, generating panic in the city, as was planned. Arbenz, fearing a bloodbath, capitulated, following almost exactly the script the CIA had planned.

That the CIA was ordered by the U.S. government to overthrow a democratically elected foreign government is not in question (although it was vigorously denied at the time, of course). But there is a significant question as to why this was done. As explained above, there were three interrelated sets of facts, any one or combination of which could have accounted for the action (and each of which has been claimed by one or another author as being the really critical one). First, Guatemala's new agrarian reform did threaten to break Guatemala free from the Third World mold of a disarticulated economy, and, with the threat of such an example spreading to the rest of the Third World in which U.S. investment opportunities were so important, could have inspired the U.S. action. Second, high U.S. officials were clearly involved with the United Fruit Company operation and stood to lose personally if Guatemala's agrarian reform were let stand. Third, the Cold War was heating up and a real fear, justifiable or not, of Communism was spreading through the United States like wildfire. The final analysis on this point may never be fully described to everyone's satisfaction, but what is clear is that a *modus operandi* was set in which the CIA was able to intervene in the internal affairs of a foreign country to depose a leader. It was a pattern that would become familiar, a striking example of which was in Nicaragua during the 1980s.

Whatever the true motives, the ultimate consequences are a matter of record. Guatemala has remained, to greater or lesser extent, ever since, stagnated in some form of military dictatorship that has maintained an impoverished peasantry. The impoverished peasantry should not really be expected to do anything else than it always does—seek land for agriculture when possible, frequently adding to the pressure on forests, almost always forced to marginal lands that quickly lose their agricultural potential, migrate to cities to live in shantytowns, creating impossible demands on an undeveloped social service apparatus, and so on. In short, all of the symptoms traditionally tied to an overpopulation crisis are chronic in Guatemala. Killing the short, hopeful, experiment of Jacobo Arbenz ensured that those problems would linger.

El Salvador: Peasants and Export Agriculture[45]

One of the classic cases frequently cited as the "basket case" of overpopulation is that of El Salvador, the smallest country in Central America, with the largest population. El Salvador's ills are well known, and the virtually continual political turmoil is tied to the fact that people are hungry. This is a point on which all sides agree. But to what extent can that hunger be attributed to the simple fact of too many people?

If we examine a graph of the size of the human population of El Salvador over time, and plot a graph of food consumption (plotted in terms equivalent to the number of people the country's corn production could support), we see a pattern that is almost identical to the one Malthus originally proposed, in which population increases much faster than food production (see Figure 14.11). It is seemingly a most spectacular verification of what Malthus had to say, and supports quite strongly the thesis that El Salvador is overpopulated. At least that is what it seems.

But a closer look changes the interpretation somewhat.[46] The first clue to the problem lies in an examination of the production areas of corn versus coffee, one of El Salvador's traditional export crops, as shown in

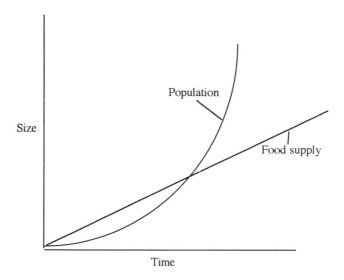

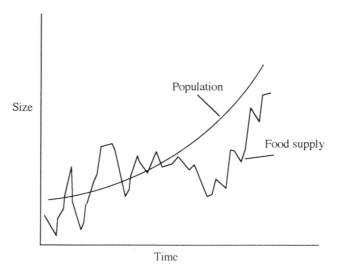

Figure 14.11. (a) The basic Malthusian position. Population growth rate is exponential and food supply is linear, leading to an inevitable "problem" of overpopulation (same as Figure 14.1). (b) Relationship between basic grain production and population size for El Salvador, seemingly an exact reflection of the Malthusian position of part a. (Data from Durham, 1979.)

Figure 14.12. The maps are virtually mirror images of one another, and reflect the basic fact that as coffee expanded in the late nineteenth century, lands that had been devoted to corn production were converted to coffee farms. Coffee is grown at relatively high elevations. Thus, when the coffee revolution hit El Salvador, all the volcanic soils in the highlands were con-

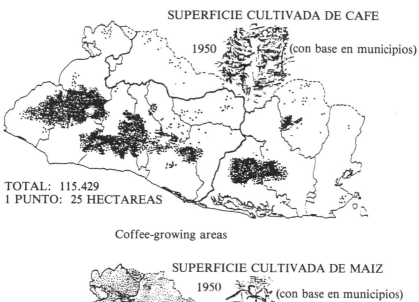

SUPERFICIE CULTIVADA DE CAFE

1950 (con base en municipios)

TOTAL: 115.429
1 PUNTO: 25 HECTAREAS

Coffee-growing areas

SUPERFICIE CULTIVADA DE MAIZ

1950 (con base en municipios)

TOTAL: 176,612
1 PUNTO: 10 HECTAREAS

Maize-growing areas

Figure 14.12. Comparison of areas devoted to coffee and maize. Note the inverse nature of the two maps. (Reprinted from *Scarcity and Survival in Central America* by William H.Durham with the permission of the publishers, Stanford University Press.© 1979 by the Board of Trustees of the Leland Stanford Junior University.)

verted to coffee. Peasant farmers, who accounted for almost all corn production, were thus displaced to the lower elevations (but mainly still able to take advantage of volcanic soils), which is what creates the pattern seen in the maps in Figure 14.12.

Then, in the 1950s, the era of cotton expansion hit El Salvador for much the same reason and with the same consequences as in Nicaragua, and further displacement of corn production took place. So, starting with coffee in the last part of the nineteenth century, and continuing with the expansion of cotton, basic grain production (here represented as corn) was continually displaced. If, instead of plotting actual corn production, as was done in Figure 14.11*b*, we plot the land-equivalent of number of people supportable along with the population (i.e., effectively supposing that instead of producing coffee and cotton, the farmers continued expanding food production), we see a graph like that presented in Figure 14.13. It is clear that agricultural expansion per se could likely have kept up with population growth. It was not the Malthusian fact of food production necessarily growing more slowly than population, but rather a sociopolitical decision to orient the society toward an agricultural export model that created the pseudo-Malthusian situation in which it seems that the popula-

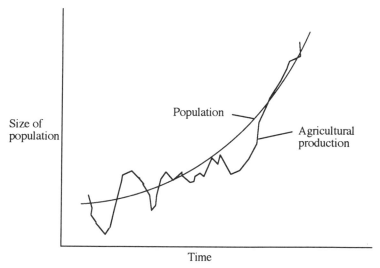

Figure 14.13. The population size and agricultural production (scaled in "people equivalents"). Compare to Figure 14.11b. (Data from Durham, 1979.)

tion grows faster than potential food production (see Figure 14.8). If different sociopolitical arrangements had been constructed (see Figure 14.9), the appearance of overpopulation could have been avoided.

A hard-core Malthusian might argue that the real world, in fact, includes such sociopolitical decisions, and that Malthus was right in the sense that sociopolitical decisions will always lead to food production increasing at a slower rate than population. Such a criticism is close to being correct, but really denies the basic Malthusian idea that there is an "essence" to the nature of humans to reproduce, and a natural limit on their ability to produce food. Indeed, the argument that sociopolitical decisions will always be involved in the picture is precisely what Malthus's critics had said back in the nineteenth century.

It is easy to see why the Malthusian argument is so attractive in the case of El Salvador. Clearly, there are great social problems there. It is also the smallest and most densely populated country in Central America. Yet, because of its position in the Lempa River valley, El Salvador has always had more agricultural potential than any of the other Central American countries, and even at the time of conquest was probably the most densely populated region of the isthmus. But El Salvador has also always had the agrarian problems so typical of other Third World countries. Possibly because of its particularly good agricultural soils, El Salvador saw the intensification of its rural problem several decades before its neighbors. As early as 1930, peasant organizations were threatening the political hegemony of the oligarchy. With full U.S. support, those peasant organizations were brutally repressed by the Salvadoran military,[47] giving rise to clandestine organizations that persisted in struggling against the Salvadoran oligarchy. The expansion of cotton in the 1950s only exacerbated an already extant problem, but memories of the repression of the 1930s coupled with a police state made it difficult for peasants to organize themselves effectively.

Buoyed by the victory of the Nicaraguan revolution in 1979, El Salvador's revolutionary movement coalesced into a potent military force in the early 1980s and threatened to topple the government. Five main military and political groups joined together under the banner of the Farabundo Marti National Liberation Movement (FMLN), which rapidly gained both internal support and international recognition. The Reagan administration responded by supplying massive military aid to the El Salvadoran government, and effectively created a military elite that even today challenges the Salvadoran oligarchy for political power. But despite U.S. advisors and huge quantities of military aid, the war stalemated by the mid-1980s, with the guerillas controlling about one-third of the country. Faced with an obvious stalemate, both the Salvadoran military and the FMLN agreed to negotiate, and in the spring of 1992 they signed a peace accord which effectively ended the war, if not the social problems that gave rise to it.

The 12 years of war produced, among other things, massive numbers of refugees. Today, Los Angeles houses more Salvadoreños than any other city except the capital, San Salvador. The massive outmigration of people during this period certainly changed the population density of the country, naturally with little direct effect on either politics or ecology. Similar to the case of Puerto Rico, reducing the effective population growth rate had little measurable effect on anything.

DISCUSSION AND CONCLUSIONS

While it is certainly true that a finite space cannot house an infinite number of people, the world is clearly far from that state, presuming that current levels of civilization and technology do not suddenly disappear. But, as neo-Malthusians would point out, if the population keeps growing, we will someday reach that point, no matter how much technology improves. They are right on that point.

But, given the truism that we wish to see populations remain within bounds that will sustain the species (that is, neither too small nor too large), it is extremely important to understand the processes that drive populations, that is, what makes populations grow and decline. And, here, there is a critical error promulgated by the neo-Malthusians that could spell disaster for all of us. This error implies that the neo-Malthusians themselves ultimately do not take the threat of overpopulation seriously. In an informative essay written over a decade ago, the geographer David Harvey took the neo-Malthusians to task for their basic essentialism, and most eloquently demonstrated how the problem is almost the reverse of what has been claimed.[48] Harvey's analysis has been repeated many times since, and has emerged as the dominant paradigm for those who take population seriously.

Harvey's argument, in a highly abbreviated and somewhat adulterated form, is as follows: First, there is simply no question about the fact that the world is finite, and there is thus some upper limit above which the human population simply cannot go (with the corollary that there is some population size that we should really try to avoid, be it 10 billion or 20 billion, or even the current 5 billion—exactly which figure is largely a value judgment, but the fact that some figure exists under a particular value system is hardly to be denied). Second, human social structures dictate both the pattern of production and the pattern of reproduction of the human species (thus setting it off from all other species, as noted previously). This second point simply confirms what the early critics said, that both population growth and utilization of resources are socially determined, and that both can thus be modified by social decisions, the production curve possibly to be higher and the population growth curve possibly to be lower, if that were the social goal of the society. Third, the sorts of social decisions that would be necessary to maintain a balance between human populations and the resources they require (be they basic foodstuffs or personal stereos) are fundamentally political in nature. Frequently, perhaps even usually, the social and political changes that are needed to save the future are in opposition to the interests of political forces that control the present. Fourth, the essentialism of the Malthusian argument (i.e., look at the fact of human reproduction and attempt to directly alter reproductive habits, rather than examine the social forces that cause high birth rates) allows its practitioners to ignore the socially unpopular and personally difficult political decisions that are necessary to avoid the situation that, all agree, could become critical in the future.

Consider the example I provided earlier of the Mexican family I came to know. The two mothers were Maria and Magnolia, with their four living children, Elena, Rene, Maggi, and Lorenzo. Recall how Elena eventually finished the third grade and brought in some income from domestic work, while Lorenzo actually had a steady job, the results of 10 years of raising this family. Recall that between the two mothers (back in the late 1970s), eight of their children had died, and the family income was virtually zero before Lorenzo and Elena became old enough to bring some money in. During my many hours of conversation with one of the mothers, Maria, I came to know her fairly well. I was always impressed with her devotion to her children. In fact, later, when I began thinking of what makes people like Maria tick, I realized that all she ever wanted to talk about were God and her children. Maria really had nothing else in life, nothing whatsoever, as far as I could tell. She was certainly a devoted mother and was devoutly religious. Each of her children was an added joy to her life, and, most importantly, the only joy to her life, outside of her religion.

It has always been of interest to me to try to figure out what makes people human. What it is that causes each of us to view ourselves as somehow different from, say, a chair? For some it may be a career, for others a family, for others some combination thereof, for others material goods, for others particular friends and/or relations. But there is always some set of things that we can point to and say, that is what makes me whole, that is the thing whose loss would mean the loss of me as a person, the thing that would literally kill me if I were to lose it. As I came to know Maria, I realized that her children—all of them, the living ones, the dead ones, and those who she planned to bear in the future—were the things that made her a human being. Having realized this, I imagined a social worker coming to Maria's house and suggesting to her that her problem in life was too many children. It would be like suggesting to a priest that he should suspend his belief in God, or that each of us discard that unique thing that we feel makes us human. Maria simply would not even hear the words.

When I compare Maria's attitudes towards children and life with those of others I know, the difference could not be more striking. Most women I know either have or want to have children, but by no means is it always the defining fact of their humanness, and none of them have lost three children. Most women I know are also far from being in Maria's social class, which, of course, is the point. My wife, for example, has a Ph.D. in biology, directs an active research program, teaches several courses at the University of Michigan, has many and varied goals for her career, and has one son. When we talk, her conversation is most stimulating on a variety of topics, and I see that she has a complex set of factors that combine to make her human, her son being just one of them. Maria's situation could not be more different. My wife had only one child because of her social class position, and Maria had more than seven because of hers. Their class position did not derive from their reproductive behavior; rather, their reproductive behavior derived from their class position. At a most general level, this is the crux of the problem with Malthusian essentialism.

The Nature of Nature

As emphasized throughout this text, part of our intellectual heritage seems to emerge from the natural structures school of thought that had developed in Europe in the late nineteenth century. This school of thought includes the urge to explain social problems as stemming from human nature (genetic determinism), the urge to explain environmental problems as stemming from the pressure of too many people (neo-Malthusianism), and the idea that there is an untrammeled thing called Nature[1] that merits our reverence (nature worship). The last is the subject of the present chapter.

Humans tend to view the environment, both social and physical, with a sense of nostalgia. Somehow, the present seems to have lost something of the truth, beauty, and goodness of the past. The northwestern forests, with their spotted owls, represent something unadulterated by modern society, something to which we someday might return to "get away from it all." Traditional family values are the things that we lost when we went down the wrong path toward modernism—how wonderful it would be if we could regain them! Yet, there is frequently a certain phoniness in nostalgia. Its definition usually entails a very selective memory of the past, either the imagined past or an experienced past. One tends to forget the negative aspects and dwell on the positive ones.

In a way, the worship of Nature is similar. At least the feelings sometimes expressed about the natural world come close to the feelings expressed in nostalgia—an escape from the problems that surround contemporary civilization. Those whose hobbies include outdoor activities will recognize these feelings immediately, and everyone will recognize them in popular cultural icons such as "born free" lions, wild rivers, and spotted-

393

owl-filled forests. These feelings are part of the modern version of Nature worship.

THE NATURE OF NATURE

The environment, from the perspective of the human animal, contains a complex concoction of good and bad, of nutrients and poisons, of regenerative structures and degenerative structures. Oxygen in the atmosphere is certainly required, and is there only thanks to the long work of photosynthesizing organisms, yet it was originally a poison. Radon seems to be an unavoidable consequence of geology, something we and most other life could certainly do without. Carbon dioxide is an indirect requirement for humans, in that the existence of green plants is a prerequisite to our own, but, as has become abundantly clear recently, too much carbon dioxide is a bad thing. And here, too, the existence of other life forms has had (and may still have) a crucial effect on the home humans call the environment. The massive limestone formations all over the world represent past biological activity of one sort or another, much like the present-day expanses of coral reefs. Simple calculations make it abundantly clear that without such biological activity in the past, the amount of carbon dioxide in the atmosphere would be sufficient to create a runaway greenhouse effect, i.e., a planet so hot that most life forms, certainly that of *Homo sapiens,* would be impossible.

More important to the immediate consciousness of the human species are the parts of the environment that have been socially produced or constructed: the interstate highway system of the United States, the pesticide residues currently spread over the entire planet, toxic waste dumps in New Jersey, the mosques of Mecca, the Taj Mahal, the strip mines of southern Illinois, plastics, cosmetics, tear gas, nuclear warheads, the latest fashions, bubble gum, hula hoops, MTV, racism, sexism, free health care in Sweden, the lack of free health care in the United States; the list goes on. This human environment is a collection of products that humans have produced with the application of social labor to natural resources. The products and by-products produced by human productive processes are thus part and parcel of the human environment.

In fact, all organisms, not only humans, create a large fraction of their own environment, through either their own actions or their genetic heritage. The beaver pond is a consequence of the beaver dam, and the overgrazed pasture a consequence of the actions of an overpopulated deer herd. The ant, because it inherited a small size, exists in a thin layer of air above the soil's surface, something that is clearly not of relevance to a lion. Gravity is an irrelevant environmental force for a bacterial cell suspended in a liquid medium but is crucial to a monkey hanging by its prehensile tail from a tree, while the Brownian motion of the molecules of the liquid medium continually thrashes the poor bacterial cell, a predicament the monkey avoids by being large. Even at very large scales, the oxygen we breathe and the fact that most of the earth's CO_2 is not in the atmosphere, are both consequences of the actions of organisms, and are relevant to those organisms that must care about O_2 and CO_2. The "environment" cannot be separated from the organism. This inevitable fact is true for all organisms, including *Homo sapiens*.

Yet the myriad forms of the environmental movement share one underlying, if sometimes tacit, assumption—there exists, external to ourselves, a material entity called "the environment," that can be either harmed or preserved.[2] There are two problems with this assumption: first, that the environment exists outside of ourselves does not fit well with modern views of ecology, as described above, and second, there may not be such a material entity in the first place, or, at least, its form may be quite different from what is normally assumed.

Part and parcel of most of the environmental movement is an underlying opposition to the unrestrained exploitation of Nature. Nature, it is thought, is what was there before human systems came to dominate and alter it. Furthermore, Nature, it is assumed, is always more beautiful than its human-modified form, and frequently forms part of the utopian vision of political action programs. This sometimes wistful yearning for innocence lost or ultimate truth and beauty is remarkably religious-like in its social manifestation—in popular culture, one can be brought to tears with visions of a burning rain forest. It is this social formation that I choose to call Nature worship, recalling the essentialist ideas of the nineteenth century.[3]

The purpose of this chapter is to challenge this viewpoint, and to argue that, while natural ecological processes were certainly operative before the evolution of *H. sapiens* and will certainly continue to operate after its extinction, that which is commonly referred to as Nature is not a collection of natural ecological processes at all, but rather an idealistic notion that had its roots in late nineteenth-century romanticism. The parallels between the discourse that included the beatification of Nature in nine-teenth-century Europe and that of today, are evident and worthy of con-siderable reflection and analysis. The intent here is to offer an interpreta-tion of Nature appreciation (rather than worship) that is more realistic than the romantic vision and, most importantly, is free of the misanthropic baggage that the nineteenth-century discourse had incorporated. With this analysis, I am hopeful not only that the potentially pernicious charac-ter of romantic Nature worship will be evident, but also that a more pro-gressive notion of Nature appreciation may take root. My thesis is that Nature is as much a social construct as is a piece of literature. Its promo-tion as a remnant of nineteenth-century romanticism is not simply an anachronism, but forms part of today's political conservatism. Yet, with an appropriate deconstruction, a more progressive "appreciation of Na-ture" can be promoted as an alternative to the romantic, reactionary, and misanthropic "Nature worship."

DECONSTRUCTING NATURE

That the nature of Nature is itself a social construction is easily seen in the historical record. For example, the tropical rain forest is

> . . . broken only by the clanging clamor of the torrents, the growling of tigers, and the swarming of infinite vipers and venomous insects. In [the mountain village of] Descanse begins the plague of vampire bats that ex-tends until Brazil, treacherously sucking in the hours of dreams the blood of men and animals. There also, by the side of the Brosymum [tree] . . . whose mere shade puffs up and scars the careless wanderer . . . one begins to suffer the privations and calamities of the wilderness, that . . . grow so as to at times make of life there scenes whose horror could figure in the Dantean pages of Purgatory and Hell.[4]

Or a tropical rain forest is

> . . . in a class of its own. It is akin to other super-size spectacles on Earth, such as the Grand Canyon and the Victoria Falls. However much you read about the scene, however many photographs or films you see of it, nothing prepares you for the phenomenon itself with its sheer scale and impact. You gaze on it and you feel your life has started on a new phase. Things will not be the same for you again after setting eyes on something that exceeds all your previous experience.[5]

So what, in point of fact, is a tropical rain forest? It is hell, heaven, something to be cleared for a farm, something to do research in, something to look for birds in, something that contains cures for cancer, an impediment to cattle, a source of poisonous snakes, a source of agricultural pests, a source of enemies of agricultural pests.

There are at least two components of the "tropical forest": (1) the plants, soil, animals, and how they are all related to one another; and (2) the observer, who may be a local farmer, a foreign industrialist, an ecotourist, or a variety of others. In short, there are text and reader (1 and 2, respectively), and the nature of the tropical forest cannot be understood as anything other than the relationship between the text and the reader.[6]

A conversation with someone who has a long history of nature-related activities (e.g., naturalists, landscape painters, hunters, bird watchers, nature photographers) usually reveals something of the discourse that defines the social construction of a "true beauty of Nature." In my youth, living in a working-class neighborhood on Chicago's northwest side, I was driven to a rejection of the environment of the city. Any foray into the non-city was a welcomed escape, such that even the empty lots across the street from my house were sources of joy, with an assortment of grasshoppers and beetles that had not succumbed to the onslaught of cement. About once a month I was treated to a Saturday trip to my cousin's house in the suburbs, where empty lots took on a totally different form (we called them prairies), with garter snakes and toads added to the basic grasshopper/beetle biodiversity array. Finally, once a year, my family was allowed a two-week respite from the city, the proverbial "vacation" of the working class. Along with thousands of other city dwellers, we went to the edge of civilization, a small resort on a small lake in northern Wisconsin. So my early formation regarding nature ranges from an empty lot on Chicago's northwest side, to a suburban "prairie," to the "wilderness" of northern Wisconsin.

It is most interesting for me to compare my present attitudes about these various forms of the natural world after working intensively in "pristine" rain forests in Costa Rica and Nicaragua for the past 20 years, having studied "scientifically" those same forests that were wilderness to me as a child, and having taught the academic subject of ecology for the past two decades. The white bark of birch trees used to signify pristine wilderness to the kid from Chicago, but now signifies early second-growth vegetation resulting from irresponsible logging of primary forest. The dense, pole-like trunks that represented impenetrable northern forest with all its mystery and hidden adventures, now are nothing more than aspen clones, again a sign of severe human intervention.[7] I now see the almost endless stands of aspen and birch of northern Michigan and Wisconsin as testament to the avaricious tendencies of petty robber barons and find it very difficult to find the same aesthetic pleasure that these habitats offered me as a child. And what of the empty lots and prairies of my childhood? These now appear to me as part of the scourge of urbanization, not the aesthetic wonder they appeared to be in my youth.

One's social class, educational level, educational quality—in short, the general sociopolitical milieu that gives life to one's personal observations—determines what is beautiful, venerable, and cherished. While my youthful sensibilities could respond with an emotional tear at miles upon miles of aspen "forests," my ecologically conscious adult responds with some contempt.

This viewpoint rather easily reconciles the dramatic opposites of the tropical forest that opened this section. The text, so to speak, is the physical elements in the area called forest, and the reader is the one who observes or "reads" that text. For the old Spanish explorer, concerned with where the gold mines might be, a reading of the trees, plants, and animals make the nature of the forest something akin to" . . . Dantean pages of Purgatory and Hell," while for the contemporary First World conservationist, reading the same text constructed the nature of the forest as something that made ". . your life [start] on a new phase." What, then, is the "nature" of the tropical forest or the Wisconsin aspen groves? It is as much a social construction as the Pyramid of the Sun in Mexico, or the Smithtown shopping center on Long Island.

There is, of course, more than just a hint of extremist relativism here. While it is imperative to "deconstruct" our notion of "Nature," probing into the social relations that give the concept meaning in the first place, this in no way should be take as a license. It is almost axiomatic that certain natural features are deserving of disdain, while others are to be treasured. It is difficult to imagine anyone seriously claiming that an Alaskan water bird covered with crude oil is aesthetically pleasing, that the ever-present bits of Styrofoam covering Puerto Rico's beaches are beautiful, or that an eroded hillside in Guatemala is to be cherished. On the other hand, a walk through a tropical rain forest or an alpine meadow, or a dive on a coral reef are among the activities that few would not find at least pleasant, if not wholly invigorating. Viewing Nature in this fashion is, as implied above, quite similar to the examination of a piece of literature with the deconstructionist's tools, as a phenomenon to be analyzed, not a religious icon. Yet, just as art can be beautiful or ugly, Nature can likewise take on such qualities. I currently cannot imagine an analysis that seriously finds an oil-covered duck to be beautiful. The fact that Nature is a human construction does not imply a crude relativism, let alone a license to destroy, but, rather, cries out for more cautious analytical thought. Furthermore, the current assumption that "pristineness" and "uniqueness" are the primary criteria for a proper appreciation of Nature derives from romantic essentialism and should be abandoned. Rather, the aesthetic sense of Nature should be continually evaluated and reevaluated, much as a piece of literature or art. Pristineness and uniqueness certainly enter the equation, but ought not be the dominant features.

THE NATURE WORTH SAVING

The above arguments cry out for a reevaluation of the appreciation of Nature. The view that a pristine Nature exists outside of the experience of *H. sapiens* is romantic idealism stemming, in part, from escapist tendencies that resulted from acknowledging the problems inherent in the modern industrial system. The alternative position is to view Nature's beauty as similar to the beauty of a poem or work of art.[8] It is the appreciation of *H. sapiens* that makes it beautiful. Nature is as much a product of human construction as a Frank Lloyd Wright building, the pirouette of a ballerina, the solution of a complex equation, or the beat of a heavy-metal rock band.[9]

Given this vantage point, two distinct models are clearly discernable. The first gives clear priority to particular readings of the text; the second conceives of the readings as emergent properties of shifting alliances. The programmatic consequences of each of these models is distinct. The "particular reading" model concludes that political liberation is a prerequisite to Nature conservation, while the "shifting alliance" model concludes that Nature conservation is a likely consequence of liberation. From a practical political point of view, the first model suggests that the goal of preserving tropical rain forests, for example, is not possible before the world's poor are taken care of, and thus has a certain pragmatic appeal for the political activist. The second model suggests something far more complicated, that the very notion of preserving Nature must be reanalyzed in line with contemporary political realities.

First, consider the particular reading model. The view that a pristine Nature exists outside of the experience of *H. sapiens* is, to some extent, romantic idealism, perhaps stemming in part from escapist tendencies that result from the problems of the modern world. An alternative position is to view Nature's beauty as similar to the beauty of a poem or work of art. It is the appreciation of *H. sapiens* that makes it beautiful. One of the consequences of this view is that only "educated" humans can appropriately appreciate Nature, much as is argued for the capacity to appreciate fine art or music. Implications of this are not as elitist as would seem at first glance, but rather acknowledge appreciation and knowledge that come from education as a human right. Peasants will likely appreciate the aesthetics of a rain forest differently when they are no longer forced to view it as a potential farm, and, rather, view it as a source of inspiration and potential knowledge (of course, today's intellectuals too may very well view it differently in a world in which former peasants hold equal political power). The former peasant farmer with a Ph.D. is not likely to read the text as an impediment to his family's betterment, as he is forced to do today.

It is tempting to go even further and formulate a program, at least in theory, for the "correct" construction of Nature. My own construction is a complex mixture including (at least) Tarzan movies, landscape paintings, Boy Scout nature lore, summer walks in the north woods with my mother, fishing with my father, adventure movies such as *King Solomon's Mines*, teaching ecology at the university, personal relationships with others who love the outdoors, sharing visions of pristine wilderness with friends and acquaintences, and so on. Obviously it is a special vision, despite my feeling that it is general. Others with different historical trajectories will have different visions. It is difficult for each of us to imagine that our view may not be the "correct" construction. But there really is no clear way to prioritize my construction over the construction of the peasant who must cut down the forest to feed her family, or the sawmill worker who must support the local lumber company to save his job (which are, of course, social constructions also). This is the conundrum of postmodernist relativism, and is the reason the prioritized reading model may not be all that useful.

We now turn to the shifting alliance model. Here, the issue of Nature construction may be brought into focus by an analysis of power structures in society. If Nature is socially constructed, similar sociopolitical conditions should produce similar social constructions. Capitalists seek to construct Nature in a way that will maximize profits. Thus, a poisoned river is not necessarily a negative in the capitalist's construction. Peasant farmers seek to construct Nature in a way that will allow them to survive. Thus, a deforested patch of land is not necessarily a negative in the peasant's construction. Workers seek to construct Nature to preserve employment conditions. Thus, global warming is not necessarily a negative in the worker's construction. The nature of the construction of Nature is based, in part, on one's power position in society.

If construction of Nature is specific to personal history, all actors will have distinct constructions, influenced by particular histories, and all constructions will necessarily be partial, since all experience is partial. As alliances form, constructions will follow, and those alliances that achieve a share of political power will, thus, contribute more to the construction of Nature than those alliances that fail. The construction of Nature thus is always a partial construction based on shifting political alliances. What is clear from this model is that the nature of Nature emerges from political alliances, and is a relatively unpredictable quantity. This suggests that the conservation of Nature is likewise contingent on current pollitical alliances. What, then, might this suggest in a practical sense?

In the same sense that one cannot envision the exact nature of an egalitarian society, yet actively engage in the struggle to attain one, one cannot see how to exactly construct the Nature that should be preserved, yet actively engage in the struggle for its preservation. The theoretical principle of egalitarianism is clear enough, and the theoretical principle of conservation is clear in the same sense. But just as the slave society of Athens was regarded as egalitarian by the non-slaves, the conservation of today's conservationists may be (I think this quite likely) unrelated to future constructions. Nature, as constructed by today's educated classes may bear little resemblance to the Nature constructed by future alliances. Because of my own historical trajectory, I have a vision of a reconstructed Nature that bears remarkable similarity to my current vision of Nature.

If we concentrate our focus on social justice, it is possible to conceive of a society in which the social construction of Nature is democratic. To the extent that my social construction of the rain forest is distinct from a local peasant farmer's construction, or that of a banana company executive, such distinctions will cease to exist in an egalitarian society. Other differences may emerge, but the differences based on class must disappear as classes disappear. When the experiences of all people are constrained by the same material forces, social constructions of nature will likely be far less variable than they are under current conditions.

Most would agree that the utopian future of an egalitarian society is hardly on the horizon. Yet, some tentative speculation may serve to initiate the debate on what might eventually constitute a "correct" construction of Nature. In that spirit, I offer a very brief speculation here.

The construction of Nature that sees much of the natural world as being worthy of preservation, reconstruction, and rational use derives mainly from privileged classes of people, mainly from the developed world. Apart from possibly specious utilitarian arguments that saving nature will find new cures for cancer, help stop global warming, and such, there is the honest argument that "I wish to save the rainforest (or coral reef, or prairie, or desert) because I find it immensely aesthetically pleasing," that cutting down rain forests is like burning Rembrandts. This argument, I believe, is the motivating argument of the vast majority of First World conservationists, utilitarian claims notwithstanding. Their view of Nature is a result of their particular reading of the text. If their particular reading is of value (and I believe it is, although that is a value judgment), it makes sense to promote that reading, such that something of a consensus on the meaning of Nature might be better approximated. Yet, the only way to reach a broader consensus on that reading is to afford all potential readers the same reading privileges. But the peasant farmer struggling to feed the family, or the sawmill worker fearful of unemployment, are not likely to construct Nature in the same way. In the end, the social construction of Nature as something beautiful and worth saving is not likely without the elimination of the impoverished peasantry in the Third World and of poverty in the developed world—in short, of those classes of people whose participation in the social construction of Nature forces them to read a negative text—to see Nature as something to be eliminated, not venerated. If my general view of the appreciation of Nature is correct, promotion of that view must take the form of the struggle for social justice.

THE NATURE WORTH SAVING, PART II

Many city dwellers will have a difficult time identifying strongly with the above reflections on Nature's beauty. But the city ultimately represents the main environmental context for almost all of us. Do the above reflections and analyses apply here also? The exuberance experienced by many from a dive on a coral reef, the tranquility and solitude of a quiet mountain cabin, the "sheer scale and impact" one gets from the first gaze at a tropical rain forest—are these feelings to be denied the city dweller? Are similar feelings not the legitimate right of those who are forced to live in the world's cities (a vast majority of the world's population today)?

In the context of the deconstruction of the present chapter, I hope the answers to these questions are clear. Indeed, it should be possible to construct the city environment in such a way that it engenders the same feelings as the "untrammeled wilderness." How is the city structured physically? Is it a safe place to be? Is one's life secure living there? Does it engender aesthetic pleasure? These are all questions that have to do with the "Nature" of the city environment and how that Nature is socially constructed.

Take, for example, Mexico City, the largest city in the world. One assessment of Mexico City, offered by a British sociologist, is as follows:

> . . . there are also serious pollution problems, due as much to the waste resulting from domestic daily activity as to wastes from large industrial zones. Pollutants are emitted from industry, motor vehicles (2,000,000 cars), and "natural" dust storms which originate in the area around the dried-up Lake Texcoco in the northeast of the city and which blow human waste from the sewage outlets all over the federal district. . . . Waste disposal is a major problem. The metropolitan area produces 6,000 tons of solid waste each day, of which only 75% is collected. The rest is scattered throughout the city, most of it on open untreated dumps. Those in "marginal" settlements near the dumping grounds are most severely affected by these wastes and there is resulting environmental degredation, through methane production, and through soil and water contamination.[10]

When I first read this passage, knowing Mexico City mainly as a tourist, I identified most strongly with these observations. They seemed right on the mark. But a Mexican friend of mine, who was born and raised in Mexico City, had quite a different response. He said (I paraphrase):

Damn Europeans. Can't see anything beyond the superficial. Sure, Mexico City has problems, so do all the world's cities. But Mexico City is a great place. It has a cultural history that traces its origins to the time Paris was a one-horse town. It has an artistic and literary tradition that rivals, and sometimes exceeds, New York even today, certainly in the past. Life there is exciting and vibrant, not like Houston or Liverpool or other megamonsters of the developed world. I would rather spend all day in Garibaldi Park then ten minutes in Oxford or Cambridge.

With his words, I recalled my own remembrances of Mexico City. I would have initially described it as the above negative reading, but I also admit that I enjoy being in that city, perhaps more so than any other city I know. As my friend said, it is the park, the cultural history, the literary tradition, the vibrant nature of street life in the center of the city. That city is indeed a beautiful, interesting, and vibrant place to be.

But what of the negative observations? Are they without merit? There are two issues here. First is the social construction of what one sees in the first place. The negative perception of the city simply sees different things than the positive one does—the text is the same, the readers different. The vibrant city center, with its parks and museums, opposes the air pollution and the sprawling shantytowns on the city's periphery. Second, of course, is the physical existence of the latter. No one, not I nor my Mexican friend, is likely to read the text of massive air pollution in a positive light, nor see the miserable, marginalized population of the peripheral shantytowns as a piece of nature's beauty. Indeed from this perspective we can read two Mexico Cities, one that reads like "Dantean pages of Purgatory and Hell," the other that could make your life start "on a new phase."

APPROPRIATE STRATEGIES FOR SAVING NATURE

At any point in time, popular constructions of Nature will exist, although they will be, as argued above, as temporary as the political alliances that make them. But once a construction is more or less fixed, the question of conservation emerges. And the practical question of strategy takes center stage. What strategies are appropriate for saving a Nature that is, admittedly, a social construction of a particular political alliance?

Perhaps the grandparent of all conservation issues is that of African wildlife. Ever since the early British explorers gazed in wonder at the herds of wildebeests and the lions that love them so much, the world has been concerned that this large mammalian fauna not go the same route as its New World counterpart.[11] A worldwide movement has thus developed to try to save this magnificent heritage. The symbol of this movement has become the elephant, majestic, powerful, mysterious, with no natural enemies other than humans.

A shocking analysis of this oldest of all conservation movements was published in 1993.[12] Former *New York Times* reporter Raymond Bonner spent four years living in Nairobi, looking at the conservation of wildlife. His analysis of what is needed to conserve wildlife, as well as what is currently being done, shocked the Western world. The major enemies of conservation, especially of the African elephant, were the major conservation organizations of the developed world. While the details are fascinating and complex, the basic story is simple. In their zeal to save the elephant, they ignored the complexity of what was causing its demise in the first place. Consequently, they had allowed the construction of political and economic forces that ultimately exacerbated the underlying social, political, and economic forces that were driving the elephant to extinction. Policies were being promoted that marginalized the African people and ignored the necessities of those who were forced to live where elephants roam. Furthermore, international policies were enacted in the name of conserving elephants that would actually take funds away from local elephant conservation efforts.[13]

While it may at first seem totally unrelated, another key book was published just three years earlier.[14] Sociologist Robert Bullard analyzed the patterns of toxic waste dumps in the United States and reported, for the first time, that people of color, especially African Americans, were far more likely to live near a toxic waste site than people of European ancestry. It was a pattern that held up even when controlling for economic status. Bullard coined the term "environmental racism" to describe this pattern, and developed a conceptual framework for thinking about solutions to it. Environmental justice, as a counterpart to social justice, has now become one of the slogans of people who, through no choice of their own, are forced to live in environmental settings that are clearly dangerous to their health.

The key to saving Nature, in my view, can be seen in the intersection of these two analyses. To save the elephants, local Africans need the political and economic power to sustain themselves and value the elephants. To remain healthy, African Americans who live next to toxic waste dumps need the political and economic power to sustain themselves and force the cleanup of the toxic dump. The notion that environmental justice, in a broad sense, should be the focus of Nature-preserving activities is not surprising, given the shifting-alliances model articulated above. The Nature that should be preserved (be it elephants or toxic waste-free space) depends on who "constructs" it, and how it should be preserved depends on the needs of those constructors. The slogan of the 1960s, "if you want peace, work for justice," may very well have its counterpart in the movement to preserve Nature—"conservation of Nature begins with environmental justice."

SIXTEEN

Conclusions?

In analyzing the post-Cold War world, one sometimes encounters a special kind of fatalism. Often dismissed in a joking manner, this fatalism takes many forms—you just can't change what Mother Nature wrought, or, people are just like that, or, why fight destiny. When faced with the obvious fact that 1 percent of Brazil's population owns almost 70 percent of the land in that country, the wizened liberal shakes his head and mumbles "What're ya gonna do," while the thinking conservative notes, quietly, "It's the nature of things." Women in most developed countries still lag behind men in participation in science and engineering, prompting the conservative to note that women have been destined that way since time immemorial, and the liberal to reluctantly admit that there may be something to this "biology is destiny" argument after all. As the tropical rain forest disappears, the liberal mind eschews the inevitable consequence of overpopulation in the Third World, while the conservative conscience accepts this inevitable price one pays for progress.

This sort of fatalism certainly is eclectic, and understanding it completely will require something of a probing analysis, not only of today's world situation, but of the way in which contemporary humans come to think they understand things. My purpose in this text has not been so ambitious. My purpose was to argue that this sort of fatalism, while perhaps perfectly logical and defensible under various religious traditions, simply is unsustainable in a secular scientific world. That is, what has in the past been a belief that God (or whatever relevant deity) controls things, and, thus, we are fools if we attempt to improve the world, is frequently expressed today as natural forces control things, thus making us fools if we attempt to improve the world. And just as religious fatalism served certain powerful interests in the past, it is my contention that the parallel secular fatalism serves similar interests now. To see how this fatalism has been constructed, and to ask to what degree its tenets are supported by relevant scientific disciplines, was the main purpose of this text. For the most part, the new secular fatalism, while retaining the spirit of and much of the analytical traditions of the older religious fatalism, takes much of its modern credibility from the field of biology, especially the subdisciplines of genetics and ecology.

Constructing a conclusion from the foregoing chapters is not an easy task. On the one hand, it seems imperative to reiterate the general theme of the text, that the vast majority of the biological essentialism that we seem to have inherited from the nineteenth century has, in fact, no biological basis to it, and that the issues we sometimes seek to understand as having an underlying biological essence are more easily understood as constructs emerging from human social institutions. On the other hand, the problems for which biological essentialism has offered these bogus solutions still exist, and to simply deconstruct a specious construction might leave one wondering, "so what should be done now?" That is, where is the new construction—the "reconstruction"?

Once again risking a charge of postmodernist relativism, I suggest that I should not be the one to suggest a recipe, nor should anyone else. While there are broad outlines that suggest themselves as antitheses to the essentialist position, the specific path to be taken in the new construction is one that must be defined by those actively engaged in making it.

Nevertheless, the broad outlines, in most general terms, are quite clear. First, the fact that ethnicity, culture, and race still determine, to a great extent, what people do must be acknowledged. Perhaps in some distant world, these constructs will cease to be diverse—a one-race, one-ethnic-group, one-culture world (of course, it is not at all clear that such a world would be either good or interesting). But our current situation is certainly very far from such a vision. It is, thus, imperative that we begin the movement toward a multicultural, multiethnic, multiracial view of social construction. One step in that direction is an understanding of where it all comes from. One purpose of this text has been to argue that little can be attributed to underlying biological factors. The deep feeling that some Croats have, for example, that Serbs are biologically different, has no basis whatsoever in biological fact. Likewise, the underlying feeling that many European Americans have that African Americans are biologically different has no basis in biological fact.[1]

Second, gender is central to all of our lives. Gender politics is one of the most active political arenas in the world today, as well it should be. True, the crude biological essentialist position has been largely discredited, but here, far more than with race or ethnicity, biology does have an influence. The exact nature of that influence is hotly debated at the present time, and it is, thus, not possible to give a final assessment. But the crude notion that biology determines gender, gender identity, sexual orientation, and gender role must be discarded, and a more nuanced analysis put forth. The challenges here are immense, and go right to the core of very basic beliefs—e.g., how many sexes are there? Nevertheless, as in the case of race and ethnicity, something akin to multiculturalism must be pursued here. Gender equality and the elimination of homophobia are fairly clear goals to which we all aspire. But by what means? That is not clear.

Third, the problems emerging from the hydrocarbon society have become too obvious to ignore. Again, the biological essentialist position that either it is in the nature of human beings to destroy the world like this, or the related idea that the problems are actually caused by too many people, can be discarded. An alternative to the hydrocarbon society can be vaguely envisioned in the evolving ideas of alternative energy sources and alternative agriculture. The vision of a solar society based on ecological agriculture is indeed an inspiring one, but its birth must await both technological and political advances. Here, modern biology has an important role to play outside of its deconstructive role.[2] Many of the problems that must be solved technologically are, in fact, biological problems, both with alternative energy and, especially, with alternative agriculture. Indeed, this is a major argument to encourage students to choose biology as a career, to say nothing of its challenge to practicing biologists to engage themselves in important practical work. Indeed, if we had as many biologists working on alternative agriculture as we have petroleum engineers in the world, we would be well on the way to solving some of the problems, at least technologically. The political questions remain.

Fourth, there is a conservative ideology suggested by this; not conservative in the sense of recent Tory ascendency in England and the United States,[3] but in the underlying meaning of the word. Beginning with the deforestation of England in the sixteenth century and extending to the production of toxic waste today, there is a sense born of the Industrial Revolution that "progress" must occur at whatever cost. One of those costs has been nature itself, at least partially. Concern over the future potential productivity of human resource transformation systems should engender something of a conservation ethic in us all. Yet, such a conservation ethic, if restricted to the sort of romantic notions inherited from the nineteenth century, may very well ignore some of the most important aspects of the environment that we ought to be conservative about. The construction of a progressive conservation discourse should be an important priority. Exactly what form that discourse should take is not exactly evident, but, clearly, we should reject the romanticism once again emerging in the conservation movements of the developed world.

Fifth, there is a certain implication that seems to emerge naturally from the above four imperatives. A harmonious, multicultural society requires equal access to power structures for the various cultures in the society. If this access does not exist, the society will not be harmonious for long. A society with equal gender relations implies a similar requisite for people associated with various gender roles and sexual orientations. An ecologically sound production system is not likely to emerge if some members of the society are locked out of society's reward structures. Finally, if a sound notion of the natural world is to be constructed, participants in that construction must have an equal voice. This implies something about democratic structure. Democracy is a goal for which any society ought to strive, especially the emerging post-industrial society. And I do not refer to the various political systems around the world parading as democracies, but, rather, to a system of politics and economics in which all members of the society have truly equal access to power.

This last point brings us to the pragmatic issue of political perspective. The politics in which we engage today will partly determine if the world of the future is to be an ecologically sound, multicultural one. But political perspective since the Cold War has not ignited much enthusiasm in either the developed world or the Third World. Indeed, radical Christians and Muslims seem intent on driving politics back to a pre-secular state of being. Nevertheless, with the social glue of anticommunism suddenly removed, political perspective has been given a sort of intellectual green light. It is thus possible, for the first time since World War II, to engage in meaningful political dialogue without the specter of anticommunism judging every word and phrase.

This dialogue of the new world order has spawned what appear to be three political perspectives regarding the issues addressed in this text. First is the belief that the industrial system[4] is fundamentally a good system, but has been corrupted by those who have sought to manage it artificially. They agree that the system tends to make the rich richer, but disagree that it makes the poor poorer. Rather, they believe that making the rich richer elevates everyone's life, on the average. They cite as evidence—and there should be no doubt that their evidence is really quite good—the difference between the life of the average person in the pre-capitalist world and that life today. Curiously, their position on racism, sexism, and the environment is very close to the position held by some liberals in the 1930s and 1940s. They believe that such problems are essentially epiphenomena, having no direct relationship to the operation of the industrial system. They sometimes have a very strong undercurrent of the natural structures school of thought, feeling that most people are in the position they find themselves largely because of the endowments they were born with. Hard work pays off, but some are born with the ability to work harder and more efficiently than others, and these are the ones who ascend to the top of the meritocracy created by the industrial system. They feel that the environment has suffered, but that such is the nature of human productive activity, not the particular way in which industrial capitalism has organized it. They tend to have romantic visions of a future in which all the bad deviations from the natural state of the system will have been defeated, and we will be able to effectively return to a more natural state. This romantic vision is usually reflected in such conservative ideals as traditional family values.

Second, there are those who believe the industrial capitalist system is fundamentally a good system, but has certain elements that generate problems. They acknowledge that the system tends to make the rich richer and the poor poorer, but feel that this aspect can be directly regulated to cushion the effects on the poor. They do not believe that making the rich richer elevates everyone's life on the average, but, rather, that it can do so if properly organized. They see racism, sexism, and environmental deterioration as emanating, at least in part, from the unregulated "cowboy" capitalism of the 1980s, and feel that resources must be redirected to actively pursue solutions to these problems. They believe that such problems are partially a consequence of the operation of the industrial system, and that is precisely why that system must be regulated. They sometimes have a very strong undercurrent of the natural structures school of thought, sometimes not. They feel that the environment has suffered and that, too, is reason to rein in the system and organize it so it functions better. They tend to have romantic visions of a future in which all the bad deviations from the natural state of the system will have been defeated and we will be able to effectively return to a more natural state. This romantic ideal is usually reflected in utopian visions of the future, in which racial harmony and environmental protection are part and parcel of everyday life.

Third, there are those who believe the industrial system was fundamentally a good system, but it has run its course and needs to be changed. They note that the system tends to make the rich richer, and the poor poorer, and that is one of its central tendencies. They cite as evidence—and there should be no doubt that their evidence is really quite good—the continual deterioration in relative quality of life of the poorest segments of the society during the past 20 or 30 years. Their position on racism, sexism, and the environment is that such problems are fundamental to the operation of the industrial system. They eschew the ideas of the natural structures school of thought, and feel that most people are in the position they find themselves largely because of the way we transform resources and deliver products. Hard work pays off, they agree, but we currently have a system in which those who work hardest (e.g., farmers and farm workers, textile mill workers, mine workers) receive the fewest of society's rewards. They feel that environmental degradation is a direct consequence of the particular way in which the resource transformation process is organized. They tend to have visions of a future in which the industrial system will have been replaced by a system that is economically just, does not promote racism or sexism, and is benign to the environment.

Making such a tripartite classification is always dangerous. People are too diverse, and the issues themselves too complex, to make such a simple categorization anything but approximate. On the other hand, poles of attraction always exist, and it seems that these three positions do represent three poles of attraction in the world today. People tend to be moving toward one or another of these three poles, perhaps never actually getting there, swerving and swaying as they analyze world problems, reflecting the complexity that is the human mind and human social organization. But within that network of interconnections, these three poles of attraction partially determine one's position in the political arena.

The material in this book has sought to make clear that the remnants of the natural structures school of thought are largely without scientific merit, that certain elements of biology need to be reconstructed so as to contribute positively to solving critical contemporary problems. To the extent that the essentialist program and the persistence of these problems are parts of one or another of these political positions, if ever so subtly, this book thus becomes a critique of those political positions. And if it is a critique of certain positions, it is, at least indirectly, an advocate of others.

Notes

CHAPTER ONE

1. Douglas, 1980, p. 13.
2. Fleck, 1935, quoted in Douglas, 1986, p. 13.
3. Burchell et al., 1991, p. 63.

CHAPTER TWO

1. Thompson, 1963.
2. The century bracketed by 1450 and 1550 saw enormous changes in energy utilization in Europe and especially in England, as described in more detail in Chapter 8. The new demand for energy, the major source of which had been charcoal, led ultimately to massive deforestation in England and a consequent search for alternative sources of energy. The source that came to dominate was coal, which began a chain of events that ultimately led to the Industrial Revolution.
3. These concepts are more fully developed in Chapter 3. Briefly, the social transformation of resources refers to the human characteristic of organizing socially for the purpose of transforming resources from one form to another: from acorn to acorn bread, from iron ore to steel, from steel to automobile (Harris, 1977; Sahlins, 1972). Social construction refers to the human habit of developing ideas, beliefs, assumptions, and traditions that determine behavior patterns, and developing these factors in social groups. Frequently, these social constructions are "reified" such that they appear to be somehow "essential" or biologically determined. Discourse is a general term that refers to the underlying assumptions, the rules of operation, the set of appropriate metaphors that we use to structure, almost subconsciously, the world in which we live. Useful references on these topics include Poster, 1984; and Foucault, 1972.
4. Wolf, 1989. The theory of evolution was not really the point of scientific debate. It had been fairly well accepted in scientific circles that the diversity of life had evolved, modern forms deriving from more primitive forms. What

Darwin provided was a mechanism for how this occurred, the mechanism of natural selection. Darwin developed the bulk of his ideas while performing the service of ship naturalist on the H.M.S. *Beagle*, as the latter traveled around the world. Darwin was a cautious worker, and had accumulated a great deal of evidence for his theory, but was less than expeditious in publishing. Alfred Russel Wallace, another world-traveling biologist, through observations he made during his travels, had developed the same theory as Darwin. It was only after Wallace's work was made known to Darwin that he finally finished his book, *On the Origin of Species by Means of Natural Selection* (1859), which was perhaps the most influential work of science ever to be published. Darwin and Wallace actually published the outlines of their theory before *The Origin of Species* was published, and the theory really ought to be attributed to the two of them rather than to Darwin alone. Several excellent comprehensive references on this history are available, for example, Mayr, 1982.

5. Genetic determinism is taken here to include the notion that biology determines various social factors such as race, gender, and individuality, a philosophy that has been criticized profusely (e.g., Lewontin, 1982, 1991; Tavris, 1992; Gould, 1981). Malthusianism is a philosophy that ties various human problems to the size of the human population (Ehrlich and Ehrlich, 1990), an idea that has been substantially criticized (e.g. Murdoch, 1980; Lappé and Collins, 1977; Lappé and Schurman, 1988; Boserup, 1965). Nature worship is an outgrowth of various forms of nineteenth-century romanticism (Burke, 1985). All are discussed at length in later chapters.

6. The Monist League was composed of like-minded intellectuals. It was an influential power in Germany during the later years of the nineteenth century and the beginning of the twentieth. A particularly devastating history of the society can be found in Gasman, 1971, while the historian Bramwell (1989) is somewhat more sympathetic.

7. Haeckel, 1900, p. 125.

8. This point is defended by Gasman, op cit.

9. Hitler, 1927, pp. 284–89. Spencer (1876) recognized this possibility explicitly: "Some facts seem to show that mixture of human races extremely unlike produces a worthless type of mind—a mind fitted neither for the kind of life led by the higher of the two races, nor for that led by the lower—a mind out of adjustment to all conditions of life."

10. Haeckel, 1868, p. 172, cited in Gasman, op cit., p. 36.

11. Haeckel, 1900, p. 125.

12. Haeckel, 1904, p. 390, cited in Gasman, op cit., p. 40.

13. Gasman, op cit., p. 91.

14. Modern molecular biology has completely dismissed the notion that the popularly defined human races are based on significant biological factors, as discussed fully in Chapter 4. Also see Lewontin, 1982.

15. For example, when *The Bell Curve* by Richard Herrnstein and Charles Murray was published in 1994, it received two cover stories in *New York Times* publications, two Sundays in a row (first in the Sunday Magazine and then in the Sunday book review), cover stories in *Forbes, Newsweek,* and *The New Republic* (at least), and enormous coverage in the broadcast media. The book offered nothing new, rehashed old ideas that had been discredited years before, received nothing but scorn from the academic community, yet was given this remarkable treatment by the media.

16. A particularly lucid description of this political phenomenon can be found in many of the works of Noam Chomsky. Especially useful is his recent *Year 501: The Conquest Continues* (1993). Specifically biological themes can readily be heard in the new fascist movement in Germany, where attacks on immigrants have burgeoned in recent years. David Duke, former president of the American Association for the Advancement of White People and senatorial candidate from Lousiana, put it this way: "All one has to do is look around this globe and see the Third World reality. Are whites holding every one of the nonwhite countries down, or are we in fact pumping billions of dollars into them along with every technological aid that the West can produce? And now the West itself is gradually being enveloped by nonwhite immigration. The exploding numbers of nonwhites are slowly wrapping formerly white nations in a dark human cocoon. Shall a butterfly emerge, or a beast that has haunted the ruins of every great white civilization that submitted to invasion by immigration and racial miscegenation?" U.S. Secretary of State William Jennings Bryan, upon encountering the Haitian elite in 1917, remarked, "Dear me, think of it, Niggers speaking French." (Chomsky, 1993, p. 201). According to President Wilson's Secretary of State Robert Lansing, "The experience of Liberia and Haiti show that the African race are devoid of any capacity for political organization and lack genius for government. Unquestionably there is an inherent tendency to revert to savagery and to cast aside the shackles of civilization which are irksome to their physical nature. Of course there are many exceptions to this racial weakness, but it is true of the mass, as we know from experience in this country. It is that which makes the negro problem practically unsolvable." (Cited in Schmidt, 1971.) And what did the so-called Roosevelt Corollary to the Monroe Doctrine imply about the "nature" of Latin Americans in stating, "Chronic wrongdoing or an impotence which results in a general loosening of the ties of civilized society, ultimately require intervention by some civilized nation, and in the Western Hemisphere the adherence of the United States to the Monroe Doctrine may force the United States, however reluctantly, in flagrant cases of such wrongdoing or impotence, to the exercise of an international police power"? (Pearce, 1982). Naturally, such intemperate language is not usually heard from government officials today, but despite the more careful use of words, the basic idea is still there. What, we might ask, did liberal policy analyst Alan Tonelson mean when he wrote, ". . . threats in Central America [should be

handled] the way that great powers have always dealt with *pesty, puny neighbors:* by laying down the law unilaterally and enforcing our will through intimidation and direct uses of military force." (emphasis added) (Tonelson, 1987). A particularly penetrating analysis of the relationship between nationalism and racism can be found in Balibar, 1991.

17. Tavris, 1992; see also Chapter 7.

18. Biologists most often abstract the problem of population growth as a two-parameter problem, with population growth and carrying capacity the two parameters of interest, the first being set by a combination of environmental forces and the inherent ability of a species to reproduce, and the second being set mainly by the environment. As noted earlier by Marx (see Parsons, 1977; Meek, 1971), and more fully appreciated by modern ecological writers (see Murdoch, 1980; or Commoner, 1992), in the human species both birth rates and carrying capacity are largely determined by human social relations. Marx specifically spoke of the "relative overpopulation" invariably caused by capitalism's need to grow and consequent disenfranchisement of one segment of the population even as production expands. Popular introductions to this topic include Lappé and Collins, 1977; Commoner, 1992. A more technical, if somewhat dated, source is Murdoch, 1980. The extensive work by Boserup has been speaking to this issue for decades (see, for example, Boserup, 1965, 1990), and a variety of recent reviews echo the same conclusion (for example, Buttel and Raynolds, 1989; Michaelson, 1981). This topic is covered in considerable detail in Chapter 12.

19. Malthus, 1960, p. 58.

20. Malthus' work helped divert attention from the problems of the working class in Britain almost as soon as it was published. Even today, the population issue serves to divert attention from the real issues. A most lucid account relevant to Latin America is given by Galeano (1973): "The human murder by poverty in Latin America is secret; every year, without making a sound, three Hiroshima bombs explode over communities which have become accustomed to suffering with clenched teeth. This systematic violence is not apparent but is real and constantly increasing: its holocausts are not made known in the sensational press but in Food and Agriculture Organization statistics . . . [The Imperium] is worried: unable to multiply the dinner, it does what it can to suppress the diners. 'Fight poverty, kill a beggar!' some genius of black humor scrawled on a wall in La Paz. What do the heirs of Malthus propose but to kill all the beggars-to-be before they are born? Robert McNamara, the World Bank president . . . has called the population explosion the greatest obstacle to progress in Latin America. . . . McNamara notes with regret that the brains of the poor do 25 percent less thinking, and the World Bank technocrats (who have already been born) set computers humming to produce labyrinthine abracadabras on the advantages of not being born. . . . The United States is more concerned than any other country with spreading and imposing family planning in the farthest outposts. [It has] nightmares about millions of chil-

dren advancing like locusts over the horizon from the Third World. Plato and Aristotle considered the question before Malthus and McNamara; in our day this global offensive plays a well-defined role. Its aim is to justify the very unequal income distribution between countries and social classes, to convince the poor that poverty is the result of the children they don't avoid having, and to dam the rebellious advance of the masses."

21. This is not to say the size of the human population in an area is irrelevant. One must understand that the world is finite and we cannot fit an infinite number of people on it. Indeed, the future clearly holds out the possibility that the world will someday become absolutely overpopulated. However, such concern should cause us to try now to change the forces that cause high population growth rates, which means dealing with the social and political issues that are so well known to plague the planet, as elaborated more fully in Chapter 12. This point has been made by Commoner (1975) in a short article with the telling title, "Does Overpopulation Cause Poverty, or Is It the Other Way Around?" One of the most articulate expression of the problem, in a slightly different context, was made by Harvey (1974), stating that ". . . failure to make use of such a method [dialectical materialism] in the face of a situation that all regard as problematic and some regard as bordering on the catastrophic, is to court ignorance on a matter as serious as the survival of the human species."

22. Burke, 1985, p. 269.

23. Shipman, 1994, p. 110.

24. The Pioneer Fund was established in 1937 by Harry H. Laughlin and Frederick Osborn. It has been instrumental in funding research oriented to the biological differences between the races, especially in the United States (Kühl, 1994, p. 6). Herrnstein and Murray's best seller, *The Bell Curve* (1994), cites a great many recipients of Pioneer Fund awards, including Herrnstein himself.

25. Osborn, 1960, p. 94.

26. Burke, 1985, p. 271.

27. The entire philosophy of *Lebensraum,* invented by the monists and key to the Nazi invasion of Poland, was based upon the underlying philosophy of Malthusianism. The German population was growing at a rate that would soon outstrip the resources of the area within its current boundaries, leading to a Malthusian crunch on the population. Since this population was a superior race, it had an obligation to seek other land, even at the expense of the people living in that other land, so as to ensure the prospering of this racially superior population.

28. Hardin, 1971.

29. Haeckel, 1900, p. 336.

30. Id., pp. 336–37.

31. Id.

32. Id.

33. These ideas are explored in detail in Chapter 15.

34. Many histories of the eugenics movement have been written. Useful recent sources are Shipman, 1994; Kevles, 1985; and Kühl, 1994.

35. Shipman, 1994, p. 123.

36. Id., p. 124.

37. Id.

38. Kevles, 1985, p. 46.

39. Id., p. 110.

40. Id., p. 329.

41. Kühl, 1994, p. 85–95.

42. Id., p. 46.

43. Stein, 1968, p. 61.

44. Id., p. 25.

45. Indeed, as Bramwell (1989) has noted, the political affiliations of the members of the Monist League ranged from right to left, with the majority probably being on the left.

46. This is discussed fully in Chapter 9.

47. The human structures school is frequently associated with the philosophical works of Karl Marx, although it was a much more general phenomenon in the nineteenth century and has become part of a wide range of political philosophies in the present century. Whatever one might feel about the current popular wave of anti-Marxism sweeping the West, this particular piece of Marx's thought ought to be regarded as independent of the political convictions commonly associated with Marxism. Marx was clearly wrong on many points, and his analysis was clearly misused in other cases. He predicted that socialist revolutions would first occur in western Europe—he was wrong. The Soviet Union claimed to base its economic structure on Marxism, something most scholars of Marx denied all along. To the extent Marxism implies a Stalinist-type command economy and anti-democratic forms of government, everyone rejects it. But the intellectual traditions of Marxism are really something else, especially regarding the methods of understanding human societies in general. Furthermore, Marx's closest collaborator, Friedrich Engels, was something of a "natural structures" thinker, although most of his work would be categorized as "human structures."

48. To claim so stridently, "it is also wrong," is done here in anticipation of the rest of the text. To a large extent the whole purpose of the text is to explore the complexities of biology and human affairs that lead to the conclusion "it is wrong."

49. This is more fully discussed in Chapter 11.

50. An especially lucid history can be found in Greenberg (1988), pp. 404–18. Also see Rist, 1992.

51. The most recent extreme neo-Malthusian view is that of Ehrlich and Ehrlich, 1990, and even they admit to the importance of non-population factors. Compare, for example, their 1990 analysis with the original analysis of Ehrlich (1968).

CHAPTER THREE

1. Morgan, 1988, p. 168.

2. The phrase "men of best quality" was first used in the context of the English Revolution of the seventeenth century, in which the radical democrats ". . . developed a kind of 'liberation theology' which, as one critic ominously observed, preached 'seditious doctrine to the people' and aimed 'to raise the rascal multitude . . . against all men of best quality in the kingdom, to draw them into associations and combinations with one another . . . against all lords, gentry, ministers, lawyers, rich and peaceable men.' " Chomsky, 1991, pp. 357–58.

3. The literature on this topic is vast. Generally there is a persistent search for the biological basis of human nature, the history of which was sympathetically summarized recently by Degler, 1991. The classic work in recent years was Wilson's popular *On Human Nature* (1978), which in turn was based on his more scientific work, *Sociobiology: The New Synthesis* (1975). More critical and skeptical views are presented by Lewontin, 1982; Kaye, 1986; and Kitcher, 1987.

4. See Chapters 3, 4, and 5.

5. This history has been repeated many times and can be found outlined in any biology text. A variety of accounts can be found in the collection edited by Stern and Sherwood, 1966.

6. It is not surprising that Mendel should be so adept at the scientific method. While here, as in other abbreviated accounts, Mendel is portrayed as a gardening monk, he was actually quite well trained in science and mathematics. His insights were unlikely due to chance and probably more due to a creative mind systematically observing nature, well trained in the scientific methods of the day, and especially knowledgeable about advanced statistical techniques.

7. At this point all the basic elements of the theory are together, and it is a wonderful example of the scientific method in its purest form, including (1) *observations* about the nature of parent-offspring relations, (2) an *abstraction* to account for information transferred from parent to offspring, and a (3) *postulate* about the nature of the transfer. All of that information may be put together to make a (4) *prediction*, which can be (5) *tested* with real plants. As simple and obvious as all of this may seem to us today, this collection of observations, abstractions, and guesses, along with the subsequent experimental verification, not only is one of the purest forms of Western science at its

best, but also forms the basis of the modern science of genetics and much of the basis of biology in general.

8. Even today, this idea is assumed without much thought by many, if not most, nonbiologists. Does not a child always look something like its father and something like its mother? Does not the child "blend" the characteristics of mother and father? In point of fact, that is not correct. The child inherits messages from father and mother, and can quite easily exhibit characteristics that are very different from either parent. Skin color is an excellent example. Because of the particularities of the inheritance of skin color, an offspring can never be darker in coloration than the darkest parent, but easily can be lighter than the lightest parent.

9. It is well to reflect on this basic idea. In a sense the most noble purpose of the scientific method is not really to understand nature, we already understand that, but rather to challenge and eventually modify what appears to be common sense. It is here that the scientific method can "rupture" the discourse, sometimes dramatically (see chapter 4).

10. Mendel's experiments are part and parcel of the mythology of modern biology, and every biology textbook recites them almost as liturgy. A different, and perhaps more historically valid, point of view, is that Mendel performed a large number of experiments, most of which have gone unreported. He developed his ideas about inheritance from these experiments, but finally published accounts either of only a small set of experiments (i.e. the ones that worked), or actually reconstructed his experiments and reported not actual experiments but reconstructed ones. The particular experiments he reported, then, may not have actually ever been done. (Di Trocchio, 1991).

11. It also should be acknowledged that Watson and Crick used the very important results of Maurice Wilkins and Rosalind Franklin, and that Franklin had already arrived at the basic double-helical form of the molecule. Her work is not usually fully acknowledged—see Sayre, 1975.

12. As discussed more fully in Chapter 6.

13. The bases get their names from various places—*adeno* is Latin for gland, and adenine was first isolated from the thymus gland; thymine also first synthesized from the thymus gland; *cyto* means cell; guanine was first isolated from bat droppings, known as guano.

14. Made up of ribose rather than deoxyribose.

15. In RNA one of the base pairs is different: Instead of adenine, it has uracil. So the uracil of RNA combines with the adenine of DNA, while the thymine of DNA combines with the adenine of RNA—it is a bit confusing. For our purposes here it is not too far off to just suppose that adenine and uracil are identical, so in all that follows we shall simply make reference to adenine even when speaking of RNA, in which case we really ought to use uracil.

16. Modern molecular genetics continues to expand our knowledge about these basic processes, and we now understand that this simple model, while correct

as a general overview, is considerably enriched with a diversity of special behaviors. An excellent popular summary of some recent findings is presented in Rennie, 1993.

17. Because the particular sequence of bases in its DNA which was delivered to it by its mother and father dictates the particular sequence on the mRNA, which causes the amino acids to form in the particular sequence that makes up this protein.

18. See Chapter 6.

19. Actually, the detailed way in which a protein is "tangled up" is determined very precisely by the sequence of amino acids. The "tangle" is not just a random ball, but has a complex structure in and of itself, so the metaphor of a tangled clothesline is very approximate and useful only for the particular application here.

20. Poly meaning many and morphism meaning structures, variability in protein structure is known as protein polymorphism. Studying protein polymorphisms is very close to studying the genetic variability itself, since single genes code for single proteins.

21. See chapter 11.

22. Of course, biologists really recognize many other types (more than 30 in all), but as a first approximation, for the kinds of animals the average reader will be familiar with, there are only 8 major types.

23. The major classification categories are called phyla (phylum in the singular). The corals and their allies are in the phylum Cnideria, the flatworms are in the Platyhelminthes, the roundworms in the Nematoda, the starfish and relatives are in the Echinodermata, the vertebrates and their relatives in the Chordata, the clams and snails and relatives in the Mollusca, the insects, spiders, crabs and relatives in the Arthropoda, the worms in the Annelida.

24. This point is discussed more fully in chapter 8.

CHAPTER FOUR

1. Harris, 1979.

2. The term rain shadow refers to the effect that a land mass (e.g., a mountain) has on the rainfall on its leeward side. As moisture is brought in on the windward side, it tends to fall as rain before the air crosses the land mass, thus making the leeward side of the mass much drier than would be expected. The ecological basis for these transformations is described in chapter 10.

3. Actually there is a fifth species, the bonobo, or pigmy chimpanzee, which is quite distinct from the common chimpanzee. Less is known about this species than the other four great apes. See Kano (1992) for the first major behavioral study of this species.

4. Leakey and Lewin, 1979, 1992; Diamond, 1992; Corbalis, 1991.

5. Blumenschine and Cavallo, 1992.

6. See later sections of this chapter and also chapter 7.

7. Leakey, 1976.

8. Corbalis, 1991, p. 39.

9. The details of biological energy transformations are fully discussed in chapter 8.

10. Bickerton, 1990.

11. The details of human resource transformation processes are developed further in chapter 9. Only an outline of the most minimal model is presented here.

12. One estimate (Pfeiffer, 1973) suggests that at its peak *H. erectus* numbered at most 40,000 bands, which would be like taking the population of Holland, Michigan, and spreading it throughout Africa, Asia, and Europe—an extraterrestrial traveler would likely have trouble even locating specimens of this species.

13. Cann, Stoneking, and Wilson, 1987; Wolpoff, 1988. There remain two general points of view on this issue: (1) *Homo erectus* migrated out of Africa about a million years ago, and regional differentiation occurred subsequently, and (2) *Homo sapiens* migrated out of Africa about a quarter of a million years ago. For the all-important question of racial distinctions, neither hypothesis offers much support to a biological interpretation of race. If hypothesis 1 is correct, there would had to have been continual mixing of genes among the three "races" in order for the observed genetic overlaps to have arisen. If hypothesis 2 is correct, even if the "races" became completely isolated from one another, 200,000 years is not very much time for evolution to have proceeded very far.

14. The following discussion of the structure and evolution of language comes mainly from Bickerton, 1990. Recently, Pinker (1994) has also provided an overview of language evolution. Pinker suggests that language might be older than previously thought, even suggesting that *Australopithecus* may have been endowed with this "organ" (p. 352).

15. A particularly good analysis of efforts to find chimp language can be found in Pinker (1994), pp. 334–42.

16. Pinker (1994), for example, jokes that ". . . Bickerton's argument . . . is reminiscent of hurricanes assembling jetliners." p. 366.

17. The literature on this topic is large and rapidly growing. Foucault's classics (1967, 1972, 1979) are dense and difficult. The introductions by Poster, 1984; Sheridan, 1980; or Philp, 1985 are excellent primers. Most recently, see the excellent analysis of Norris, 1993.

18. Galbraith, 1958.

19. Kuhn, 1970. See especially the addendum to the second edition.

20. Chomsky, 1989.

21. This section follows closely the arguments of Poster, 1984.

22. This notion is referred to as "reification," the tendency for humans to think of things that are really social constructions as if they were truly material things.

23. Dawkins, 1976.

24. This is discussed more fully in chapter 6. Also see Kitchner, 1987; and Sober, 1994.

CHAPTER FIVE

1. The quote is from the famous Lincoln–Douglas debates, as quoted by Gould, 1981.

2. *New York Times,* Aug. 15, 1994.

3. The original classic on the definition of human races, now largely discredited, is Coon, 1962. A modern treatment of the difficulties, much of which is repeated in this chapter, is Lewontin, 1982. Other useful references, all of the same mind on the issue, can be found in Marshall, 1969, and Harding, 1993.

4. The terminology is actually a bit anachronistic, even in plant breeding—most plant breeders would refer to "varieties" rather than races, but the basic idea is the same.

5. The word "miskins" here comes from the humorous writings of Molly Ivins, 1991.

6. This point has most recently been repeated in the best seller, *The Bell Curve,* by Herrnstein and Murray (1994).

7. Or a million years ago, depending on your interpretation of the anthropological and biochemical evidence, as discussed in chapter 3.

8. Fagen, 1977; Mulvaney, 1969.

9. Sokal, 1991.

10. This, in fact, was what Lewontin found in his classic study (Lewontin, 1972).

11. See chapter 2.

12. See chapter 1.

13. It is of interest to note that several of the best studies on racial differences in IQ are hardly ever cited—they report that blacks score *higher* than whites. In one study on IQ scores of English orphans, some of whom were from black parents, some from white parents, and some from "mixed" parents, blacks scored 105.7, "mixed" scored 109.8, and whites scored 101.3. This, of course, is no better evidence for a biological basis of racial differences than is the oft-cited performance of African Americans versus European Americans on IQ tests (Lewontin, 1982). It is, on the other hand, quite interesting that these data are rarely cited. In the recent popular book, *The Bell Curve,* only passing reference is made to these studies.

14. USA Today, 1991; Dyson, 1992. It is with understandable irritation that many black scholars have noted that the main proponent of the "black race is inherently better" theory, Dr. Leonard Jeffries of City College of New York

is routinely vilified by the press, and legally harrassed by his own school, while the more common, though equally absurd, theory that the "white race is inherently better" receives a dignified hearing—witness the cheerleading by the New York Times in its coverage of *The Bell Curve* in 1994 (Browne, 1994; DeParle, 1994).

15. Jensen, 1969.

16. Many subtle, yet horrible social consequences can result from this sort of deterministic ideology. A close friend of mine once told me that since he understood that females' roles were determined partly by their genes, he had learned to expect less of his daughters than of his son. Another acquaintance, a white man who had adopted an African baby, told me that he no longer puts the kind of pressure for academic performance on his African son as he did on his Anglo sons since he discovered the strong genetic basis for intelligence.

17. For all the reasons discussed above, this is a very unlikely occurrence. It is nevertheless conceivable.

18. Biologists have been debating the meaning of biological species for many years. Probably the classic statement of "reproductive isolation" as a determining factor is Mayr, 1963. The first serious criticism of this criterion was by Sokal and Crovello, 1970. The problems with the biological species concept have not been resolved despite many years of debate. How does one tell, for example, that a jaguar and a leopard are truly different species? Presently they live on different continents (South America vs. Africa) so are not able to interbreed simply because they never encounter one another. Would they interbreed if brought into contact with one another? But would bringing them into contact with one another violate the "under normal circumstances" criterion? It is still a murky concept in its philosophical particulars, yet for most practical applications it is really quite obvious when two species are distinct.

19. It is of interest to the present text since the biological notion of subspecies is virtually identical to the notion of race characterized by "deep" biological differences. Indeed, biologists used to think of subspecies as precursors to species, the latter being defined by reproductive isolation and characterized by the so-called genetic revolution. That is, once isolated and "speciated," the two populations would become very different from one another genetically. It is not too much of an extrapolation to suggest that "subspecies," as precursors to species, might also be represented by these very large genetic differences. Today, we know that the formation of species does not involve a genetic revolution in the first place, largely rendering moot the question as to whether subspecies also represent such a revolution. See any textbook on evolution, for example, Futuyma, 1979.

20. Refer to Figure 5.1. In the first case, it was simple to define two subspecies, northern and southern. In the second case, it was not possible to define two subspecies, since their characters were not concordant. If we had forced a northern and southern subspecies definition anyway, clearly for all of the char-

acters the within-group (subspecies) diversity will be much larger than the between-groups diversity (i.e., the diversity of snout length is higher within each of the defined species than between them, and likewise for tail length).

21. While the basic idea of this comparison is quite simple, the details are not. The statistical technique is known as the analysis of variance, and allows one to guess the likelihood that a particular difference might happen simply by accident.

22. Indeed, the notion that there is some rule of thumb will cause my statistician friends to groan. One cannot formally make such a rule, since it all depends on the sample size of the populations being compared. If the percentage between groups is only 10 percent (say), that could easily be statistically significant if the sizes of the samples of the populations are very large, while if the percentage is 80 percent that might simply be due to chance if the samples of the populations are very small.

23. As discussed in detail in chapter 2.

24. Lewontin, 1972.

25. Note how these classifications, based principally on language and appearance, correspond reasonably with the known migratory patterns. The Africans migrated into Europe and Asia, making the (1) "African race," (2) Caucasoid (Indo-European) race, and (3) Mongoloid (Asian) race. In turn, the Asians migrated to south Asia and north Asia (giving rise to the Mongoloid and south Asian races), and the northern part of the population migrated to the Americas to form the Amerinds. Other migrations of both Mongoloid and south Asian races presumably formed the Oceanian race.

CHAPTER SIX

1. Kühl, 1994.

2. Id., p. 7.

3. Jensen, 1969.

4. Herrnstein, 1973, p. 221.

5. Wilson, 1978, cited in Fausto-Sterling, 1985.

6. Wright, 1994, pp. 347–348. Wright also seems to have scooped my intent to satirize the sociobiologists by suggesting that post-modernism itself is a consequence of evolutionary biology:

> . . . if Freud stressed people's difficulty in seeing the truth about themselves, the new Darwinians stress the difficulty of seeing truth, period. Indeed, Darwinism comes close to calling into question the very meaning of the world *truth*. For the social discourses that supposedly lead to truth—moral discourse, political discourse, even, sometimes, academic discourse—are, by Darwinian lights, raw power struggles. A winner will emerge, but there's often no reason to expect that winner to be truth. A cynicism deeper than

Freudian cynicism may have once seemed hard to imagine, but here it is." (p. 325)

Once again, I am overwhelmed by the ability of the sociobiology paradigm to "explain everything."

7. Itzkoff, 1994, pp. 108–109.

8. Rushton, 1995, pp. xii–xiv.

9. Robertson, 1981, pp. 226–227.

10. E.g., one could always say, "Did you used to cheat on your boyfriend, and if so, are you still doing it?"

11. Here I do not speak of legitimate witches among modern women, but rather to the conceptualization of sixteenth-century New England.

12. The lac operon is now a standard example in many elementary biology courses, and its description can be found in many standard biology texts. See for example Purves et al., 1992. The significance of *Acetabularium* development has recently been brilliantly expounded by Goodwin, 1994.

13. Many base triplets code for the same amino acid anyway, and many changes in amino acid sequence in the protein will not affect the protein function. See chapter 3.

14. It is probably good to repeat what has been implied several times already in this text. In a deep philosophical sense, all human behavior is ultimately genetic, since without heredity we simply would not exist. So the fact that genes probably stipulate, in some complicated and totally unknown fashion, the developmental sequence in which language is acquired by children, implies that in an ultimate sense all social forces must also be so determined—if language determines social forces, and language is determined by genes, social forces are thus ultimately genetic. This form of the argument is obviously trivial and will not be pursued further.

15. From Freud's classical essay, "The Psychical Apparatus and the Theory of Instincts," reprinted in Lemert, 1993, p. 138.

16. Bouchard et al., 1990, p. 227.

17. Kamin, 1974.

18. See the introductory comments to chapter 14.

19. This particular elementary transformation is discussed in fascinating detail, and extended to what may very well be a new way of looking at biology altogether, by Goodwin, 1994.

20. Lewontin, 1977a, 1977b, 1991; Kitcher, 1987; Howe and Lyne, 1992.

21. The theory of evolution through natural selection was explained in chapter 3. It might appear remarkable that anyone could ever have doubted a theory that seems so self-evident. But the reader must recall the times in which the theory was first introduced. So little was known of genetics, and the dominant paradigm in genetics was even quite wrong, to the point that Darwin actually had

to have been wrong, in that climate. It turns out that what was thought to be true of genetics was incorrect, and it is only our modern understanding of a great many more details that makes the theory so self-evident.

22. Goodwin (1994) makes this point in a very explicit fashion (see pp. 30, 31).

23. The current (1995) resurgence of attacks from the religious right in the United States is just such an example.

24. There are a wide array of selective patterns that have been demonstrated, and many more that have been theoretically articulated. In the context of individual behavior three forms of selection are usually cited: individual selection, kin selection, and reciprocal altruism, although the last form remains controversial. Individual selection simply means that an individual organism will behave in ways that will maximize its probability of survival and reproduction. Kin selection means that an individual organism will behave in ways that will maximize the probability of its closest kin to survive and reproduce. Reciprocal altruism means that an individual will behave altruistically toward another individual (sacrifice a certain percentage of its own survival and reproductive probabilities) at one point in time, if the probability of the other individual returning that altruistic action in the future is sufficiently high.

25. This refers to a comment made in the preface.

26. Refer to chapter 4 for a fuller discussion.

27. A summary of the characteristics that have been strongly suspected of having a genetic basis in recent history (schizophrenia, criminality, IQ, and homosexuality, among others) was presented in a brief article in *Scientific American* in 1993. The general conclusion was that most announcements that the gene for this or that behavior had been found were later judged to be erroneous, and that thus far the holy grail of genes for human behavior remains elusive.

28. The noted biologist T. H. Huxley, Darwin's principal defender against attacks from the church, stated the principle quite clearly in 1894: ". . . progressive modification of civilization which passes by the name of the 'evolution of society,' is, in fact, a process of an essentially different character, . . . from that which brings about the evolution of speces, in the state of nature . . ." Huxley, 1894, p. 37. More recently, Sober (1994) has provided an exhaustive treatment of the inapplicability of Darwinian natural selection to human cultural characteristics.

CHAPTER SEVEN

1. In the United States, women are notoriously underrepresented in science and math. Other countries are different. For example, in Puerto Rico, 57 percent of math majors are women and 62 percent of natural science majors are women (*San Juan Star,* May 31, 1993).

2. Money and Ehrhart, 1972.

3. Id., p. 119.

4. Id., p. 122.

5. People frequently have difficulty understanding the gender "ambivalent." As explained in the rest of this chapter, it is usual, but not inevitable, that one identifies with the socially defined role of male or female. One should also realize that it is not even clear that there are really only two sexes.

6. Actually, there are two types of organisms on the earth, those that have a nucleus in the cells, called eukaryotes, and those that have no nucleus, called prokaryotes, as discussed in chapter 3.

7. See chapter 2.

8. The biological summary of gender development is taken principally from Money and Ehrhart, 1972.

9. Lewontin, 1982, p. 5.

10. Money and Ehrhart, 1972, p. 119.

11. Fausto-Sterling, 1993. In addition to male and female, she defines three other types, hermaphrodites that have external genitalia more female-like, which she calls femes, those that have external genitalia more male-like, which she calls memes, and those that have external genitalia truly intermediate, which she calls hemes. She notes that it is strictly a social phenomenon that we decided to force all five of these types into just two categories. Her ideas may seem radical, but from a biological point of view there is really nothing at all unusual about her proposal. It is not uncommon for other animals to have more than two sexes. For example, the single-celled *Paramecium* has as many as seven distinct sexes, with various rules as to who can mate with whom.

12. Tavris, 1992.

13. The bulk of this section comes mainly from Greenberg, 1988.

14. Greenberg, 1988, p. 111.

15. For example, two studies (Levay and Hammer, 1994) were subjects of reports in the *New York Times* in 1992. They were both subjected to a devastating critique by William Byne (1994). Byne's critique was ignored by the popular media. Also see Rist, 1992.

Chapter Eight

1. Eaton, 1973.

2. McNaughton, 1976; McNaughton and Wolf, 1979, pp. 549–554.

3. Formally, these types are known as endothermic and exothermic reactions. Endothermic reactions store energy in chemical bonds and exothermic reactions release energy from chemical bonds.

4. That is, it is easier for me to write "C-H-O" than "the huge collection of atoms of carbon, hydrogen, and oxygen connected by chemical bonds that contain the energy that will be later used in life's processes."

5. Molecular oxygen simply means oxygen connected with itself as opposed to either unconnected or connected with other elements, and is the main form in which oxygen occurs in the air.

6. These organs in most plants are called chloroplasts, and they contain the chemical chlorophyll, which has a green color and is responsible for the green coloration of all photosynthetic plant tissue.

7. This shock has to do with the problem of global warming and the reduction of the ozone layer, fully discussed later in this chapter and in chapter 8.

8. This is treated in somewhat more detail in chapter 8.

9. Tucker and Richard, 1983.

Chapter Nine

1. See chapter 4.

2. Much like that advocated by Harris, 1979.

3. As already outlined in chapter 3.

4. This term, as well as "simple commodity production and exchange" and "production for exchange value," are terms commonly associated with the economic writings of Karl Marx (see, e.g., Marx, 1867). In fact they go back at least as far as Ricardo before him, and, at least in conceptualization, even further back.

5. Seeing some things as unquestionably natural is part of the prevailing discourse; the process whereby something that is socially constructed becomes transformed into something that we think is natural is called reification (Eagleton, 1991).

6. The "other form of production," of course was feudalism, and Shylock's avariciousness was justly punished, even though his activities then were substantially less harmful to the general population than are those of many respected financial institutions today (see, for example, Stewart, 1991; Burrough and Helyar, 1990; Day, 1993; O'Shea, 1991).

7. This is actually quite a difficult and value-laden term to try to define. Some people have a knee-jerk reaction that all capitalists are similar to the criminals responsible for the S&L crisis, filled with avariciousness and greed. For these people, the very word capitalism signifies something evil. To others, the word signifies a system that efficiently distributes goods and services, based on certain principles that most regard as good, such as freedom and democracy. For these people, the capitalist system won the Cold War because it was a better system than socialism or Communism, and judging someone to be a "good capitalist," in fact, is meant to be a compliment. In this text, I try to eschew either of these usages and simply refer to the world political-economic system that began in late feudal Europe, characterized by those who control the bulk of economic and political activities being those who own the means of production, operating under the underlying philosophy of M-P-M. It is also the

world system, in that from my point of view, it does not make much sense to talk of the U.S. capitalist system versus the British capitalist system, since the entire economic system is globally interconnected (as so eloquently described by current Labor Secretary Reich, (1991)). My usage thus corresponds broadly with Wallerstein, 1980.

8. Here, I avoid calling the owners capitalists, since from an environmental/ecological point of view, it matters little whether the owners are capitalists or the state, if both are trying to maximize profit from the factory.

9. It is a somewhat different problem when the production facility is cooperatively owned by those who work in it. Here, the workers and owners are the same, and the classic confrontation between labor and management theoretically cannot occur. Yet if production facilities are in competition with one another, reducing the cost of production has to be a goal of the owner, whether he or she is a worker or not in that same production facility. This problem is most interesting in some areas where cooperative production is common, most notably in the Basque area of Mondregon, where almost all economic activity is based on economic cooperation. (Milbrath, 1983; Oakehott, 1978). In general it is not a common phenomenon in today's world.

10. Wallerstein, 1980; Chomsky, 1993; deJanvry, 1983; Galbraith, 1994; also see discussion below.

11. In many indigenous production systems, however, an ethic seems to have evolved in which one does not interfere with the production processes of others.

12. See, for example, Martinez-Alier, 1987; Sahlins, 1975.

13. While this idea is not always covered in elementary economics courses, it is certainly a universal among economic systems, pre-capitalist, capitalist, and post-capitalist systems. It is a force that happens, and is routinely accepted by the general population as something not out of the ordinary (which is what is meant by a "social contract"—it is part of the general discourse).

14. Herber, 1965.

15. Everest, 1986.

16. This is currently a focus of intense debate. In recent years, legal and political maneuvering have, in fact, caused producers to pay for part of these costs.

17. Thrupp, 1990.

18. After a destructive process such as logging, the formerly forested area begins the process of recuperation (see chapter 10). If the area is left alone long enough, it will eventually be harvestable again. But "leaving it alone" implies certain opportunity costs, which are hidden costs of the wood that are not paid for by the lumberer, usually (Westoby, 1989; Poore, 1989).

19. Hardin, 1968; for a critique see Murdoch and Oaten, 1975. Curiously, some of Hardin's other writings clearly recognize "externalities" rather than "commons," e.g., Hardin, 1969.

20. One of the better introductions to this field is Clark, 1976.

21. See Eagleton, 1991.

22. To Native Americans, suggesting that individuals can "own" land is much like suggesting that one can own pieces of the air.

23. Murdoch and Oaten, 1975.

24. In a detailed analysis of many true "commons" situations involving land and a variety of other resources, Ostrom (1990) demonstrates that it is the rule more than the exception that local communities develop mechanisms to ensure responsible behavior for common goods.

25. In its original formulation, Hardin 1968 asserted that privatization was the only solution.

26. The normal course of ecological succession will "renew" the pasture automatically, albeit only after some time passes, as discussed in chapter 10.

27. (1) If we develop a social contract to preserve the commons, we run the risk of all that is implied about "regulation," especially if the commons has been routinely treated as an externality before. Those regions that are responsible and develop a sound social contract will be at a competitive disadvantage to those regions who do not develop the social contract. In our modern context, this means that if the social contract does not cover all commons that enter the competitive sphere, they are likely to drive responsible parties out of the production system in question. (2) To privatize the commons could be even worse, in that the competitive edge may be felt sooner. (3) Eliminating the system that requires externalization in the first place would obviously work, but with what would it be replaced?

28. This point is discussed fully by Chomsky, 1993, chapter 11.

29. See chapter 12.

30. Quoted in deJanvry, 1981, p. 10.

31. The analysis of the Berkeley economist Alain deJanvry, specifically applicable to Latin America, but perhaps having some bearing on Africa and parts of Asia as well (deJanvry, 1983).

32. For the sake of heuristics in this abbreviated explanation, I use the word crisis in a very broad sense. In his original analysis, deJanvry noted that the center economy was constantly facing "barriers" to accumulation. Rather than explain the notion of accumulation in the theory of capitalist development and then discuss the various barriers that all capitalists must face, I chose to simply cast the system as one that creates crises, sometimes large sometimes small. Broadly speaking my use of crisis can be thought of as equivalent to barriers, i.e. one faces a crisis when encountering a barrier to accumulation.

33. Interviewed in the film *Controlling Interest*.

34. Obviously, today we do not usually think of owners in the same vein, since most modern production facilities are public and the owners are really the stockholders, who mandate that the managers make the economic decisions

to maximize their profits. In many ways, then, the managers of the modern corporation make the same sorts of decisions as the "owners" of the factories made during the early years of industrialization, while the concerns of the stockholders are the same as the concerns investors have always had—maximize return on investment. For heuristic purposes, to see the bare bones of First World-Third World connections, it still makes sense to think of the "owners," even though such a characterization is not precise for a modern industrial system.

CHAPTER TEN

1. See chapter 4.
2. See chapter 9.
3. The normal biological processes that keep our bodies warm operate by burning the food we eat. Most of that food went to obtaining the energy we burn over a period of less than a year (the agricultural cycle). In burning a piece of wood, we may be utilizing 100 years' worth of biological energy storage during the same time period we used the equivalent of one year's storage by eating and digesting a tortilla (the one year that it took to produce the corn that went into making the tortilla).
4. See chapter 13.
5. Albion, 1926; Maczak and Parker, 1978; Tucker and Richard, 1983.
6. This is actually a debatable point, but for purposes of this chapter, that debate matters rather little. In comparison with the energy use subsequent to this period, the use for cooking and heating was extremely low and much closer to sustainable than what followed.
7. See chapter 9.
8. Bernal, 1965.
9. Herber, 1965.
10. Palmer and Colton, 1950.
11. Bernal, 1965.
12. See chapter 9.
13. The historical narrative on oil comes mainly from Bernal, 1965, and Yergin, 1991.
14. Native Americans had used rock oil for caulking their canoes, and it was well known as a popular remedy for all sorts of ailments.
15. As presented in any elementary economics textbook, prices are set by a balance between supply and demand. A very large number of forces determine the exact nature of the supply and demand, and that very large number of forces is mostly determined by human social constructions. Managing both supply and demand simply means trying to influence the social constructions that affect the particular levels of demand and supply. For example, advertising is

generally a demand management technique. Supply management is accomplished by, for example, hoarding surpluses, holding back on production, or forming cartels to reduce production. While some elementary economics texts do not emphasize this issue, and, indeed, sometimes even eschew its discussion since it represents a deviation from free-market assumptions, I know of no actual businessman or woman who does not actively engage in some sort of supply or demand management.

16. Yergin, 1991, p. 31.
17. Ford's most important contribution was obviously not the automobile, since he wasn't its inventor in the first place. In 1885, Karl Benz built the first prototype of the automobile, and in 1903 Henry Ford founded the Ford Motor Company.
18. The Taxi Brigade happened in 1914. The French government had already evacuated Paris, leaving only a small military contingent to defend it. It seemed that the capital would fall rapidly. But the French commander felt that an attack on the German lines would stop their advance. On September 6, he launched a series of attacks with much success, only to convince the Germans that they had to call in reinforcements. French soldiers in Paris could have overwhelmed the German forces that were actually there, but only if they attacked before the reinforcements came. But the soldiers were in Paris and the front was a considerable distance away. If the troops marched, they would never get there in time, and the French railroad system had already been completely destroyed by the Germans. So the French commander ordered the three thousand available taxicabs to report for duty. The brigade of taxis transported the French soldiers to the front and began their attack on September 8. On September 9, the Germans began their retreat.
19. The purpose of the suit was to eliminate the cartel and all the negative effects its existence implied. The initial consequences were clearly as intended, but what happened subsequently was arguably not so healthy, as the independent companies formed from Standard's breakup began to cooperate with one another and with the large international companies.
20. As elaborated fully in chapter 9, the Third World's role was to be one of "paying the costs of externalities" in a broad sense. The Third World would have to remain suppliers of cheap raw materials and labor, and the occasional market, to maintain investment opportunities for First World corporations, especially in times of economic downturns in the First World. Third World nationalists, like Cardenas in Mexico and Mossadegh in Iran, and later Arbenz in Guatemala, Ho Chi Minh in Vietnam, and the Sandinistas in Nicaragua, represented a threat to that arrangement. See Chomsky, 1992, for more historical details, and deJanvry, 1983, for a particularly lucid explanation of the phenomenon in the specific case of Latin America.
21. The history of agricultural development in the First World is treated in depth in chapter 13.

22. For example, in manufacturing birchbark canoes, woodland Indians cut down birch trees. The waste product was the core of the trunk that was left after the bark was stripped. The core of the trunk decayed at a rate that was certainly much faster than the rate at which cores were produced in the manufacture of canoes—for example, a single canoe may have lasted five to ten years, while the core left after its manufacture would have completely decayed in one or two years. Or, simply in the course of household activities, early farmers normally threw kitchen scraps onto the ground, where animals would eat them, or bacteria and fungi would decompose them. The rate of decomposition of the kitchen scraps was larger than the rate of discarding them. Consequently, the world did not see a continual buildup of mountains of birch cores or kitchen scraps.

23. The Bhopal disaster has become something of a paradigm for this problem, but certainly is not the only example.

24. The problem of global warming is actually still quite controversial. Useful references are Bridgman, 1990 and Beckerman, 1992. The general consensus seems to be that yes, if global emissions of greenhouse gasses continue, the world will become warmer, with a host of negative effects. But considerable debate exists about the need to curtail emissions now, and how rapidly the warming will occur.

25. As discussed in chapter 8, before there was an ozone layer the ultraviolet radiation from the sun did not permit the evolution of terrestrial life. Only after the evolution of photosynthesis did marine organisms begin pumping oxygen into the atmosphere, thus permitting the formation of an upper ozone layer to intercept the ultraviolet radiation, permitting terrestrial life to evolve.

26. Recently, farm animals in Chile have been developing cataracts, something some scientists feel could be a result of UV damage. Since Chile is the nearest populated area near to where the southern ozone hole forms, speculation has been that these cataracts are warnings of might come in the future. This could be the first warning sign of problems associated with ozone destruction.

27. There are now only six sisters, since Chevron purchased Gulf in 1983. Furthermore, one must make mention of some of the important independent companies, such as Occidental. Space does not permit a full treatment of this company, but, headed by the far-thinking Armand Hammer, Occidental reached a size in which it actually could challenge some of the market control of the seven sisters. Furthermore, Occidental reached a creative agreement with Libya in which petroleum could be produced in a cooperative manner. See Yergin, 1991, for further details.

28. Maull and Pick, 1989.

29. After all, Iraq argued, admittedly with some credibility, these countries were set up by the Europeans as an outgrowth of the fall of the Ottoman Empire anyway, so their boundaries are arbitrary. Today's Kuwait was actually admin-

istered by the same British entity that administered today's Iraq, so even by the Europeans' rules, Kuwait was part of Iraq.

30. For example, the success of conventional U.S. weaponry was on the order of 30 percent, a figure not available to the press during the war, while the success of the "smart" bombs was regularly and triumphantly reported in the press to be close to 100 percent, and even that, we now know, was wildly exaggerated as part of wartime propaganda.

CHAPTER ELEVEN

1. Recall those basic categories from chapter 8.
2. The material in this section can be found in most standard ecology textbooks, e.g., Krebs, 1985.
3. This section is based on the original work of Noy-Meir (1975), who developed it in the context of large African grazers.
4. Wright, 1992; Jennings, 1975.
5. Gilpin, 1979; Hastings and Powell, 1991; Vandermeer, 1993.
6. The hard scientific evidence on this point, however, is hardly overwhelming.
7. Lotka, 1925: Volterra, 1926.
8. Gause, 1935.
9. Boucher, 1985.
10. Risch and Boucher, 1976.
11. The technical details on this point are found in Vandermeer and Boucher, 1978.
12. This topic is discussed further in chapter 13.
13. In fact, lions tend to eat larger herbivores, such as antelope, zebras, and giraffes, while cheetahs eat smaller ones like gazelles. They still potentially compete with one another, since a lion will eat a gazelle if it can catch it while a cheetah will occasionally bring down a young antelope, even though it is not strong enough to deal with an adult.
14. Connell, 1978; Huston, 1979; Hubbell and Foster, 1986.
15. Yih et al., 1991; Connell, 1978.

CHAPTER TWELVE

1. Haller and Balarin, 1982; Wood, 1987.
2. Griffiths and Driscoll, 1982; Rice and Vandermeer, 1990.
3. Which is another way of saying the somewhat more technical, "a low-pressure area is thus created at the base of the Himalayan mountains."
4. Drurey and Nisbet, 1973; Connell and Slayter, 1977.
5. Recall the discussion of competition in chapter 2.

6. Some would argue that all the oak-hickory forest will eventually be replaced by beech-maple forest, since the oak-hickory forest itself slowly modifies the soil and makes it more water-retentive, but such details are debatable.

7. Ehrenfield, 1980; Denslow, 1987.

8. Dunn et al., 1983; Yih et al., 1991.

9. Vandermeer, et al., 1990; Yih et al., 1991; Vandermeer and Perfecto, 1991.

10. Mooney and Gordon, 1983.

11. Including savannahs, woodlands, steppes, and other similar formations.

12. For example, not just grassland but short grass prairie, long grass prairie, acacia woodland, asian steppe, and a great variety of other subcategories of grassland. Or not just temperate forest but eastern deciduous forest, northern boreal forest, taiga, southern mixed deciduous forest, pine forest, and a great variety of other subcategories of temperate forest.

Chapter Thirteen

1. The background for this material was covered in chapter 11.

2. See point 1 in Figure 13.1. For all points to the left, the rate of harvest is lower than the rate of resource increase and therefore the resource population increases, while for all points to the right of point 1 the reverse is true.

3. Martin, 1973; Janzen and Martin, 1982.

4. Flannery, 1973; Minc and Vandermeer, 1990.

5. Harris, 1977; Minc and Vandermeer, id.

6. Minc and Vandermeer, id.

7. See chapter 12.

8. This is not a very well established fact, but most ecologists think it is at least approximately true. See Nadelhoffer, 1983.

9. Boserup, 1965, 1990.

10. Minc and Vandermeer, 1990.

11. Recall from above, when *Homo sapiens* arrived in America some 12,000 years ago, it apparently hunted the large herbivorous mammals to extinction. Thus, the large ungulates that used to roam the savannahs of America were not available to be domesticated as draft animals, a not exactly trivial example of how driving things to extinction can limit one's options for the future.

12. Sugar production required the slave system. Since the former was partly the basis of European expansion into the new world, slavery itself was also a necessary basis.

13. See chapter 9.

14. Schob, 1975.

15. For example, tomato farmers in the midwestern United States refused to adopt the mechanical harvesting of tomatoes despite a relentless campaign

waged by various state extension services and propaganda provided by universities such as Ohio State, Purdue, and Michigan State. Rosset and Vandermeer, 1986a; Vandermeer, 1982, 1986.

16. Of course, its effect on the world in general were enormous, as described in chapter 10.

17. Russell, 1993.

18. Morgan, 1979.

19. Morgan, 1979, p. 29.

20. Palmer and Colton 1950, pp. 314–318.

21. These soils correspond to the three extensive areas of temperate zone grassland in the world. In is not an accident that this is also where the richest soils in the world are found. The thousands of years of annual burning that maintained these grassland areas had resulted in the incorporation of a large amount of stable nutrient material into the soils. These are some of the only soils in the world in which the depletion of nutrients because of agriculture is not really a problem.

22. *Biocide* is a collective term for insecticides, fungicides, nematocides, and other chemicals designed to kill particular life forms.

23. Carson, 1962. It should be noted that Carson's brilliance was in bringing all of this information to the attention of the public. It all had been previously published, but usually in obscure scientific publications not generally available.

24. For example ". . . the statement on page 17 that arsenic in chimney soot is the cause of cancer; many, though not all, scientists believe it is the tars in soot that are the chief carcinogens." Graham, 1970, p. 67. It is, of course, well established that arsenic is a potent carcinogen. The point was that even though arsenic is found in chimney soot, and chimney soot is known to cause cancer, one cannot conclude that it is the arsenic that is the cause.

25. Graham, 1970.

26. Much of the following is based on material presented in chapter 11.

27. As presented in chapter 11, a population interaction of this sort results in an indirect positive effect by combining two negative effects, similar to the effect of ants on the *Cecropia* trees. The basic idea is really quite obvious—an enemy of my enemy is my friend.

28. Bollworms are actually moth larvae and are continually appearing in the cotton bolls because adult moths continually fly into the cotton fields and lay eggs. Thus the group of worms killed today will be replaced by new worms next week. When the wasps are around they kill some fraction of the bollworms, thus maintaining this pest at a relatively low level. By killing both bollworms and wasps with pesticides, the technicians eliminated the effects of the pest initially. But when the adults of the bollworm flew in and laid their eggs during the next week, there were no wasps around to kill them. Thus, there was a resurgence.

29. Russell, 1993.

30. Refer to chapter 3 for the elementary operation of evolution through natural selection.

31. Chapter 3.

32. Each mating includes a male and a female. The male may be AA or Aa and the female may be AA or Aa. Thus the possible matings include AA male with AA female, AA male with Aa female, Aa male with AA female, and Aa male with Aa female. The AA × AA matings produce all AA genotypes. The Aa × Aa matings produce 25 percent AA, 50 percent Aa, and 25 percent aa. The AA × Aa matings produce 50 percent AA and 50 percent Aa. Assuming perfectly random matings, 25 percent of all matings will be AA × AA, 25 percent will be Aa × Aa, and 50 percent will be AA × Aa. Put it all together, and you get 56 percent AA (from all the offspring of the 25 percent AA × AA matings, plus 50 percent of the offspring of the 50 percent AA × Aa matings, plus 25 percent of the offspring of the 25 percent Aa × Aa matings = $1.00 \times .25 + 50 \times 50 + .25 \times .25 = .25 + .25 + .06 = .56$).

33. Van den Bosch, 1978, p. 24.

34. Russell, 1993.

35. This is still a rapidly evolving discipline, known as integrated pest management (IPM). It involves two components: First, agricultural fields are scouted for the presence of the pests of concern, and pesticides are applied only when the pests reach a predetermined density that the farmer knows will cause damage. Second, various techniques, such as interplanting other plants to attract predators, are used to reduce the natural population densities of the pests as much as possible (Vandermeer and Andow, 1986).

CHAPTER FOURTEEN

1. Garcia Barrios and Garcia Barrios, 1988.

2. The Penan are an indigenous group of people that live on the island of Borneo. They have become something of a symbol for the rain forest preservation movement because the Malasian government's forestry program was cutting the tropical rain forest in which they made their home.

3. CIES, 1985.

4. Buttel and Raynolds, 1989.

5. Buttel and Raynolds conceive of production as simply food production, but their analysis is really more general.

6. The classic book on this position is Simon, 1981. Also see Simon and Kahn, 1984.

7. See, for example, Plucknett and Smith, 1982.

8. Lappe and Schurman, 1988; Murdoc, 1980; de Janvry, 1983; Commoner, 1992; Boserup, 1990; Mass, 1976.

9. Ehrlich, 1968; Ehrlich and Ehrlich, 1990; Brown, 1992; Vitouseck et al., 1986; Homer-Dixon, 1993.

10. Many studies have examined the issue of population and natural resources at the level of particular countries, usually supporting the non-Malthusian position to one degree or another. For example, El Salvador, Durham, 1979; Kenya, Kitching, 1980; India, Mamdani, 1972. Many other examples can be cited.

11. Since the most enthusiastic Malthusians have tied almost everything to population density at one time or another, several studies have examined the issue from the point of view of particular problems. For example, relative to soil degradation, Blakie and Broomfield, 1987; relative to health and social disorganization, Chadwick, 1972.

12. This point was fully developed in chapter 9.

13. Galbraith, 1994, p. 233.

14. See chapters 4 and 9.

15. The theoretical background for this exercise was presented in chapter 11.

16. Diez, 1986.

17. Birdsey and Weaver, 1982.

18. As explained in chapter 11.

19. The best statement of the general principle is still Boserup, 1965.

20. The two islands in this example are Madagascar, with 12 million people on 58 million hectares, and Japan with 120 million people on 38 million hectares. Infant mortality in Madagascar is 110 per 1,000 live births, while it is 5 per 1,000 live births in Japan (figures projected for 1990–1995). Life expectancy in Madagascar is 56 years, compared to 79 years in Japan. People in Madagascar consume 51 grams of protein per day. The figure is almost twice as high in Japan. (All data from Brown, 1992.)

21. Hecht and Cockburn, 1992.

22. La Operación, produced by CINGLD, 1982.

23. Diez, op cit.

24. Indeed, the outmigration certainly had a far greater effect on the island's population size than the sterilization program had.

25. Hardin, 1971; recently, Hardin (1993) has repeated this same basic argument.

26. This point is driven home eloquently by Kaplan in his famous *Atlantic Monthly* article (1994).

27. Volpe, 1993, p. 460.

28. The history of U.S. intervention in the Third World is long. An excellent recent summary, including most of the examples mentioned here, is Chomsky's *Year 501: The Conquest Continues* (1993).

29. Lappé and Collins, 1977, p. 36.

30. This quick summary of soils is relatively standard fare. For a similar but slightly more technical introduction see Vandermeer and Perfecto, 1995a. For a yet more technical introduction see Richter and Babbar, 1991.

31. CUSUCA, 1977, pp. 11–21.

32. Williams, 1986.

33. Von Braun et al., 1989.

34. This concept was fully presented in chapter 11. Van den Bosch, 1978; Pedigo, 1989.

35. An exception to this pattern was the highly successful program of integrated pest management for insects in the United Fruit Company plantations near Golfito, Costa Rica (Stevens, 1984).

36. Van den Bosch, op cit.

37. Rosset, personal communication. The pesticide treadmill was clearly operative in Nicaraguan cotton production, beginning with the introduction of this crop in the 1950s. It is speculation to suggest that the whitefly is also a consequence of this pesticide treadmill, but the circumstantial evidence is considerable. Furthermore, it is also speculation that the whitefly that now decimates the tomato fields of the interior of the country are a result of those that were produced by the pesticide treadmill in cotton. Thus, the entire story is based on weak hard evidence, but supported by a large body of circumstantial evidence.

38. Barry, 1987; Williams, op cit.

39. Chomsky, op cit.; de Janvry, op cit.; Grindle, 1986.

40. Melville and Melville, 1971; Fried et al., 1980.

41. For a particularly lucid account of this period see Melville and Melville, id.

42. "Controlling Interest: The World of the Multinational Corporation," producer California Newsreel. See chapter 7 for full context.

43. Rabe, 1988.

44. The first significant documentation of the facts of this episode was published by NACLA (North American Committee on Latin America, 1974). Later, based on Freedom of Information suits, Immerman (1982) provided a much more complete picture.

45. Gettleman et al., 1981.

46. Durham's exhaustive study of this issue (1979) suggests quite a different interpretation, and is the basis for most of this section.

47. The so-called matanza of 1930 is the most vivid reminder. An estimated 30,000 peasants were murdered by the El Salvadoran military—U.S. gunboats were floating just offshore, ready to come to the aid of the military in case that was necessary (see Gettleman et al., 1981).

48. Harvey, 1971.

CHAPTER FIFTEEN

1. In this chapter I follow the style of Evernden (1992) and use the capitalized Nature when refering to the idealized structure of the natural world (e.g., the worship of Nature) and the uncapitalized nature in its more colloquial use (e.g. it is in the lion's nature to be fierce).

2. This is, the reader will recall, the third component of the essentialist argument, as presented in chapter 2.

3. See chapter 2.

4. Rocha, 1905.

5. Meyers, 1985, p. 22.

6. The parallel between this focus and postmodern literary criticism is not accidental. Much of the inspiration for this analysis comes from Eagleton's masterful *Literary Theory* (1983).

7. Aspen trees are the dominant trees in the early stages of succession after the climax forest has been cleared in these areas—see chapter 12.

8. Palmer (1992) has recently written eloquently on this issue, casting the problem perceptively in the context of diversity, with humans and their creations another form of diversity, equally deserving of preservation. As he notes, "the more convinced we are that our species is a plague, the more we are obliged to yearn for disasters."

9. There is a great deal of historical literature on the development of ideas of wilderness, especially in the context of the North American wilderness, much of which is similar to the analysis presented here. For example, Turner's (1983) treatise on how European settlement transformed the conceptual framework in which the environment is viewed from the native peoples to the dominant form of European nature domination, carries with it an implicit assumption that nature itself is a socially defined characteristic. Duerr's (1985) massive compilation of cross-cultural myths concerning wilderness, demonstrates how many cultures, by constructing barriers between themselves and the wilderness, in fact socially constructed "nature" in the same way as I suggest here. Ponting's (1991) exploration of Judeo-Christian thought (chapter 8) also suggests a strong social constructionist view of the natural world. See especially Evernden's (1992) bibliographic essay (pp. 167–174).

10. Sanchez de Carmona, *Man in the Biosphere Program,* pp. 107–108, as cited in Redclift, 1987. As discussed in Chapter 16.

11. Recall that the early migrants to the New World, arriving only about 12,000 years ago, apparently caused the massive extinctions of the large mammalian fauna through overhunting.

12. Bonner, 1993.

13. Several African countries (e.g., Zimbabwe and South Africa) had been funding many of their conservation programs through the sale of ivory. Since elephants frequently overpopulate areas, they must be culled anyway. Using the ivory sales to fund conservation efforts was thus seen as a logical way to make use of elephants that had to be killed anyway. International conservation organizations found it far more difficult to raise funds with a slogan such as "buy ivory and support local development," but received record contributions when they developed the slogan "ban the bloody ivory trade." By promoting a ban on international trade in ivory, they consequently cut off the very funds that were being used in local conservation efforts.

14. Bullard, 1990.

CHAPTER SIXTEEN

1. Of course, the various cues used to classify people as African American may have a genetic basis, but the notion that there are deep biological differences between European and African Americans is simply not tenable scientifically. See chapter 5.

2. It was a careful biological analysis that revealed the operation of the pesticide treadmill, for example (see chapter 13). The utilization of hybrid corn, one of the centerpieces of modern technified agriculture, turns out to be an unnecessary and wasteful technology (Lewontin and Berlan, 1990), something we now understand due to a careful biological analysis (i.e. a deconstruction of the myths that surround hybrid corn). Many other examples could be cited.

3. It is sometimes stated, as acerbic political humor, that the U.S. system really has only a Tory party with two wings—the republican wing and the democratic wing. The election of Bill Clinton and his subsequent performance might be cited by a cynic as further support for this interpretation.

4. Many authors refer to the "industrial capitalist" system. In conjunction with previous chapters (especially chapters 9, 10, and 13), the points of view represented here are relevant to the world system as it exists today. Some might call that industrial capitalism, but I prefer to refer to it simply as the industrial system. The former (and present) socialist systems had similar attitudes as the capitalist systems and, from a world system point of view, the former socialist bloc of eastern Europe and the Soviet Union were simply a slight deviation from the basic rules of the game. All of the analyses of this book thus refer equally to the command economies of eastern Europe and the "capitalist" economies of France and Britain.

References

Albion, R. G. 1926. *Forests and Sea Power: The Timber Problem of the Royal Navy 1652–1862*. Harvard University Press, Cambridge, MA.

Allen, T. W. 1994. *The Invention of the White Race: Racial Oppression and Social Control*. Verso, London.

Balibar, E. 1991. "Racism and Nationalism." in Balibar, E. and I. Wallerstein. *Race, Nation, Class: Ambiguous Identities*. Verso, London and New York.

Barry, T. 1987. *Roots of Rebellion: Land and Hunger in Central America*. South End Press, Boston.

Beckerman, W. 1992. "Economic Growth and the Environment: Whose Growth? Whose Environment?" *World Development* 20: 481–496.

Bernal, J. D. 1965. *Science in History: The Scientific and Industrial Revolutions*. The MIT Press, Cambridge, MA.

Bickerton, D. 1990. *Language and Species*. University of Chicago Press, Chicago.

Birdsey, R. A. and P. L. Weaver. 1982. "The Forest Resources of Puerto Rico." USDA Forest Service, Southern Forest Experiment Station, Resource Bulletin SO-85, October, 1982.

Blakie, P. and P. Broomfield. 1987. *Land Degredation and Society*. Methuen, London and New York.

Blumenschine, R. J. and J. A. Cavallo. 1992. "Scavenging and Human Evolution." *Scientific American*, October, 90–96.

Bonner, R. 1993. *At the Hand of Man: Peril and Hope for Africa's Wildlife*. Alfred A. Knopf, New York.

Boserup, E. 1965. *The Conditions of Agricultural Growth*. All and Unwin, London.

Boserup, E. 1990. *Economic and Demographic Relationships in Development*. Johns Hopkins Univ. Press, Baltimore.

Bouchard, T. J., D. T. Lykken, M. McGue, N. L. Segal, and A. Tellegen.

1990. "Sources of Human Psychological Differences: The Minnesota Study of Twins Reared Apart." *Science* 250: 223–250.

Boucher, D. H. 1985. *The Biology of Mutualism: Ecology and Evolution.* Croom Helm, London, 388 pp.

Bramwell, A. 1989. *Ecology in the 20th Century.* Yale Univ. Press, New Haven, CT, and London.

Brown, L. 1992. *State of the World,* W. W. Norton, New York.

Bridgman, H. 1990. *Global Air Pollution: Problems for the 1990s.* Belhaven Press, London.

Browne, M. W. 1994. "What is Intelligence, and Who Has It?" *New York Times Book Review.* October 16, 1994; 3, 41–45.

Bullard, R. D. 1990. Dumping in Dixie: *Race, Class, and Environmental Quality.* Westview, Boulder, CO.

Burchell, G., C. Gordon, and P. Miler. 1991. *The Foucault Effect: Studies in Governmentality.* Univ. of Chicago Press, Chicago.

Burke, J. 1985. *The Day the Universe Changed.* Little, Brown and Co., Boston and Toronto.

Burrough, B. and J. Helyar. 1990. *Barbarians at the Gate: The Fall of RJR Nabisco.* Harper Perennial, New York.

Buttel, F. H. and L. T. Raynolds. 1989. "Population Growth, Agrarian Structure, Food Production, and Food Distribution in the Third World." in Pimental, D. and C. W. Hall, eds. *Food and Natural Resources.* Academic Press, New York.

Byne, W. 1994. "The Biological Evidence Challenged." *Scientific American,* May, 50–55.

Cann, R. L., M. Stoneking, and A. Wilson. 1987. "Mitochondrial DNA and Human evolution." *Nature* 325: 31–36.

Chadwick, B. A. 1972. "In Defense of Density: Its Relationship to Health and Social Disorganization." in Bahr, H. M., B. A. Chadwick, and D. L. Thomas. *Population, Resources, and the Future: Non-Malthusian Perspectives.* Brigham Young Univ. Press, Provo, Utah.

Childress, J. J., H. Selbeck, and G. Somero. 1987. "Symbosis in the Deep Sea." *Scientific American* 256: 114–120.

Chomsky, N. 1989. *Necessary Illusions: Thought Control in Democratic Societies.* South End Press, Boston.

Chomsky, N. 1991. *Deterring Democracy.* Hill and Wang, New York.

Chomsky, N. 1993. *Year 501: The Conquest Continues.* South End Press, Boston.

CIES (Centro de Investigaciones Ecologicos del Sur). 1985. *Los Agroecosisemas del Altiplano de Chiapas.* CIES.

Clark, C. 1976. *Mathematical Bioeconomics.* John Wiley, New York.

CNS (Capitalism, Nature, Socialism). 1992. Symposium on the Second Contradiction of Capitalism. CNS 3 (3): 77–100; 3(4): 109–119.

Commoner, B. 1992. *Making Peace with the Planet*. The New Press, New York.

Commoner, B. 1975. "How Poverty Breeds Overpopulation (And Not the Other Way Around)." *Ramparts* 31: 21–25, 58–59.

Connell, J. H. 1978. "Diversity in Tropical Rain Forests and Coral Reefs." *Science* 199: 1302–1310.

Connell, J. H. and R. D. Slayter, 1977. "Mechanisms of Succession in Natural Communities and Their Role in Community Stability and Organization." *Am. Nat.* 111: 1119–1144.

Connor, J. 1988. "Capitalism, Nature, Socialism: A Theoretical Introduction." *CNS* 1 (Fall, 1988).

Connor, J. 1991. "On the Two Contradictions of Capitalism." CNS 2 (3): 107–109.

Coon, C. 1962. *The Origin of Races*. Alfred A. Knopf, New York.

Corbalis, M. C. 1991. *The Lopsided Ape: Evolution of the Generative Mind*. Oxford Univ. Press, Oxford.

CUSUCA (Programa Centroamericano de Ciencias Sociales), 1977. *Estructura Agraria, Dinámica de Población y Desarrollo Capitalista en Centroamérica*. EDUCA Editorial Universitaria, Centro Americana, San José, Costa Rica.

Darwin, C. 1859. *On the Origin of species by Means of Natural Selection*. London: John Murray.

Davidson, B. 1991. *African Civilization Revisited: From Antiquity to Modern Times*. Africa World Press, Trenton, NJ.

Davidson, B. 1992. *The Black Man's Burden*. Times Books, Random House, New York.

Dawkins, R. 1976. *The Selfish Gene*. Oxford University Press, Oxford.

Day, K. 1993. S & L Hell: *The People and the Politics Behind the $1 Trillion Savings and Loan Scandal*. W. W. Norton, New York.

Degler, C. N. 1991. In Search of Human Nature: The decline and revival of Darwinism in American social thought. Oxford University Press, Oxford.

deJanvry, A. 1983. *The Agrarian Question and Reformism in Latin America*. Johns Hopkins Univ. Press, Baltimore.

Denslow, J. S. 1987. "Tropical Rainforest Gaps and Tree Species Diversity." *Ann. Rev. Ecol. Syst.* 18: 431–451.

DeParle, J. 1994. "Daring Research or 'Social Science Pornography'?" *New York Times Magazine*, October 9, 1994: 48–53; 62; 70–71; 74; 78–80.

Diamond, J. 1992. *The Third Chimpanzee: The Evolution and Future of the Human Animal*. HarperCollins, New York.

Diez, J. 1986. *Economic History of Puerto Rico: Institutional Change and Capitalist Development*. Princeton Univ. Press, Princeton, NJ.

DiTrocchio, F. 1991. "Mendel's Experiments: A Reinterpretation." *J. of the History of Biology* 24: 485–519.

Douglas, M. 1986. *How Institutions Think*. Syracuse Univ. Press, Syracuse, NY.

Drury, W. B. and I. C. T. Nisbet. 1973. "Succession." *J. Arnold Arbor.* 54: 331–368.

Duerr, H. P. 1985. *Dreamtime: Concerning the Boundary between Wilderness and Civilization*. Basil Blackwell, Oxford.

Dunn, C. P., G. R. Guntenspergen, and J. R. Dorney. 1983. "Catastrophic Wind Disturbance in an Old-Growth Hemlock-Hardwood Forest, Wisconsin." *Can. J. Bot.* 61: 211–217.

Durham, W. 1979. *Scarcity and Survival in Central America: The Ecological Origins of the Soccer War*. Stanford Univ. Press, Palo Alto, CA.

Dyson, E. D. 1992. "Melanin madness." *Emerge,* February, p. 37.

Eagleton, T. 1983. *Literary Theory: An Introduction*. Univ. of Minnesota Press, Minneapolis.

Eagleton, T. 1991. *Ideology, an Introduction*. Verso, London.

Eaton, R. L. 1973. *The World's Cats. Vol 1*. World Wildlife Safari, Winston, OR.

Edelman, M. and J. Kenen. 1989. *The Costa Rica Reader*. Grove Weidenfeld, New York.

Ehrenfield, J. G. 1980. "Understory Response to Canopy Gaps of Varying Size in Mature Oak Forest." *Bull. Torrey Bot. Club* 107: 49–41.

Ehrlich, P. R. 1968. *The Population Bomb*. Ballantine, New York.

Ehrlich, P. R. and A. Ehrlich. 1990. *The Population Explosion*. Simon and Schuster, New York.

Everest, L. 1986. *Bhopal: The Anatomy of a Massacre.*Banner Press, New York.

Evernden, N. 1992. *The social Creation of Nature*. Johns Hopkins University Press, Baltimore.

Fagen, B. M. 1977. *People of the Earth: An Introduction to World Prehistory*. Little, Brown and Co., Boston.

Fausto-Sterling, A. 1985. *Myths of Gender: Biological Theories about Women and Men*. Basic Books, New York.

Fausto-Sterling, A. 1993. "The Five Sexes." *The Sciences,* March/April, 1993.

Flannery, K. V. 1973. "The Origins of Agriculture." *Annual Review of Anthropology,* 2: 271–310.

Foucault, M. 1967. *Histoire de la Folie (Paris 1961);* trans. as *Madness and Civilization.* Random House, New York.

Foucault, M. 1972. *The Archaeology of Knowledge and the Discourse on Language.* Pantheon Books, New York.

Foucault, M. 1979. *History of Sexuality, Vol I.* Random House, New York.

Franklin, R. S. 1991. *Shadows of Race and Class.* Univ. of Minn. Press, Minneapolis.

Fried, J. L., M. E. Gettleman, D. T. Levenson, and N. Peckenham. 1980. *Guatemala in Rebellion: Unfinished History.* Grove Press, New York.

Futuyma, D. J.1979. *Evolutionary Biology.* Sinauer Associates Press, Sunderland, MA.

Galbraith, J. K. 1958. *The Affluent Society.* Houghton, New York.

Galbraith, J. K. 1993. *A Short History of Financial Euphoria.* Viking, New York.

Galbraith, J. K. 1994. *A Journey Through Economic Time.* Houghton-Mifflin Co., Boston.

Galeano, E. 1973. *Open Veins of Latin America: Five Centuries of the Pillage of a Continent.* Monthly Review Press, NY.

Garcia-Barrios, E. and L. Garcia-Barrios. 1988. "La tecnología de producción de una agricultura en crisis." *Comercio Exterior* 38: 578–585.

Gasman, D. 1971. *The Scientific Origins of National Socialism: Social Darwinism in Ernst Haeckel and the German Monist League,* Macdonald & Co., London and New York.

Gause, G. F. 1934. *The Struggle for Existence.* Waverly Press, Baltimore.

Gettleman, M. et al. 1981. *El Salvador: Central America in the New Cold War.* Grove Press, New York.

Gilpin, M. E. 1979. "Spiral Chaos in a Predator-Prey Model." *Am. Nat.* 107: 306–308.

Goodwin, B. 1994. *How the Leopard Changed Its Spots: The Evolution of Complexity.* Charles Scribner's Sons, New York.

Gould, S. J. 1981. *The Mismeasure of Man.* W. W. Norton, New York.

Gould, S. J. 1989. *Wonderful Life: The Burgess Shale and the Nature of History.* W. W. Norton, New York.

Gould, S. J. and R. C. Lewontin. 1979. "The Spandrels of San Marco and the Panglossian Paradigm: A Critique of the Adaptationist Programme." *Proceedings of the Royal Society of London* b 205: 581–598.

Greenberg, D. 1988. *The Construction of Homosexuality.* University of Chicago Press, Chicago.

Griffiths, J. F. and D. M. Driscoll. 1982. *Survey of Climatology*. Merrill, Columbus, OH.

Grindle, M. S. 1986. *State and Countryside: Development Policy and Agrarian Politics in Latin America*. Johns Hopkins Univ. Press, Baltimore.

Hacker, A. 1992. *Two Nations: Black and White, Separate, Hostile, Unequal*. Ballantine Books, New York.

Haeckel, E. 1868. *The History of Creation: Or the Development of the Earth and Its Inhabitants by the Action of Natural Causes. A Popular Exposition of the Doctrine of Evolution in General, and that of Darwin, Goethe and Lamarck in Particular*. 2 vols. Appleton, New York.

Haeckel, E. 1900. *The Riddle of the Universe*. Harper, New York.

Haeckel, E. 1904. *The Wonders of Life*. Harper, New York.

Haller, R. D. and J. D. Balarin. 1982. "Agroforestry for Wasteland Reclamation." *Ecoforum* 10: 5.

Handlin, O. and M. F. Handlin. 1950. "Origins of the Southern Labor System." *William and Mary Quarterly*, 3rd Series, 7: 220–221.

Hardin, G. 1968. "The Tragedy of the Commons." *Science* 162: 1243–1248.

Hardin, G. 1969. "Not Peace, but Ecology." In *Diversity and Stability in Ecological Systems*. Brookhaven Symposium, May 26–28, 1969.

Hardin, G. 1971. "The Survival of Nations and Civilization." *Science*, 172: 1297.

Hardin, G. 1974. "Living on a Lifeboat." *Bioscience* 24:561–568.

Hardin, G. 1993. *Living within Limits: Ecology, Economics, and Population Taboos*. Oxford Univ. Press, Oxford.

Harding, S. 1993. *The "Racial" Economy of Science: Toward a Democratic Future*. Indiana Univ. Press, Bloomington, IN.

Harris, M. 1979. *Cultural Materialism: The Struggle for a Science of Culture*. Random House, New York.

Harris, D. R. 1977. "Alternative Pathways Toward Agriculture." in C. A. Reed, ed. *Origins of Agriculture*. Mouton, The Hague, pp. 179–244.

Harvey, D. 1974. "Population, Resources, and the Ideology of Science." *Economic Geography* 50: 256–277.

Hastings, A. and T. Powell. 1991. "Chaos in a Three-Species Food Chain." *Ecology* 72: 896–903.

Hecht, S. and A. Cockburn. 1989. *The Fate of the Forest: Developers, Destroyers and Defenders of the Amazon*. Verso, London and New York.

Hecht, S. and A. Cockburn. 1992. "The Rhetoric and the Reality in Rio." *The Nation*, June 22, pp. 848–852.

Herber, L. 1965. *Crisis in our Cities.* Prentice-Hall, Inc., Englewood Cliffs, NJ.

Herrnstein, R. 1973. *IQ and the Meritocracy.* Little Brown, Boston.

Herrnstein, R. and C. Murray. 1994. *The Bell Curve: Intelligence and Class Structure in American Life.* The Free Press, New York.

Hitler, A. 1927. *Mein Kampf.* Houghton Mifflin, Boston (1971 edition).

Homer-Dixon, T. F., J. H. Boutwell, and G. W. Rathjens. 1993. "Environmental Change and Violent Conflict." *Scientific American,* February, Vol. 268:38–45.

Howe, H. and J. Lyne. 1992. "Gene Talk in Sociobiology." *Social Epistemology* 6: 109–163.

Hubbell, S. P. and R. B. Foster. 1986. "Biology, Chance, and History and the Structure of Tropical Rain Forest Tree Communities." In J. Diamond and T. J. Case, eds. *Community Ecology,* pp. 314–329. Harper and Row Publishers Inc., New York.

Huston, M. 1979. "A General Hypothesis of Species Diversity." *Am. Nat.* 113: 81–101.

Huxley, T. H. 1894. *Evolution and Ethics. Prolegomena.* Reprinted, 1970, in *Anglistica & Americana,* Georg Olms Verlag, Hildesheim, New York.

Immerman, R. H. 1982. *The CIA in Guatemala: The Foreign Policy of Intervention.* Univ. of Texas Press, Austin.

Itzkoff, S. W. 1994. *The Decline of Intelligence in America: A Strategy for National Renewal.* Praeger, Westport, CT.

Ivins, M. 1991. *Molly Ivins Can't Say That, Can She?* Vintage Books, New York.

Janzen, D. H. and P. S. Martin. 1982. "Neotropical Anachronisms: Fruits the Gomphotheres Ate." *Science* 215: 19–27.

Jennings, F. 1975. *The Invasion of America: Indians, Colonialism, and the Cant of Conquest.* W. W. Norton, New York.

Jensen, A. 1969. "How Much Can We Boost IQ and Scholastic Achievement?" *Harvard Educational Review* 39: 1–123.

Jordan, W. D. 1968. *White over Black: American Attitudes Toward the Negro 1550–1812.* Univ. of North Carolina Press, Chapel Hill.

Kamin, L. 1974. *The Science and Politics of IQ.* Erlbaum, Potomac, MD.

Kano, T. 1992. *The Last Ape: Pygmy Chimpanzee Behavior and Ecology.* Trans. by E. O. Vineberg. Stanford Univ. Press, Palo Alto, CA.

Kaplan, R. D. 1994. "The Coming Anarchy." *Atlantic Monthly,* February: 44–76.

Kaye, H. L. 1986. *The Social Meaning of Modern Biology.* Yale University Press, New Haven, CT.

Kevles, D. J. 1985. *In the Name of Eugenics: Genetics and the Uses of Human Heredity.* Univ. of California Press, Berkeley.

Kitcher, P. 1987. *Vaulting Ambition: Sociobiology and the Quest for Human Nature*. The MIT Press, Cambridge, MA.

Kitching, G. 1980. *Class and Economic Change in Kenya: The Making of an African Petite-Bourgeoisie*. Yale Univ. Press, New Haven, CT.

Kühl, S. 1994. *The Nazi Connection: Eugenics, American Racism, and German National Socialism*. Oxford University Press, Oxford, UK.

Krebs, C. J. 1985. *Ecology*. Harper and Row, New York.

Kuhn, T. 1970. *The Structure of Scientific Revolutions*. 2nd ed. Univ. of Chicago Press, Chicago.

Lappé, F. M. and J. Collins. 1977. *Food First: Beyond the Myth of Scarcity*. Houghton Mifflin, Boston.

Lappé, F. M. and R. Schurman. 1988. *Taking Population Seriously*. Institute for Food and Development Policy, San Francisco.

Leakey, M. D. 1979. "Footprints in the Ashes of Time." *National Geographic* 155: 446–457.

Leakey, M. D. 1976. "A Summary and Discussion of the Archaeological Evidence from Bed I and Bed II, Olduvai Gorge, Tanzania." In G. L. Isaac and E. R. McGowan, eds. *Human Origins: Louis Leakey and the East African Evidence*. Benjamin Pub. Co., Menlo Park, CA, pp. 431–59.

Leakey, R. E., and R. Lewin. 1979. *Origins*. Rainbird Pub. Group, London.

Leakey, R. E., and R. Lewin. 1992. *Origins Reconsidered: In Search of What Makes Us Human*. Doubleday, New York.

Leiman, M. M. 1993. *The Political Economy of Racism: A History*. Pluto Press, London.

Lemann, N. 1991. *The Promised Land: The Great Black Migration and How It Changed America*. Alfred A. Knopf, New York.

Lemert, C. 1993. *Social Theory: The Multicultural and Classic Readings*. Westview Press, Boulder, CO.

LeVay, S. and D. H. Hamer. 1994. "Evidence for a biological Influence in Male Homosexuality." *Scientific American,* May, pp. 44–49.

Levinton, J. S. 1992. "The Big Bang of Animal Evolution." *Scientific American,* November, pp. 84–91.

Lewis, W. A. 1954. "Economic Development with Unlimited Supplies of Labor." *The Manchester School* XXII: 139–191.

Lewontin, R. C. 1972. "The Apportionment of Human Diversity." *Evolutionary Biology* 6: 381–398.

Lewontin, R. C. 1977a. "Caricature of Darwinism." Review of *The Selfish Gene* by R. Dawkins. *Nature* 266: 283–294.

Lewontin, R. C. 1977b. "Sociobiology—A Caricature of Darwinism." in F. Suppe and P. O. Asquith, eds. *Proceedings of the 1976 Biennial Meeting of the Philosophy of Science Association,* Vol. 2 pp. 22–31. Philosophy of Science Association, East Lansing, MI.

Lewontin, R. 1982. *Human Diversity.* Scientific American Books, New York.

Lewontin, R. C. 1991. *Biology as Ideology: The Doctrine of DNA.* Harper Perennial, New York.

Lewontin, R. C., S. Rose, and L. Kamin. 1984. *Not in our Genes.* Pantheon, New York.

Lewontin, R. C., and Berlan, J. P. 1990. "The Political Economy of Agricultural Research: The Case of Hybrid Corn." In Carroll, Vandermeer, and Rosset, eds. *Agroecology,* McGraw-Hill, New York.

Lotka, A. 1925. *Principles of Physical Biology.* Waverly Press, Baltimore.

Maczak, A. and W. N. Parker, eds. 1978. *Natural Resources in European History.* Resources for the Future, Washington, DC.

Malthus, T. 1960. *A Summary View of the Principle of Population* (originally published in 1830). The New American Library, New York.

Mamdani, M. 1972. *The Myth of Population Control.* Monthly Review Press, New York.

Marshall, G. A. 1969. "Racial Classificationes: Popular and Scientific," in Mead, M., ed. *Science and the Concept of Race,* Columbia Univ. Press, New York, pp. 149–164.

Martin, P. S. 1973. "The Discovery of America." *Science* 179: 969–974.

Martinez-Alier, M. 1987. *Ecological Economics: Energy, Environment and Society.* Basil Blackwell, Oxford.

Marx, K. 1967. *Capital.* 3 Vols. Edited by Frederick Engels. (Originally published, 1867.) International Publishers, New York.

Mass, B. 1976. *Population Target: The Political Economy of Population Control in Latin America.* Latin American Working Group, Toronto.

Maull, H. and O. Pick, eds. 1989. *The Gulf War.* St. Martin's Press, New York.

Mayr, E. 1963. *Animal Species and Evolution.* Harvard Univ. Press, Cambridge, MA.

Mayr, E. 1982. *The Growth of Biological Thought: Diversity, Evolution, and Inheritance.* Belknap Press of Harvard Univ., Cambridge, MA.

McNaughton, S. J. 1976. "Serengeti Migratory Wildebeest: Facilitation of Energy Flow by Grazing." *Science* 191:92–94.

McNaughton, S. J. and L. L. Wolf. 1979. *General Ecology.* Holt, Rinehart and Winston, New York.

Meek, R. L. 1971. *Marx and Engels on the Population Bomb.* The Ramparts Press, Berkeley, CA.

Melville, T. and M. Melville. 1971. *Guatemala: The Politics of Land Owner-ship*. Free Press, New York.

Meyers, N. 1985. *The Primary Source: Tropical Forests and Our Future*. W. W. Norton, New York and London.

Michaelson, K. L., ed. 1981. *And the Poor Get Children: Radical Perspectives on Population Dynamics*. Monthly Review Press, New York.

Milbrath, B. 1983. "Lessons from Mondragon." *Science for the People* 15: 7–11.

Minc, L. D. and J. H. Vandermeer. 1990. "The Origin and Spread of Agri-culture." In Carroll, Vandermeer, and Rosset, eds., *Agroecology*, McGraw-Hill Pub. Co., New York, pp. 65–112.

Mintz, S. W. 1985. *Sweetness and Power*. Elisabeth Sifton Books, Viking, NY.

Mulvaney, D. J. 1969. *The Prehistory of Australia*. Praeger, New York.

Money, J. and A. A. Ehrhardt. 1972. *Man and Woman, Boy and Girl: Differ-entiation* and Dimorphism of Gender Identity from Conception to Matu-rity. Johns Hopkins Univ. Press, Baltimore.

Mooney, Harold A. and M. Gordon, eds. 1983. *Disturbance and Ecosystems*. Springer-Verlag, Berlin.

Morgan, E. 1975. *American Slavery, American Freedom: The Ordeal of Colo-nial Virginia*. W. W. Norton, New York.

Morgan, E. S. 1988. *Inventing the People*. W. W. Norton, New York.

Morgan, D. 1979. *Merchants of Grain*. Viking, New York.

Murdoch, W. 1980. *Poverty of Nations: Population, Hunger, and Develop-ment*. Johns Hopkins Univ. Press, Baltimore.

Murdoch, W. and A. Oaten. 1975. "Population and Food: Metaphors and Realities." *Bioscience* 25: 561–567.

Nadelhoffer, K. J. 1983. "Leaf-Litter Production and Soil Organic Matter Dynamic along a Nitrogen-Availability Gradient in Southern Wiscon-sin," *Canadian Journal of Forestry Research* 13: 12–21.

Norris, C. 1993. *The Truth about Postmodernism*. Blackwell, Oxford.

North American Committee on Latin America. 1974. *Guatemala*. S. Jones and D. Tobis, eds. NACLA, New York.

Noy-Meir, E. 1975. "Stability of Grazing Systems: An Application of Pred-ator-Prey Graphs." *J. Ecol.* 63: 459–481.

Oakeshott, R. 1978. *The Case for Workers' Co-ops*. Routledge and Kegan Paul, London.

Osborn, F. 1960. *Population, An International Dilemma*. (First published in 1958.) New American Library, New York.

O'Shea, J. 1991. *The Daisy Chain*. Pocket Books, New York.

Ostrom, E. 1990. *Governing the Commons*. Cambridge Univ. Press, Cambridge.

Pacey, A. 1990. *Technology in World Civilization*. The MIT Press, Cambridge, MA.

Palmer, R. R. and J. Colton. 1950. *A History of the Modern World*. Alfred A. Knopf, New York.

Palmer, T. 1992. "The Case for Human Beings." *Atlantic Monthly,* January, pp. 83–88.

Parsons, H. L., ed. 1977. *Marx and Engels on Ecology*. Greenwood Press, Westport, CT.

Pearce, J. 1982. *Under the Eagle: U.S. Intervention in Central America and the Caribbean*. South End Press, Boston.

Pedigo, 1989. *Entomology and Pest Management*. Macmillan, New York.

Pfeiffer, J. E. 1973. *The Emergence of Man*. Book Club Associates, London.

Philp, M. 1985. "Michel Foucault." in Q. Skinner, ed. *The Return of Grand Theory in the Human Sciences*. Cambridge Univ. Press, Cambridge, pp. 65–81.

Pinker, S. 1994. *The Language Instinct*. William Morrow, New York.

Plucknett, D. K. and N. J. H. Smith. 1982. "Agricultural Research and Third World Food Production." *Science* 217: 215–220.

Ponting, C. 1991. *A Green History of the World: The Environment and the Collapse of Great Civilizations*. St. Martin's Press, New York.

Poore, D. 1989. *No Timber without Trees: Sustainability in the Tropical Forest*. Earthscan Publications, London.

Poster, M. 1984. *Foucault, Marxism and History: Mode of Production versus Mode of Information*. Polity Press, Cambridge.

Purves, W. K., G. H. Orians, and H. C. Heller. 1992. *Life: The Science of Biology*. Sinauer Associates, Sunderland, Mass.

Rabe, S. G. 1988. *Eisenhower and Latin America: The Foreign Policy of Anticommunism*. Univ. of North Carolina Press, Chapel Hill.

Redclift, M. 1987. *Sustainable Development: Exploring the Contradictions*. Methuen, London.

Reich, R. 1991. *The Work of Nations: Preparing Ourselves for 21st Century Capitalism*. Vintage Books, New York.

Rennie, J. 1993. "DNA's New Twists." *Scientific American,* March: 122–132.

Ricardo, D. 1817. *Principles of Political Economy and Taxation*. Dent, London.

Rice, R. A. and J. H. Vandermeer. 1990. "Climate and the Geography of Agriculture." In Carroll, R. C., J. H. Vandermeer, and P. Rosset, eds. *Agroecology*, McGraw-Hill, New York.

Richter, D. D. and L. J. Babbar, 1991. "Soil Diversity in the Tropics." *Advances in Ecological Research* 321: 315–389.

Risch, S. J. and D. H. Boucher. 1976. "What Ecologists Look For." *Bull. Ecol. Soc. Am.* 57: 8–9.

Rist, D. Y. 1992. "Sex on the Brain: Are Homosexuals Born That Way?" *The Nation,* Oct. 19: 424–429.

Robertson, W. 1981. *The Dispossessed Majority.* Howard Allen, Cape Canaveral, Fla.

Rocha, J. 1905. *Memorandum de un Viaje.* Editorial El Mercurio, Bogota, Colombia.

Roediger, D. R. 1991. *The Wages of Whiteness.* Verso, London.

Rosenzweig, M. L. and R. H. MacArthur. 1963. "Graphic Representation and Stability Conditions of Predator-Prey Interactions." *Am. Nat.* 97: 209–223.

Ross, A. 1994. *The Chicago Gangster Theory of Life: Nature's Debt to Society.* Verso, London.

Rosset, P. and J. H. Vandermeer. 1986a. "The Confrontation between Processors and Farm Workers in the Midwest Tomato Industry and the Role of the Agricultural Research and Extension Extablishment." *Ag. and Human Values* 3:26–32.

Rosset, P. and J. H. Vandermeer. 1986b. *Nicaragua: Unfinished Revolution.* Grove Press, New York.

Rushton, J. P. 1995. *Race, Evolution, and Behavior: A Life History Perspective.* Transaction Pubs., New Brunswick, NJ.

Russell, E. 1993. *War on Insects: Warfare, Insecticides, and Environmental Change in the United States, 1970–1945.* Ph.D. dissertation, Univ. of Michigan, Ann Arbor.

Sachs, J. D. 1987. "Trade and Exchange Rate Policies in Growth-Oriented Adjustment Programs." In Corbo, V., M. Goldstein, and M. Kahn, eds. *Growth-Oriented Adjustment Programs.* IMF and World Bank Symposium Procedings, Feb 25–27, Washington, DC.

Sahlins, M. 1972. *Stone Age Economics.* Aldine, Chicago.

Sayre, A. 1975. *Rosalind Franklin and DNA: A Vivid View of What It Is Like to Be a Gifted Woman in an Especially Male Profession.* W. W. Norton, New York.

Schmidt, H. 1971. *The United States Occupation of Haiti, 1915–1934.* Rutgers Univ. Press, New Brunswick, NJ.

Schob, D. E. 1975. *Hired Hands and Plowboys: Farm Labor in the Midwest, 1815–60.* Univ. of Illinois Press, Urbana, IL.

Serafini, T., T. E. Kennedy, M. J. Galko, C. Mirzayan, T. M. Jessell, and M. Tessier-Lavigne. 1994. "The Netrins Define a Family of Axon Outgrowth-Promoting Proteins Homologous to *C. Elegans* UNC-6." *Cell* 78: 409–424.

Sheridan, A. 1980. *Michael Foucault: The Will to Truth.* Tavistock, London.

Shipman, P. 1994. *The Evolution of Racism: Human Differences and the Use and Abuse of Science.* Simon and Schuster, New York.

Simon, J. 1981. *The Ultimate Resource.* Princeton Univ. Press, Princeton, NJ.

Simon, J. and H. Kahn, eds. 1984. *The Resourceful Earth.* Blackwell, Oxford.

Sober, E. 1994. *Models of Cultural Evolution.* pgs 477–492. in Sober E. (ed) Conceptual issues in Evolutionary Biology. MIT Press, Cambridge, Mass.

Sokal, R. and T. J. Crovello. 1970. "The Biological Species Concept: A Critical Evaluation." *Amer. Nat.* 104: 127–153.

Sokal, R. 1991. "Ancient Movement Patterns Determine Modern Genetic Variances in Europe." *Human Biology* 63:589–606.

Spencer, H. 1876. The Comparative Psychology of Man *Mind,* 1: 7–20.

Stanley, H. M. 1878. *Through the Dark Continent. Vol II.* Sampson Low, Marston and Co. Ltd., London.

Stein, G. H. 1968. *Hitler.* Prentice-Hall, Englewood Cliffs, N.J.

Stephens, C. S. 1984. "Ecological Upset and Recuperation of Natural Control of Insect Pests in Some Costa Rican Banana Plantations." *Turrialba* 34: 101–105.

Stern, C. and E. R. Sherwood, eds. 1966. *The Origin of Genetics: A Mendel Source Book.* W. H. Freeman, San Francisco.

Stewart, J. B. 1991. *Den of Thieves.* Simon and Schuster, New York.

Tarbell, I. M. 1904. *The History of the Standard Oil Company.* 2 vols. Mc-Clure, Phillips, New York.

Tavris, C. 1992. *The Mismeasure of Woman.* Simon and Schuster, New York.

Thompson, E. P. 1963. *The Making of the English Working Class.* Vintage Books, London.

Thrupp, L. A. 1991. "Sterilization of Workers from Pesticide Exposure: Causes and Consequences of DB CP-induced Damage in Costa Rica and Beyond." *Intl. J. of Health Services.* 21: 731–757.

Tonelson, A. 1987. "Give 'Em Hell." *The New Republic* Oct. 5, 1987: 20–24.

Tucker, R. P. and J. F. Richard. 1983. *Global Deforestation and the Nineteenth Century World Economy.* Duke University Press, Durham, NC.

Turner, F. 1983. *Beyond Geography: The Western Spirit Against the Wilderness.* Rutgers Univ. Press, New Brunswick, NJ, and London.

USA Today, 1991. "Black Professor Called a Racist." August 14: 2A.

van den Bosch, R. 1978. *The Pesticide Conspiracy*. Doubleday, New York.

Vandermeer, J. H. 1980. "Indirect Mutualism: Variations on a Theme by Stephen Levine." *Amer. Nat.* 116: 441–448.

Vandermeer, J. H. 1982. "Science and Class Conflict: The Role of Agricultural Research in the Midwestern Tomato Industry." *Studies in Marxism* 12: 41–57.

Vandermeer, J. H. 1986. "Mechanized Agriculture and Social Welfare: The Tomato Harvester in Ohio." *Ag. and Human Values* 3: 21–25.

Vandermeer, J. H. 1991. "The Political Economy of Sustainable Development: The Southern Atlantic Coast of Nicaragua." *The Centennial Review*, XXXV: 265–294.

Vandermeer, J. H. 1993. "Loose Coupling of Predator-Prey Cycles: Entrainment, Chaos, and Intermittency in the Classic MacArthur Consumer-Resource Equations." *Am. Nat.* 141:687–716.

Vandermeer, J. H. and D. Andow. 1986. "Prophylactic and Responsive Components of an Integrated Pest Management Program." *J. Econ. Entom.* 79: 299–302.

Vandermeer, J. H. and D. Boucher. 1978. "Varieties of Mutualistic Interaction in Population Models." *J. Theor. Biol.* 74: 549–558.

Vandermeer, J. H., N. Zamora, K. Yih, and D. Boucher. 1990. "Regeneracion Inicial en una Selva Tropical en la Costa Caribeña de Nicaragua después del Huracan Juana." *Revista Biología Tropical (Costa Rica)* 38:347–359.

Vandermeer, J. H., I. Perfecto, and D. Boucher. 1991. "Conservation in Nicaragua and Costa Rica: Indirect Consequences of Social Policy." INTECOL Bulletin, January.

Vandermeer, J. H. and I. Perfecto. 1991. "Los Bosques del Caribe de Nicaragua Tres Años despues del Huracan Joan." *Wani* 11:79–102 (1991).

Vandermeer, J. H. and I. Perfecto. 1995. "Deforestation in Central America." To appear in Taylor P. and Y. Haila, eds. *Natural Contradictions*.

Vandermeer, J. H. and I. Perfecto. 1995a. "A Breakfast of Biodiversity: How Food Insecurity Causes the Destruction of Tropical Rain Forests." Institute for Food and Development Policy, Oakland, CA.

Vitousek, P. M., P. R. Ehrlich, A. H. Ehrlich, and P. A. Matson. 1986. "Human Appropriation of the Products of Photosynthesis." *BioScience* 36: 368–373.

Volpe, E. P. 1993. *Biology and Human Concerns,* 4th ed. Wm. C. Brown, Dubuque, IA.

Volterra, V. 1926. "Variations and Fluctuations of the Number of Individuals in Animal Species Living Together. *J. Cons. perm. int. Ent. Mer.* 3: 3–51.

von Braun, J., D. Hotchkiss, and M. Immink, 1989. "Nontraditional Export Crops in Guatemala: Effects on Production, Income and Nutrition." International Food Policy Res. Inst., Research Report 73: 1–99.

Wallerstein, I. 1980. *The Modern World System II: Mercantilism and the Consolidation of the European World-Economy, 1600–1750.* Academic Press, New York.

Westoby, J. 1989. *Introduction to World Forestry.* Basil Blackwell Ltd., Oxford.

Williams, E. 1944. *Capitalism and Slavery.* Univ. of North Carolina Press, Chapel Hill.

Williams, R. G. 1986. *Export Agriculture and the Crisis in Central America.* Univ. of North Carolina Press, Chapel Hill.

Wilson, E. O. 1975. *Sociobiology: The New Synthesis.* Harvard Univ. Press, Cambridge, MA.

Wilson, E. O. 1978. *On Human Nature.* Harvard Univ. Press, Cambridge, MA.

Wolf, E. 1989. *Europe and the People Without History.* Univ. of Calif. Press, Berkeley, CA.

Wolpoff, M. H. 1988. "Multiregional Evolution: The Fossil Alternative to Eden." In Stringer, C. B. and F. Andrews, eds. *The Origins and Dispersal of Modern Humans.* Cambridge Univ. Press, Cambridge.

Wood, C. V. 1987. *Trees for Wastelands: The Baobab Farm Handbook.* Baobab Farm Ltd, Mombasa, Kenya.

World Bank. 1994. *World Development Report, 1994.* Oxford University Press, Oxford.

Wright, R. 1992. *Stolen Continents: The Americas through Indian Eyes since 1492.* Houghton Mifflin, Boston.

Wright, R. 1994. *The Moral Animal.* Pantheon Books, NY.

Yergin, D. 1991. *The Prize: The Epic Quest for Oil, Money, and Power.* Simon and Schuster, New York.

Yih, K., D. Boucher, J. H. Vandermeer, and N. Zamora. 1991. "Recovery of the Rainforest of Southeastern Nicaragua after Destruction by Hurricane Joan." *Biotropica* 23: 106–113 (1991).

Index